Black Abolitionists in Ireland

The story of the anti-slavery movement in Ireland is little known, yet when Frederick Douglass visited the country in 1845, he described Irish abolitionists as the most 'ardent' that he had ever encountered. Moreover, their involvement proved to be an important factor in ending the slave trade, and later slavery, in both the British Empire and in America.

While Frederick Douglass remains the most renowned black abolitionist to visit Ireland, he was not the only one. This publication traces the stories of ten black abolitionists, including Douglass, who travelled to Ireland in the decades before the American Civil War, to win support for their cause. It opens with former slave, Olaudah Equiano, kidnapped as a boy from his home in Africa, and who was hosted by the United Irishmen in the 1790s; it closes with the redoubtable Sarah Parker Remond, who visited Ireland in 1859 and chose never to return to America. The stories of these ten men and women, and their interactions with Ireland, are diverse and remarkable.

Christine Kinealy gained her PhD in Trinity College, Dublin. In 2013, she was appointed the founding Director of Ireland's Great Hunger Institute at Quinnipiac University. She has lectured and published extensively on various aspects on modern Irish history, most particularly on the Great Famine and the Irish abolition movement. Her previous publications include *Frederick Douglass. In his own words* (2 vols. Routledge, 2018).

Routledge Studies in Modern European History

73 Interwar East Central Europe, 1918–1941
The Failure of Democracy-building, the Fate of Minorities
Edited by Sabrina Ramet

74 Free Trade and Social Welfare in Europe
Explorations in the Long 20th Century
Edited by Lucia Coppolaro and Lorenzo Mechi

75 Immigrants and Foreigners in Central and Eastern Europe during the Twentieth Century
Edited by Włodzimierz Borodziej and Joachim von Puttkamer

76 Europe between Migrations, Decolonization and Integration (1945–1992)
Edited by Giuliana Laschi, Valeria Deplano, Alessandro Pes

77 Steamship Nationalism
Ocean Liners and National Identity in Imperial Germany and the Atlantic World
Mark Russell

78 Transatlantic Anarchism during the Spanish Civil War and Revolution, 1936–1939
Morris Brodie

79 Emotions and Everyday Nationalism in Modern European History
Edited by Andreas Stynen, Maarten Van Ginderachter and Xosé M. Núñez Seixas

80 Black Abolitionists in Ireland
Christine Kinealy

www.routledge.com/history/series/SE0246

Black Abolitionists in Ireland

Christine Kinealy

LONDON AND NEW YORK

First published 2020
by Routledge
2 Park Square, Milton Park, Abingdon, Oxon OX14 4RN

and by Routledge
605 Third Avenue, New York, NY 10017

First issued in paperback 2021

Routledge is an imprint of the Taylor & Francis Group, an informa business

© 2020 Christine Kinealy

The right of Christine Kinealy to be identified as author of this work has
been asserted by her in accordance with sections 77 and 78 of the
Copyright, Designs and Patents Act 1988.

All rights reserved. No part of this book may be reprinted or reproduced
or utilised in any form or by any electronic, mechanical, or other means,
now known or hereafter invented, including photocopying and recording,
or in any information storage or retrieval system, without permission in
writing from the publishers.

Trademark notice: Product or corporate names may be trademarks or
registered trademarks, and are used only for identification and
explanation without intent to infringe.

Publisher's Note
The publisher has gone to great lengths to ensure the quality of this
reprint but points out that some imperfections in the original copies may
be apparent.

British Library Cataloguing-in-Publication Data
A catalogue record for this book is available from the British Library

Library of Congress Cataloging-in-Publication Data
A catalog record has been requested for this book

ISBN 13: 978-1-03-223626-1 (pbk)
ISBN 13: 978-0-367-22533-9 (hbk)

Typeset in Times New Roman
by Integra Software Services Pvt. Ltd.

To Saoirse Rose ... and all others who seek to be free

Contents

	Acknowledgements	viii
	Introduction	1
1	Olaudah Equiano (1745–1797): 'In every respect on par with Europeans'	41
2	Moses Roper (1815–1891): 'A religious turn of mind'	60
3	Charles Lenox Remond (1810–1873): 'A mission of humanity'	76
4	Frederick Douglass (1818–1895): 'Agitate, Agitate, Agitate!'	106
5	William Wells Brown (c.1814–1884): 'A cultivated fugitive'	135
6	Henry Highland Garnet (1815–1882): 'A staunch new organizationist'	162
7	Edmund Kelly (1817–1884): 'A family redeemed from bondage'	188
8	Samuel Ringgold Ward (1817–c.1866): 'A Christian abolitionist'?	201
9	Benjamin Benson (1818–?): 'Drunkenness … worse than slavery'	226
10	Sarah Parker Remond (1826–1894): 'Remarkably feminine and graceful'	240
	Bibliography	266
	Index	279

Acknowledgements

The origins of this book lie in research on Daniel O'Connell that I carried out about 15 years ago. At that stage, I was a 'Daniel-sceptic', my sympathies lying more with 'Young' rather than 'Old' Ireland. As I researched, however, my opinion changed and I came to admire O'Connell for his pioneering stand on international human rights, particularly his uncompromising stance on abolition. As I explored more deeply, I came to regard O'Connell's speeches denouncing slavery as the finest that he made—no mean feat given his skills as an orator.

And it was O'Connell who led me to another remarkable champion of social justice—Frederick Douglass. In 1845, Douglass visited Ireland as a 27-year-old fugitive slave. His meeting with his 70-year-old hero, O'Connell, helped him to define and craft his own political philosophy, changing him from being simply a spokesperson for abolition, to an advocate for the oppressed everywhere. And it was another life-long campaigner for social justice, Don Mullan, who suggested that I should transcribe the speeches made by Douglass while he was in Ireland. When I agreed, I did not realize that there were over 50 speeches, none of them written down, and that this project would take me almost ten years to complete. It became a labour of love. Moreover, as a result of this research, I came to understand that Douglass was only one of several talented black abolitionists who made the journey across the Atlantic to Britain to win support for their cause. A smaller number of these men and women then travelled onwards to Ireland, the home of the most 'ardent' abolitionists in Europe. These are the circuitous origins of this publication. Dan, Frederick and Don, thank you all for leading me to these remarkable, and a largely forgotten, stories.

A number of other debts have been incurred during the writing of this book. Many librarians, archivists and curators on both sides of the Atlantic have shared their expertise and their knowledge with me. Special thanks are due to Robert Young and Sandy O'Hare of Quinnipiac University, Dr Alan Delozier of Seton Hall University, Martin Fagan, formerly of the National Archives of Ireland, now with Strokestown Park, Brian McGee of Cork City and County Archives and Liz Fitzpatrick and her colleagues at Glasnevin Trust in Dublin. I am grateful also to Robert Langham of Routledge Publishers for having faith in this project.

Many friends and colleagues have cast a critical eye over the text for which I am truly grateful. This includes, Francine Sagar, Lynn Bushnell, Peter Murphy,

Acknowledgements ix

Turlough McConnell, Professor Rebecca Abbott, Dr Gerard Moran, Dr Jason King and Dr Maureen Murphy. Their comments and insights have been invaluable, but any mistakes and omissions are my own.

The publication has benefitted from discussions and exchanges with a group of incredible people who not only share my interest in this aspect of Irish history, but who combine it with an ongoing commitment to social justice. They are Don Mullan, human rights activist; Nettie Washington Douglass, Ken Morris, and Kristin Leary of the Frederick Douglass Ireland Project; and Dr Richard W. Thomas and Dr William Smith of the National Center for Race Amity. They each live their lives in the generous, inclusive spirit of Frederick Douglass and his less well-known colleagues in the abolition movement. Gerry Adams and Jim Gibney in Ireland, Andrew Edwards in England, Todd Allen in New Jersey and John Muller in Washington are also working to preserve the legacy of the early abolitionists and to promote their desire for freedom and equality. By doing so, they are recreating the spirit of transatlantic co-operation that was at the heart of the anti-slavery movement.

Finally, a thank you to my friends and family who have supported me during the researching and writing of this book—you know who you are and I am eternally grateful.

Christine Kinealy

Introduction

> I tell it, to let English people know the truth; and I hope they will never leave off to pray to God, and call loud to the great King of England, till all the poor blacks be given free, and slavery done up for evermore.[1]
>
> (Mary Prince)

> We look very much to Great Britain and Ireland for help. Whenever we hear of the British or Irish people doing good to black men, we are delighted and run and tell each other the news.[2]
>
> (Moses Grandy)

From the 1760s to the 1860s, the campaign to end enslavement was one of the most organized, visible and effective movements in the world. From its origins in the late-eighteenth century, it slowly but steadily gained momentum, achieving public recognition and engagement as it sought initially to end the slave trade, and then slavery itself. The chapters that follow examine the struggle to end enslavement through the stories of a small number of black abolitionists who crossed the Atlantic before the American Civil War and who travelled to Ireland to win support for their cause.

This publication provides a brief overview of the lives of ten black abolitionists, nine men and one woman, and their interactions with the anti-slavery movement in Ireland. With few exceptions, their remarkable personal stories have been largely forgotten and their time spent across the Atlantic, ignored. Yet, during their life-times, although deemed to be intellectually and socially inferior, these intrepid travellers dined with ambassadors, lectured alongside politicians and advised several Presidents. Moreover, despite being largely self-educated, they lectured to hundreds and thousands of people and wrote narratives of their lives that were reprinted multiple times. Most of these narratives were written long before they travelled to Ireland.

It has been suggested that the main purpose of both the narratives and the lectures was to serve as 'performative manifestos', that is, to create a network of sympathetic activists. They do much more. By revealing the similarities and differences between these ten abolitionists, they provide an insight into the

2   Introduction

diversity of the movement and of the actors within it. The lectures are particularly interesting. These abolitionists were generally excellent public speakers, and some could speak for over two hours and did so without notes. The contents of their lectures, therefore, have been culled from a large variety of newspapers, both hard copies and online. It is from these detailed reports that the hopes, aspirations and frustrations of the various abolitionists emerge, while insights are provided into the impact that they had on their audiences. Regardless of lives spent in the public eye, and spending thousands of hours lecturing and writing, these abolitionists remain hard to define or to categorize, they each bringing their unique skills and abilities to the movement. Ireland proved to be an important staging post on their individual and collective journeys.

It has been estimated that at the height of transatlantic anti-slavery activities, that is, between 1830 and 1860, over 80 black abolitionists visited Britain, but only half a dozen of them crossed the Irish Sea.[3] The following chapters suggest that the number who travelled to Ireland is higher than has been suggested and that many other stories may remain to be re-discovered. This publication follows the contributions of nine men and one woman, namely, Olaudah Equiano (1745–1797), born in Africa and kidnapped as a young boy; Moses Roper (1815–1891), born into enslavement in North Carolina to mixed race parents; Charles Lenox Remond (1810–1873), born a free man in Massachusetts; Frederick Douglass (1818–1895), born into enslavement in Maryland, to mixed race parents; William Wells Brown (c.1814–1884), born into enslavement in Kentucky of mixed race parents; Henry Highland Garnet (1815–1882), born in Maryland to two enslaved parents; Edmund Kelly (1817–1884), born into enslavement in Tennessee to mixed race parents; Samuel Ringgold Ward (1817–1866), born into enslavement in Maryland to two enslaved parents; Benjamin Benson (1818–?), born into enslavement in Bermuda, freed and re-enslaved; and Sarah Parker Remond (1826–1894), born a free woman in Massachusetts. They all visited Ireland in their quest to end slavery, although their expectations, motivations and interactions were very different.

The early movement to end the slave trade was largely associated with William Wilberforce, an English reformer who championed anti-slavery both inside and outside of the British parliament. He embodied a first generation of moderate abolitionists who favoured a gradualist approach and who viewed abolition within an evangelical Christian framework. Wilberforce and his 'apostle' colleagues regarded the trade as unchristian, not simply because of its cruelty, but because the enslaved were deprived of knowledge of God.[4] Similarly, a number of abolitionists who visited Ireland used an evangelical lens for arguing against enslavement. They included Samuel Ringgold Ward, Henry Garnet, Edmund Kelly and Benjamin Benson. Despite being in an overwhelmingly Catholic country, these men for the most part only lectured in Protestant venues. In contrast, several other visitors spoke out against the role of Protestant churches in not condemning slavery but, as Frederick Douglass and Sarah Remond found, such criticisms were not welcomed by members of the church hierarchies.

In 1807, a victory came to the abolitionists with the ending of the slave trade by Britain and the United States. This partial triumph represented the first phase

Introduction 3

of anti-slavery. However, the continuation of human trafficking and slavery led to a new wave of agitation in the 1820s, with a fresh generation of male and female abolitionists, who were generally more militant than their predecessors. Again, they achieved some successes.[5] Britain's ending of slavery within her Empire in 1833 (except for in 'British' India) was heralded as an example of how peaceful the process could be.[6] Following this, abolitionist eyes increasingly focused on the United States. The American Civil War in the 1860s, and President Abraham Lincoln's 1863 Proclamation to end slavery, appeared to mark the end of this century-long struggle. Tragically, segregation, Jim Crow Laws and lynchings followed, demonstrating, as Charles Remond and Douglass had feared, that prejudice and racism would fill the vacuum created by ending enslavement. This battle proved to be a harder one to win.

In the long struggle to end enslavement in the British Empire and in North America, Britain and Ireland both played a special part. Britain's role in abolition was complicated by the fact that, until 1807, she was a major slave trading nation. In Ireland, while some individual towns and merchants may have benefitted from the trade, anti-slavery was more traditional than in the rest of the United Kingdom.[7] Leading Irish abolitionists, including Daniel O'Connell and his son John, liked to state that Ireland had never benefitted from the slave trade, while abolition had a long pedigree. In 1853, John O'Connell, informed an anti-slavery society meeting that:

> He desired to make known to the citizens of Dublin that their city was the first place in the United Kingdom to raise the voice of indignant and outraged humanity against the practices of the slave trade (cheers) ... One hundred and twenty-five years ago, in that very city, the voice of Ireland was raised in condemnation of slavery, and it was not until nearly fifty years after that a similar movement was attempted in either England or Scotland (cheers)![8]

This claim may not have been totally accurate, but it provided an insight into how Irish abolitionists viewed their historic role. Generally overshadowed by what happened in Britain, Irish engagement with the abolition movement and with black abolitionists was unique within transatlantic anti-slavery, more particularly for often placing the struggle within the larger desire for social justice. Involvement was complicated by Ireland's ongoing colonial status—the trope of Irish people being slaves was a frequently used part of the discourse. As many American abolitionists realized, Ireland was not independent, her people did not enjoy full civil or religious rights, while political power, land ownership and culture were disproportionately the preserve of the minority Protestant Ascendancy. Furthermore, the majority of visitors were shocked by the endemic poverty and subsistence crises that were a feature of Irish life and, to some, a visible manifestation of British misgovernment.[9] Ireland, therefore, more than any other part of the United Kingdom, could understand oppression, marginalization and racism—yet, as Frederick Douglass pointed out—while the Irish

4   *Introduction*

were oppressed and impoverished, they were *not* slaves. What was not in dispute, was that each of these visiting abolitionists viewed Ireland as a place of sanctuary, where they knew they would be assured of support.

Ireland's role in anti-slavery had a long pedigree. It was set against the backdrop of the country's perennial poverty and intermittent famines and the desire for political reform, if not full independence. There was frequently a confluence between Irish politics and transatlantic abolitionism. In the 1790s, several of the people who hosted former slave Olaudah Equiano were leaders of the republican United Irishmen, many of whom were to die or be exiled as a result of the 1798 Rising. The failed Rising had another unintended consequence. In its wake, the Dublin parliament was forced to vote itself out of existence, thus allowing Ireland to be absorbed into a new political entity, the United Kingdom. Consequently, after 1801, Ireland was governed from Westminster in London, with only 100 MPs (who were all Protestant) representing Irish interests in the House of Commons. The majority of Irish politicians favoured ending the slave trade and so they strengthened the abolitionist lobby. Their support contributed to the successful passage of the 1807 Act to end Britain's involvement in the Slave Trade.[10] In the wake of this legislation, and as war with Napoleonic France intensified, the slave question was put on the back-burner, not to re-emerge until the 1820s.

Transatlantic co-operation

While their reasons for travelling and their impact when overseas varied, the visiting abolitionists all agreed that transatlantic cooperation was vital to end enslavement. For them, especially those who had been formerly enslaved, Britain and Ireland were sanctuaries. In 1772, Granville Sharp, an English evangelical lawyer,[11] had won the Somerset case, which established that an enslaved person could not be forcibly removed from England.[12] This judicial decision was applied to Ireland (which then had its own parliament) and other British colonies.[13] It is thought that news of this decision was taken quickly across the Atlantic, probably by black mariners, to the delight of enslaved people.[14] The impact of this news is hard to measure, but a rare letter in the National Archives of Ireland reveals a tantalizing glimpse into the story of one escaped slave who made it to Ireland, albeit not to lecture. William Taylor, formerly a slave in the British West Indies, escaped to Dublin. He claimed that his master, Daniel Camp, had mistreated him, and that his back and arms provided proof of this. Writing to an unidentified recipient in December 1832, Taylor said that he was determined to 'make Dublin my Place of residence', hoping that he would be given a passport for protection. The letter somehow made its way to Richard Greene, the Law Advisor to the Lord Lieutenant, who told Taylor that being on Irish soil, he was safe, and that, 'If any violation of his personal liberty be attempted, he can procure his liberation upon application to any Judge'.[15] Taylor then disappeared. His letter had been written on the eve of Britain emancipating the enslaved people in the West Indies. A similarly touching story was reported in March 1833 in a Belfast newspaper, of a slave from Bermuda whose ship had docked in the port. He had been put in touch with the secretary of the anti-slavery society 'who entered warmly into the man's case'. The unnamed slave was 'delighted with his newly acquired freedom' and expressed his desire to seek employment.[16] He too then disappeared from public view. In addition to offering a safe haven, extending the struggle across the Atlantic was crucial, with public opinion being regarded as a vital weapon in winning the moral force argument against enslavement. To this end, abolitionist speakers often spoke of the 'weight of moral power'.[17] American abolitionists knew that events in Britain and Ireland were closely monitored in the United States, believing that 'the literature of Great Britain exercises so vast an influence over the public opinion of America'.[18] The holding of the first international Anti-Slavery Convention in London 1840 was a further indication of the central role that non-American abolitionists would play.[19] The presence of black abolitionists, who crisscrossed the United Kingdom to tell their stories, was crucial in keeping the support energized and engaged.

When in Belfast in 1841, Charles Remond informed his audience that he had come to Ireland because, '... he had advocated the abolition of slavery in America; he was now endeavouring to stimulate England, Ireland, and Scotland to raise their voices against it'.[20] Almost 20 years later, his sister, Sarah Remond, speaking in Waterford, stated:

> The abolitionists of America looked for sympathy to the British people; they looked to them for an expression of opinion in favour of the slave; such opinion would be listened to in America with great attention, and help to strike the fetters from the slave.[21]

At another meeting, when appealing on behalf of enslaved women, she ended by pointing out:

> ... the value to the American anti-slavery cause of those expressions of sympathy which it was in the power of the people England to send across the Atlantic, which would cheer the hearts of those engaged in the great struggle now going on and tend greatly to advance the cause of negro emancipation.[22]

Just as important as raising awareness in Ireland and Britain was the impact that these speakers had on their adversaries back home. Thus, in the decades before the Civil War, 'Britain's aid was seen by all sides, from the strongest supporters of slavery to the fiercest abolitionists, as decisive in empowering African Americans as political actors at home, despite their enormous disabilities'.[23] According to one historian, Britain's 'courting of escaped slaves such as Douglass ... receiving the adulation of crowds and the friendship of genteel white women, constituted the gravest possible insult'. Moreover, this

6 Introduction

was set against a backdrop of unequal power, at a time when the strength and reach of the British empire 'weighed on Americans, especially Southerners ... [and] their sense of inferiority when confronting John Bull's navy, factory complex, and vast well of investment capital, and his cultural and institutional sophistication'.[24] As a civil war seemed inevitable, the battle for hearts and minds in the battle to end enslavement had become a struggle in which the very future of America was at stake.

While transatlantic co-operation was most evident in the decades between 1830 and 1860, its origins lay in the late-eighteenth century. In the early 1790s, Equiano arrived in Ireland as the guest of the United Irishmen. These republicans, inspired by events in America and France, redefined what it meant to be Irish, urging that religious differences be put to one side. The fact that they also supported the abolition of slavery put them far ahead of other contemporary radicals. Their unsuccessful rising in 1798 was not only brutally put down, but resulted in the dissolution of the Irish parliament and direct rule from London under the umbrella of the Act of Union between Great Britain and Ireland. One consequence was that the city of Dublin went into decline, while decisions regarding the future of Ireland were made 300 miles away. The physical distance, however, was of less significance than the ideological one. Only seven years later, while the Napoleonic War raged, Britain abolished the Slave Trade—the act's passage through Westminster being assisted by the addition of 100 Irish MPs, who generally favoured abolition.

Anti-slavery agitation revived in the 1820s. In Britain, a new association was formed known as 'The Society for the Mitigation and Gradual Abolition of Slavery throughout the British Dominions'. It had the support of the ailing Wilberforce. As its name suggested, the focus of the society was on the British Empire, not America, and it advocated gradual, rather than immediate, abolition. In America, the 1820s were marked by the emergence of free black communities who established their own educational institutions and churches. In 1829, the inaugural Black Negro Convention was held in Philadelphia. It was the first of many and provided a valuable platform for many young black lecturers.[25] During this period of regrouping and reorientations, David Walker emerged as the most influential black abolitionist in America.[26] His powerful 1829 'Appeal to coloured people' demanded that slave-owners reform their ways, while exhorting enslaved people to take action to change their situation. He warned that bloodshed would be the alternative. As a new generation of activism was getting underway, Walker foregrounded the value of overseas support, while acknowledging the complexities of the situation:

> The English are the best friends the coloured people have upon earth. Though they have oppressed us a little and have colonies now in the West Indies, which oppress us *sorely,* — Yet notwithstanding they (the English) have done one hundred times more for the melioration of our condition, than all the other nations of the earth put together. The blacks cannot but respect the English as a nation, notwithstanding they have treated us a little cruel.

Introduction 7

There is no intelligent *black man* who knows anything, but esteems a real Englishman, let him see him in what part of the world he will—for they are the greatest benefactors we have upon earth. We have here and there, in other nations, good friends. But as a nation, the English are our friends.[27]

Changes were also taking place on the other side of the Atlantic. By this stage, prolonged illness meant that Wilberforce had retired from parliament and largely disappeared from the public stage, while his former mentor, the aged Thomas Clarkson, had reduced his active participation. They had, however, been replaced by a new abolitionist spokesperson—Irishman, Daniel O'Connell. In 1824, O'Connell had been persuaded to lend his support to abolition by Liverpool abolitionist, James Cropper. From the outset, O'Connell proved to be fearless, unrelenting and uncompromising on the issue, supporting an immediate and total ending to enslavement, wherever it existed.

In many ways, O'Connell was uniquely placed to champion enslaved and subjugated people.[28] As an Irish Catholic, he understood oppression, segregation and exclusion. The backdrop to his involvement was the campaign for Catholic Emancipation, namely, for the right of Catholics to sit in the British parliament. However, it would not be until 1829 that Catholics, led by O'Connell, would win this right. This success propelled him to celebrity status as the Liberator of his people. The victory also meant that O'Connell would sit in the House of Commons from 1829 until his death in 1847. For almost 20 years, he proved to be a an unrelenting defender of oppressed people from America to India, and from the West Indies to New Zealand, with the abolition of slavery being one of his priorities.

Ireland contributed to the anti-slavery revival in the 1820s in a number of other ways. Although small in number, Irish Quakers were at the forefront of reform and progressive movements, including abolition. The Webb family, who welcomed many abolitionists to their Dublin home between 1840 and 1860, came from this liberal Quaker tradition. In 1827, an Anti-Slavery Society had been founded in Dublin by local Quakers and other religious dissenters. O'Connell gave them his early support.[29] In 1830, they presented a petition to the British House of Commons calling for slavery to end.[30] This was the first of many petitions, which increased as the debate intensified in the early years of the decade.[31] In the first five months of 1833, the number of petitions presented to the British House of Commons had risen to 570.[32] It was not only Irish Quakers who opposed slavery. In 1829, the same year that O'Connell helped to achieve Catholic Emancipation, the Dublin Negro's Friends Society was formed by Charles Orpen.[33] Within a year, they had changed their name to the Hibernian Negro's Friend Society. Reflecting the new spirit of militancy, they demanded an immediate and total abolition of slavery. The Society was overtly Protestant, with several of its founders being openly anti-Catholic. Its objectives being:

To promote the utter abolition of Negro slavery, and also the moral improvement of the Negro Slave, by the means of the establishment of schools, the establishment of the Sacred Scriptures, and the employment of Scripture Readers.[34]

8   *Introduction*

The Society was successful enough to employ the pious, and eccentric, Captain Charles Stuart, 'an evangelist of the immediatist gospel', as their agent in England in 1831.[35] The close association between abolition and evangelicalism meant that O'Connell's insertion and prominence in the movement was a challenge to the traditional Protestant leadership. Moreover, he proved to be indefatigable. In 1830, O'Connell attended numerous anti-slavery meetings in Dublin and Cork. In Cork, O'Connell linked the issue of slavery to oppression on both sides of the Atlantic, telling his audience, 'he who was liberated himself may have the pleasure of striking the chain from others'.[36] Many of the other speakers were Protestant, including the Rev. J. McCrea, who claimed to have opposed O'Connell regarding 'feelings, religious and political', but admitted that he now felt 'gratifying pleasure to share a platform with him'.[37] Abolition, it seemed, was capable of transcending historic antagonisms.

The 1830s witnessed a more radical approach to anti-slavery on both sides of the Atlantic. In America, the publication of Walker's appeal and the founding by William Lloyd Garrison of the *Liberator* newspaper in January 1831, suggested a new level of militancy and organization. On the other side of the Atlantic, new leaders were also emerging who were similarly combative and favoured an immediate ending to the system. Enslaved people were also taking their own actions. At the end of 1831, a peaceful protest in Jamaica transformed into a large-scale revolt. This became known as the Baptist War after its leader, the Rev. Samuel Sharpe, an enslaved Baptist minister. The rebellion lasted around ten days and involved 60,000 slaves. The insurgents were aware of the debates taking place in the British parliament and believed that their emancipation was imminent, if not already granted. The suppression and subsequent reprisals against the slaves were brutal. Significantly, the resulting official enquiries were highly critical of the actions of the slave-owners, thereby contributed to speeding up the passing of the abolition legislation in 1833. Historian Gordon Barnes has identified in this revolt, a sophisticated revolutionary thinking that was part of a longer continuum of enslaved people seeking to liberate themselves, while locating themselves firmly within the 'age of revolutions'. He argued that, 'The Baptist War was able to lay the foundation for a socially revolutionary process, one that ended chattel slavery while failing to bring a political revolution to fruition'.[38] Almost 35 years later, there would be another revolt in Jamaica that was also viciously repressed and which, in turn, would draw the public wrath of both Samuel Ringgold Ward and Sarah Remond, but for very different reasons.

The much-awaited legislation to end slavery was passed in 1833,[39] but it disappointed those who had fought for it, they disapproving of the £20 million compensation given to slaveowners, and of the transition period known as 'apprenticeship', which effectively prolonged enslavement for up to 12 years. Even as the bill was passing through parliament, protests were being held. A large meeting of the Hibernian Negro's Friend Society was held in Dublin at the end of May to express 'dissatisfaction with the proposed plan' regarding apprenticeship. The speakers pointed out that as the legislation had declared slavery to be illegal, it made no sense that apprenticeship could be legal.[40] Nor

Introduction 9

were Irish women any less active or visible than men, philanthropy and abolition being areas in which females could enter into the public sphere. In Dublin, 5,000 women signed a petition to parliament on the same topic.[41] Additionally, they paid the *Dublin Evening Post* to reprint a speech made by veteran English abolitionist, Fowell Buxton, arguing against the system of apprenticeship.[42] In 1837, the Dublin Ladies' Association was founded as an auxiliary to the men's society. The following year, they sent a petition to Queen Victoria, signed by 75,000 Irish women, describing apprenticeship as being worse than slavery.[43] As Sarah Remond was to do 20 years later, they made a special appeal to their fellow women. O'Connell too, proved to be an outspoken critic of apprenticeship, both inside and outside of parliament. At a mass meeting held in Birmingham in February 1836, he was praised by Joseph Sturge, an English Quaker and founder of the British and Foreign Anti-Slavery Society, who described his speech as 'an address of extraordinary power by Daniel O'Connell, whose fidelity to the cause of the slave never faltered for an instant during his long and stormy public career'.[44]

In August 1837, a large meeting was held in the Rotundo Concert Rooms in Dublin at which the Webb brothers spoke.[45] The following month, the Hibernian Anti-Slavery Society was founded by Richard Webb, James Haughton and Richard Allen, which marked the beginning of a new phase of activity in the capital city. At the inaugural meeting, they drew up a 'Solemn Protest' against apprenticeship, describing it as 'merely transferring the whip from the Master to the Magistrate'. They also published, 'An Address to the People of Ireland', written with 'feelings of deep and bitter disappointment', claiming:

> Every principle of humanity and justice is flagrantly and systematically outraged by the general treatment of the Colonial Negro population, for whose emancipation our nation has liberally paid their Masters Twenty Million sterling, with interest.[46]

Although meetings were held in Belfast to condemn apprenticeship,[47] the failure of other parts of Ireland to take up the cause led the *Freeman's Journal* to issue a public rebuke in May 1838:

> The people of England are advocating the cause of the oppressed negro with an energy and perseverance equally honourable to them as men and Christians. We wish we could say as much for our own country, but on this subject there seems to be the most unaccountable—we were going to say disgraceful— apathy. The meeting of the citizens of Dublin at the Rotundo has not had the good effects we anticipated. We thought the seed sown on that occasion would have produced an abundant harvest—we fear it has fallen on a barren soil. What is Cork, and Limerick, and Waterford, and Galway, and Kilkenny, about? Why do the citizens of these influential towns not meet and forward petitions to the legislature in favour of their suffering brethren? We earnestly call upon them to bestir themselves in time; every law of humanity, every principle of justice, demand their interference.

10   Introduction

The paper went on to praise the people of the West Indies for the dignified way in which they had handled their liberation:

> Some thought that the negro would have broken loose and revenged himself upon his persecutors for the recollection of the planters' villainy was fresh in the mind of every man. Some thought that the sudden transition might prove too strong for his uncultivated mind, and render him dangerous to the public peace. But now no such pretext exists that the experiment has been made successfully. In Antigua and the Bermudas there was no preparatory step, and yet neither anarchy nor indolence prevailed amongst the entirely emancipated negroes. On the contrary, tranquility and religious thankfulness and willing industry everywhere prevailed, and is every day increasing. Experience has shown that the negro is as fit for freedom as the white man, and that his liberation would be not only safe, but productive of great benefit to his master. How could it be otherwise?[48]

Again, people in the West Indies played an important role in bringing the system to an end. In 1837, a first-hand account of apprenticeship had been published in London: *A Narrative of Events, since the First of August, 1834, by James Williams, an Apprenticed Labourer in Jamaica*.[49] The 26-page pamphlet was co-authored by Dr Archibald Leighton Palmer, a Scottish doctor working in Jamaica. The *Narrative* was sold in both the United Kingdom and Jamaica and had to be reprinted many times. Tellingly, the title page featured a speech made by O'Connell in 1833:

> Oh! The slave who toils from the rising sun to sundown—who labours in the cultivation of a crop whose fruits he may never reap—who comes home at nightfall, weary, faint, and sick of heart, to find in his hut creatures that are to run in the same career with himself—will you not tell him of a period when his toil will be at an end? Will you not give him a hope for his children?[50]

The outrage caused by the *Narrative* resulted in the British government appointing a commission of enquiry led by Special Magistrate, Sir John Daughtrey, and local justice, George Gordon. Their findings, which were made public swiftly, largely corroborated Williams' claims.[51] Around the same time, on 25 July 1838, Dr Jean Baptiste Phillipe, the first black member of the Trinidad and Tobago Council, introduced a motion demanding the ending of apprenticeship. It was successful.[52] In 1838, shortly after the report on William's findings was made public, the Apprenticeship System was ended, after only four years, not the intended twelve. Once again, anti-slavery forces on both sides of the Atlantic were in alignment. Following this victory, the interests of Irish and British abolitionists turned eastwards to British India and westwards to America. It was within this highly charged atmosphere that the first international anti-slavery convention was held in 1840, which brought abolitionists from all over the world to London.

In his capacity as a Member of the British parliament, O'Connell had played a pivotal role in bringing about the ending of slavery in the British

Introduction   11

Empire in 1833. However, he regarded the legislation as a tainted victory, objecting to the £20-million compensation paid to slave-owners and the imposition of a transition period for the enslaved, euphemistically referred to as apprenticeship. He spoke out against both. In the same year that apprenticeship was ended, O'Connell was involved in a public dispute with the American Ambassador to England, Andrew Stevenson, whom he openly accused of slave-breeding. The prolonged dispute polarized opinion on both sides of the Atlantic and led to O'Connell being challenged to a duel—which he declined.[53] When Charles Remond visited Ireland in 1841, he referred to this matter and called on people throughout the country to sign a petition, 'praying that Mr. Stevenson, the American slave-holding Ambassador, should be recalled from the Court of St. James's'.[54] Therefore, for abolitionists who visited Ireland and Britain in the 1830s and 1840s, O'Connell was the man to meet. The so-called 'King of the Beggars' may have been the nemesis of the British government and slave-holders alike, but he was the champion of the oppressed. As a politician, a lawyer, a skilled orator and a humanitarian, O'Connell was proving to be unparalleled as an international spokesperson for the enslaved.[55]

O'Connell's pre-eminent status was confirmed by his appearance at the first International Anti-Slavery Convention in London in June 1840. The holding of this convention was further evidence of the reinvigoration of the abolition movement and the desire for transatlantic unity in this fight. For visiting Americans, invoking the example of the British government's peaceful ending of slavery in the West Indies, and having the support of British and Irish abolitionists, was a powerful moral argument to send back home.[56] The 500 delegates who attended the Convention were overwhelmingly—and perhaps inevitably—drawn from Britain, Ireland and America.[57] The veteran, and at this stage, venerable, octogenarian British abolitionist, Thomas Clarkson was the Chairman of proceedings, but the undoubted star was O'Connell:

> When O'Connell made his appearance, the applause was absolutely deafening. He made a speech of great power, and denounced American slave-holders in blistering language—at the same time, paying the highest compliments to American abolitionists.[58]

O'Connell was joined by 17 delegates from Ireland, representing Cork, Dublin and Belfast. They included James Haughton, Richard Webb and Richard Allen, the founders of the Hibernian Anti-Slavery Society, and Dr Richard Madden, who, after 1833, had been employed by the British government as a Justice of the Peace in the West Indies, to oversee the ending of enslavement.[59]

The decision to hold an international Anti-Slavery Convention in London was a bold initiative. But if a purpose of the convention was to unify the international abolition movement, it was not totally successful; only months earlier, there had been a split in the American Anti-Slavery Society, with the more moderate American and Foreign Anti-Slavery Society being established. It was their sister group, the British and Foreign Anti-Slavery Society, that hosted the

12 *Introduction*

Convention. More radical attendees also wanted to tie the demand for abolition in with the quest for women's rights. Negotiating these differences and divisions within the movement would prove to be one of the challenges facing abolitionists visiting the United Kingdom. Perhaps unsurprisingly, on the first day, a vote was taken on the question of whether women could have full delegate status. The outcome was that they could only be observers and would have to watch the proceedings from a gallery. Their exclusion was to sow the seeds for the seminal Seneca Falls Convention in 1848, with its demand for women's suffrage.[60] Garrison, arriving late to the convention and accompanied by a young black abolitionist, Charles Lenox Remond, chose to sit with the women, meaning that they too could not participate in the proceedings. O'Connell had initially opposed women delegates, but quickly regretted his 'unworthy' action. He visited the women every day, much to their delight.[61] One of the excluded women, Elizabeth Cady Stanton, described him as, 'tall, well-developed and a magnificent looking man, and probably one of the most effective speakers Ireland ever produced'.[62] Regardless of the divisions, the gathering was successful in terms of attendance, audience and impact. A further outcome was that during the convention, O'Connell agreed to lend his name to a petition imploring the Irish in America to support abolition. It would fall to Remond to promote the project in Ireland and to physically carry the document back to America. The mixed, and largely negative, response to the 'Irish Address' revealed how deeply controversial and problematic this issue was for Irish immigrants to America.

Following the Convention, several American abolitionists availed themselves of the opportunity to visit Ireland. They included Lucretia Mott, a colleague of Garrison and one of the women who had been denied delegate status in London. She and her husband, as so many visiting abolitionists would be, were the guests of Richard and Hannah Webb in their home on Great Brunswick Street.[63] Like so many others, she found her time in Ireland to be liberating. Writing from Dublin, Mott informed Maria Weston Chapman of the lack of prejudice regarding her gender:

> Since we came to Dublin I have accepted an invitation to speak in a Temperance Mg.–not the least manifestation of dissatisfaction—although unexpected to most present—but on the contrary 'cheers long & loud'—& not merited neither—but such is the custom in this land—and I mention it as proof that the objections to our admission were all hollow.[64]

Richard Webb confirmed Mott's description, agreeing that while hearing a woman lecturer was 'altogether new', she had been listened to 'with good respect and attention'.[65] The Motts were also delighted with 'the generous hospitality extended', which Lucretia described as 'genuine Irish'.[66] They dined with the Webb brothers, James and Thomas, as well as the Haughton and the Allen families. While the Motts were in Dublin, three more American abolitionists arrived in the Webb household: Parker Pillsbury, Nathaniel Peabody and William Garrison.[67] Webb told Garrison that he was 'deeply gratified at having

Introduction 13

an opportunity of meeting with you once more and showing you some little attention in our own country'.[68] Garrison stayed with the Webb family for three days in late July.[69] After he left, Webb wrote to him, 'you have wound yourself round our memories in a way which it will give old Father Time a mighty troublesome job to twist off again'.[70] It was the start of a life-long friendship and, for the next half century, followers of Garrison would be warmly welcomed by the Webbs.

Cady Stanton and her husband, Henry, also visited Dublin. Like Lucretia, she had been denied delegate status at the Convention. Not all visitors to Ireland were followers of Garrison. At the end of August, James Birney from America and John Scoble from England arrived in Dublin. One of their purposes was to attend an anti-slavery meeting at which O'Connell would speak. Birney had resigned from the American Anti-Slavery Society because he disagreed with equal rights for women.[71] Scoble was one of the founders of the British and Foreign Anti-Slavery Society. In advance of their visit, information was provided about them in the Irish press, suggesting a general interest in anti-slavery:

> Mr. Birney removed from Alabama, emancipated and settled all his slaves, giving them education in defiance of the laws of Kentucky, and himself setting up a newspaper in Cincinnati, standing his ground there against many and awful attempts upon his life, and at length gaining complete victory, and establishing freedom of speech and the press ... Mr. Bimey [sic] is about to deliver lectures in the principal English towns on American slavery ... We may well mention, in conclusion, that Mr. Birney's father was an Irishman, and that it is his intention to visit the land of his fathers before he goes to America. We hope to see the time when the advent of such a man on our shores will be hailed by tens of thousands with hearty respect and gratification.[72]

On 26 October, Birney, Stanton and Scoble addressed a large anti-slavery meeting in the Adelphi Theatre in Dublin. Haughton was in the chair. O'Connell had been invited but was away travelling. Regardless, he was singled out for praise for his principled stance on slavery in general and his latest statements criticizing the continuation of slavery in 'British' India. Scoble, who had recently visited the West Indies, spoke first about 'the present condition of the liberated negroes'.[73] The major talking point, however, which had also been discussed at the Convention, was the lack of support from Irish Americans—and sometimes, outright hostility to abolition. Stanton informed the 'numerous' audience that:

> there were nearly two thousand abolition societies, containing about three hundred thousand members ... They asked for the sympathy of Irishmen, because they could do much to help them in their enterprise ... He would ask Irishmen what could they do for the abolition of slavery? They had no idea of the amount of service they could render (hear). They could exert

14 *Introduction*

a social influence on America (loud cries of hear, hear). America is filled with Irishmen; they have not forgotten their country; and if appeals came to them from Dublin and Belfast, Cork and Limerick, they would not be deaf to the call so made upon them; they could exercise a legislative influence in America ... He would ask them to rise above a religious influence, and to put beyond the pale of their good opinion any Irishman in America who had anything to do in the support of slavery.

The seasoned Irish abolitionist, Dr Madden, spoke in support of Stanton:

From his own knowledge he could say that Irishmen in America were hostile to the abolitionists there. He begged that Irishmen would warn their friends going to the United States to avoid the contamination of slavery— that few could escape.[74]

Although the subject matter was disheartening, the attendance at the meeting and the press coverage suggested that regardless of what was happening in Irish America, within Ireland, anti-slavery was strong. Interest continued even after Birney and Scoble had left Ireland, one newspaper reporting that they had:

mixed extensively in private society during their short sojourn here. They alluded to Wm. Lloyd Garrison, of Boston, and N. P. Rogers of Concord, New Hampshire; and they embraced this opportunity of bearing record to the value of their visit spreading true anti-slavery principles amongst those with whom they associated.[75]

As a result of the Convention, therefore, new friendships had been forged and old enmities confirmed. A particularly enduring partnership had been created between William Lloyd Garrison and abolitionists in Dublin, one consequence of which was that a steady stream of abolitionists travelled to Ireland over the subsequent two decades. A second Convention was held in London in 1843. Although it was not as successful as the first one, within the space of only three years, it appeared that a momentum had been created to make abolition not simply a transatlantic question, but an international one. Significantly, the United Kingdom was the location of both meetings. In the intervening years, a petition, signed by almost 70,000 Irish men and women, had been sent across the Atlantic, chastising Irish Americans for their lack of support. More importantly, during the decade, 1833 to 1843, enslaved people in the West Indies had been emancipated, the Apprenticeship System had ended and, in 1843, slavery had been abolished in India. Irish abolitionists had been at the forefront of each of these campaigns. At this stage, however, American slavery appeared to be as entrenched as ever. American abolition, however, had a new rising star. In 1845, Frederick Douglass made his way to Ireland, following in the footsteps of Equiano and Charles Remond, but creating a new pathway that would become a benchmark for black abolitionists who followed.

Introduction 15

Irish America

The 1840 Convention had agreed that lack of support by Irish Americans should be tackled directly by the creation of a mass petition. The Convention had also determined that if O'Connell's name was attached to the document, and he appealed directly to Irish emigrants, it would be treated with respect.[76] Thus, the idea of an 'Irish Address' had been born. O'Connell, however, had little direct involvement with the project. At this stage, he was preoccupied with a new political initiative to repeal the Act of Union.[77] Nonetheless, he continued to lend his name to the Address and to allow agents of the new Repeal Association to collect signatures. It was left to Irish supporters of Garrison to help bring the idea to fruition. A black American abolitionist had been charged with the task of overseeing the creation of the Irish Address. Charles Lenox Remond, born free and from an affluent abolitionist family, had been employed by Garrison since 1838 as the first black agent of the American Anti-Slavery Society. It fell to Remond to champion the Address in Ireland and to convey it to the United States. Yet, despite the perceived urgency of the situation, it would take a year before any concrete action was taken and Remond visited Ireland. This mission meant that Remond was following in the footsteps of Equiano, while forging a new pathway that Douglass and other abolitionists would later take.

In August 1841, the Address was unveiled at a meeting of the Hibernian Anti-Slavery Society in Dublin. Remond was present, he being a guest of the Webb family. The petition stated:

> The object of this address is to call your attention to the subject of SLAVERY IN AMERICA, that foul blot upon the noble institutions and the fair-name of your adopted country. But for this one stain, America would indeed be a land worthy of your adoption; but she will never be the glorious country that her free constitution designed her to be, so long as her soil is polluted by the footprint of a single slave.[78]

Initially, it had been hoped that 100,000 signatures would be collected, but by the time Remond returned home, fewer than 70,000 people had signed—still an impressive number—and more were collected following Remond's departure. To O'Connell's head-lining signature had been added that of another influential Irish man—Father Mathew, the 'apostle of temperance'. Richard Allen explained to Garrison that only these two illustrious signatures had been included on the grounds that: 'We have not sought for many other *great* names, although we could get plenty. It is emphatically *the voice of the people* we wanted and send'.[79]

Remond returned to the United States at the end of 1841 with his precious cargo. It was unveiled in Faneuil Hall in January 1842. A newcomer to the anti-slavery lecturing circuit was present on the stage—Frederick Douglass. If there was disappointment that the 100,000 signatures hoped for had not been collected, it was not evident. A resolution was passed thanking O'Connell and Father Mathew, immediately followed by one:

16 *Introduction*

That we receive, with the deepest gratitude, the names of the sixty thousand Irishmen, who, in the trial-hour of their own struggle for liberty, have not forgotten the slave on this side of the water; that we accept, with triumphant exultation, the *Address* they have forwarded to us, and pledge ourselves to circulate it through the length and breadth of our land, till the pulse of every man, and specially every man who claims *Irish* parentage, beats true to the claims of patriotism and humanity.[80]

Opponents to the Address, however, were unequivocal in their condemnations, the following appearing in several American newspapers:

For some time past there has been a statement going the rounds, that the great O'Connell and Father Mathew had signed a memorial to the Irish of the United States, urging them to embrace the views of the abolitionists. *This is a foul slander.* Such a meeting was got up in Dublin, under the influence of Dr. Madden, an Irishman, who has sold himself to England, and his soul to the States; but neither of the great Irish champions had anything to do with it. Abolition is a British, not an Irish doctrine, and there is not in the United States as we believe, a single Irish abolitionist.[81]

The largely negative response to the petition revealed how controversial and problematic this issue was for Irish immigrants to America, who were being asked to criticize the Constitution of the country that had given them shelter.[82] Despite the vocal opposition of pro-slavery advocates and several leading Irish Americans, Garrison and his supporters put a positive, if tepid, slant on its reception, telling their followers at the end of 1843 that, 'O'Connell's denunciations of slavery are producing some good effects in the States'. Moreover, the struggle for abolition was being linked directly to Ireland's struggle for independence and the wider search for human rights:

The friends of universal liberty, who sympathize with the American slave, and with the oppressed people of Ireland in their peaceful struggles against British tyranny, of whatever sect or party, are invited, one and all, to assemble in Faneuil Hall, on Saturday evening, Nov. 18, 1843, at seven o'clock, to listen to a voice from Ireland, in the form of an Address on the subject of American Slavery, written by Daniel O'Connell, and unanimously adopted by the Dublin Repeal Association ... and to take such action respecting said address as its character and the circumstances in which it has been put forth may require. Irishmen, if you revere the name of your great leader and champion, come to the old cradle of liberty and listen to what he has so recently said of American slavery, and of those who, under the guise of a pretended zeal for the welfare of your native country, are endeavouring to blind your eyes to the enormities of that diabolical system, and keep you from espousing the cause of mercy and

Introduction 17

justice in the land of your adoption. Several distinguished friends of human rights will address the meeting.[83]

This and other appeals fell on deaf ears. Regardless of the intervention of O'Connell and other Irish abolitionists, the role of many Irish Americans remained indifferent or antagonistic towards abolition. Consequently, black abolitionists who visited Ireland remained perplexed that the ardency of abolitionists in Ireland did not survive the Atlantic crossing.

Possibly out of politeness, many black abolitionist visitors avoided mentioning the role of Irish Americans in upholding slavery or not supporting abolition. A small number, however, including Douglass and Samuel Ringgold Ward, did tackle it head on. In his *Narrative*, Ward referred to the issue, stating, 'Englishmen, Irishmen, and Scotchmen, generally become the bitterest of Negro-haters, within fifteen days of their naturalization—some not waiting so long'.[84] He juxtaposed the stance of the Irish in America against the support of abolition in Ireland:

> How I wish that the immigrant from the Emerald Isle understood the doctrine of the brotherhood of man and practiced it towards his coloured fellow citizen! If he did, one of the most serious obstacles to the cause of the Negro would disappear in America. I do hope that Irish abolitionists will be true to emigrants, exhorting them to save themselves from the abominations of proslaveryism, and rebuking those who ruthlessly trample upon the Negro, who found friends in O'Connell and Madden, and who now, for the best of reasons, blesses the names of Richard Webb, Mr. Jennings, the Marquis of Sligo, and the Right Honourable John Wynne.[85]

Ward followed this extortion with a warning:

> If, however, the present hostility of the Irish towards the black continue, it may pass the bounds of even a Negro's endurance and provoke such a reaction as all must regret. The increasing numbers, growing intelligence, and advancing progress, of the Negro in America, will one day make him no mean foe for the Celt to contend against. Before such disaster befall both races, and that a spirit of mutual good will may [sic] prevail,
>
> > *let us pray, that come it may,*
> > *An' come it will for a' that;*
> > *That man to man, the warld all o'er,*
> > *Shall brithers be, an' a' that.*[86]

Henry Highland Garnet, when in Ireland in 1851, took a different approach, appealing to Ireland's long tradition of demonstrating 'an undying attachment to the principles of liberty' and urging the Irish who emigrated to America to carry this moral value with them.[87]

18   *Introduction*

Transatlantic crossings

The 1840s witnessed the emergence of a new generation of black abolitionist leaders who were public intellectuals, powerful orators and personally charismatic. They included William Wells Brown, Frederick Douglass, Henry Highland Garnet, Moses Roper and Samuel Ringgold Ward. Their speaking and writing talents were even more remarkable given that they had received no formal education but were largely self-taught. Their motivations for travelling to Ireland varied, and they each experienced the country and its people in different ways. The 1850 Fugitive Slave Act resulted in a wave of escaped slaves travelling to Britain and Ireland, traversing the country sometimes in competition for the same audiences and—in some cases—for the same financial resources. This group included Edmund Kelly, William and Ellen Craft, Henry Box Brown and Benjamin Benson. The decade ended with the visit of Sarah Parker Remond, Charles' younger sister, whose poise, intelligence and charm were universally admired. Douglass, Wells Brown and Sarah Remond were unusual in that their first encounters with non-American abolitionists were with Irish—not British—colleagues. This allowed them to see Ireland with their own eyes, and not through a prism of British prejudice.

Even when safely on British or Irish soil, and regardless of experiencing any overt prejudice, black abolitionists were often viewed through a racialized lens, especially when it came to describing their appearance. The language of enslavement was present in many other ways, including how to self-identity. On freeing themselves from enslavement, an early action was to change name—partly for safety but also as an act of redefinition. Equiano was unusual in being remembered by his African name, despite his personal preference for his given name, Gustavus Vassa. When overseas, the question of being denied American citizenship also became central to the question of how to self-identity. In Belfast, Douglass reflected on this issue:

> I have no end to serve, no creed to uphold, no government to defend; and as to nation, I belong to none. I have no protection at home, or resting-place abroad. The land of my birth welcomes me to her shores only as a slave, and spurns with contempt the idea of treating me differently. So that I am an outcast from the society of my childhood, and an outlaw in the land of my birth.[88]

For Wells Brown, Garnet and Sarah Remond, the possession of a passport and travel visa were central to how they viewed themselves. Garnet was the first black person to be given a passport since the 1857 Dred Decision, which had ruled that black people, free or enslaved, had no rights to citizenship. For Sarah Remond, the issue of obtaining a travel visa became a means of holding the American government up to public ridicule. Language was again important. Garnet was insistent that the word 'Negro' be used to describe him in his passport. Wells Brown came to reject that word, preferring African. By making this choice, he came full circle to the term used by Equiano in the 1780s. Douglass and Harriet Jacobs frequently referred to themselves as 'Fugitive' or 'Fugitive Slave', thus inverting their status and simultaneously challenging the authorities.[89]

Introduction 19

The various abolitionists who travelled to Britain, and then onwards to Ireland, hoped to win support for abolition by telling their personal life stories to hundreds, if not thousands, of strangers. They relied on audiences—both for their lectures and publications—to enable them to earn a livelihood. Writing their life stories became an accepted way of doing this. The genre of slave narratives, of which Equiano had been an early and successful proponent, was an important way of reaching larger audiences than simply through lecturing. It also provided a much-needed source of income. While Frederick Douglass's narrative became the most famous, and proved to have the most longevity, there were many more. Other authors, however, never enjoyed the public profile accorded to Douglass. Narratives that predated Douglass's included those by William Grimes in 1825,[90] Mary Prince in 1831 and one of the first to be written by a woman,[91] and Lunsford Lane in 1842.[92] Harriet Jacobs's narrative published in 1862, written while her country was engaged in a brutal war to end slavery, was amongst the number that were lost from public view for decades.[93]

Several of the more successful narratives were reprinted numerous times, some having sold out within months. Reprints provided an opportunity to change or make additions to the original version. Several were enlarged with different images being included. Equiano, who in the space of five years published eight further reprints, used later editions to include letters of introduction and articles praising him as a way of countering false assertions, including suggestions that he had not penned the narrative himself.[94] Many narratives included similar endorsements, generally from white patrons. Douglass and Wells Brown, when publishing Irish editions of their life stories, possibly emboldened by being 3,000 miles away from their mentor Garrison and from danger of recapture, felt liberated enough to insert their own Prefaces. In addition, the second Irish edition of Douglass's narrative allowed him to demonstrate his agency and independence by taking control of the editorial process, even to the point of disagreeing with Webb about what should be included.

Not all abolitionists wrote narratives. Charles Remond and his sister Sarah, although both born free and both well educated, published little. While in England, Sarah gave an interview in 1861, which was the closest she came to revealing her personal history in written form. In the same year, a biographical sketch appeared.[95] Similarly, Garnet, born into enslavement around 1815 and regarded as an intellectual of the movement, chose not to publish a memoir.[96] Benjamin Benson's narrative was written by a third party, who, with little evidence, accepted his story as true. Providing a written account of a personal life story was not without its perils. Both at the time and subsequently, accusations of distortion, dishonesty, exaggeration and plagiarism were directed at some of the narratives.[97] Importantly though, these publications extended and embedded support for anti-slavery, while engaging the readers in this cause. An analysis of the first major narrative, by Equiano, which became a prototype for many that followed, described its text as being a 'performative manifesto'. The author's 'careful construction of information' to tell the 'interesting' life history of the former slave, was a central part of 'his nationwide effort to convert sympathetic

20 *Introduction*

actors into political actors'.[98] Sympathy for the enslaved then needed to be transformed into sustained political activity or, as Douglass informed his audience in Dublin, 'Agitate, agitate, agitate'.[99]

Narratives were written for a predominantly white audience who brought their own sensitivities to the reading process. For those who lived outside of the States, they were a powerful antidote to pro-slavery propaganda, especially as they were told by people who had first-hand experience. Thus, in 1848, several British newspapers reprinted a quote from Theodore Parker that:

> The lives of Moses Roper, of Lunsford Lane, of Moses Grundy, Frederick Douglass, and W. W. Brown, are before the public and prove what could easily be learned from the advertisements of southern newspapers, conjectured from the laws of the southern states, or foretold outright from a knowledge of human nature itself: that the sufferings of three millions of slaves form a mass of misery which the imagination can never realize, till the eye is familiar with its terrible details.[100]

While slave narratives proved to be popular with the reading public, it was a novel, written by a free, privileged white woman, Harriet Beecher Stowe, which proved to be the best seller of the nineteenth century, far outselling any of the narratives. Ten thousand copies of *Uncle Tom's Cabin* were purchased in the United States in its first week of release, and one and a half million copies in Great Britain within one year.[101]

In addition to publishing their life stories, lecturing was essential to promote the visiting abolitionists and help the sales of their narratives. They each proved to be skilful and creative in devising ways to engage—and entertain—their audiences. Many of the fugitive slaves exhibited instruments of torture—whips, manacles, neck collars—often linking them in with the cruel treatment that they had personally received. Many proved to be powerful speakers, making their arguments clearly and cogently, demonstrating a knowledge of history and of contemporary issues. They also had a great command of vocabulary, making biblical and literary allusions and using sophisticated rhetorical devices—all the most impressive from speakers who were self-educated.[102] Furthermore, they were clearly refuting the stereotype that black people were intellectually inferior to white people. Many lecturers would quote poetry, the English poet, William Cowper, and Scottish poet, Robbie Burns, being favourites. More unusually, Moses Roper when lecturing in the north of England, chose a local poet, James Montgomery, to recite, doing so in a 'soul-stirring fashion'.[103] Frequent references were made to the Bible, even by abolitionists who were critical of organized religion. In particular, Benjamin Benson, although not a minister, became renowned for the pious tone of his lectures. More light-heartedly, Douglass and Wells Brown would delight their audiences by spontaneously bursting into song. Douglass also brought his singing friends, the Hutchinson family, to an anti-slavery meeting in Dublin, it being the first time there had been music at such an event. The

Introduction 21

two acknowledged masters of public speaking, Douglass and Ward, charmed their audiences with their humility, self-deprecation and humour, but also with their skill at mimicry, usually parodying American slave-owners. Unusually, when in Ireland, an experience that Ward did not totally enjoy, he mimicked his hosts, 'it's meself to blame for niver remimbering the gintlemen's name at all, at all'.[104] A small number of the speakers made use of a new visual craze, that of the panorama. Wells Brown was a pioneer in this form of performance, one newspaper stating that, 'the last new move in this movement is the exhibition of a new "moving" panorama consisting of a series of 25 views'.[105] Panoramas were also used by Henry Box Brown, Presley Ball and Anthony Burs.[106] More unusually, Edmund Kelly sold woodcuts that featured images of his family and four children as a way of raising money.[107]

The period from 1840 to 1860 was marked by massive public interest in the issue of slavery as audience attendance figures and book sales attested. Moreover, the personal stories were reinforced in popular culture, with songs, musicals, plays, performances and visual images about enslavement abounding, which overwhelmingly sided with the enslaved people. A number were racially offensive, something that Douglass challenged when in Limerick, arguing that a local 'blackface' performance was not entertaining, but was perpetuating negative stereotypes.[108] Many of the visitors proved adept at using the media to promote themselves and their publications. Equiano, for example, placed self-promoting articles in newspapers in each location where he was lecturing, ostensibly to thank his subscribers and supporters but, more importantly, to keep himself and his narratives in public view. Almost 70 years later, Sarah Remond made use of the press to draw attention to instances of prejudice and to ridicule the American government for denying her a travel visa. Nor was coverage of these activities confined to newspapers in Ireland or Britain, as the actions of the visiting abolitionists were followed by newspapers across the Atlantic, on both sides of the divide.

Although frequently relying on white patronage for endorsements and introductions, several black visitors increasingly demonstrated their desire not only to tell their own stories, but also to shape their own destinies. In this regard, Wells Brown proved to be pioneering, organizing commemorations to celebrate West Indian Emancipation Day, using London as his stage. At the 1851 event, the 'American Fugitive Slaves in the British Metropolis' association was formed by Wells Brown and other exiled American slaves. The aim was to assist fellow fugitives find employment or education, and to adjust to their new lives.[109] Several leading British and American abolitionists were present including George Thompson and Maria Chapman. Wells Brown, however, made it clear that the black abolitionists present were there to be listened to, not to listen to others speaking on their behalf, later writing:

> In different parts of the hall were men and women from nearly all parts of the kingdom, besides a large number who, drawn to London by the Exhibition, had come in to see and hear these oppressed people plead their own cause.[110]

22 *Introduction*

According to Joel Schor, too few scholars have communicated sufficiently 'the infighting, passionate conflicts and mutual suspicions which came to generate permanent dislikes among black abolitionists'.[111] Although seeking the same goal—the ending of enslavement—in crucial ways these men and women were very different, with their experiences, aspirations, political and religious outlooks being neither united nor homogeneous. Their individual stories demonstrated that the abolitionist movement was far from monolithic and that black abolitionists were individually diverse. Inevitably, there were multiple points of conflict and opinions that could change over time, but key points of contention included the fact that some abolitionists supported emigration and colonization abroad, others did not, but favoured integration; some embraced women as equals, for others, this was a step too far; some believed moral suasion would win the day, others favoured engagement in politics; some advocated the necessity of force, others preferred non-resistance; some were integrationists, others championed black nationality. All, however, desired the self-elevation of the black population. They wanted to free their people from enslavement and uplift them in their own eyes and in the eyes of the world. The influence of black abolitionists on each other's political outlook has not always been fully appreciated either. In this regard, three of the intellectual giants—Douglass, Garnet and Ward—stand out. They each took a different position on the Constitution, religion, colonization and the path to liberation, but through constant debating, either face to face or in the columns of newspapers, they challenged and helped refine each other's views. Although Douglass often criticized Ward, he also wrote of his debt to his fellow abolitionist for helping him to hone his own political outlook.[112]

Douglass's meteoric rise to prominence was noted both by the public and his fellow abolitionists. When Douglass and Remond lectured together in 1842, one newspaper posed the question, as to whether the older man was jealous of the younger one, forcing Remond to issue a public rebuttal.[113] Following the success of his time overseas, Douglass was paid more money by the *Liberator* than either Wells Brown or Remond, as the paper wanted to keep his services and name association, even though Douglass intended to start his own newspaper.[114] Garnet, who was considered by some to be the equal, if not superior, to Douglass in terms of his logical and oratorical skills, in 1849 accused Douglass of falling prey to the 'green-eyed monster' of jealousy.[115] In 1850, fellow black abolitionist Martin Delany, chastised his colleagues for their very public bickerings, warning Ward, Garnet and Douglass that:

> … while others are writing you into fame, you are writing each other down!
>
> The public has announced you as aspirants—jealous of each other's popularity … with a determination to accomplish the design of personal ambition, though it be done over the ragged fragments of the liberties of your almost hopeless struggling people. The friends of Mr Douglass say, 'Ward is jealous of Douglass's popularity', while the friends of Mr Ward, on the other hand, say, 'Douglass is jealous of Ward and Garnet, lest they become as popular throughout the country as himself'. And in this sir, you give them good reason to say, while you continue this personal hostility to each other.[116]

Introduction 23

There were also instances of jealousy among white abolitionists towards their black colleagues, they rarely having the same oratory skills, charisma or compelling life story.[117] While in Ireland, Douglass was aware that his white travelling companion, James Buffum, resented the attention that he was receiving. In a private letter to a friend in America, Douglass admitted, 'My old friend Buffum finds the tables turned on him completely—the people lavish nearly all of their attention on the negro'.[118]

Abolitionists also differed when it came to making financial appeals. Equiano, the Remonds, Douglass and Wells Brown never asked for money for themselves from their audiences, but suggested that they should support the women's bazaars in Boston or Rochester. In sharp contrast, Roper, Benson, Kelly and others appealed for financial contributions for themselves, their families, their churches or schools. Early in his tour, Roper explained that his appeal for money was so that he could train to become a missionary. His failure to ever do so, led to him being accused publicly of 'genteel begging' by a former ally.[119] Another major fault-line concerned the role of churches and organized religion. Criticizing the churches in America and elsewhere for being complicit with enslavement was central to Douglass's mission; for others, this represented a heresy. Since the late-eighteenth century, Wilberforce and his 'apostle' colleagues (so called because of their evangelical beliefs) had viewed slavery as unchristian, part of its cruelty arising from the fact that the enslaved were being deprived of knowledge of God through the Scriptures.[120] Abolitionists from Wilberforce to Ward, therefore, believed that Christianity was the way to end the unchristian evil of slavery. Consequently, the moral and spiritual improvement of enslaved people was an integral part of the mission. However, this vision sometimes was allied with an evangelical Protestantism that was overtly anti-Catholic. A number of abolitionists who visited Ireland used an evangelical lens for arguing against enslavement. They included Ward, Garnet, Kelly and Benson. Tellingly, these men avoided contact with Catholic audiences and lectured in Protestant venues. Nor were their attitudes unique. In 1851, the Rev. William Munroe, a black Anglican minister from Detroit, spoke in several Protestant church halls in Belfast. His purpose in Ireland was to raise money to build a church for his congregation at home. In one of his lectures, he attacked the Catholic Church, claiming, 'both the Pope and his priesthood had ever been the abettors of slavery'.[121] It was a gratuitous and unfounded insult but was revealing of the complexity of divisions and alliances within abolition.

Rather than view enslavement through a Christian lens, several abolitionists including Equiano, Douglass and the Remonds, framed their arguments in terms of social justice and the quest for universal civil rights. In this regard, visiting Ireland and observing its poverty and its struggle for independence was critical in helping them to refine their own political outlook. This was most evident in the intellectual development of Douglass. Shortly after leaving the country, he wrote to Garrison:

> I see much here to remind me of my former condition, and I confess I should be ashamed to lift up my voice against American slavery, but that I know the cause of humanity is one the world over. He who really and only feels for the

24 *Introduction*

American slave, cannot steel his heart of the woes of others; and he who thinks himself an abolitionist, yet cannot enter into the wrongs of others, has yet to find a true foundation for his anti-slavery faith.[122]

Douglass's championing of the black republic of Haiti in 1893, was an indication of his life-time commitment to international human rights. For other abolitionists, the rising in Jamaica in 1865 showed how diverse attitudes could be, the brutal response by the British authorities being opposed by all supporters of Garrison. Observing from England, both Sarah Remond and Ellen Craft personally chastised the controversial Governor of the island for his cruelty to the insurgents. In Ireland, Webb was also appalled by the brutality of the response, believing it demonstrated, 'how little mercy a coloured population have to hope for either of justice or mercy at the hands of white planters who have full power in their hands'.[123] In contrast, from his new ministry in Jamaica, Ward roundly condemned the native population. These tensions and divisions were not unique to black abolitionists but were a microcosm of the divisions regarding the best way to end slavery and segregation in the United States and elsewhere.

Due to the restrictions on both enslaved and free black people receiving a formal education, many of the visitors were self-taught. Regardless, as their writings and lectures attested, they were articulate, well informed, widely read and intellectually refined. Douglass and Wells Brown in particular, proved to be talented writers in diverse genres. For others, travelling overseas provided an opportunity to acquire an education. Moses Roper, who first came to England in the 1830s, attended college in London for two years.[124] William and Ellen Craft, who had made a dramatic escape from enslavement disguised as master (Ellen) and slave (William), were illiterate. Ellen, therefore, pretended to have an injured arm so that she would not be expected to write.[125] When they eventually found themselves in England, several benefactors paid for them to receive a formal education. This enabled William (with the assistance of his good friend, Wells Brown) to write a narrative of their dramatic experiences.[126] Both Charles and Sarah Remond, born into a free and affluent family, had attended school but still felt their education to be lacking as, even in the free states, prejudice against black people receiving an education was deep rooted. Garnet, an acknowledged intellectual, had been driven with five other black students out of Canaan Institute in New Hampshire when the local people objected to their presence.[127] Despite these challenges, the academic achievements of many black abolitionists challenged all negative stereotypes. Late in life, Sarah Remond and Wells Brown chose medicine as their profession, joining Harriet Tubman, James McCune Smith, David Ruggles and Martin Delany in this calling.[128] Sarah received her qualifications in Italy and chose to practice there too.

One thing that most visiting black abolitionists agreed on was the absence of prejudice based on colour in either Ireland or Britain. The journey there, however, could be a grim reminder of their status; neither Charles Remond nor Douglass, for example, were allowed to have cabins on the Atlantic crossing, even though they had paid for them. Remond related to an audience in Belfast that, as a result

Introduction 25

of this treatment, he had suffered from sea-sickness throughout the journey.[129] Within weeks of being in England, however, Remond wrote to a friend in America that 'prejudice ... this hydra-headed personage, thanks be to God, has but few advocates in this country; if any, I have it to learn'.[130] Similarly, Harriet Jacobs, a fugitive slave who arrived only months before Douglass, not to lecture, but as companion to a white family, wrote:

> My visit to England is a memorable event in my life ... I remained abroad ten months, which was much longer than I had anticipated. During all that time, I never saw the slightest symptom of prejudice against color. Indeed, I entirely forgot it, till the time came for us to return to America.[131]

For Douglass, the absence of prejudice, which he first experienced in Ireland, proved to be 'transformative':

> Instead of a democratic government, I am under a monarchical government. Instead of the bright blue sky of America, I am covered with the soft grey fog of the Emerald Isle. I breathe, and lo! the chattel becomes a man. I gaze around in vain for one who will question my equal humanity, claim me as his slave, or offer me an insult.[132]

The large influx of black exiles after 1850 had a less palatable consequence— fraud. While several black abolitionists had been accused of some self-invention when telling their life stories, it was clear a small number had indeed made them up. In March 1854, the Dublin-based *Freeman's Journal* reported the case of Reuben Nixon who had been found guilty in Brighton of passing himself off as a fugitive slave. Upon his arrival in Liverpool he had sought out local Quakers for shelter. He had then moved to Birmingham, carrying with him a photograph, allegedly of his enslaved mother. In the city, he met with the experienced abolitionist, Joseph Sturge, who gave him a sovereign—a gold coin worth one-pound sterling. From there, Nixon travelled to London where he met the Secretary of British and Foreign Anti-Slavery Society, Louis Chamerovzow, who also gave him money. During this time, Nixon attended numerous temperance meetings where he again received financial support. At some stage, it was realized that he was not telling the truth, but not before he had hood-winked some of the leading voices in British abolition. Nixon was convicted of being 'a rogue and vagabond' and he received three months hard labour. The paper reported that he had cried when confessing to his deceit.[133]

Clearly, having patronage was an important asset in ensuring a comfortable transition to anti-slavery circles. The powerful British and Foreign Anti-Slavery Society backed James Pennington, Garnet and Ward, but rejected Wells Brown and William Craft, supporters of Garrison. Douglass and Sarah Remond, although also supporters of Garrison, proved to be skilled in working with both sides of the divide in Britain and Ireland. In England, the wealthy Harriet, Duchess of Sutherland, and confidante of Queen Victoria, used her influence and rank

26 *Introduction*

to promote a number of philanthropic issues, including abolition.[134] She met and befriended several female abolitionists including Lucretia Mott, Elizabeth Cady Stanton, Elizabeth Greenfield and Harriet Stowe.[135] Encouraged by the success of *Uncle Tom's Cabin*, the Duchess created an address 'To the Christian Women of America' in 1852, signed by half a million women, making it the largest anti-slavery petition ever.[136] On the other side of the Atlantic, it elicited a response from Julia Tyler, wife of a former President, which defended the institution of slavery.[137] Tyler's intervention was an indication that the transatlantic slavery movement was causing concern in the United States. Supporters of Garrison in Britain and Ireland, however, were bemused by the attention received by Stowe's novel and by the Duchess's Address, which exceeded any interest that they had generated in their intense 20 years of activities.[138] Veteran abolitionist John Estlin, who had hosted many visiting lecturers at his home in Bristol, informed Maria Chapman in Boston that, 'the Duchess of Sutherland's Address amuses me; it is useful for exciting discussion ... Of course, we *oppose* none of these harmless amusements'.[139] Webb, writing from Dublin, was more cynical, describing 'all this fuss about pennies and memorials—*soda water*', but he acknowledged that, as a consequence, interest in anti-slavery was probably higher than it had ever been before.[140] The renewed interest was evident at a meeting convened in Exeter Hall on 16 May 1853 by the British and Foreign Anti-Slavery Society. Both Harriet Stowe and the Duchess attended, their entrances allegedly causing several women admirers to faint. Supporters of Garrison had been invited to attend, but not to speak. They included Wells Brown, William and Ellen Craft, William and Mary Allen, and Parker Pillsbury. The lecturers included Harriet's husband, the Rev. Calvin Stowe, and Ward. Wells Brown was dismissive of the former's speech for its failure to criticize American churches, but said of the latter:

> Mr Ward did himself great credit, and exposed the hypocrisy of the American pro-slavery churches in a way that caused Professor Stowe to turn more than once in his seat. I have but little faith in the American clergy—either coloured or white; but I believe Ward to be not only the most honest, but an uncompromised and faithful advocate of his countrymen. He is certainly the best coloured minister that has yet visited this country.[141]

In 1852 and 1853, largely as a result of the recent passage of the Fugitive Slave Law, there were probably more black abolitionists in the United Kingdom than ever before, yet it was the interventions of two white privileged women that had galvanized anti-slavery sentiment on both sides of the Atlantic.

Undoubtedly, the abolitionists who travelled to Ireland and Britain reinvigorated the movement on both sides of the Atlantic. In doing so, they also rediscovered their own voices and agency. There was a price to be paid, however. Many were separated from their wives and children for months, if not years. Being a spokesperson for such a controversial cause, meant they were often subject to ridicule and physical attacks. Ward wrote that his appointment in 1839 as an anti-slavery lecturer 'cost me a great deal of effort and self-denial'.[142] In 1843, Douglass and his associates were attacked by a mob in Pendleton, Indiana. Douglass's right hand was broken and, because the bones were not properly set, it never regained its 'natural strength and dexterity'.[143] Although welcomed warmly when travelling overseas, feelings of isolation must have intensified, especially for abolitionists who were also 'fugitives'. Their status, however, meant that returning to America was full of risks. Touring Ireland and Britain, although safe from recapture and treated with respect, black abolitionists were displaced and homeless. While they were often publicly feted, privately, their day-to-day existence could be financially precarious, especially if they did not have the backing of one of the main anti-slavery societies. Even the talented and resourceful Wells Brown experienced this vulnerability and, at times, his loneliness and isolation were profound. His encounter with an impoverished fugitive slave on the streets of London was a reminder that success and notoriety were not universal.[144] Moreover, at that stage, Wells Brown only had a farthing in his possession. This small coin had been given to him by a little girl at a meeting in Croyden, who told him, 'This is for the slaves'. As he pondered on his situation, Wells Brown reflected, 'Where on earth is a man without money more destitute?'[145]

While seeking publicity was essential, constant exposure could also be uncomfortable. Through their narratives, their tours, their letters and even when being invited into the homes of local supporters, abolitionists lived their lives in public view, and often under intense scrutiny. Their hosts were not always sensitive to the personal cost of this life. Webb, host to so many American abolitionists, said of Remond, 'he need not be so depressed as I see him at times'.[146] For Douglass, homesickness only affected him after he had left Ireland and was in Scotland. In May 1846, he confided to his 'sister' that he was feeling out of sorts and that it was affecting his health.[147] Douglass, a lover of music, broke his despondent mood by purchasing a second-hand fiddle, which he would play whenever he felt depressed.[148] Despite his freedom being 'purchased' by English abolitionists at the end of the year, Douglass would not return to his family until April 1847.[149] Even white abolitionists experienced this loneliness. Parker Pillsbury first visited Dublin in the 1840s with Peabody and Garrison. They were hosted by the Webbs. In total, Pillsbury stayed in Europe for two years on behalf of American Anti-Slavery Society, during which time he was often ill and lonely—a situation that was not uncommon.[150] His autobiography, published in 1884 about his fellow anti-slavery lecturers, was entitled, 'Acts of the Anti-Slavery Apostles', in which he singled out Charles Remond, William Wells Brown and Frederick Douglass for praise.[151] For him, Douglass in particular was the personification of a 'self-made man'.[152]

Sometimes the visiting abolitionists were called on to comment on issues that were potentially controversial or divisive. In Ireland, two topics that recurred were the role of Irish Americans in not supporting slavery, and the constant references to Irish people as slaves. Ireland's position as a colony and, after 1801, as a reluctant partner in the United Kingdom, meant that she occupied an unusual middle ground in the debate about what constituted freedom and independence. Since the seventeenth century, Catholics and other Protestant dissenters had been discriminated against in a range of areas, including not being allowed to build churches or schools, to vote, purchase or inherit land, own a horse or a weapon, etc. At the end of the eighteenth century, at the time when

28   *Introduction*

Equiano was visiting, many of these restrictions had been lifted, but Catholics remained excluded from political involvement in the Westminster parliament until 1829, while Jews and Quakers were excluded until 1858. Significantly, Quakers were the main hosts of many of the abolitionists who visited between 1840 and 1860. The Irish context, therefore, served to complicate the issue of white privilege and British liberty.

The trope of slavery was frequently used by Irish nationalists and republicans when talking about their relationship with Britain. This was particularly evident during the visits of Equiano, Remond and Douglass, when agitation for independence was at its peak, with the rise of the United Irishmen and the Repeal movement respectively. Many of those involved in the struggle for Irish independence were also ardent abolitionists. Moreover, the theme of the Irish being slaves because of their colonial status and thus having a common cause with other enslaved peoples was frequently invoked. This link had a long pedigree: in the late-eighteenth century, Thomas Addis Emmet, who would later be exiled in America for his involvement in the 1798 Rising, engaged with the issue of how both black slaves and the Irish people were subject to patronizing attitudes that depicted them as being incapable of freedom. He wrote:

> Some supposed—what had been asserted of the negro race—that the Irish were an inferior, semi-brutal people, incapable of managing the affairs of their country, and submitted, by the necessity of their nature, to some superior power, from whose interference and strength they must exclusively derive their domestic tranquility.[153]

The question of Irish people being slaves arose when Charles Remond was in Dublin and a member of the audience called out, 'What will we do with the slaves at home?', which was greeted with 'cries of shame'. The ever-polite Remond did not respond, but a fellow Irish man did, saying, 'This man, whoever he was, knew not what he said; for if he knew what slavery was, he would not insult the people of Ireland "by telling them that any of them were in slavery (hear.)"'[154]

It was not until he had been some weeks in Ireland that Douglass, lecturing in Limerick, tackled the question publicly, stating unequivocally that, 'there was nothing like American slavery on the soil on which he now stood. Negro-slavery consisted not in taking away a man's property, but in making property of him'[155] In her 1861 narrative, fugitive slave Harriet Jacobs also addressed the issue, saying, 'I WOULD ten thousand times rather that my children should be the half-starved paupers of Ireland than to be the most pampered among the slaves of America'.[156]

The civil war

The passage of the more stringent Fugitive Slave Law in 1850 had led to renewed anti-slavery activity throughout Ireland, even as the country was slowly recovering from a devastating famine. Many of those involved were the same people who had welcomed Douglass to the country five years earlier, including Francis Calder

Introduction 29

and James Standfield in Belfast; James Haughton, Richard Allen and Richard Webb in Dublin; and Andrew Roche and Richard Dowden in Cork. In the latter city, at a specially convened meeting, a number of condemnatory resolutions were passed, including one to give 'every assistance to those noble-minded men who are labouring to efface from the national escutcheon so deep and foul a stain'.[157] By the late 1850s, at the time when Sarah Remond visited Britain and Douglass returned there, anti-slavery sentiment was largely on the wane, with only pockets of activity surviving. Douglass was appalled by the apparent apathy that had replaced the outrage evident during his visit 14 years earlier.[158] Chamerovzow, who toured Ireland shortly afterwards, witnessed a similar decline, attributing it to the fact that, 'Disease, and other causes, have removed from the scene the society's chief co-adjutors of past times', while those remaining, 'were incapacitated by age and infirmities from taking part in a public movement'.[159] What he may not have realized was that Ireland was on the verge of another period of crop failures. The early years of the 1860s witnessed the worst subsistence crisis in Ireland since the Great Famine, leading to an inevitable spike in emigration, with thousands of poor Irish seeking succour and survival in the United States. This latest period of hunger coincided with increasing polarization in America as the North and the South tumbled towards a civil war that proved to be divisive and deadly.

The early phase of the American Civil War proved to be disappointing for abolitionists as President Abraham Lincoln placed maintaining the Union before ending slavery. Their despondency was consolidated by Queen Victoria's early Proclamation of Neutrality, issued on 21 May 1861. Observing from Ireland, Richard Webb, a life-long pacifist, was doubly despairing, writing at the end of 1861 that the War was not 'a bona fide anti-slavery war', a view shared by Douglass, Wells Brown and others.[160] Webb believed that many people in the north and within the federal government were showing 'virtual pro-slavery complicity and want of anti-slavery principle', which he found, 'at once sorrowful, disheartening and amazing'.[161] He blamed America's aggressive stance towards Britain for the British lack of overt support for the North.[162]

It was not until two years into the war that President Lincoln issued a Proclamation ending slavery. By 1863, public opinion, if not the British government, had changed for the most part in favour of the North, helped by Lincoln's Proclamation, by the publication of an Address to the Women of England by Beecher Stowe, and through the selfless support of workers through Britain for the ending of slavery, most notably in Manchester and the rest of Lancashire.[163] In regard to the latter, the action taken by local cotton workers and others demonstrated the opposition to the Confederacy. According to historian Joel Schor, 'English abolition as supported by Douglass, Ward, the Crafts, William Wells Brown, and Garnet had done its work successfully'.[164] If this was the case, it had taken two years of violent warfare before this spirit of opposition was manifested. This revival of support led George Thompson to found an Emancipation Society in order to provide a platform for the revival of anti-slavery feeling.[165] Within America, Douglass and Wells Brown, along with several other black abolitionists, worked tirelessly to recruit black men to the Union army.

30 Introduction

The War had led to a trade depression throughout the United Kingdom, concurrently with repeated crop failures in Ireland. The increase in emigration meant that, by May 1863, an estimated 5,000 emigrants were travelling to the northern states of America from the United Kingdom every week.[166] The majority were Irish. Their arrival coincided with a new conscription regulation.[167] It led to riots in many northern cities in the summer of 1863, most particularly in New York, white workers having been warned that newly emancipated black workers would soon take their jobs and would depress wages. Irish immigrants, encouraged by the pro-slavery Democratic Party, targeted black people in openly racist attacks.[168] The news was treated with dismay by Irish abolitionists, who blamed the Democratic Party leaders and Catholic 'Ultramontane clergy' for inciting Irish Catholics.[169] It was an inglorious episode in the history of the Irish in America and one that did not augur well for the enslaved who had finally been freed.

At the end of 1864, the American Anti-Slavery Society split over the issue of Lincoln's re-election bid, with the traditional allies Garrison and Wendell Phillips coming out on opposing sides. Harriet Martineau, a long-time supporter of Garrison, from her home in the north of England, urged that they keep the dispute as contained as possible, fearing that it would damage the cause 'to set the abolitionists before the world as breaking asunder and wrangling, now when their exceptional work is done'.[170] The North won the War, but the human cost was high in terms of loss of life, the dead including the President. The ending of the War was used by some abolitionists as an opportunity to end their activities. Symbolically, after over 30 years of publication, Garrison closed the *Liberator* newspaper. Post-Bellum America, however, was a country filled with discrimination, prejudice, Jim Crow restrictions and lynchings—demonstrating that freedom was not the same as equality, just as Remond and others had long recognized. For Douglass, therefore, a new phase of the struggle was underway. In this fight, he was joined by a new generation of activists, including the fearless Ida Bell Wells. In 1893, two years before his death, Douglass, now aged 75 and the most well-known abolitionist of the nineteenth century, made an impassioned speech in defence of Haiti, the world's first black republic. He explained to his audience why:

> ... after Haiti had shaken off the fetters of bondage, and long after her freedom and independence had been recognized by all other civilized nations, we continued to refuse to acknowledge the fact and treated her as outside the sisterhood of nations ...
>
> A deep reason for coolness between the countries is this: Haiti is black, and we have not yet forgiven Haiti for being black [Applause] or forgiven the Almighty for making her black. [Applause.] In this enlightened act of repentance and forgiveness, our boasted civilization is far behind all other nations. [Applause.] In every other country on the globe a citizen of Haiti is sure of civil treatment. [Applause.][171]

Douglass's words were a sad reminder of how deep the divisions still were.

Introduction 31

Conclusion

Writing in 1941, Herbert Aptheker, an American scholar of African American history, argued that black people needed to be made central to the story of slavery and abolition rather than ignored or marginalized. He contended that even liberal historians, 'fail to consider the vital importance of the Negro people in breaking their own chains, both by independent work and by work within and through mixed groups', adding:

> Because of these authors, the Abolitionist movement has been dealt with, when at all sympathetically considered, as a white man's benevolent association. The Negro, when mentioned, has been presented as an alms-taking, passive, humble, meek, individual.[172]

Aptheker could have added that this interpretation was mirrored in many visual representations. Designed by Josiah Wedgwood in the late-eighteenth century, the ubiquitous and enduring image of a kneeling supplicant slave, with hands in manacles and including the words, 'Am I not a man and a brother?', being a case in point—it suggesting that black people were victims who begged for their freedom, rather than agents in achieving their own self-emancipation. The cameo had been created to support the work of the Society for the Abolition of the Slave Trade, which had been founded in 1787, Wedgwood being one of its members.[173] This image long outlasted both the Society and its creator.

In an English journal published in 2007 to mark the 200th anniversary of the ending of the slave trade in the British Empire, Kevin Shillington wrote, 'It is now widely acknowledged that Africans played an important role in responding to the demands of the slave traders; but their role in resisting slavery and in achieving its eventual abolition has often been overlooked'.[174] He further highlighted the cynicism in the British government's action, arguing that:

> As the world's leading super-power, Britain developed the self-serving myth of an imperial mission to spread 'freedom and civilization' throughout the pre-industrial world. In this way, an on-going mission to eradicate slavery became a tool to justify to colonial conquest of Africa at the end of the nineteenth century.[175]

To some extent, Shillington was following in the footsteps of Trinidadian historian Eric Williams who, in his seminal 1944 book, *Capitalism and Slavery*, had claimed that both the 1807 legislation, and again in 1833, had been motivated by economic factors rather than humanitarian ones.[176] His interpretation proved to be contentious and continues to be debated. While some of Williams's assertions have since been refined, there is no doubt that the sugar economy was in massive decline in the 1820s and interest in Africa was changing from her being a supplier of enslaved people to a market for Europe's surplus manufacture.[177] However, black abolitionists who came to Britain and Ireland as a place of

32   *Introduction*

sanctuary and support, overwhelmingly framed their mission in humanitarian, rather than economic terms. What was the contribution of abolitionists—black and white—to the ending of enslavement? How did they engage with changing economic and political contexts in which slavery existed? Just as importantly, why have so many of these men and women and their roles in ending enslavement been forgotten or marginalized for so long? The involvement of so many remarkable black abolitionists has been, until recently, largely air-brushed out of the narrative. Moreover, Ireland's involvement in transatlantic abolition has generally been ignored by historians or subsumed under British involvement. An exception is the story of Frederick Douglass, the towering giant of transatlantic abolition. Sadly, many other stories have been lost. According to historian Nell Irvin Painter, writing in 2014, 'The main problem was that 20th-century American culture accommodated only one 19th-century black man, a spot already taken by the monumental, best-selling Frederick Douglass'.[178]

The chapters that follow provide insights into the complexity of the abolition movement and the diversity of those who regarded it as a major weapon in the ending of enslavement. The interactions of white abolitionists with both free and self-emancipated black people enriched, energized and enlightened them and their cause. More importantly, black abolitionists, especially those who had been formerly enslaved, brought an energy, empathy, authenticity, sensitivity and intellectualism, that was often self-taught, to the movement, making them powerful agents of change. Their life stories, individually and collectively, are remarkable. For those black abolitionists who did make the 3,000-mile journey across the Atlantic, it proved to be a transcendent experience. They not only grew in stature, but 'From a position of great weakness, they derived a startling degree of political agency'.[179] Furthermore, in doing so, they helped to forge a powerful international movement that not only wanted to end enslavement wherever it existed, but also sought to reach out to oppressed groups everywhere, from America to New Zealand, from Haiti to India, from Australia to Ireland. It is no coincidence that today, self-emancipated slave Frederick Douglass is remembered not simply an abolitionist, but as a champion of international human rights. His story might be the most famous, but it is not unique.

Notes

1 Mary Prince, *The History of Mary Prince, a West Indian Slave. Related by Herself* (London: published by F. Westley and A. H. Davis, Stationers' Hall Court; and by Waught & Innes, Edinburgh: and supplied at trade price to Anti-Slavery Associations by Joseph Phillips, 18, Aldermanbury, 1831), p. 23.
2 Moses Grandy, *Narrative of the Life of Moses Grandy; Late a Slave in the United States of America* (London: C. Gilpin, 5, Bishopsgate-Street, 1843), p. 71.
3 This figure was suggested by Jeffrey Kerr-Richie, 'Black Abolitionists, Irish Supporters, and the Brotherhood of Man', in *Slavery & Abolition. A Journal of Slave and Post-Slave Studies*, vol. 37, no. 3 (2016), pp. 599–621, 600.
4 Ian Bradley, 'Wilberforce the Saint', in Jack Hayward (ed.), *Out of Slavery: Abolition and After* (London: Frank Cass, 1985), pp. 79–81.

Introduction 33

5 In his seminal work, *Capitalism and Slavery* (1944), Eric Williams argued that it was declining economic returns rather than humanitarian reasons or abolitionist activity that led to the ending of the slave trade and slavery. His interpretation caused a long-running debate: William A. Darity, 'Eric Williams and Slavery: A West Indian Viewpoint', *Callaloo*, vol. 20, no. 4 (Fall 1997), pp. 801–16.

6 Black abolitionists were in the forefront of organizing annual commemorations to celebrate on 1 August, West Indian Emancipation Day.

7 See writings by Irish scholars, Nini Rodgers and William Rolston.

8 According to John O'Connell, *Freeman's Journal*, 15 February 1853.

9 Although shocked by Irish poverty, both Douglass and Benson attributed it to intemperance. Douglass later revised this opinion, attributing it to centuries of colonial oppression.

10 An Act for the Abolition of the Slave Trade, 47° Georgii iii, session 1, cap. xxxvi, 25 March 1807: Available at: www.bbc.co.uk/history/british/abolition/abolition_tools_gallery_08.shtml.

11 Granville Sharp (1735–1813), was a Civil Servant. In 1787, he was a founder of the 'Society for Effecting the Abolition of the Slave Trade' and was its first chairman.

12 William R. Cotter, 'The Somerset Case and the Abolition of Slavery in England', in *History*, vol. 79, no. 255 (Feb. 1994), pp. 31–56. In early October 1771, James Somerset ran away from his master, a Virginia businessman named Charles Steuart, while they were in England on business. Less than two months later, Somerset was captured, locked in shackles and placed on a ship bound for Jamaica where he was to be sold. While he was free, Somerset had made contact with British abolitionists. Upon hearing of Somerset's plight, the abolitionists petitioned the British court for a writ of *habeas corpus*. In February 1772, Somerset's case was heard by the Court of the King's Bench. In June, Chief Justice Lord Mansfield ruled that Somerset should go free. Available at: https://www.history.org/History/teaching/enewsletter/volume7/feb09/teachstrategy.cfm.

13 Daniel J. Hulsebosch, 'Nothing but Liberty: "Somerset's Case" and the British Empire', in *Law and History Review*, vol. 24, no. 3 (Fall 2006), pp. 647–57, 651.

14 Van Gosse, 'As a Nation, the English Are Our Friends: The Emergence of African American Politics in the British Atlantic World, 1772–1861', in *The American Historical Review*, vol. 113, no. 4 (Oct. 2008), pp. 1003–28, 1008.

15 Reference: CSO/RP/1832/6266, 21 December 1832, Chief Secretary's Office, Letter from William Taylor, former slave, Dublin, to unidentified recipients, addressed 'Gentleman', noting that he had been a 'slave in the East Indias' [sic] to a man called [Daniel Camp] who mistreated him; adding that his 'back and arms will show the traitment' he was subjected to; stating that he was determined to 'make Dublin my Place of residence' and hoping that he would be given a passport for protection. The annotation from Richard Greene, [the Crown Law Advisor] stated that, 'This man being in Ireland, his former master cannot retake him' and, 'If any violation of his personal liberty be attempted, he can procure his liberation upon application to any Judge'.

16 'A Slave Emancipated in Belfast', Belfast *News-Letter*, 19 March 1833.

17 'Hibernian Anti-Slavery Society', *Nenagh Guardian*, 14 August 1841.

18 *Proceedings of the General Anti-Slavery Convention* (London: British and Foreign Anti-Slavery Association, 1840), p. 121.

19 Ibid.

20 'LECTURES on AMERICAN SLAVERY', *Northern Whig*, 21 October 1841.

21 'American Slavery', *Waterford Mail*, 19 April 1859.

22 'MISS SARAH P. REMOND IN LONDON', *Anti-Slavery Advocate*, 1 July 1859, no. 31, vol. 2, 1 July 1859.

23 Gosse, 'As a Nation, the English Are Our Friends', p. 1005.

24 Ibid., p. 1016.

34   *Introduction*

25 Howard Holman Bell, *A Survey of the Negro Convention Movement, 1830–1861* (New York: Arno Press, 1969).
26 Depending on the source, David Walker was born in North Carolina in 1785 or 1786 to a free mother and an enslaved father. As a result of his mother's status, he was born free but, from early on, found the enslavement of other black people to be unbearable: 'If any are anxious to ascertain who I am, know the world, that I am one of the oppressed, degraded and wretched sons of Africa, rendered so by the avaricious and unmerciful, among the whites' (*Appeal*, p. 81). Walker died in 1830, less than a year after his Appeal had originally appeared. He had opposed colonization, arguing that black people were fully entitled to be regarded as American citizens.
27 David Walker, *Walker's Appeal, in Four Articles; Together with a Preamble, to the Coloured Citizens of the World, but in Particular, and Very Expressly, to Those of the United States of America, Written in Boston, State of Massachusetts, September 28, 1829* (Boston, MA: Revised and Published by David Walker, 1830). Walker's unequivocal *Appeal* polarized opinion and led to Georgia offering an award of $10,000 if he was captured alive. For some, it marked the start of a black nationalist tradition in America.
28 See Christine Kinealy, *Daniel O'Connell and the Anti-Slavery Movement. The Saddest People the Sun Sees* (London: Routledge, 2011), passim.
29 *Freeman's Journal*, 2 November 1847; *Anti-Slavery Reporter*, October 1829, pp. 93–5.
30 'House of Commons—28 June', *Tralee Mercury*, 4 July 1832.
31 'House of Commons—28 June', *Telegraph or Connaught Ranger*, 4 July 1832.
32 Ibid., 'Miscellaneous', 22 May 1833.
33 Cork-born Charles Edward Herbert Orpen (1791–1856) was an Irish physician who opened a school for Deaf and Dumb children in Dublin. In line with his evangelical views, he wrote a number of tracts suggesting how the Irish language should be used to convert Irish Catholics to the Scriptures.
34 Maurice Bric, 'Daniel O'Connell and the Debate on Anti-Slavery, 1820–1850', in *History and the Public Sphere* (2005), pp. 65–82, 71.
35 Stuart had toured with the East India Company's Army. He subsequently travelled to North America where he came in contact with a number of abolitionists, including with Theodore Dwight Weld. See, Allen P. Stouffer, *Light of Nature and the Law of God: Antislavery in Ontario, 1833–1877* (Montreal: McGill-Queen's Press, 1992), pp. 23–7.
36 *Anti-Slavery Reporter*, September 1830, p. 391.
37 Ibid., May 1830, p. 215.
38 Gordon Barnes, 'Revolutionary Jamaica: Interpreting the Politics of the Baptist War'. Available at: https://ageofrevolutions.com/2017/01/23/revolutionary-jamaica-interpreting-the-politics-of-the-baptist-war/.
39 The Slavery Abolition Act (3 & 4 Will. 4 c.73), which received Royal Assent on 28 August 1833.
40 Gordon Barnes, 'Declaration of Anti-Slavery Friends in Ireland', *Northern Whig*, 3 June 1833, in *Age of Revolutions*, Available at: https://ageofrevolutions.com/2017/01/23/revolutionary-jamaica-interpreting-the-politics-of-the-baptist-war/.
41 'House of Commons', *Warder and Dublin Weekly Mail*, 14 May 1833.
42 Clare Midgely, *Women against Slavery: The British Campaigns, 1780–1870* (London: Routledge, 1995), p. 59.
43 'Hibernian Negro's Friend Society', from the *Irish Temperance Shield*, reprinted in the *Liberator*, 20 October 1837. The women formed their own society following a visit by George Thompson.
44 Alexandrina Peckover, *Life of Joseph Sturge* (London: Swan Sonnenschein, 1890), p. 29.
45 *Kerry Evening Post*, 16 August 1837.

Introduction   35

46 Hibernian Anti-Slavery Society, *Address of the Hibernian Anti-Slavery Society to the People of Ireland* (Dublin: Webb and Chapman, 1837), pp. 1–2.
47 Belfast *News-Letter*, 7 November 1837.
48 'Anti-Slavery Meetings', *Freeman's Journal*, 1 May 1838.
49 James Williams, *A Narrative of Events, since the First of August, 1834, by James Williams, an Apprenticed Labourer in Jamaica* (London: Rider, 1837).
50 Ibid., title page.
51 'Investigations by the Commissioners of Enquiry into the case of James Williams, and other Apprenticed labourers', *Papers presented to Parliament ... for the abolition of slavery throughout the British Colonies*, British Parliamentary Papers, part v, Jamaica, 1838, vol. xlix (1837–1838).
52 John Dryden, 'Pas de Six Ans!', in Anthony de Verteuil, *Seven Slaves & Slavery: Trinidad and Tobago 1777–1838* (Port of Spain, 1992), pp. 371–9.
53 There are number of versions of this conflict, with some accounts having the men meeting face to face, but the dispute was more probably carried out in the newspapers. See, Francis F. Wayland, 'Slave-Breeding in America: The Stevenson-O'Connell Imbroglio of 1838', in *The Virginia Magazine of History and Biography*, vol. 50, no. 1 (Jan. 1942), pp. 47–54.
54 'American slavery', *Northern Whig*, 23 October 1841.
55 In addition to defending slaves in the Caribbean and America, O'Connell spoke in defence of the Maoris, the Aborigines, slaves in 'British India' and Jews everywhere. For more, see, Kinealy, *The Saddest People*.
56 'Hibernian anti-slavery society', *Nenagh Guardian*, 14 August 1841; *Proceedings ... Anti-Slavery Convention*, p. 121.
57 Belfast *News-Letter*, 19 June 1840.
58 William Garrison to Helen Garrison, 29 June 1840, Clare Taylor, *British and American Abolitionists: An Episode in Transatlantic Understanding* (Edinburgh University Press, 1974), p. 92.
59 Samuel Haughton, *Memoir of James Haughton with Extracts of His Letters* (Dublin: E. Ponsonby, 1877).
60 Frederick Douglass attended and signed the Declaration of Sentiments in 1848.
61 O'Connell to Lucretia Mott, 20 June 1840, James Mott, *Three Months in Great Britain* (Philadelphia, PA: J. Miller McKim, 1841), p. 20.
62 'Obituary of E. Cady Stanton', *New York Times*, 27 October 1902.
63 Now known as Pearse Street. The Webb house has been demolished and is the site of Trinity College's Science Building.
64 Frederick B. Tolles Mott, *Slavery and 'The Woman Question'. Lucretia Mott's Diary of Her Visit to Great Britain to Attend the World's Anti-slavery Convention of 1840* (Philadelphia, PA: Friends' Historical Association & Friends Historical Society, 1952), p. 62. On 22 July, Mott had spoken at a temperance meeting and she recorded that the 'people appeared satisfied', Mott to Maria Chapman, Dublin. 7 Mo. 29th. 1840 (written on stationery of the British & Foreign Anti-Slavery Society). Available at: http://womhist.alexanderstreet.com/socm/doc16.htm.
    William Lloyd Garrison (1805–1879) was the Boston editor of the *Liberator* and New Hampshire Nathaniel P. Rogers (1794–1846) was the editor of the *Herald of Freedom*. Both were delegates to the World's Anti-Slavery Convention. They protested against the exclusion of the women delegates and so refused to participate. They left Ireland on 29 July and sailed from Liverpool to the United States on 4 August 1840.
65 Letter from Richard Davis Webb, Dublin, to William Lloyd Garrison, 1840 [July] 23rd, BPL: www.digitalcommonwealth.org/search/commonwealth:2z10zc651.
66 Anna Davis Hallowell (ed.), *James and Lucretia Mott: Life and Letters* (Boston, MA: Houghton, Mifflin and Company, 1890), p. 168.

36 Introduction

67 According to Lucretia's 'skeletal diary', the men arrived on 29 July 1840. She only mentions Rodgers and Garrison. Hallowell, *Life and Letters*, p. 169.

68 Letter from Richard Davis Webb, Dublin, [Ireland], to William Lloyd Garrison, 1840 [July] 23rd, BPL: www.digitalcommonwealth.org/search/commonwealth:2z10zc651.

69 Parker Pillsbury, *Acts of the Anti-Slavery Apostles* (Boston, MA: Cupples, Upham, & Company, 1884), p. 26. They left Glasgow the morning of 28 July 1840 but, before departing, they filled their pockets with 'Scottish cakes'.

70 Letter from Richard Davis Webb, Dublin, [Ireland], to William Lloyd Garrison, 1 [August] 1840, BPL: www.digitalcommonwealth.org/search/commonwealth:2z10zc70w.

71 James Gillespie Birney (1792–1857). In 1840, he stood as candidate for the newly formed Liberty Party.

72 'Anti-slavery movement', *Dublin Monitor*, 20 August 1840.

73 *Freeman's Journal*, 27 October 1840.

74 'Belfast Miscellaneous', *Dublin Morning Register*, 20 August 1840.

75 Ibid., 'Hibernian Anti-Slavery Society', 13 October 1841.

76 *Proceedings ... Anti-Slavery Convention*, p. 13.

77 In 1840, O'Connell had launched a new political initiative, the Loyal National Repeal Association, with the aim of winning a repeal of the Act of Union and the restoration of the Irish parliament.

78 'The Anti-Slavery Cause. Slavery in America', *Nenagh Guardian*, 11 August 1841.

79 'The Disgrace of America', Letter from Allen to Garrison, 1 December 1841, the *Liberator*, 14 January 1842.

80 Ibid., 'GREAT MEETING IN FANEUIL HALL, 4 February 1842.

81 Ibid., 'Irish address' 25 October 1842, from the *St. Louis Reporter* of March 1842.

82 See chapter on Charles Lenox Remond.

83 'Letter from FRANCIS Jackson, WM. LLOYD GARRISON, etc', Belfast *News-Letter*, 12 December 1843. O'Connell had written in 1843 to Repealers in Cincinnati, chastising them for not condemning slavery.

84 Samuel Ringgold Ward, *Autobiography of a Fugitive Negro: His Anti-Slavery Labours in the United States, Canada, & England* (London: John Snow, 1855), p. 39.

85 Ibid., p. 384.

86 Ibid.

87 'Belfast Anti-Slavery Society. Lecture by the Rev. Henry Highland Garnet', Belfast *News-Letter*, 22 January 1851.

88 'LETTERS FROM FREDERICK DOUGLASS, NO. V', Victoria Hotel, Belfast, 1 January 1846, the *Liberator*, 30 January 1846.

89 Harriet Ann Jacobs was born into enslavement in North Carolina in 1813. Her escape necessitated a number of years spent in hiding, she only reaching the North in 1842. Harriet travelled to England in January 1845.

90 William Grimes (1784–1865), *Life of William Grimes, the Runaway Slave. Written by Himself* (New York: W. Grimes, 1825).

91 Mary Prince (1788–? Post 1833) *The History of Mary Prince, a West Indian Slave. Related by Herself. With a Supplement by the Editor. To Which Is Added, the Narrative of Asa-Asa, a Captured African* (London: Published by F. Westley and A. H. Davis, 1831).

92 Lunsford Lane (1803–1879), *The Narrative of Lunsford Lane, Formerly of Raleigh, N.C. Embracing an Account of His Early Life, the Redemption by Purchase of Himself and Family from Slavery, and His Banishment from the Place of His Birth for the Crime of Wearing a Colored Skin* (Boston, MA: J.G. Torrey, 1842). Similar to Equiano, Lane purchased his freedom.

93 Harriet Jacobs, under the pen name Linda Brent, published her memoir, *Incidents in the Live of a Slave Girl, Written by Herself* (1862). In the late 1930s, as part of the Works Project Administration, field workers from the Federal Writers' Project

Introduction 37

endeavoured to interview elderly Americans who had lived as slaves. More than 2,300 people provided recollections, which were then transcribed and preserved as typescripts.

94 Equiano, *Narrative* (ed. nine, 1794), p. xvii.
95 Sarah's story had first appeared in Sarah Parker Remond, 'Lives of Distinguished Women', in *English Woman's Journal*, vol. vii, no. 37, 1 March 1861. In the same year also, Matthew Davenport Hill, *Our Exemplars Poor and Rich: Or Biographical Sketches of Men and Women Who Have by an Extraordinary Use of Their Opportunities Benefited Their Fellow-creatures* (London: Cassell, Petter and Galpin, 1861), pp. 276–86. This writing of Sarah's life-story in the former is sometimes referred to as her 'narrative'.
96 Garnet's 1848 'The Past and the Present Condition, and the Destiny, of the Coloured Race', was widely published, but little that was personal was written by him.
97 Wells Brown was latterly accused on plagiarism in many of his writings.
98 John Bugg, 'The Other Interesting Narrative: Olaudah Equiano's Public Book Tour', in *PMLA. The Journal of the Modern Language Association of America*, vol. 121, no. 5 (Oct., 2006), pp. 1424–42, 1426.
99 Douglass made this speech when talking alongside Daniel O'Connell in Conciliation Hall in Dublin on 29 September 1845.
100 'The Evils of Slavery', *Manchester Times*, 19 February 1848; *Newcastle Guardian and Tyne Mercury*, 26 February 1848.
101 *Uncle Tom's Cabin* had started life as a serial in *The National Era*. In 1852, it was published as a two-volume book. See, 'Harriet Beecher Stowe Center': www.harriet beecherstowecenter.org/harriet-beecher-stowe/uncle-toms-cabin/.
102 As a teenager, Douglass, for example, had obtained a copy of the *Columbian Orator*, which had included some of the most powerful public speeches made, as a way of training readers the skills of great oratory.
103 'Moses Roper', *Bradford Observer*, 5 March 1840. James Montgomery (1771–1854), a hymn writer and poet, had been born in Scotland but moved to Sheffield in the 1790s. He supported a range of humanitarian causes including abolition.
104 Ward, *Autobiography*, p. 249.
105 'American Slavery', *North and South Shields Gazette*, 8 November 1850.
106 Teresa A. Goddu, 'Anti-Slavery's Panoramic Perspective', in *Multi-Ethnic Literature of the U.S.*, vol. 39, no. 2 (Summer 2014), pp. 12–41.
107 'COLLECTIONS IN ENGLAND FOR THE BENEFIT OF AMERICAN SLAVE-HOLDERS', *Anti-Slavery Advocate*, 1 April 1853.
108 See chapter on Douglass.
109 Richard J. M. Blackett, *Building an Antislavery Wall: Black Americans in the Atlantic Abolitionist Movement, 1830–1860* (Baton Rouge: Louisiana State University Press, 2002), p. 5.
110 Wm. Wells Brown, *The American Fugitive in Europe. Sketches of Places and People Abroad, with a Memoir of the Author* (Boston, MA: John P. Jewett and Company, 1855), pp. 216–7.
111 George Washington William, quoted in Joel Schor, 'The Rivalry between Frederick Douglass and Henry Highland Garnet', in *Journal of Negro History*, vol. 64, no. 1 (Winter, 1979), pp. 30–8, 30.
112 *North Star*, 13 June 1850.
113 'MY DEAR FRIEND, W.L. GARRISON', the question was first posed in the *Daily Bee* and reprinted in the *Liberator*, 2 December 1842.
114 Connie A. Miller, *Frederick Douglass. American Hero: And International Icon of the Nineteenth Century* (Bloomington, IN: Xlibris, 2008), p. 118.
115 'Calling him out', *North Star*, 7 September 1849.
116 Robert S. Levine (ed.), *Martin R. Delany: A Documentary Reader* (Chapel Hill: University of North Carolina Press, 2003), p. 177.

38   *Introduction*

117 Miller, *Frederick Douglass. American Hero*, p. 118.
118 Douglass to Francis Jackson, Holist Street, Boston, 29 January 1846, Anti-Slavery Collection, BPL, MS. A. 1.2. v. 16, p. 13.
119 Quoted in the *Berkshire Chronicle*, 28 November 1840. Also, see chapter on Moses Roper.
120 Ian Bradley, 'Wilberforce the Saint', in Jack Hayward (ed.), *Out of Slavery: Abolition and After* (London: Routledge, 1985), pp. 79–81.
121 'Address by Rev. C. Munroe. The Slave Population of America', Belfast *News-Letter*, 14 May 1851.
122 'LETTER FROM FREDERICK DOUGLASS', Frederick Douglass, Scotland, to Garrison, 26 February 1846, the *Liberator*, 27 March 1846.
123 Webb to Edmund Quincy, 8 December 1865, Taylor, *British and American*, p. 536.
124 'AMERICAN SLAVERY', *Carlisle Journal*, 18 April 1840.
125 Craft lectured on slavery in Winslow about his escape, *Bucks Herald*, 15 May 1858. According to Blackett, fugitive slave, William Watson, had enrolled in school.
126 William Craft, *Running a Thousand Miles for Freedom; or, the Escape of William and Ellen Craft from Slavery* (London: William Tweedie, 1860).
127 Obituary in the *New York Times*, 11 March 1882.
128 Leslie A. Falk, 'Black Abolitionist Doctors and Healers, 1810–1885', in *Bulletin of the History of Medicine*, vol. 54, no. 2 (Summer, 1980), pp. 258–72, 259.
129 'American slavery', *Northern Whig*, 21 October 1841.
130 *The Colored American*, 30 June 1840.
131 Jacobs, *Incidents in the Life of a Slave Girl*, p. 8.
132 'LETTERS FROM FREDERICK DOUGLASS, NO. V', Frederick Douglass, Belfast to W. L. Garrison. 1 January 1846, reprinted in the *Liberator*, 30 January 1846.
133 *Freeman's Journal*, 31 March 1854.
134 The enterprising Stowe had presented a copy of her book to Prince Albert when it was released in March 1852, but at the time of writing this letter, the Queen had not read it: Queen Victoria to the Duchess of Sutherland, 29 October 1852, Gilder Lehrman Institute of American history. Available at: www.americanhistory.amdigi tal.co.uk/Documents/Details/Queen-Victoria-to-the-Duchess-of-Sutherland-about– Uncle-Tom-s-Cabin—the-death-of-Wellington-/GLC01587.
135 The Duchess had met Mott, Stanton and Garrison following the 1840 Anti-Slavery Convention. Her home in London, Stafford House, became a centre of anti-slavery activities. Elizabeth Cady Stanton in 'Eighty Years'. Available at: https://digital. library.upenn.edu/women/stanton/years/years.html.
136 Evelyn L. Pugh, 'Women and Slavery: Julia Gardiner Tyler and the Duchess of Sutherland', in *The Virginia Magazine of History and Biography*, vol. 88, no. 2 (April 1980), pp. 186–202, 186.
137 Julia Gardiner Tyler, *The Women of England Versus the Women of America. Mrs. Ex-President Tyler's Letter to the Duchess of Sutherland on American Slavery* (London: W. Davy and Son, 1853).
138 During her time in Britain, Stowe was honoured with many public banquets, with high demand for tickets, 'Banquet in Honour of Mrs H.B. Stowe', *Illustrated London News*, 30 April 1853.
139 J.B. Estlin, Bristol to Maria Chapman, December 1852, in Taylor, *British and American*, p. 392.
140 Ibid., Webb was quoted in Mary Estlin to Maria Chapman, 10 January 1853; partial letter from Richard Davis Webb, Dublin, to Emma Forbes Weston [27 April 1853?]. Available at: www.digitalcommonwealth.org/search/commonwealth:cv43pr53zx.
      A suggestion had been made that everybody who read *Uncle Tom's Cabin* should contribute one penny to anti-slavery.

Introduction 39

141 Wells Brown to Garrison, London, 17 May 1853, quoted in C. Peter Ripley (ed.), *The Black Abolitionist Papers, 1830–1865* (Chapel Hill: University of North Carolina Press, 1987), pp. 344–6.
142 Ward, *Autobiography*, p. 52.
143 'Casting of Frederick Douglass' Right Hand, 1895'. Available at: www.nps.gov/museum/exhibits/douglass/exb/visionary/FRDO497_deathHand.html.
144 W. Wells Brown, *Three Years in Europe: Or, Places I have Seen and People I have Met* (London: Charles Gilpin, 5 Bishopsgate Street, Without; Edinburgh: Oliver and Boyd. 1852), pp. 113–4.
145 Ibid.
146 Webb to Garrison, the *Liberator*, 24 September 1841.
147 In the letter, Douglass uses the *n*—word.
148 Douglass to Harriet Bailey, 16 May 1846, Frederick Douglass Collection, Library of Congress. Available at: www.loc.gov/resource/mfd.03002/?sp=93.
149 Ibid. The process was complicated and expensive. Some of the documents are available in the Collection, pp. 93–100.
150 Stacey M. Robertson, *Parker Pillsbury: Radical Abolitionist, Male Feminist* (New York: Cornell University Press, 2000), p. 77.
151 Pillsbury, *Anti-Slavery Apostles*, pp. 237–8.
152 Ibid., pp. 482–4.
153 Thomas Addis Emmet quoted in *Memoir of Thomas Addis and Robert Emmet: With Their Ancestors and their immediate family*, vol. 2 (New York: The Emmet Press, 1915), p. 11.
154 'Hibernian anti-slavery society. Speech by Councilor Moore', *Nenagh Guardian*, 14 August 1841.
155 'Frederick Douglass', *Limerick Reporter*, 11 November 1845.
156 Jacobs, *Incidents*, p. 49.
157 'AMERICAN FUGITIVE SLAVE LAW at a Meeting of the CORK ANTI-SLAVERY Society', *Freeman's Journal*, 5 June 1851.
158 *Frederick Douglass' Monthly*, July 1861. The *Monthly* was the successor to *Frederick Douglass' Paper*.
159 Quoted in Richard J. M. Blackett, *Divided Hearts: Britain and the American Civil War* (Baton Rouge: Louisiana State University Press, 2000), p. 50.
160 Ibid. Queen Victoria had issued a Proclamation of Neutrality. Downing Street, London, 1 February 1862.
161 Webb to Samuel May, 21 December 1861; Webb to Miss Weston, 31 December 1861, Taylor, *British and American*, pp. 469–71.
162 Blackett, *Divided Hearts*, p. 50.
163 'Address to President Lincoln by the Working-Men of Manchester, England, 31 December 1862', *Manchester Guardian*, 1 January 1863. The President responded on 19 January 1863. Not all workers were sympathetic, however, the actions of those who were meant that, in 1919, a statue of Lincoln was erected in Manchester, the inscription reading, 'Lancashire friendship to the cause for which he lived and died'.
164 Schor, 'The Rivalry between', p. 20.
165 F. W. Chesson, Emancipation Society, London, to Garrison, 9 January 1863, in Taylor, *British and American*, pp. 493–5.
166 This estimate was provided by Webb who added, 'I wish the immigrants were likely to add as much to your moral strength as to your material ability'. In the same letter, he said that he was ending his newspaper, the *Advocate*, as circulation was small and he was supported financially by Miss Estlin, Webb to Samuel May, 30 May 1863, Taylor, *British and American*, pp. 506–7.

40   *Introduction*

167 The new Conscription Law made all male citizens between 20 and 35, and all unmarried men between 35 and 45, subject to military duty. It was possible to purchase an exemption or hire a substitute.

168 Leslie M. Harris, *In the Shadow of Slavery: African Americans in New York City, 1626–1863* (University of Chicago Press, 2003), pp. 279–88.

169 Unknown person, Co. Dublin, to Samuel May, 3 August 1863, Taylor, *British and American*, p. 510.

170 Ibid., Harriet Martineau to an unknown recipient, 10 August 1864, pp. 525–6.

171 'LECTURE ON HAITI', delivered on 2 January 1893 at the World's Fair, Chicago (Chicago, IL: Violet Agents, 1893).

172 Herbert Aptheker, *The Negro in the Abolitionist Movement* (New York: International Publishers, 1941), p. 4.

173 Cynthia S. Hamilton, 'Hercules Subdued: The Visual Rhetoric of the Kneeling Slave', in *Slavery and Abolition. A Journal of Slave and Post-Slavery Studies*, vol. 34, no. 4 (2013), pp. 631–52.

174 Kevin Shillington, 'British Made. Abolition and the Africa Trade', in *History Today* (January 2007), pp. 21–2.

175 Ibid.

176 Eric Williams, *Capitalism and Slavery* (Chapel Hill: University of North Carolina Press, 1944).

177 Shillington, 'British made', p. 22.

178 Nell Irvin Painter, 'William Wells Brown', *New York Times*, 16 November 2014.

179 Gosse, 'As a Nation', p. 1006.

1   Olaudah Equiano (1745–1797)

'In every respect on par with Europeans'

Gustavus Vassa, more popularly remembered as Olaudah Equiano, was a pioneering black abolitionist who visited Ireland and Britain at a time of revolutionary turmoil across the world.[1] After Frederick Douglass, he is probably the best-known abolitionist to tour these countries. Unusually, Equiano lectured there in the 1790s, at a time when the slave trade was still operative, and 50 years before Douglass. He was pioneering in other ways, too. The publication of *The Interesting Narrative of the Life of Olaudah Equiano, or Gustavus Vassa, the African. Written by himself*, is generally hailed as the first successful memoir of an enslaved person.[2] Following its release, he lectured extensively throughout Britain and Ireland for almost five years, before disappearing from view. Unfortunately, the contents of his speeches have not survived. The nine editions of the *Narrative*, each subsequent one enlarged and updated, tell the story of Equiano during these years.

During Equiano's lifetime, there were accusations that he was not the author of the *Narrative*, with suggestions that a white person had been involved.[3] As a way of pre-empting doubters, the opening sentence of the *Narrative* stated:

> I believe it is difficult for those who publish their own memoirs to escape the imputation of vanity; nor is this the only disadvantage under which they labour: it is also their misfortune, that what is uncommon is rarely, if ever, believed, and what is obvious we are apt to turn from with disgust, and to charge the writer with impertinence.[4]

The persistence of such accusations led Equiano to include testimonials of his character and abilities in later editions.[5] A revival in interest in Equiano's story occurred around the 200th anniversary of the ending of the slave trade in 2007. At this time, misgivings appeared about the authenticity of his early life story. Doubts about whether he had really been born in Africa were raised by his biographer, Vincent Carretta. Carretta, in turn, was robustly challenged by a number of other scholars, notably Paul Lovejoy.[6] The debate served to raise a number of issues, including those of memory, identity, accuracy, distortion and motivation, which are pertinent to the writing of any memoir or narrative.[7] To what extent was Equiano, or any other visiting abolitionist, a 'virtuoso self-fashioner' as has

42 *Olaudah Equiano (1745–1797)*

been suggested?[8] If so, would it make his contributions to anti-slavery any less valid? Significantly, British abolitionists who met Equiano, including Granville Sharp, believed his story. His origins were also accepted by fellow African, Ottobah Cugoano, who had been born in what is now Ghana. He lectured with Equiano and was a subscriber to the first edition of the *Narrative*.[9] Overall, Equiano's publication provided a unique insight into one man's journey from enslavement to freedom in the eighteenth century. Moreover, as a free man, he devoted his adult life to fighting oppression, beyond simply the ending of enslavement.

Unlike later generations of visiting abolitionists, Equiano lived at a time when the slave trade was still being practised by the major transatlantic powers, including Britain and America. The timing of his visit meant that he belonged to a first wave of activists who sought to end the trade, believing that if it was ended, slavery itself would wither and disappear. The years that Equiano was active in Ireland and Britain coincided with a flowering of anti-slavery activity, associated with the so-called 'twelve apostles', who included Granville Sharp, Thomas Clarkson and William Wilberforce. By working alongside these white activists, writing a narrative and lecturing throughout Ireland and Britain, Equiano unwittingly forged a path that would be followed by later black abolitionists. Moreover, publishing and lecturing proved necessary in order to provide the visiting abolitionists with an income. Equiano's narrative provided a template for many later slave narratives; generally, the title made it clear that it was written 'by himself or herself'; an image of the narrator was provided; testimonials were included by white patrons; a quote, usually biblical or poetic, appeared on the opening pages; the author's chosen name was given; and the cruelties of slavery were outlined in the text.

Equiano was unique in a number of ways, most notably that he was a 'first-generation' slave who had been born in Africa, kidnapped and enslaved. Consequently, he was able to devote a large part of his narrative to writing about the customs and traditions of Africa and the brutality of the 'middle passage'. As a reminder of his origins, the title of his *Narrative* referred to him as 'the African'. Equiano did liberate himself, but he did so by paying for his freedom. Upon becoming free, he did not change his name, always signing himself as Gustavus Vassa, the name he had been given when enslaved, but followed by 'the African'. It was also the name he chose when he was baptized in London. When writing his *Narrative*, however, Equiano used his African name, Olaudah Equiano, explaining, 'I was named Olaudah, which, in our language, signifies vicissitude or fortune also, one favoured, and having a loud voice and well spoken'.[10] Regardless of being remembered by his pen-name, he continued to sign his letters as 'Gustavus Vassa, the African'.[11] This marked him as different from many other black abolitionists who adopted new names, moreover, names that suggested anglicized roots. While all abolitionists were Christian, Equiano's image at the front of the *Narrative*, depicting him holding a Bible, followed by a quote from Isaiah, was a clear statement of his devotion to Christianity.[12] Because of the way in which his books were funded, each of the editions included a list of subscribers. The list in the first

Olaudah Equiano (1745–1797) 43

edition was headed by 'His Royal Highness the Prince of Wales. His Royal Highness the Duke of York', which was a pointed reminder that anti-slavery—and Equiano—had support at the highest level of society.

Early life

What is known about Equiano's early life is based on his *Narrative*. He was born in what is now Nigeria. He was captured when aged about 11 and, along with his sister, enslaved. They were soon separated, never to see each other again. Equiano was initially taken to Virginia, but then sold to a ship's captain. He spent his teenage years at sea, during which time he visited England and served on vessels engaged in fighting in the Seven Years' War. Importantly also, during this time, he learned the basics of reading and writing. Equiano witnessed the brutality of enslavement first-hand on a visit to the West Indies—a traumatic experience that he never forgot. While enslaved, he visited England with his owner. His initial fears about being amongst Europeans were alleviated quickly, and instead he 'relished their society and manners'.[13] While there, Equiano's desire for more education was realized when two kindly sisters arranged for him to attend school. They also were responsible for his baptism.[14] Equiano's owner agreed, reluctantly, to this. Equiano later wrote that:

> Shortly after my arrival, he sent me to wait upon the Miss Guerins, who had treated me with much kindness when I was there before; and they sent me to school. While I was attending their servants told me I could not go to Heaven unless I was baptized. This made me very uneasy; for I had now some faint idea of a future state: accordingly, I communicated my anxiety to the eldest Miss Guerin, with whom I was become a favourite, and pressed her to have me baptized; when to my great joy, she told me I should. She had formerly asked my master to let me be baptized, but he had refused; however she now insisted on it; and he being under some obligation to her brother complied with her request; so I was baptized in St. Margaret's Church, West-minster, in February 1759, by my present name.[15]

At this stage, St Margaret's Church was the official church of the British House of Commons and, therefore, one of the most prestigious locations for a baptism ceremony to take place—more especially for a 14-year-old slave.[16] Equiano remained a devout Methodist for the remainder of his life. However, unlike a number of abolitionists who came after him, his religious outlook did not make him either conservative or anti-Catholic.[17]

Aged 20, Equiano achieved his self-emancipation by purchasing his freedom with money that he had saved. He came to England as a free man around 1768, taking a variety of jobs including as a waiter and a hairdresser. Because of the precariousness of his existence, he decided to return to sea. While at sea, Equiano travelled both to Turkey and to the Artic in 1772 and 1773. Overall, Equiano's early life and his experiences at sea meant that he was truly cosmopolitan, unlike

44   *Olaudah Equiano (1745–1797)*

many later abolitionists whose time in Ireland and Britain marked their first time outside America. Fearing re-capture, Equiano returned to London in the 1780s with a view to settling in England. A legal ruling in 1772 had decreed that slavery was illegal in England. The man responsible for the ruling was an English lawyer, Granville Sharp, whom Equiano had first met in 1774. In London, he became involved with the abolitionist movement, including the Sons of Africa. Ottobah Cugoano, also formerly enslaved, was a member. Equiano proved to be a fearless champion of enslaved people when, in 1783, he brought to Sharp's attention an incident that had occurred two years earlier when the crew on board a British slaving ship had thrown more than 130 slaves overboard and then tried to claim insurance. Although Sharp did not win the case, the 'Zong Massacre' increased sympathy for ending the slave trade.[18] It also propelled Equiano into prominence within the movement. In November 1786, Equiano was appointed commissary for the British government's Sierra Leone settlement plan, which aimed to transplant impoverished black people living in England.[19] However, he lost his job when he accused some of his fellow officials of being corrupt.[20] Undaunted, Equiano entered the public arena in England, using the press to defend his accusations. The *Public Advertiser* published his letters, but simultaneously included rebuffs accusing him of 'falsehoods as deeply black as his jetty face'.[21] Such comments were a reminder of the deep-seated prejudice and racism that existed side by side with a growing support for abolition. As this issue was playing out in the newspapers, in 1787, the Society for the Abolition of the Slave Trade was founded. Equiano remained central to the public agitation, attending:

> … debates in the House of Commons on slavery and the abolition of the slave trade in 1788 and address[ing] the government directly through published letters on the subject. He corresponded with parliamentarians and one of his letters to Lord Hawkesbury was presented to a Parliamentary Committee as evidence in 1789.[22]

The timing was perfect for Equiano to write his narrative. In 1789, as a republican revolution was unfolding in France, Vassa published *The Interesting Narrative of the Life of Olaudah Equiano* or *Gustavus Vassa the African, written by himself*. It became a best-seller, helping to turn many people against slavery. The final three words of the title, 'written by himself', pre-empted the inevitable criticisms that the volume must have been ghost written by a white person. Some decades later, Douglass would write a narrative to prove that his lectures had been authentic; in contrast, Equiano now undertook a lecture tour to prove that his *Narrative* was authentic. For these two men and other abolitionists, publications provided a means of securing an income from sales. Although Equiano's lectures have not survived, his skill as a lecturer was praised. Occasionally, this was done through a racialized lens, one newspaper stating, 'his manners polished, his mind enlightened, and in every respect on par with Europeans'.[23]

In August 1790, a 'second and corrected' version of Equiano's two-volume *Narrative* was published in England. In the accompanying notices in newspapers,

Equiano thanked 700 persons 'of all denominations' for supporting the work.[24] While volume one had only included a portrait of the author, volume two included a plate showing the manner in which Equiano had been shipwrecked in 1767, thus adding to the drama of his life story. The *Narrative* covered many other topics ranging from the countries of Africa and their customs and traditions, to his kidnapping, the cruel treatment of slaves, his escape and his conversion to 'the faith of Christ Jesus'.[25] Despite handling sales himself, purchases were buoyant and, in December of the same year, a third edition—'corrected and enlarged' was announced. Publicity—also handled by Equiano—included a favourable review of the book from the *General Magazine* of July 1790.[26] Proving to be a gifted self-publicist, Equiano followed up each new edition with letters to the regional papers where he happened to be speaking, by thanking people for their interest and stating:

> 'Tis now the duty of everyone who is a friend to religion and humanity, to assist the different Committees engaged in this pious work. Those who can feel for the difficulties of their own countrymen, will also commiserate the case of the poor Africans.—Since that it does not often fall to the lot of individuals to contribute to so important a moral and religious duty as that of putting an end to a practice which may, without exaggeration, be stiled [sic] one of the greatest evils now existing on the earth; it may be hoped, that each one will now use their utmost endeavour for that purpose. ... Permit me, dear friends, on behalf of myself and countrymen, to offer you the warmest effusions of a heart replete with gratitude.[27]

Ireland

In April 1791, in a speech lasting for four hours, William Wilberforce introduced the first parliamentary bill to abolish the slave trade.[28] It was easily defeated, to some extent falling victim to a conservative backlash as revolutions raged from Europe to the West Indies. In a letter published in numerous newspapers, Sharp asked supporters, including those in Ireland, to regard the outcome of the vote as 'a delay rather than a defeat'.[29] Shortly following this, in May 1791, Equiano sailed to Dublin to oversee the fourth edition of his *Narrative*. He stayed in the country for eight months. Like Douglass 50 years later, Equiano was in Ireland at a time of heightened political tension. For the most part, the revolution in France had been welcomed by Irish people, committees had been formed in the main cities and towns to celebrate the anniversary of the Fall of the Bastille on 14 July 1789. Within only weeks of being in the country, Equiano would have witnessed massive demonstrations celebrating the second anniversary of the revolution, hailing it as a harbinger of liberty for all. At the time of his visit, there were large parades through the streets of Dublin. The organizers claimed that the widespread support was suggestive of 'their good will to the general liberties of mankind, and of the sentiments they entertain on the RIGHTS OF MEN'. Banners were displayed stating, 'We do

46   *Olaudah Equiano (1745–1797)*

not rejoice because we are slaves, but because Frenchmen are free'.[30] In Belfast, the large and elaborate celebrations in 1791 included a preamble stating:

> Twenty-six millions of our fellow creatures (near one-sixth of the inhabitants of Europe), bursting their chains and throwing off, almost in an instant, the degrading yoke of slavery—is a scene so new, interesting and sublime, that the heart which cannot participate in the triumph, must have been vitiated by illiberal politics, or be naturally depraved ...
>
> The inhabitants of Belfast and its neighbourhood, the more strongly to mark their abhorrence of despotism; their love of liberty; and their attachment to their brethren of mankind—dedicated this day to the commemoration of the greatest event in human annals.[31]

At the end of the day, numerous toasts were drunk, commencing with one to 'The King of Ireland' and including another to 'The Society for Abolishing the Slave Trade'.[32] Ironically, 'Irish Volunteers', a militia brought into existence by the British government in case of an invasion by France during the American Revolutionary War, played a prominent role in the processions.[33] Worryingly for the British government, the celebrations that were taking place in England linked the revolutions in America and France with the position of Ireland, drinking toasts to 'Ireland and her Band of Patriots'.[34]

It was to this cauldron of political activity, and the forging of bonds between disparate oppressed groups, that Equiano arrived in Ireland. His visit also coincided with the formation of the Society of the United Irishmen in October 1791, marking a new departure in Irish politics, and an unwelcome one for the British government. Inspired by the American and French revolutions, the United Irishmen were republican nationalists who wanted a complete political separation from Britain. They also promoted the Enlightenment concepts of liberty, independence and popular sovereignty. Many of the movement's leaders were radical Protestants who urged an alliance with Catholics in order to unite under the common name of Irish men. Although Catholics represented over 80 per cent of the country's population, centuries of repression by the Protestant minority had systematically denied them of their basic civil rights. In his *Argument on Behalf of the Catholics of Ireland* (1791), Theobald Wolfe Tone employed a trope repeatedly used in nationalist discourse, referring to Irish people as slaves.[35] He argued that the minority Protestant Ascendancy in Ireland (of which he was a member) had held 'three millions of our fellow creatures, and fellow subjects, in degradation and infamy, and contempt, or to sum up in one word, in *slavery*'.[36] Tone's pamphlet was published in the same year that Equiano visited Ireland and the arguments that it promulgated would have suggested some similarities with his own situation. Even if Equiano did not read it, he inevitably would have come into contact with its ideas as several of his Irish hosts were also leading members of the United Irishmen.

Equiano wrote little about his time in Ireland; in the later editions of the *Narrative*, he explained that although he could write about his travel experiences, it

Olaudah Equiano (1745–1797)   47

would 'swell the volume too much'. Instead, he just gave a brief overview of his travels, writing:

> I shall only observe in general, that, in May 1791, I sailed from Liverpool to Dublin where I was very kindly received, and from thence to Cork, and then travelled over many counties in Ireland. I was everywhere exceedingly well treated, by persons of all ranks. I found the people extremely hospitable, particularly in Belfast, where I took my passage, on board of a vessel for Clyde, on the 29th of January, and arrived at Greenock on the 30th.[37]

Similar to Douglass and William Wells Brown 60 years later, Equiano travelled to Ireland to oversee the publication of an Irish edition of his life story. On 31 May 1791, the *Freeman's Journal* announced the arrival of the fourth edition of the *Narrative*, 'corrected and enlarged', and stating that it was on sale in bookshops in Capel Street, Dame Street and Grafton Street.[38] The Irish publication was also announced in British newspapers.[39]

The Dublin edition was 359 pages in length. The cover was

> half calf over marble boards, spine gilt with blind tooled ornaments.[40] As usual, it was 'Printed for, and Sold by, the Author.' The Frontispiece also stated that the book was available at the *Dublin Chronicle* Office and other booksellers in Dublin.

A separate page was dedicated to 'Robert, Lord Archbishop of Dublin'.[41] Equiano had attracted enough Irish subscribers to warrant including separate lists of British and Irish subscribers. The Irish list showed the extent of Equiano's patronage, included the Archbishop of Dublin, the Duke of Leinster, the Earl of Ormonde, the Lord Bishop of Cork, the Lord Bishop of Meath and Henry Howison, the Lord Mayor of Dublin.[42] Subscribers also included three leading members of the United Irishmen—Oliver Bond, Napper Tandy and Samuel Neilson. The women donors were Lady Louth, Lady Miltown, Lady Moira and Lady Cecilia La Touche.[43] In total, there were 70 subscribers from Ireland, including ministers and women, and drawn from all parts of the country: Armagh, Athlone, Belfast, Carlow, Clonmel, Cork, Drogheda, Kilkenny, Limerick, Lisburn, Lurgan, Mote, Mullingar, Tandragee and Waterford. The fact that the subscribers were overwhelming Protestant, reflected the nature of Ireland's political and economic inequalities.

Towards the end of his time in Ireland, Equiano travelled to the northern town of Belfast, then a stronghold of radical Protestantism. On 16 December 1791, when he was in the town, the *Belfast News-Letter* announced that on that day the *Narrative* was available—'in one handsome volume ... on good paper, price 4 shillings, sewed ... written by himself, with an elegant print of the author'.[44] On the same day, an editorial in the paper reported on societies being formed in Britain to boycott rum, sugar and coffee, concluding with an appeal that:

48   Olaudah Equiano (1745–1797)

Whoever reflects on the well attested instances of cruelty to the blacks, torn from their country for the purpose of raising luxuries unknown to former times, must, if he appeal to the native feelings of the heart, wish for a speedy abolition of a traffic which is a disgrace to every country which sanctions it.[45]

In Belfast, Equiano stayed with the family of Samuel Neilson, founder and one of the most radical of the United Irishmen, which had earned him the nickname, 'the Jacobin'. Born in County Down in 1761, the son of a Presbyterian minister, Neilson was also a successful businessman. His home was a hub of political activity and, inevitably, Equiano would have met other leading members and engaged with them on political issues. Neilson was also editor of the bi-weekly *Northern Star* newspaper, which first appeared on 4 January 1792—while Equiano was still a guest in Neilson's home. The paper was a mouth-piece for the United Irishmen, urging its readers, 'Unite and be Free—Divide and be Slaves'.[46] A large part of its columns were devoted to events unfolding in France. Its support for the rights of man were not limited simply to Irishmen but extended to ending the slave trade. The first edition of the paper included an anonymous poem called 'The Negroe's [sic] Complaint', which commenced:

Forced from home and all its pleasures,
Afric's coast I left forlorn …[47]

Readers were urged not to consume West Indian produce, especially rum and sugar, describing its consumption as 'positive and downright murder'.[48]

The success of Equiano's time in Belfast led to a Letter of Introduction being sent on his behalf on 25 December 1791 to a Mr O'Brien in Carrickfergus. The letter was penned by Thomas Digges, a Catholic born in Maryland, who had moved to England during the American Revolution to work as an agent for American prisoners. Digges had subsequently moved to Ireland, where he ended up advising the leaders of the United Irishmen.[49] Throughout his life, suspicion dogged him that he was a double agent and engaged in industrial espionage. Digges, however, had met Equiano on a number of occasions and each man appeared impressed by the other. Digges's letter was reprinted in subsequent editions of the *Narrative*:

The bearer of this, Mr Gustavus Vassa, is an enlightened African, of good sense, agreeable manners, and of an excellent character, and who comes well recommended to this place, and noticed by the first people here, goes to-morrow to your town, for the purpose of vending some books, written by himself, which is a Narrative of his own Life and Sufferings, with some account of his native country and its inhabitants. He was torn from his relatives and country (by the more savage white men of England) at an early period in life; and during his residence in England, at which time I have seen him, during my agency for the American prisoners, with Sir William Dolben, Mr. Granville Sharp, Mr. Wilkes, and many other distinguished

Olaudah Equiano (1745–1797) 49

characters; he supported an irreproachable character, and was a principal instrument in bringing about the motion for a repeal of the Slave-Act. I beg leave to introduce him to your notice and civility; and if you can spare the time, your introduction of him personally to your neighbours may be of essential benefit to him.[50]

On 29 January 1792, Equiano sailed to Scotland. The day before he left Belfast, a large meeting had been convened in the town for the purpose of presenting to the Dublin parliament a petition on behalf of Catholic Emancipation.[51] The notice informing the public about the meeting had included the signatures of Samuel Neilson and Thomas McCabe, and explained:

As MEN and as IRISHMEN, we have long lamented the degrading state of slavery and oppression in which the great majority of our Countrymen, the ROMAN CATHOLICS, are held—nor have we lamented it in silence.[52]

During the course of the meeting, reference was made to ending the slave trade, on the grounds that freedom was 'an inheritance and a right'.[53] A number of the speakers attacked the radicalism of the newly formed United Irishmen. Neilson spoke in its defence.[54] The meeting also disagreed as to whether Catholic Emancipation should be immediate or gradualist, the latter being in the majority.[55] Similar divisions were common within the abolitionist movement. It is highly probable that Equiano attended given his close association with Neilson. The similarity between Irish progressive politics and anti-slavery would not have been lost on Equiano as he brought his Irish sojourn to a close.

During his eight months in Ireland, Equiano had sold 1,900 books, which almost equalled the Irish sales of Thomas Paine's *Rights of Man*.[56] However, his time in Ireland had also coincided with news of a slave revolt in Haiti (St Domingo), with early reports in the Irish and British newspapers focusing on the violence of the insurgents.[57] Several even blamed the abolitionists for emboldening them.[58] Sections of the Irish press were more sympathetic. The Belfast *News-Letter*, for example, informed its readers:

The late disasters in this unfortunate colony, particularly the burning of Port-au-Prince, are to be ascribed solely to the direct breach of faith with the People of Colour, on the part of the Whites ... as soon as the Negroes appeared to be quelled, the Whites refused to execute the agreement.

Such instances of folly, treachery and insolent cruelty ... ought to make those who have roundly charged the advocates for the abolition of the Slave Trade with being the authors of all the calamities of St Domingo, somewhat more guarded in their future assertions, if not ashamed of the past.[59]

Regardless of some negative reporting about the revolt in Haiti, abolitionists in Ireland and Britain, including Equiano, remained faithful to agitating to end the slave trade.[60]

50   *Olaudah Equiano (1745–1797)*

Later life

The year 1792 proved to be a momentous one for Equiano. In April, a provincial British newspaper announced in its Marriage section that:

> On Monday the 9th inst. Soham, Cambridgeshire, Gustavus Vassa, the African (well known in England as the champion and advocate for procuring a suppression of the slave trade), to Miss Cullen daughter of Mr. Cullen, of Ely.[61]

The wedding was also noted by newspapers in Ireland, who described him as 'well known in England as the champion and advocate for the suppression of the slave trade'.[62] They added that the ceremony had taken place 'in the presence of a vast number of people assembled for the occasion'.[63] Being mentioned in this way was indicative of Equiano's acceptance into, and stature within, British and Irish society. Also, unlike the opprobrium that Douglass would later face for marrying Helen Pitts, a white woman, there appeared to be no negative reaction to this inter-racial union. Later editions of the *Narrative* included a section on his marriage, Equiano simply noting that after hearing a debate in parliament on the slave trade, 'I then went to Soham in Cambridgeshire, and was married on the 7th of April to Miss Cullen, daughter of James and Ann Cullen, late of Ely'.[64] Susannah had been a subscriber to the third edition of the *Narrative*. They probably had met when Equiano was lecturing in Cambridgeshire in 1789. They both shared similar Christian views.[65]

The year of the marriage coincided with several debates in the British parliament and elsewhere to end the slave trade, with numerous petitions being presented.[66] In May 1792, Equiano thanked the General Assembly of the Church of Scotland for condemning the trade. In a letter published in a number of papers, he said, 'It filled me with love towards you'.[67] Similar debates were taking place in Ireland. In June 1792, at the annual meeting of the General Synod of Ulster, an address on the slave trade was drawn up, to be forwarded to Wilberforce.[68] Yet, regardless of extensive public support for abolition, Granville Sharp, now chairman of the Committee of the Society for the Abolition of the Slave Trade, frequently appealed for funding for their depleted finances. These requests appeared in the Irish press.[69] A letter by Sharp to the editor of the Belfast *News-Letter* in October 1792 called on the people of Ireland to join with those in Britain 'in the cause of humanity'.[70]

By this stage, Equiano's interest in human rights extended beyond abolition. He had become involved with another radical society, the London Corresponding Society, which had been founded in 1792 with the aims of reforming parliament and introducing universal male suffrage. Its founder, Thomas Hardy, was also a long-term champion of the ending of the slave trade. Hardy and his wife Lydia had a close friendship with Equiano. In addition to their mutual political outlook, they shared a deep commitment to Christianity. Before travelling to Ireland, Equiano had stayed at their home where he made revisions to the Irish edition of his *Narrative*.[71] In April 1792, Lydia had written to her husband asking about the progress of Wilberforce's latest bill in parliament, adding that she hoped that

Equiano's tour of Scotland, where he was promoting a new edition of the *Narrative*, would be successful.[72] The *Narrative* was published in Scotland in May 1792.[73] However, Equiano had a further mission. From Scotland he reported back to Hardy about the state of reform societies in the country.[74]

The rapid growth of the London Corresponding Society and of radicalism in general, at a time that Britain was at war with France and slave revolts were taking place in Haiti, worried the British authorities. It led to Hardy's arrest for High Treason in 1794. He was acquitted but, from this point, Hardy ceased his involvement with radical politics.[75] Around this time, Equiano also disappeared from public view. He was possibly concerned by the government's backlash against British and Irish radicals, which had included the suspension of Habeas Corpus in May 1794. Equiano's public profile and links with radical groups on both sides of the Irish Sea made him particularly vulnerable to arrest. One of his letters, revealing his membership and desire that the Corresponding Society's influence would spread further, had been seized by the government during Hardy's arrest.[76] Equiano was not only close to a republican movement that was uniting Protestants and Catholics in Ireland, but he was actively involved with radical groups in England. These connections and networks, which cut across traditional enmities and boundaries, would have made Equiano appear highly dangerous in a time of heightened apprehension. Significantly also, no more editions of the *Narrative* were published.[77] By this stage, however, Equiano's lucrative lecture tours and book sales meant that he was wealthy enough, 'to live the life of a gentleman'.[78] This financial security remained elusive to many later visiting abolitionists.

In his personal life, Equiano experienced tragedy. Susannah died in 1796. In her will, she left everything to her husband.[79] Equiano did not long outlive her, dying on 31 March 1797, aged 52. Although it was recorded that he died in London, his burial place has remained unknown.[80] A number of English newspapers noted his death, but with a sting: 'On Friday last died in London, Mr Gustavus Vassa, the African, well known to the public for his "Interesting Narrative of his Life," supposed to have been written by himself'.[81] Similar notices appeared in Irish newspapers.[82] Equiano and Susannah had two daughters— Anna Maria, born in January 1793, and Joanna, born in April 1795. Sadly, Anna Maria died in July 1797. She was buried in St Andrew's Church in Chesterton in Cambridgeshire. An elaborate memorial was erected in her honour, which referred to her father's origins:

> Should simple village rhymes attract thine eye,
> Stranger, as thoughtfully thou passest by,
> Know that there lies beside this humble stone,
> A child of colour, haply not thine own.
> Her father born of Afric's sun-burnt race,
> Torn from his native fields, ah! foul disgrace;
> Through various toils at last to Britain came,
> Espoused, so heaven ordain'd, an English dame,

52   *Olaudah Equiano (1745–1797)*

And follow'd Christ their hopes two infants dear,
But one, a Hapless Orphan, slumbers here.
To bury her, the village children came,
And dropp'd choice flowers, and lisp'd her early fame;
And some that lov'd her most, as if unblest.
Bedew'd with tears the white wreath on their breast.
But she is gone and dwell's in that abode,
Where some of ev'ry clime shall joy in God.

The inscription above the stone read: 'Near this place lies interred ANNA MARIA VASSA, Daughter of GUSTAVUS VASSA, the AFRICAN. She died July 21, 1797. Aged 4 years'.[83] Joanna Vassa lived until March 1857.[84] When she reached 21, she received a substantial inheritance of £950, left by her father. In 1821, Joanna married Henry Bromley, a Congregationalist minister.[85]

In the same year that Equiano died, the British government closed down the *Northern Star*. The following year, a rising by the United Irishmen was brutally put down resulting in the death of many of its leaders including Wolfe Tone and Henry Joy McCracken. Henry's sister, Mary Ann, would be one of the women who welcomed Douglass to Belfast in 1845 and helped found the Belfast Ladies' Anti-Slavery Society in honour of his visit.[86] Neilson, in turn, was indicted for High Treason, imprisoned and deported. From his exile in America he planned to revive the *Northern Star* but died of yellow fever in 1803, the year in which Robert Emmet led another unsuccessful rising for a democratic Irish republic.

The United Irishmen had universally opposed the slave trade and slavery while in Ireland, but a number of those who survived the risings and sought exile in the United States did not continue to support these principles. As Craig Landy has suggested:

> Once on American soil, few remained committed to the immediate abolition of slavery and many gradually turned more conservative on the issue of slavery, as they strove to become part of the fabric of white America.[87]

The relationship of Irish Americans with slavery and anti-slavery was something that would vex abolitionists throughout the nineteenth century. Early exceptions included Thomas Addis Emmet, William James MacNevin and William Sampson.[88] Thomas Emmet, a United Irishman, lawyer, abolitionist and older brother of the doomed Robert Emmet, had been one of the most vocal opponents of slavery while in Ireland. Using the pen-name *Montanus*, he had written in *The Press* that all enslaved people needed to join together to fight again oppression.[89] In the wake of the failed 1798 rebellion, Emmet spent time in prisons in Ireland and Scotland. Following a brief spell in France, he sought exile in America where he joined the New York Bar. His first case involved the prosecution of the captain of a slave ship from Newport in Rhode Island, the case aligning with his anti-slavery beliefs, first honed in Ireland.[90] Throughout his distinguished legal career,

Olaudah Equiano (1745–1797)   53

Emmet continued to act on behalf of fugitives slaves, and to oppose the expansion of slavery within the United States. Moreover, he did so for no payment.[91] Consequently, the men who had hosted Equiano when he visited Ireland, demonstrated their ongoing commitment to social justice and to ending enslavement, but now from the other side of the Atlantic.

Conclusion

Equiano is one of the small number of black abolitionists whose contributions have been remembered, and his legacy has been honoured in Britain. Moreover, he has featured in popular culture in a number of ways. During his lifetime, he was referred to in an anti-slavery poem by Manchester-born John Lowe, in which Equiano features as the go-to hero:

> Fly to England! and tell 'Vassa'
> To Desist 'Tis all in vain.
> Destruction save us! from a Massa
> Of your kindred—*on this plain.*[92]

More recently, it has been suggested that the eponymous hero of Caryll Phillips 1992 historical novel, *Cambridge*, was based on Equiano.[93] The 2006 British-made film, *Amazing Grace*, which included Equiano in a number of scenes, was both critically and commercially successful.[94] Unusually, Equiano's one surviving daughter was also the object of a film in 2012, the low budget, *Joanna*.[95] Nor has Equiano's daughter who died in infancy been forgotten. The memorial to Anna Maria became part of a human rights walk for school children in Cambridgeshire.[96] In 1996, the Equiano Society was formed in London, 'to celebrate and publicize' Equiano and others 'who made outstanding contributions to the African literary heritage'.[97] His work in the capital has further been commemorated by a number of plaques placed upon his various residences in that city.[98] In 2009, an oval memorial tablet was unveiled in St Margaret's Church in Westminster where Equiano had been baptized. The Inscription reads: 'THE AFRICAN, OLAUDAH EQUIANO, Baptized Gustavus Vassa in this church 9 February 1759, Author and Abolitionist'.[99] Despite this public recognition, Equiano's place of burial remains unknown. In contrast, a historian of Equiano discovered Joanna's grave in 2005, thus enabling it to be restored in time for the 200th anniversary of the ending of the slave trade, to which her father had contributed so much. Equiano's contributions to changing the political landscape have been remembered at the highest levels. His ongoing relevance was apparent during a debate in the British House of Lords in 2002 on Human Trafficking when, 'They drew upon evidence and experiences supplied by a remarkable African who had himself been sold into slavery. Olaudah Equiano was that slave'.[100] His contributions to bringing about legislative changes in the first phase of abolition were acknowledged when, in September 2019, a bronze bust was acquired for the Parliamentary Art Collection by

54   Olaudah Equiano (1745–1797)

the Speaker's Advisory Committee on Works of Art. It referred to him as, *Olaudah Equiano—African, slave, author, abolitionist*. The art was by sculptor Christy Symington.[101] To date, there are no memorials to this trail-blazing abolitionist and human rights activist in Ireland, Douglass being the only black abolitionist to have been publicly commemorated.[102]

As would later be the case for Douglass, even before he arrived in Ireland, Equiano had encountered Irish people at significant junctures in his life. It was an Irishman who not only helped to bring about his religious conversion but also consolidated his desire to be free. In the Irish edition of his *Narrative*, Equiano wrote that a 'messmate, the Irishman Daniel Quin, taught him to read the Bible and to think of nothing "but being free"'.[103] Equiano's time in Ireland is revealing because while he was there, he moved comfortably in radical, republican circles. As a result of close contact with its leaders, Equiano was enabled to make, 'significant interventions in linking anti-slavery positions to United Irish democratic cultures', which, in turn, gave him a central role in the politics of the 'Black Atlantic'.[104] Moreover, it could be argued that he was also influential in the politics of a 'Green Atlantic' as 'his connections with radicals associated with the United Irishmen contributed to the prominence of anti-slavery themes in United Irish writing and thought'.[105] Again, Equiano was not unique in placing abolition within a wider demand for human rights, but he was the first black abolitionist to openly seek partnerships with radical groups in both Ireland and in Britain. Although in the public eye for a relatively short period of time, Equiano not only contributed to the abolition movement, but, perhaps more than any other visiting black abolitionist, he left a mark on progressive thought on both sides of the Irish Sea.

For a number of reasons, Equiano was one of the most important black abolitionists of the Ante-Bellum period. Unusually, although his time in Ireland attracted far less attention at the time than that of many later abolitionists, it has been more widely acknowledged as significant by historians.[106] Equiano died in 1797. It would take another decade before the slave trade was abolished, and three further decades more before slavery was ended in the British Empire. His contributions to both were many. Equiano pioneered the concept of an author's book tour—something that would be replicated by later visiting abolitionists. His *Narrative* provided a prototype for subsequent slave narratives, and these publications, in turn, became an important tool in ending slavery. Moreover, his involvement with radical political groups in Ireland and Britain placed abolition in the context of the wider desire for the universal rights of man. In this capacity, Equiano provided a unique link that stretched across the Irish Sea and, through the continued involvement of several exiled United Irishmen in America, across the Atlantic.

Notes

1   As a young man, he was given a variety of names, but his second owner gave him the name Gustavus Vassa, which became his preferred name. Olaudah Equiano, by which he is generally remembered, was his African name and the name he used as author of his *Narrative*.

Olaudah Equiano (1745–1797)   55

2 Other memoirs were written, but they did not have the same commercial success or legacy of Equiano's: for example, *Letters of the Late Ignatius Sancho* (1782); Ottobah Cugoano, *Thoughts and Sentiments on the Evil and Wicked Traffic of the Slavery and Commerce of the Human Species* (London: July 1787). In 1831, *The History of Mary Prince, a West Indian Slave* helped to revive this tradition.

3 Equiano Olaudah, *The Interesting Narrative of the Life of Olaudah Equiano, or Gustavus Vassa, the African. Written by himself* (London: Author, 1794, ninth edition), p. xvii.

4 Equiano, *Narrative* (London: 1789, first edition), p. 2.

5 This accusation followed him to his death, see 'Died', *Norfolk Chronicle*, 15 April 1797.

6 Vincent Carretta, 'Olaudah Equiano or Gustavus Vassa? New Light on an Eighteenth-Century Question of Identity', in *Slavery and Abolition*, vol. 20, no. 3 (1999), pp. 96–105; Paul E. Lovejoy, 'Autobiography and Memory: Gustavus Vassa, Alias Olaudah Equiano, the African', in *Slavery and Abolition*, vol. 27, no. 3 (2006), pp. 317–47. Nini Rodgers, author of *Equiano and Anti-Slavery in Eighteenth-Century Belfast* (Belfast: Belfast Society, 2000), accepts the early account of his life as true.

7 The prolific William Wells Brown, for example, writing almost 60 years after Equiano first published his narrative, has recently been accused of plagiarism. See chapter on Wells Brown.

8 John Bugg, 'The Other Interesting Narrative: Olaudah Equiano's Public Book Tour', in *Journal of Modern Language Association*, vol. 121, no. 5 (October 2006), pp. 1424–42, p. 1424.

9 *Ottobah Cugoano, or John Stewart, was listed in the first edition*, p. viii; The Abolition Project: http://abolition.e2bn.org/people_26.html.

10 Equiano, *Narrative* (1789), p. 31.

11 Letter to the printer of the *Leeds Intelligencer*, in *Northampton Mercury*, 18 December 1790.

12 The quote is: 'Behold, God is my salvation; I will trust and not be afraid, for the Lord Jehovah is my strength and my song; he also is become my salvation. And in that day shall ye say, Praise the Lord, call upon his name, declare his doings among the people'. *Isaiah* xii. 2, 4.

13 Equiano, *Narrative* (1789), p. 132.

14 The plaque on St Margaret's Church in Westminster gives 1759 as the date, which allies with the date in the *Narrative*: www.westminster-abbey.org/st-margarets-church.

15 Equiano, *Narrative*, pp. 133–4. The Church of St Margaret is located on the grounds of Westminster Abbey on Parliament Square in London. It was, until 1972, the Anglican parish church of the British House of Commons.

16 See: https://www.westminster-abbey.org/abbey-commemorations/commemorations/olaudah-equiano-gustavus-vassa.

17 See chapters on Benson, Kelly and Ward.

18 The Zong Case:http://www.understandingslavery.com/index.php-option=com_content&view=article&id=373&Itemid=236.html.

19 The settlement plan was organized by the Committee for the Relief of the Black Poor, which had been found by Granville Sharp. Sixty years later, William Wells Brown would suggest a similar solution, but to the West Indies.

20 Records relating to 'The Black Poor', in the National Archives, England: www.nationalarchives.gov.uk/pathways/blackhistory/work_community/poor.htm.

21 Quoted in Jon Mee, 'Print, Publicity, and Popular Radicalism in the 1790s, The Laurel of Liberty', May 2016, 17–110, p. 1427, at: www.cambridge.org/core/books/print-publicity-and-popular-radicalism-in-the-1790s/publicity-print-and-association/37844739FBF1520AE0FD504718F886A9/core-reader.

56   *Olaudah Equiano (1745–1797)*

22 September Artwork of the Month, Christy Symington, 'Olaudah Equiano—African, slave, author, abolitionist', at: www.parliament.uk/about/art-in-parliament/news/2019/september/september-artwork-of-the-month-olaudah-equiano-by-christy-symington/.

23 *Sheffield Register, Yorkshire, Derbyshire, & Nottinghamshire Universal Advertiser*, 27 August 1790.

24 'This day is published', *Manchester Mercury*, 20 July 1790.

25 'This day is published', *Sheffield Register, Yorkshire, Derbyshire, & Nottinghamshire Universal Advertiser*, 20 August 1790.

26 'This day is published', *Northampton Mercury*, 18 December 1790.

27 'Letter to the printer of the *Leeds Intelligencer*', *Northampton Mercury*, 18 December 1790. The letters are all similar, see, *Newcastle Courant*, 6 October 1792.

28 Seymour Drescher, 'People and Parliament: The Rhetoric of the British Slave Trade', in *Journal of Interdisciplinary History*, vol. 20, no. 4 (Spring, 1990), pp. 561–80.

29 'Committee for effecting the abortion of the slave trade', Belfast *News-Letter*, 6 May 1791; *Finn's Leinster Journal*, 11 May 1791.

30 Ibid., 'Dublin. Anniversary of Revolution in France', 20 July 1791.

31 Ibid., 'Belfast. Commemoration of the French Revolution', 24 July 1791.

32 Ibid., The Volunteers, a militia originally founded in Belfast in 1788 to defend against a French invasion, regularly toasted 'Wilberforce and the abolition of the slave trade', Belfast *News-Letter*, 20 May 1791.

33 From their origins as a Protestant-only militia force, the Volunteers developed into an engine for political change, especially in regard to Irish independence.

34 'French Revolution', *Sheffield Register, Yorkshire, Derbyshire, & Nottinghamshire Universal Advertiser*, 22 July 1791. One of the largest meetings took place in the Crown and Anchor Tavern in London, chaired by George Rous. The tavern was located in the Strand and associated with English radicals from the 1790s to the Chartists. On 17 August 1846, the first meeting of the transatlantic Anti-Slavery League was held there, with Garrison and Douglass in attendance. It had been founded a week earlier, see, William Lloyd Garrison, *The Letters of William Lloyd Garrison: No Union with the Slaveholders, 1841–1849* (Cambridge: Harvard UP, 1973), p. 327.

35 William Drennan, one of founders of United Irishmen, in his 'Letters of Orellana' commenced each letter with 'Fellow Slaves'.

36 Theobald Wolfe Tone, *An Argument on Behalf of the Catholics of Ireland* (Belfast: Society of United Irishman of Belfast, 1791), p. 28.

37 Equiano, *Narrative* (ninth edition), pp. 258–359.

38 'This day is Published', *Freeman's Journal*, 31 May 1791; a thank-you letter in which he personally thanked the local subscribers, appeared in places that Vassa visited, for example, 'To the printer of Sheffield Register', *Sheffield Register*, 3 September 1790; *Yorkshire, Derbyshire, & Nottinghamshire Universal Advertiser*, 3 September 1790.

39 'This day is published', *Caledonian Mercury*, 21 May 1792.

40 For sales of the fourth edition, see: www.maggs.com/the-interesting-narrative-of-the-life-of-olaudah-equiano-or-gustavus-vassa-the-african_205332.htm.

41 Fourth edition of the *Narrative*, Dublin, 1791.

42 'List of Subscribers in Ireland', The Mayor's surname was incorrectly given as Howlon, *Narrative*, fourth edition, p. xxxi.

43 Ibid., List of Subscribers, pp. xxxi–xxxii.

44 No title, Belfast *News-Letter*, 16 December 1791.

45 Ibid., 'Belfast, December 16', 13 December 1791.

46 *Northern Star*, 21 July 1892.

47 Ibid., 4 January 1792.

48 'Slave Trade', *Northern Star*, 14 April 1792.

49 Nini Rodgers, *Equiano and Anti-Slavery in Eighteenth-Century Belfast* (Belfast: Ulster Historical Foundation, 2000), p. 6.

Olaudah Equiano (1745–1797) 57

50 Equiano, *Narrative*, ninth edition, 1794, p. xii.
51 'Town Meeting', *Northern Star*, 28 January 1792; Catholic Emancipation had the support of the Leader of the Irish Parliament, Henry Grattan, who repeatedly spoke in its favour. Grattan also used the trope of slavery to describe the condition of Irish Catholics, see, Belfast *News-Letter*, 24 March 1797. In 1800, Ireland lost its parliament in Dublin as a result of the Acts of Union. Instead, 100 (Protestant) MPs sat in the Westminster Parliament in London.
52 'To the Principle Inhabitants of the Town of Belfast', Belfast *News-Letter*, 24 January 1792.
53 'Town Meeting', *Northern Star*, 1 February 1792.
54 Richard Robert Madden, *The United Irishmen: Their Lives and Times*, etc., vol. 4 (Dublin: James Duffy, 1860), p. 8.
55 'Town Meeting', *Northern Star*, 1 February 1792.
56 Rodgers, *Equiano*, p. 4.
57 'Extract from a Letter from Montego Bay', *Northern Star*, 8 February 1792.
58 *Bath Chronicle and Weekly Gazette*, 10 November 1791.
59 'St Domingo', Belfast *News-Letter*, 27 January 1792.
60 The Haitian rebellion began in 1791. Slavery was abolished in the French colonies in 1794 and reintroduced by Napoleon in 1802. Haiti secured independence in 1804. See, Robin Blackburn, 'Haiti, Slavery, and the Age of the Democratic Revolution', in *The William and Mary Quarterly*, Third Series, vol. 63, no. 4 (Oct. 2006), 643–74, p. 670.
61 'Marriages', *The Scots Magazine*, 1 April 1792; 'Married', *Northampton Mercury*, 28 April 1792.
62 No title, Belfast *News-Letter*, 24 April 1792.
63 Ibid.
64 Equiano, *Narrative*, Chapter xii (NINTH EDITION ENLARGED. *LONDON*: PRINTED FOR, AND SOLD BY, THE AUTHOR. 1794), p. 359.
65 Vincent Carretta, *Equiano, the African: Biography of a Self-Made Man* (University of Georgia Press, 2005), p. 347.
66 For example, 'The Slave trade', Belfast *News-Letter*, 2 February 1790; Ibid., 'British House of Commons—slave trade', 7 June 1790; Ibid., 'British house of commons', 17 February 1792; Ibid, 'House of Commons—slave trade', 22 April 1791; Ibid., 'House of Commons—slave trade', 6 April 1792; Ibid., 'British house of commons—slave trade', 1 May 1792; Ibid., 'British House of Lords—Slave Trade', 8 May 1792; 'House of Commons—slave trade', *Finn's Leinster Journal*, 24 December 1790; Ibid., 'House of commons, Adjourned debate on the slave trade', 27 April 1791; Ibid., 'Slave trade', 11 May 1791; Ibid., 'House of commons—slave trade', 28 March 1792; Ibid., House of Commons—slave trade', 25 April 1792; 'House of commons—slave trade', *Freeman's Journal*, 20 March 1792.
67 'To the General Assembly', *Caledonian Mercury*, 26 May 1792.
68 No title, Belfast *News-Letter*, 3 July 1792.
69 'The Committee', *Freeman's Journal*, 1 May 1792; Ibid., 24 October 1793; No title, *Dublin Evening* Post, 3 May 1792.
70 'To the editor', Belfast *News-Letter*, 30 October 1792.
71 Clare Midgley, *Women against Slavery: The British Campaigns, 1780–1870* (London: Routledge, 1995), p. 39.
72 Jon Mee, 'Print, Publicity, and Popular Radicalism in the 1790s', in *The Laurel of Liberty* Online publication, May 2016, 17–110: www.cambridge.org/core/books/print-publicity-and-popular-radicalism-in-the-1790s/publicity-print-and-association/37844739FBF1520AE0FD504718F886A9/core-reader.
73 *Caledonian Mercury*, 21 May 1792.
74 Mee, 'Popular Radicalism'.

58   *Olaudah Equiano (1745–1797)*

75   E.P. Thompson, *The Making of the English Working Class* (New York: Vintage Books) p. 20.
76   Mee, 'Popular Radicalism', p. 1426.
77   At this stage, Equiano had produced nine editions of the *Narrative*: (London: printed and sold for the author, 1789), the first edition; (London: printed and sold for the author, 1789), the second edition; (London: printed and sold for the author, 1790), the third edition; (Dublin: printed and sold for the author, 1791), the fourth edition; (Edinburgh: printed and sold for the author, 1792), the fifth edition; (London: printed and sold for the author, 1793), the sixth edition; (London: printed and sold for the author, 1793), the seventh edition; (Norwich: printed and sold for the author, 1794); the eight edition; (London: printed and sold for the author, 1794), the ninth and last edition to be produced during Equiano's lifetime. In 1791, an unauthorized edition was published in America (New York: W. Durell, 1791). See also, 'Olaudah Equiano. A Bibliography' at: www.brycchancarey.com/equiano/biblio.htm#editions.
78   Carretta, *Self-Made Man*, p. 363.
79   Ibid., Susannah, in turn, had inherited two acres of land from her sister, which Equiano also inherited. It is probable that Susannah was buried in St Andrew's Church in Soham where the children were baptized and the family lived: 'Remembering Equiano': www.equiano.soham.org.uk/family.htm.
80   'Died', *Ipswich Journal*, 15 April 1797.
81   'Died', *Oxford Journal*, 25 March 1797, reprinted in the *Norfolk Chronicle*, 15 April 1797.
82   'Died', *Freeman's Journal*, 22 April 1797; Belfast *News-Letter*, 21 April 1797.
83   St Andrew's Church: www.standrews-chesterton.org/church-history/olaudah-equiano/.
84   Monument to Joanna Vassa in Abney Park Cemetery: https://historicengland.org.uk/listing/the-list/list-entry/1392851
85   A. Osborne, 'Equiano's Daughter, The Life & Times of Joanna Vassa Daughter of Olaudah Equiano, Gustavus Vassa, The African', *Dictionary of National Biography* (2007).
86   See chapter on Frederick Douglass.
87   Craig T.A. Landy, 'Society of United Irishmen Revolutionary and New-York Manumission Society Lawyer: Thomas Addis Emmet and the Irish Contributions to the Antislavery Movement in New York', in *New York History*, vol. 95, no. 2 (Cornell University Press, Spring 2014), 193–222, p. 217.
88   On arrival in New York in 1804, one of Emmet's first acts was to join the Manumission Society, and he served as a Counsellor for the rest of his life. Landy, 'Society', p. 194. 'The New York Society for the Manumission of Slaves and the Protection of such of them as had been or wanted to be Liberated' had been founded in 1785. Alexander Hamilton was a member.
89   Landy, 'Society', p. 195.
90   Ibid., p. 193.
91   Ibid., pp. 209–13.
92   John Lowe (of Manchester), 'The Ship-Wreck of a Slave-Ship', *Poems* (Manchester: R. and W. Dean, 1803), p. 56.
93   John Bugg, 'The Other Interesting Narrative: Olaudah Equiano's Public Book Tour', in *PMLA*, vol. 121, no. 5 (October 2006), 1424–42, p. 1424.
94   'Joanna Vassa' (2012). The Production Company was Queensbury Methodist Church. They describe the Storyline thus: England, 1821. Joanna Vassa—the daughter of Gustavus Vassa, otherwise known as Olaudah Equiano, a Wesleyan Methodist —marries Rev. Henry Bromley, who becomes the Minister of Clavering Congregational Church between 1826–1845. Their marriage represents the integrated history between the Methodist Church and the Congregational Church now known as the United Reformed Church.
      For more information, see: www.imdb.com/title/tt0454776/.

Olaudah Equiano (1745–1797)   59

95 See: www.imdb.com/title/tt1727320/.
96 'Footprints of Faith': footprintsfaith.wordpress.com/the-walks/human-rights-ks1/human-rights-walk-ks1-stop-1-the-round-church/.
97 The Equiano Society at: www.brycchancarey.com/equiano/eqs.htm.
98 For example, at his home on Riding House Street: www.waymarking.com/waymarks/WMP9DR_Olaudah_Equiano_Riding_House_Street_London_UK.
99 See: https://www.westminster-abbey.org/abbey-commemorations/commemorations/olaudah-equiano-gustavus-vassa.
100 'Trafficking: Children', *Hansard*, House of Lords Debates, 13 March 2002, vol. 632, cc. 877–914.
101 'September Artwork of the Month: Olaudah Equiano—African, slave, author, abolitionist by Christy Symington': www.parliament.uk/about/art-in-parliament/news/2019/september/september-artwork-of-the-month-olaudah-equiano-by-christy-symington/.
102 For example, Douglass is the central person in a mural honouring human rights' activists on the Peace Wall in West Belfast.
103 The Quinn story is not included in the early versions of his narrative but coincides with his visit to Ireland and appears in later editions, Equiano, *Narrative* (1791), p. 91.
104 David Featherstone, '"We will have equality and liberty in Ireland": The Contested Geographies of Irish Democratic Political Cultures in the 1790s', in *Historical Geography*, vol. 41 (2013), 121–36, p. 121.
105 Ibid., p. 126.
106 For example, the academic research on Equiano by Irish historians Nini Rodgers and Bill Rolston.

2 Moses Roper (1815–1891)
'A religious turn of mind'

Moses Roper was one of the most enigmatic abolitionists to visit Ireland. Similar to Samuel Ringgold Ward and others, he viewed the ending of slavery in religious and moral terms, rather than ideological or political ones. He also chose to lecture only in small, Protestant venues. Yet, unlike Ward, he belonged to a small group of abolitionists who used their personal stories to raise money in ways that were questionable.

Despite not being allied to any of the main abolitionist organizations, Roper spent more time on the British lecture circuit than any other American abolitionist, being active in the 1830s, 1840s and 1850s. There, he quickly established a public reputation because, as early as 1840, British newspapers were describing him as the 'celebrated Moses Roper'.[1] His narrative, written during his first visit, outsold that of many other black abolitionists who came to the United Kingdom, with 30,000 copies being printed. Nonetheless, like several other black abolitionists, he was largely forgotten subsequently, on both sides of the Atlantic. In 2011, the Introduction of his reprinted autobiography stated that, after 1844, 'Most details concerning the rest of Roper's life, including the date and place of his death, remain unknown'.[2]

Early life

Roper's early life had parallels with that of the more famous Frederick Douglass. He was born in Caswell County in North Carolina in 1815. Like Douglass, he did not know the year or month of his birth. Like Douglass and Edmund Kelly, Roper was born of mixed parentage—an enslaved mother and a white planter father.[3] Unlike Douglass, however, Roper used the surname of his father, Henry Roper, throughout his life.[4] Roper's mother was half white, and Roper had a light complexion.[5] His skin tone enabled him to 'pass' as a white person, he possibly being one of the first escaped slaves to do so.[6] When aged about 6, Roper and his mother were sold to a new master. Roper was to be sold multiple times. As a teenager, he began to plan his escape, finally escaping from his Florida master in 1832. He did this by literally jumping from a ship he was employed on, and then walking—an estimated 350 miles—to his freedom. His travels took him to Boston where he met William Lloyd Garrison and became a signatory to the constitution of the American Anti-Slavery Society.[7] Fearing recapture, Roper sailed to Liverpool in England in 1835, arriving there at the end of November. He made his way to London, where he met with John Scoble, one of the founders of the British and Foreign Anti-Slavery Society. Scoble found him accommodation and introduced him to other leading abolitionists.[8]

Roper claimed that one of his reasons for wanting to be in Britain was to obtain an education to work in African missions. To this end, he first attended boarding schools in England, then moving to University College in London.[9] Roper had a few influential backers. One of his main financial sponsors was the wealthy Baptist minister, Rev. Dr Francis Cox. Cox helped Roper attend a school to get a basic education. During this time also, Roper attended Cox's ministry, 'to which I ascribe the attainment of clearer views of divine grace than I had before'.[10] Roper was admitted into the Baptist Church in March 1846.[11] Cox was a controversial figure within anti-slavery circles, however. He had refused to speak out against slavery when attending a Baptist Convention in Virginia in 1835, a fact remembered by the audience when Roper was called on to address an anti-slavery meeting in London in May 1836. Despite some opposition, Roper was allowed to speak, but the incident provided him with an early insight into the sensitivities of the wider abolitionist movement. During his speech, he explained his relationship with the minister:

> Dr Cox did pay a portion towards his education, but that should not hinder him from advocating the cause of his mother, brethren, and sisters now in bondage (Loud cheers). He was grateful to Dr Cox for that which he was doing for him; but at the same time his principles were not to be bought.[12]

Regardless of this early controversy, Roper was given shelter, education and introductions by English abolitionists, as he toured. For the most part, he only lectured in Protestant chapels in Britain, and, where possible, Baptist ones.[13]

Like Douglass was to do, Roper apologized frequently to his audiences for his lack of formal education, explaining, 'He could not make an eloquent speech; for they must know that the slaves in America were not allowed to read or write; but he had received two year's education since he came to England'.[14] In reality, Roper proved to be a talented public speaker who could alternatively thrill his audience, make them laugh or upset them with his stories and visual aids. He also could talk for two and a half hours at a time.[15] This fact was commented on by the press, 'Allowing for his adult education, which was commenced since his escape, his address and language are highly interesting and impressive'.[16] In 1839, Roper was able to inform his audiences that, 'he is now pursuing his studies at a college in London, and by sale of his printed narrative providing himself with the means of education in order to make himself useful to the African race'.[17]

After only a year in England, Roper's supporters had helped him to produce his life story, entitled *A Narrative of the Adventures and Escapes of Moses Roper from American Slavery*, which was published in London in 1837, a year before the American edition.[18] As had been the case with Equiano, the title

62 *Moses Roper (1815–1891)*

suggested that the reader was in for a thrilling read. Unlike Equiano, who had witnessed the brutality of the system largely second-hand, Roper's *Narrative* provided an unflinching first-hand account of the cruelty of slavery. Similar to many other narratives, the Preface was written by, and thus 'authenticated' by, a white man, in this case, the British minister, Rev. Thomas Price of Brighton. The 1838 edition contained five illustrations, possibly making it the first slave narrative to include images depicting the harshness of slavery.[19] The images of torture reinforced Roper's uncompromising text describing the inhumanity of the system. Within the United States, copies of the book were sold by the American Anti-Slavery Society.[20] In March 1838, the *Liberator* published a long article about Roper's *Narrative* and his two years in England, saying that the paper could 'testify to the uprightness of his character and the intelligence of his mind' as before embarking for England he had resided in Boston.[21] The book was also favourably reviewed in the *London Christian Advocate*, the journal praising Roper for the 'soundness of his religious views' and recommending Christians and the anti-slavery public to spend two shillings to purchase it, thus allowing Roper to become partially financially independent.[22] Between 1837 and 1856, Roper's *Narrative* was reprinted in ten different editions.[23] Unusually—and perhaps uniquely—an edition was produced in the Welsh language in 1842.[24] However, at Price's insistence, his Preface was removed in later editions.[25] Consequently, versions printed after March 1846 were printed under the direction of Roper. The 1848 edition included both a Preface and an Appendix that had been written by Roper.[26] Around this time, Douglass was also taking over editorial control of his own narrative. By doing so, both men were demonstrating that enslaved people were active participants not only in the process of liberation, but also in telling their stories.

Although there is no evidence that Roper visited Ireland during his first stay in the United Kingdom, he was clearly aware of Irish abolitionists, writing in his *Narrative*:

> I intend now, before I return to Canada, to visit Scotland and Ireland, and deliver lectures, as I have not been in many towns in those countries … My dear and kind friends, throughout Great Britain and Ireland, farewell![27]

His comment indicated the value of transatlantic support to American abolitionists, including to enslaved people who were able to read. Moreover, Roper's story and activities were being followed by Irish abolitionists, with interest and sympathy. This was evident from a long poem written by Mary Tuckey of Ferney in County Cork, named *Lines Written on Occasion of the Escape to England of Mr. Moses Roper, Late an American Slave, now a Freeman of Great Britain*. The poem was published in the *Limerick Chronicle* of 17 November 1838. It was also reprinted in full in the Appendices of the 1848 publication of the *Narrative*.[28] The poem read:

> Who is my brother? Ask the waves that come
> From Africa's shores to greet our island home.
> Who is my brother? Ask the winds that stray

Moses Roper (1815–1891)   63

From Indian realms, to chase our clouds away.
Who is my brother? Ask the suns that shine
On southern seas, then turn to smile on thine.
Who is my brother? Ask the stars that roll
Their nightly journey round from pole to pole.
These with one voice shall answer that they find
But one vast family in all mankind;
Nor colour, clime, nor caste can e'er efface
The kindred likeness of the wide-spread race,
Or break the chain that at the first began
To bind in one the family of man.
Come then, awake thy sympathies to feel
A brother's interest in thy brother's weal.
God's wisdom and his goodness both decreed
That from one stock all nations should proceed;
That wheresoe'er he cast his creatures' lot,
Kindness and love might consecrate the spot,
Behold thy brother! On his form, confess'd,
Thy nature's dignity is seen imprest,
In every look—in every gesture—man!
Wipe off the stamp of manhood, ye who can!
Beats not his breast with warm affection's glow!
Breathes not his mind with thoughts impassion'd flow?
Is there a joy—a grief man ever knew,
But in his bosom has a birth-place too?
What though a tyrant's hand might strive to bind,
With iron grasp, the energies of mind,
As well might chains and stripes control the wave,
The soul!—the soul!—can never be a slave!
Brother, by that Creative Power whose word
One common nature on our race conferred;
Brother, still closer by the love that sent
The Son of God to bear sin's punishment;
Brother, by grace divine which poured its light
On the dark horrors of our heathen night,
We give the hand of fellowship to thee,
We bid thee welcome, and we hail thee Free!
Thou art a slave no longer! On thy brow
The air of Freedom breathes in triumph now!
Thine heart rejoices o'er thy broken chain,
Whose links are sever'd ne'er to meet again.
But sweeter still, that liberty to know
Which Christ, the Saviour, only can bestow,
And feel, whate'er thy future lot may be,
The truth! The truth has made thy spirit free!

64 *Moses Roper (1815–1891)*

Through all thy touching story, glad we trace
The ways of Providence, the power of grace;
And see thy countless trials join to prove
The God of glory is the God of love.
Go, then, still guided by his mighty hand,
Where'er His will, his wisdom may command.
His love direct thy steps, as when of old
He led the shepherd of His chosen fold.
Thy tale, like his whose name is borne by thee,
Mark'd out for death in helpless infancy,
Like him, the child of servitude and shame.
Born of a race that bear the captive name;
Daily indebted to a tyrant's nod,
For the free mercies of a bounteous God;
Holding the very life He gave, at will
Of those who, though they cannot save, can kill,
Like him, cast from the land that gave thee birth,
And driven a wanderer on the face of earth.
(Like him, in all thy wanderings may'st thou find
The stranger's kindness soothe and cheer thy mind,)
Like him, when come to years, by grace divine,
Led to embrace a Saviour's cross as thine.
Still be thy tale like his;—to thee be given
To bear on earth the messages of heaven;
To tell the Pharaohs who enslave thy race
That God will scatter plagues on every place
Where proud oppression dares His wrath defy,
And brave his arm, and scorn His searching eye.
Sound out his thunders till the dead in sin
Shall hear the voice of conscience speak within.
Believe, and tremble at the dread decree,
Break every chain—bid every slave be free.
Then, when thy brethren forth from bondage come,
Be thine to lead them to their better home—
The Land of Promise, where their souls shall rest,
With peace and liberty for ever blest,
And through the wilderness that lies between
Their wearied spirits and the joys unseen,
Be God to thee and them a shade by day,
A light by night to mark their future way,
Till all the freemen of the Lord shall meet,
To cast their crowns at Jesus's sacred feet,
And own the link that shall for ever bind,
Even as one soul, all nations of mankind.
  M. B. TUCKEY. Ferney, Cork, 31 October 1838.[29]

Moses Roper (1815–1891) 65

By 1839, Roper was attracting as many as 2,000 people to his lectures, with people being turned away at smaller venues.[30] Like many former slaves, Roper engaged his audiences by displaying 'several instruments of torture', stating that 'he explained the system from personal experience, having himself escaped from slavery in the United States'.[31] These items including the 'floppa' or 'flapper'—a particularly vicious whip, and a 'negro paddle'. The latter resembled a cricket bat with holes and was used to give beatings.[32] The 'flapper' was 'a ponderous whip, more adapted for the back of an elephant than that of any other animal. It is loaded with lead, and the handle-like hammer is used to knock down refractory slaves'.[33] Roper also displayed collars, padlocks and chains.[34] These, combined with stories of this own cruel treatment, 'roused the liveliest sympathy in the breasts his hearer'.[35] Unlike many other speakers, however, Roper avoided speaking about politics. On occasion, he was critical of churches in the United States, although he regarded the Quakers and the Reformed Presbyterians as exceptions, on the grounds that they alone did not enslave people.[36] Unusually, Roper criticized English, rather than Irish, emigrants for their behaviour when they arrived in America, explaining, 'He found that in this country the English were warm friends to the slaves; but he must say that when out of this country they were the greatest oppressors'.[37] On a more personal note, he informed one audience that, 'Had it not been for the English who sold his parents, the individual who then addressed them would never have been a slave'.[38] This statement conflicted with his more usual assertion that his father was a white planter.

Roper's early travels in Britain and his lectures received extensive coverage in both American and British press.[39] From reports in the latter, a description of his physical appearance and presence emerged. One paper described him as being of 'gigantic proportions', estimating his height to be six-feet five inches.[40] Not to be outdone, another described him as being almost seven foot tall, with 'pleasing manners'.[41] He was commonly described as being 'athletic' and 'muscular'.[42] Like Douglass, his mixed race background was commented on, he being 'but little darker in complexion than Europeans, but his hair and features indicate consanguinity to the African race'.[43] Early in the *Narrative* he described his mother as 'half white', but elsewhere as being, 'part Indian, part African'.[44] His mixed heritage led one newspaper to describe him as 'a scion of Europe, Africa, and America, and mixture of the white, black and red men'.[45] Roper occasionally used his own mixed heritage family history to challenge stereotypes about race and demonstrate its complexity. In one lecture, he stated,

> since his first arrival in England, he had married a lady whose father was a native of Wales, while her mother was sprung from an English family, and they had two children, who thus had part of English, Welsh, American, Negro, and Indian blood in their veins.[46]

Not all welcomed or believed Roper and his dramatic life story. The *Hampshire Advertiser*, while demonstrating unbridled racism, repeatedly attacked Roper. In July 1839, they printed a long offensive article that commenced:

66   *Moses Roper (1815–1891)*

Sambo Munchausen, the itinerant lecturer, who, under the cognomen of Moses Roper, delivered such marvels at the Baptist Chapel last week, held forth in favour of freedom and fighting at the Above Bar Chapel, on Wednesday evening last. Our doubts of his veracity it seems had excited Sambo's wrath most intensely, and by way of proving the truth of his statements he exhibited a 'Negro-Hopper', (a whip with a handle as thick as a man's arm, loaded with lead, and having a very long and heavy lash attached) which he was prepared to use on our reporter's back, if he denied their accuracy. Our reporters' gout, therefore, if Sambo Munchausen be not indeed a poltroon as well as an anti-truth telling and unbelieving-nigger, has stood him in good case, inasmuch as it deprived him of a gout-deflopper. It seems we were wrong in imagining the various instruments of torture he exhibited were brought by him from America,—as Sambo had them forged for his own special use at Birmingham. We have heard of a cat having nine lives, but Sambo must have had at least eighteen and his fingers and toes, doubtless, possess the re-producing power of the crab.[47]

The paper also claimed that while Roper was often well received, at times, 'He was hissed and called to order'.[48] The paper claimed to be opposed to slavery but averred, 'it is not the monstrous perversions and lying inventions of Moses Roper that will either enlist English sympathies or effect change in the American character'.[49] In a long editorial comment, it attacked the character of Roper and the authenticity of his story:

Now, if there be one sin on earth calling more loudly than another to the throne of Heaven for punishment, if there is one degree of suffering more agonising and more pathetically calling for relief than another, that sin and that suffering is 'Slavery'. Slavery is the foul blot which obscures and defiles all that is great and good among men who achieved freedom for themselves, but denied it to their fellow men. We have the evidence of better authorities than Moses Roper for the real treatment of slaves in the United States, namely—Mrs. Trollope, Miss Martineau, Judge—, Captain Marryatt, and others. We must reserve further remarks on Moses Roper till we have had an opportunity of hearing him in person.[50]

Two weeks later, having attended Roper's lecture, the paper again attacked him, opining, 'We have seldom heard such mystification, delivered with such bold a face', accusing him of 'reaping a rich harvest at the expense of the gullibility of John Bull'. Roper had, in turn, attacked the newspaper during the lecture with, 'as incoherent a harangue as was ever delivered out of Bedlam'.[51] Attacks were not always confined to the printed word. When lecturing in Hitchin in Hertfordshire, two men attended and shouted, 'opprobrious epithets towards the speaker', with the ensuing chaos leading some women to faint.[52] Such incidents were rare, but a reminder of the perils of being the public face of enslavement.

Regardless of these criticisms and controversies, Roper's lectures continued to be, 'crowded to excess'.[53] Women—the invisible engine of the anti-slavery movement—always formed a large part of his audiences.[54] However, in 1840, a further and more damaging public rebuke was made by somebody who had previously been a supporter of Roper. The Rev. Price publicly denounced Roper on the grounds that, 'his original intention had been to raise money to enable him to become a teacher of Christianity in Africa' but instead, he was leading a 'desultory and mendicant life', and 'pursuing a system of genteel begging'. Price asked that the Preface he had written for the *Narrative*, be 'wholly expunged from publication'.[55] It was an unsavoury insight into Roper's character but did not deter him from continuing to lecture and republish his *Narrative*. After 1840, Roper's public appearances were reduced, but he continued to tell audiences that he intended to use the income from his lecturing and books sales to move to the Cape of Good Hope (now South Africa), so that he could 'lend a helping hand in the extinction of that monstrous system which spoils all that is good in America'.[56]

In 1844, following almost nine years of continuous lecturing in Britain, Roper left the country. At this stage, he estimated that he had given almost 2,000 lectures; however, his travels had not extended to Ireland.[57] His education at a London college and his living expenses had been paid for from a combination of sources: benevolent patrons, money raised at lectures and buoyant sales of his book—25,000 English and 5,000 Welsh copies had been printed.[58] Roper, together with his English wife, Ann Stephen Rice, whom he had married in 1839, purchased land in Canada.[59] For a number of years, Roper had told audiences that he wanted to move with his wife and child to the Cape. To this end, he had written to the Committee of the British and Foreign Anti-Slavery Society in London asking if they would pay their fares. Roper explained that

> I have been brought up to cultivating, Cotton, Tobacco, Indian corn (and to farming) and which I find from a work recently written by Mr. Chase on the Cape, they will grow very well at the Cape of Good Hope, and I am very anxious to settle in some part of Africa, as I have a strong desire to be useful to that race.[60]

It appears that his request was not agreed to and hence Canada became the destination of the Roper family. In the 1848 printing of the *Narrative*, Roper provided a different interpretation of his decision to settle in Canada stating:

> ... at the commencement of 1844, I left England with my family for British North America, and have taken up my future residence in Canada West, it being as near as I can get to my relations (who are still in bondage) without being again taken.[61]

Roper's stay in Canada proved to be short, he sailing to England in December 1845. He arrived in Liverpool in January 1846. The reason for his return is not known, Roper simply explaining that, 'Having some matters of a private

68   *Moses Roper (1815–1891)*

nature to settle in this country'.[62] While there, he oversaw another reprinting of his *Narrative*. He also stated that, 'I intend now, before I return to Canada, to visit Scotland and Ireland, and deliver lectures, as I have not been in many towns in those countries'.[63] Roper did resume lecturing immediately, predominantly in Scotland. There is no evidence that he visited Ireland on this trip either.[64] Again, his lectures were well attended.[65] In another change of direction, however, when appealing for support, Roper told his audiences that his mother and his nine brothers and sisters were still in bondage and he wanted to purchase their freedom.[66] His earlier desire to 'become a teacher of Christianity to his brother natives in Africa', was no longer mentioned.[67] Moreover, there were other inconsistences in his stories; in some earlier reports he had stated that his mother was dead.[68] He later claimed that his mother's master had deliberately lied to him.[69]

Roper's time in Scotland coincided with that of Douglass, who was often accompanied by George Thompson and Henry Clarke Wright. By this time, Douglass's focus was on the 'Send Back the Money' campaign, which proved to be both divisive and damaging.[70] Roper assiduously kept away from this topic, winning him praise when in Kennoway, the local paper reporting:

> Mr R. did not meddle with the questions regarding this subject which have excited so much discussion on the platform and from the press but stated what he had seen and felt, and his details of the soul sickening cruelties committed by slaveholders.[71]

Although Roper was lecturing in Scotland at the same time as Douglass, there is no evidence that they ever met. Newspapers, however, did make the connection:

> We understand that Mr Moses Roper, runaway American slave, is to address a meeting of the inhabitants of Cupar in the Secession Church, Burnside, tomorrow evening. Roper has recently visited various towns in Scotland, and at meetings of their inhabitants has made fearful exposures of the horrors of American slavery both as experienced in his own person, and as witnessed in the suffering of others. His labours, in addition to those of Messrs Douglass, Buffum, and Thompson, will doubtless awaken such a powerful feeling against slavery as will ultimately force the American people take steps for removing this dark stain from their national character.[72]

Not all Scottish newspapers were as positive, some newspapers warning that Roper would likely speak 'in the same spirit' as Douglass—namely, being fiercely Garrisonian and condemnatory of the Free Church. They were relieved to find he was neither, with his lectures focusing on his own life story. Although he occasionally criticized the American churches, he did not do so in the inflammatory way that Garrison himself did. This led one paper to describe Roper as having 'a religious turn of mind'.[73] One anonymous commentator believed that this initial fear may have accounted for the relatively small audience at Roper events.[74] Like Douglass

Moses Roper (1815–1891)   69

and Ward, Roper could talk for over two hours without notes. Similarly, his lectures were infused with religious and biblical imagery and similar rhetorical devices— he including quotes from the poems of Cowper and Burns—favourites of many abolitionists, in his lectures.[75] Roper continued to have a powerful impact on his audiences, especially when recounting the story of his own escape, which could bring audiences, especially the women, to tears.[76] By mid-1847, Roper was back lecturing in England, he shocking audiences by telling them that he had been sold by his own father when only 6 years old.[77] Little is known about Roper's personal life during his return to Britain. A small notice appeared in several English newspapers in the middle of 1848, reporting the marriage of Moses Roper to Miss Margaret Hunter in Stockton on 28 May.[78]

Ireland

Roper returned to Britain in 1854. He explained the reason for his return was that he was now far more educated than he had been previously.[79] Those who had heard him lecture when he first escaped from slavery agreed on how more fluent he had become when lecturing.[80] Interestingly, he was now described as being 'Moses Roper of Canada'.[81] On this visit, Roper did visit Ireland, lecturing there over a period of nine months.

Although Roper spent a longer period of time in Ireland than other visiting abolitionists, unusually, he did not visit the country's main towns and cities or follow the route of other black lecturers. In early October 1854, Roper lectured to the Clogher Anti-Slavery Association in County Tyrone.[82] Clogher had a large active organization that was well supported by local gentry and ministers.[83] The Clogher women, led by the energetic Isabella Waring Maxwell, were especially active.[84] They specialized in producing 'fancy work', which they sent to the New York Anti-Slavery Society for the aid of fugitive slaves.[85] At a meeting the day before Roper attended, the women had raised £5–6s-5d to send to New York, which included a donation from 'servants at Daisy Hill' and the proceeds from the sale of 'Uncle Tom handkerchiefs'.[86] A Dublin newspaper reported that, 'The meeting was very numerously attended, and comprised a very large display of the beauty and fashion of the surrounding neighbourhood'.[87] By 1857, the Clogher women were also supporting Douglass in his endeavours, sending him a donation of £20.[88] Unusually, the Clogher abolitionists met in a private home, Killyfaddy House, the residence of Robert Waring Maxwell, Esquire, who chaired the meeting with Roper.[89]

Later in the same month, Roper lectured in the small town of 'Tubbermore' (probably Tobermore) in Ulster, in the local Baptist Chapel, where he spoke about the horrors connected with slavery.[90] He was described as being 'a tall, keen-eyed mulatto, calling himself Moses Roper'.[91] Roper spoke for almost two hours to an audience that was described as 'large and well-conducted'. At the end of his talk, a collection was made and £1–5s—3d was raised. He appeared to have made a deep impression on the audience who left the lecture, 'sorrowing for the down-trodden sons of Africa'.[92] On 27 November, Roper lectured in the First Presbyterian Church in Derry. Again, the lecture was well attended. He outlined

70 *Moses Roper (1815–1891)*

his unusual life story and explained that his motive for lecturing was because he wanted to help his mother and siblings escape from slavery. As seems to have become the usual practice, 'A collection was taken up at the close of the address, for the purpose of assisting Mr. Roper in this undertaking'.[93]

On 27 March 1855, Roper lectured in the Presbyterian Church in Downpatrick.[94] He spoke for two and a half hours. He shocked the Irish audience by repeating the story of having been sold by his own father, his white master. In addition, Roper entertained his audience by singing 'some negro hymns, both of an affecting and cheerful character'.[95] More unusually—and strangely—the story of his escape was made even more thrilling by the additional information that he had 'combatted wolves, tigers, alligators, and other dangerous obstructions, in making his escape'. These exotic creatures had not featured in his early lectures or in his *Narrative*.[96] At the conclusion of the meeting, a collection was made on his behalf. Two months later, Roper had moved further south, lecturing in a Presbyterian church in Westmeath to a 'large' audience. A local newspaper reported that, 'the account of his sufferings and many hair breath escapes were very interesting'.[97] On 2 July, Roper lectured in the Court House in Maryborough in County Laois (then known as Queen's County), and the following evening at Abbeyleix. The next evening, he spoke in Portarlington, all of which were in the Midlands—areas not generally visited by American abolitionists. A newspaper notice advertising the three meetings stated, 'A Collection will be taken at the close in aid of the object the Lecturer has in view, and which will be explained at the Meeting'.[98] Shortly after these lectures, Roper returned to England where he traversed the lecture circuit for more than a year.[99]

In total, Roper had spent eight months in Ireland, which was longer than most other visiting abolitionists, yet his impact on the country, and the country's impact on him, seemed minimal. For the most part, he did not attract large audiences in Ireland, but this partly reflected the choice of venues, which were small and provincial. Like several other evangelical abolitionists, he chose only to lecture in Protestant lecture halls. Consequently, he took a very different approach from the usual lecture route followed by Equiano, Remond, Douglass and others, who chose to visit the main towns and cities, which had strong traditions of anti-slavery, where they spoke to audiences comprised of all religions.[100] Tellingly, at the conclusion of each lecture, a collection was made and a new reason was proffered for Roper's needing this money.[101]

Later life

Roper returned to the United Kingdom in 1860, staying and lecturing there into 1861. The venues, and presumably the audiences and revenue, however, had become smaller with each subsequent visit, he now lecturing mostly in school rooms.[102] Nonetheless, Roper continued to be praised, one paper admiring, 'his wondrous energy and determination, combined with a gifted and cultivated mind, gives practical denial to the alleged predestined inferiority of the African race'. The same report also suggested that the ebullient lecturer who had first arrived

Moses Roper (1815–1891) 71

in England in the 1830s, had been replaced by a middle-aged more despondent man. One newspaper noted Roper's sadness, pointing out, 'And no wonder he should be depressed when he knows that his mother, if living, besides nine brothers and sisters, are all still at the mercy of the overseer's lash'.[103] It seemed that he never succeeded in his declared mission to purchase their freedom. At this stage, it appears that Roper was estranged from his wife and family. At some stage, Roper returned to the United States, but by himself. He became an itinerant lecturer and any other job he could find, but mostly he was no longer on public view. He reappeared briefly in 1881, publishing the largely forgotten, *An Intellectual Entertainment! Moral, Instructive and Amusing, Spiced with Humor.*[104] It seemed a strange choice given Roper's personal history, but was consistent with Roper's track record of inconsistency.

Conclusion

Roper died in April 1891 in Boston City Hospital following a collapse in the train station. He was alone, except for his faithful dog, Pete.[105] The *New York Times* briefly noted his passing in a paragraph entitled, 'A Coloured Lecturer Dead':

> Boston—April 16—MOSES Roper, aged about sixty-five, died at the hospital last evening from kidney and heart troubles. Roper was born a slave in Caswell County, N.C. and when quite young he escaped to England, where he was educated. In after-years, he became a lecturer.[106]

This brief tribute did not do justice to a man born enslaved, who was read, listened to and feted by leading British abolitionists, although he was only in his early twenties. Roper was a flawed champion, whose motives were often self-serving and dubious. His early successes were not sustained and he gradually disappeared from public sight, making only a brief re-appearance at his death. His tragic final years belie the potential and contributions made by the young fugitive slave who arrived in Britain in the mid-1830s. Roper was one of the first of a new generation of black abolitionists to cross the Atlantic and enthrall British audiences. In doing so, he paved the way for later anti-slavery activists, including Douglass.

Notes

1 'American Slavery', *Carlisle Journal*, 18 April 1840; *Cambridge General Advertiser*, 12 August 1840. The latter referred to him as 'the celebrated refugee American slave'. From 1841 to 1844, his public appearances were less frequent, but he was still referred to in this way, *Nottingham Review and General Advertiser for the Midland Counties*, 26 February 1841.

2 Harry Thomas, *Summary of Moses Roper's Narrative* (2011): https://docsouth.unc. edu › neh › roper › summary.

3 At a large anti-slavery meeting in London in 1836, Roper was introduced by seasoned abolitionist, George Thompson, as being the son of an American General, 'ENGLAND. MEETING AT LONDON', the *Liberator*, 20 August 1836.

72 *Moses Roper (1815–1891)*

4 Ibid., 30 March 1838; Moses Roper, *A Narrative of the Adventures and Escapes of Moses Roper from American Slavery, with a Preface by the Rev. T. Price, D.D.* (London: Darton: Harvey, and Darton, 55 Gracechurch-Street; Birmingham: B. Hudson, 18, Bull-Street, and of the Author, 31, Cherry-Street, 1837), p. 15.

5 Ibid.

6 Moses Roper, *A Narrative of the Adventures and Escape of Moses Roper, from American Slavery. With an Appendix, Containing a List of Places Visited by the Author in Great Britain and Ireland and the British Isles; and Other Matter* (Berwick-upon-Tweed: Published for the Author, and Printed at the Warder Office, 1848), p. 22. When he arrived in Boston, Roper shaved his head to disguise his origins; Ibid., p. 47.

7 Although this claim is frequently repeated by his biographers, there is no evidence he did so and the dates do not fit. For example, Paul Roper, 'Moses Roper (1815–?) An African-American Baptist in Victorian England (1835–44)', 296–302, takes Roper at face value. Available at: www.tandfonline.com/doi/abs/10.1179/bqu.2007.42.4.004?journalCode=ybaq20.

8 Roper, *Narrative* (1848), p. 49.

9 Elsewhere, Roper was described as having attended Westminster College in London, which had opened in 1838 as the first polytechnical college. See, 'AMERICAN SLAVERY', *Carlisle Journal*, 18 April 1840.

10 Roper, *Narrative* (1848), pp. 49–50.

11 Ibid.

12 Meeting at Finsbury Chapel, 30 May 1836, reprinted in C. Peter Ripley, *The Black Abolitionist Papers. The British Isles, 1830–1865*, vol. 1 (Chapel Hill: University of North Carolina Press, 2015), p. 61.

13 *Hampshire Chronicle*, 15 July 1839. Roper's second lecture in the Independent Chapel was described as 'crowded to excess', 'Slavery', *Cambridge Independent Press*, 28 September 1839.

14 'American Slavery', *Carlisle Journal*, 18 April 1840.

15 Ibid.

16 *Bradford Observer*, 5 March 1840.

17 'American Slavery', *Sheffield Independent*, 12 October 1839.

18 The first English edition was published by 'London: Darton, Harvey, and Darton, 55 Gracechurch-street. Birmingham: B. Hudson, 18, Bull-street, and of the Author, 31, Cherry-street'; the American edition was published in Philadelphia in 1838 by Merrihew & Gunn.

19 Martha J. Cutter, 'Revising Torture: Moses Roper and the Visual Rhetoric of the Slave's Body in the Transatlantic Abolition Movement', in *ESQ: A Journal of the American Renaissance*, vol. 60.no. 3 (2014) (No. 236 O.S.) 371–411, p. 372.

20 *National Anti-Slavery Standard*, 27 August 1846.

21 'Narrative of Moses Roper', the *Liberator*, 30 March 1838.

22 The review was also reprinted in the *Liberator*, 30 March 1838.

23 Harry Thomas, *Summary of Moses Roper's Narrative* (2011): https://docsouth.unc.edu › neh › roper › summary.

24 *Hanes bywyd a ffoedigaeth Moses Roper, o gaethiwed* Americanaidd (Aberystwyth: Argraphwyd dros y cyhoeddwr gan; J. Cox., 1842).

25 Douglass's *Narrative* (Boston, 1845) was endorsed by Garrison who wrote the Preface. Roper's was written by Rev. Thomas Price, a British abolitionist. In later editions, this was eliminated.

26 Roper, *Narrative* (1848).

27 Ibid., (1848), p. 52.

28 The poem appeared in the 1848 version of the *Narrative*, pp. 57–9. Tuckey was a poet who also wrote a poem commemorating Douglass's visit to Cork: https://library.duke.edu/rubenstein/findingaids/tuckeymaryb/.

Moses Roper (1815–1891) 73

29 'Very long poem dedicated to M. Roper by M. B. Tucket [sic], Ferney, Cork, 31 October 1838', *Limerick Chronicle*, 17 November 1838.
30 'Moses Roper's Lectures', *Worcestershire Chronicle*, 11 December 1839.
31 'Slavery', *Cambridge Independent Press*, 28 September 1839.
32 'American Slavery', *Carlisle Journal*, 18 April 1840.
33 'Moses Roper', *Bradford Observer*, 5 March 1840.
34 *Salisbury and Winchester Journal*, 22 July 1839.
35 'Moses Roper', *Bradford Observer*, 5 March 1840.
36 'AMERICAN SLAVERY—LECTURE BY MR MOSES ROPER', *Carlisle Journal*, 18 April 1840; 'American Slavery', *Fife Herald*, 18 June 1846.
37 'American Slavery', *Carlisle Journal*, 18 April 1840.
38 Ibid.
39 'REV. R. J. BRECKINRIDGE AND *MOSES ROPER*', the *Liberator*, 24 September 1836, reprinted from the *Emancipator*.
40 *Bradford Observer*, 5 March 1840.
41 'American Slavery', *Hereford Journal*, 27 November 1839.
42 'AMERICAN SLAVERY—LECTURE BY MR MOSES ROPER', *Fife Herald*, 18 June 1846.
43 *Bradford Observer*, 5 March 1840.
44 Roper, *Narrative* (1848), p. 42.
45 *Bradford Observer*, 5 March 1840.
46 'AMERICAN SLAVERY—LECTURE BY MR MOSES ROPER', *Fife Herald*, 18 June 1846.
47 'American Slavery', *Hampshire Advertiser*, 13 July 1839.
48 Ibid.
49 Ibid.
50 Ibid.
51 Ibid., 27 July 1839.
52 'Letter to the editor of the Reformer', *Hertford Mercury and Reformer*, 1 August 1840.
53 *Hampshire Chronicle*, 15 July 1839; *Cambridge General Advertiser*, 12 August 1840.
54 'AMERICAN SLAVERY', *Carlisle Journal*, 18 April 1840.
55 *Berkshire Chronicle*, 28 November 1840.
56 'American Slavery', *Stamford Mercury*, 9 December 1842.
57 Appendix, Roper, Narrative (1848).
58 Letter from Moses Roper to The Committee of the British and Foreign Anti-Slavery Society, 9 May 1844, in 'Documenting the American South': https://docsouth.unc.edu/fpn/roper/support3.html.
59 Roper married Rice in December 1839, Roper, *Narrative* (1848), p. 52.
60 Letter from Roper to the British and Foreign Anti-Slavery Society, 9 May 1844: in Documenting the American South:https://docsouth.unc.edu/fpn/roper/support3.html.
61 Roper, *Narrative* (1848), p. 52.
62 Ibid.
63 Ibid.
64 Alastair Pettinger says Roper did visit Ireland at this time but he provides no evidence.
65 *Northern Warder and General Advertiser for the Counties of Fife, Perth and Forfar*, 22 October 1846; Ibid., 'Monday—Rose Street Chapel—well filled', 5 November 1846.
66 'American Slavery', *Elgin Courier*, 31 July 1846.
67 *Berkshire Chronicle*, 28 November 1840.
68 *Bradford Observer*, 5 March 1840.
69 Roper, *Narrative* (1848), pp. 7, 50.

74   *Moses Roper (1815–1891)*

70   Iain Whyte, *'Send Back the Money!': The Free Church of Scotland and American Slavery* (Cambridge: James Clarke & Co, 2012).
71   *Northern Warder and General Advertiser for the Counties of Fife, Perth and Forfar*, 5 November 1846.
72   'American Slavery', *Fife Herald*, 11 June 1846.
73   *Dumfries and Galloway Standard*, 25 March 1846.
74   This incident was quote in Alasdair Pettinger, *Frederick Douglass and Scotland, 1846: Living an Antislavery Life* (Edinburgh University Press, 2018) p. 88. The anonymous correspondent was the Rev. Chalmers of the Free Church.
75   'American slavery', *Elgin Courier*, 31 July 1846.
76   'AMERICAN SLAVERY—LECTURE BY MR MOSES ROPER', *Fife Herald*, 18 June 1846.
77   'American Slavery', *Leeds Times*, 20 February 1847; 'American Slavery', *Bradford Observer*, 11 March 1847.
78   'Marriage', *Newcastle Courant*, 2 June 1848; *Newcastle Guardian and Tyne Mercury*, 3 June 1848.
79   *Hereford Times*, 4 August 1855.
80   *Wells Journal*,12 January 1856—this paper observed that, 'Those who heard him some 15 years ago were surprised at the improvement he has obtained in making a public address'.
81   *Hereford Times*, 4 August 1855.
82   'CLOGHER ANTI-SLAVERY ASSOCIATION', *Dublin Evening Mail*, 18 October 1854, reprinted from the *Tyrone Constitution*. The Association had only been founded two years earlier.
83   Jeffrey Kerr-Ritchie, 'Black abolitionists, Irish supporters, and the brotherhood of man', in *A Journal of Slave and Post-Slave Studies*, vol. 37, no. 3 (2016), 'Ireland, Slavery, Anti-Slavery and Empire'. Available at: www.tandfonline.com/doi/abs/10.1080/0144039X.2016.1208912?src=recsys&journalCode=fsla20.
84   By 1863, the once active society was moribund, but Isabella continued her activities, in the summer of 1865 contributing £30 to the Freed-Men's Aid Society in the United States, *The Freed-man. A Monthly Magazine devoted to the interests of the Freed Colored People*, vol. 2 (London: S. W. Partridge, 1866), p. 40.
85   'CLOGHER ANTI-SLAVERY ASSOCIATION', *Dublin Evening Mail*, 18 October 1854.
86   Ibid.
87   Ibid.
88   Douglass, Rochester to Mrs Maxwell, Treasurer of Clogher Anti-Slavery Society, 10 October 1857, in *Anti-Slavery Reporter*, 1 December 1857, p. 279.
89   'CLOGHER ANTI-SLAVERY ASSOCIATION', *Dublin Evening Mail*, 18 October 1854.
90   'ANTI-SLAVERY LECTURE AT TUBBERMORE', *Coleraine Chronicle*, 28 October 1854. Tobermore is a small village in County Derry in Ulster. It lies 2.5 miles south-south-west of Maghera and 5.5 miles north-west of Magherafelt. Tobermore lies within the civil parish of Kilcronaghan and is part of Mid-Ulster District. The Baptist church was established in the early nineteenth century. Roper lectured there on 21 October 1854.
91   Ibid.
92   Ibid.
93   'Lecture on Negro Slavery', *Londonderry Standard*, 30 November 1854.
94   *Downpatrick Recorder*, 31 March 1855. Roper was hosted by the Rev. Dr William White.
95   Ibid.
96   Ibid.

97 *Westmeath Independent*, 2 June 1855. Roper lectured in Westmeath in May 1855.
98 'AMERICAN SLAVERY', *Leinster Express*, 30 June 1855.
99 *Hereford Times*, 4 August 1855.
100 In the 1848 edition of his *Narrative*, Roper provides a long list of the places where he had lectured. They were overwhelmingly Baptist Church Halls, pp. 63–8.
101 *Sherborne Mercury*, 15 January 1856; 21 August 1856.
102 *Bury Free Press*, 29 June 1861.
103 *Bury and Norwich Post*, 12 March 1861.
104 Moses Roper, *An Intellectual Entertainment! Moral, Instructive and Amusing, Spiced with Humor* (Rutland, VT: Tuttle & Co., 1882).
105 'Mother Was A Slave; Death of Moses Roper in the City Hospital—Was Suffering from Skin Disease and a Kidney Complaint', *Boston Globe*, 16 April 1891.
106 'A COLORED LECTURER DEAD', *New York Times*, 17 April 1891.

3 Charles Lenox Remond (1810–1873)

'A mission of humanity'

Charles Lenox Remond has been described as 'The Lost Prince of Abolitionism'.[1] The same author further suggests that:

> Remond does not receive the credit due him for such achievements as paving the way for other black abolitionists on the speaking circuit, breaking the ice for future European speaking tours by other blacks, and forcing changes in northern discriminatory policies.[2]

Remond was born into an affluent, free, black family in Massachusetts and educated in public schools; thus, his life experiences were different from those of other black abolitionists who travelled overseas. Although free, Charles Remond and, later, his sister Sarah Parker Remond, devoted their lives to campaigning on behalf of enslaved peoples and more broadly for social justice for all. Both were to visit Ireland, although almost 20 years apart.

Early life

Remond started lecturing at abolitionist meetings when a teenager. In 1832, he was employed by William Lloyd Garrison as an agent for the *Liberator*. As a founding member of the New England Anti-Slavery Society, created in January 1832, and of the American Anti-Slavery Society, formed in New York in December 1833, Remond quickly established himself as part of a new wave of radical abolition activity in America, often associated with Garrison. In 1838, he was employed as an agent of the Massachusetts Anti-Slavery Society, becoming the first paid black anti-slavery lecturer in the United States.[3] However, it was Remond's 18 months in Britain and Ireland that propelled him into prominence as an anti-slavery orator.[4] At a time when the abolition movement was overwhelmingly white, Remond broke through multiple barriers, and created a slip stream for black abolitionists who came after him.

Like other abolitionists, Remond realized that it was not enough to end slavery, but that it was necessary to fight what he called:

> slavery's grand hand-maiden ... *prejudice* that acts the part to slavery of second king at arms, and exercises its authority by assisting in kidnapping

Charles Lenox Remond (1810–1873) 77

the innocent and free at the capital, disfranchises the citizens of Pennsylvania, proscribes the colored man in Rhode Island, abuses and gives him no resting place as a man in New-Hampshire, which murders in Illinois, cries out amalgamation in Maine, mobs him in New York, and stones him in Connecticut.[5]

By 1840, Remond was one of the most highly regarded and influential abolitionists in America. He was one of four delegates to travel to London on behalf of American Anti-Slavery Society, along with Garrison, Lucretia Mott and Nathaniel Peabody Rogers, editor of the *Herald of Freedom*. Remond, Rogers and Garrison all sailed together, leaving Boston in mid-May on board the *Columbus*, bound for Liverpool.[6] Regardless of his status and his finances, when sailing to Britain, Remond had to travel in steerage simply because of his colour.[7]

The anti-slavery convention

The first World Anti-Slavery Convention met at Exeter Hall in London, between 12 and 23 June 1840. Veteran campaigner and octogenarian Thomas Clarkson was the chairperson; Daniel O'Connell was the superstar. When O'Connell entered the room, he was greeted with 'enthusiastic applause'.[8] One of the early actions of the meeting was to pass a vote of thanks to the Irish man 'for the unvarying interest he has exhibited in the cause of the oppressed natives of British India and his valuable and spontaneous assistance on the present occasion'.[9]

Remond was one of only a handful of black men to attend the Convention. In the official Proceedings, he was described as 'a gentleman of colour from the United States'.[10] However, Remond did not play a direct role at the Convention. Remond and his party had not attended the opening sessions of the Convention as bad weather had delayed their sailing from Boston. When the three men arrived, they found that one of the first actions of the meeting had been to vote to exclude women. Together with Garrison and Rogers, Remond refused to sit with male delegates or to speak during the Convention.[11] For Remond, this was an especially sensitive issue:

> In view of the fact that I was almost entirely indebted to the kind and generous members of the Bangor Female Anti-Slavery Society, the Portland Sewing Circle, and the Newport Young Ladies' Juvenile Anti-Slavery Society, for aid in visiting this country. And I can assure you it was among my most happy reflections to know, that in taking my seat in the World's Convention, I should do so, the honored representative of three female associations.[12]

Initially, O'Connell had opposed the admission of women delegates on the grounds it would lay the Convention open to ridicule. Following a public challenge by Mott, he apologized, saying that he now realized that it was 'an unworthy, and indeed cowardly, motive'. O'Connell became one of a small group of delegates who visited the women each day in the gallery.[13] In these unusual

78   Charles Lenox Remond (1810–1873)

circumstances, Remond would have met O'Connell, the hero of so many American abolitionists. A number of other Irish abolitionists were also present.[14] The role of Ireland, which provided America with so many emigrants, was recognized and it was proposed that more be done to develop anti-slavery sentiment within the country to ensure that emigrants would be 'ready-made abolitionists'.[15] For those already there, it was suggested that O'Connell should issue an Address, exhorting them to support the abolitionists.[16] The task of bringing the Address back to America would fall to Remond.

On 24 June, immediately following the ending of the Convention, a further meeting was convened by the British and Foreign Anti-Slavery Society in Exeter Hall. The Duke of Sussex was the chairman, but O'Connell was the main speaker. Remond, Garrison and Mott were present. Remond was impressed with the Irishman, writing to Charles Ray, the editor of the *Colored American* newspaper:

> My Friend, for thirteen years I have thought myself an abolitionist, but I had been in a measure mistaken, until I listened to the scorching rebukes of the fearless O'Connell, [...] when before that vast assemblage, he quoted American publications, and alluded to the American declaration, and contrasted theory with practice; then I was moved to think, and feel, and speak [as an abolitionist]'.[17]

In a letter to the *Liberator*, Remond stated: 'No nation or people possess a superior to DANIEL O'CONNELL as a political advocate.'[18]

Following the Convention, Remond stayed on in Britain, initially travelling with Garrison, but remaining after his mentor had left. Remond's arrival in Britain, and then in Ireland, coincided with a re-energized abolition movement and a revived nationalist movement. All this activity, combined with the warmth of the welcome and the lack of prejudice towards his skin colour,[19] must have proved to be a liberating and unique experience for the American visitor.

During his twelve months in Britain, Remond became a noted presence on the abolitionist circuit, sharing the platform with the world's leading abolitionists, including O'Connell. He was present at the meeting to found the British India Society in Manchester in August 1840, where he was described as 'a delegate from the United States'.[20] Thomas Clarkson was made the President, although he was not present. Clarkson had requested that this position to be honorary only, because of his age and infirmities. At times, Remond was asked about the differences within the American movement and split that had occurred in 1840, giving rise to the founding of the American and Foreign Anti-Slavery Society, also known as the 'New Organization'. Remond spoke in defense of Garrison and the 'Old Organization', but he made it clear that he wanted his focus to be on ending slavery, the aim of both bodies.[21] Public opinion was also largely in favour of what he was promoting, Remond informing Garrison that four out of six British newspapers were reporting positively on the movement.[22]

On 14 May 1841, Remond attended the second annual meeting of the British and Foreign Anti-Slavery Society in London. It was held in Exeter Hall, which

Charles Lenox Remond (1810–1873)

could hold 3,000 people. Remond was noted in the press as being one of the platform party. O'Connell also was present. In his long and much-cheered speech, Remond described the need for cooperation between the British and American anti-slavery movements and he was critical of 'the impetus which Great Britain still gives to slavery'. In contrast, Remond praised O'Connell for the fact that,

> the Irish agitator, is invoked to agitate his countrymen against slavery on this side of the water, while, both in Ireland and England, his roaring voice is perpetually lifted up in abuse of the noble-hearted, the independent, and the fearless Southern planters, as well as the American character at large.[23]

Ireland

Remond toured Britain for over a year, raising awareness about slavery, before travelling to Ireland. Even before setting foot in the country, he was impressed, not only with O'Connell's ardency, but with the staunchness of other Irish abolitionists. In May 1841, he had sent a report back to the *Liberator*, stating, 'Nobly do our Irish friends contest for truth and justice. I expect to go over in a few weeks to Ireland'.[24] A key purpose of Remond's visit to Ireland was to collect signatures to the Address—the appeal to Irish Americans to support abolition—that had been discussed at the Convention in the previous year. Remond's hosts in Dublin were the Hibernian Anti-Slavery Society. James Haughton was impressed with their visitor, describing him as:

> An extraordinary young fellow, singularly gifted and well-suited by his talents and the admirable tendency of his mind to assist in the progress of human improvement. He disarms prejudice by his amiable manners, and he reaches the heart by his eloquence and the truthfulness of his statements.[25]

Remond's first public appearance in Dublin was at a meeting in the Royal Exchange to talk about British India. It was an issue that Remond had gained knowledge of while in Britain. Haughton and Richard Allen were the first speakers. Haughton, the Chairman, explained that they wanted to fight against slavery wherever it existed, but the continuation of slavery within the British Empire 'left her in the position of being taunted by the American slaveholder'.[26] When called on to speak, Remond, who was described as 'a *very* prepossessing gentleman of colour', used the opportunity to explain that his purpose in leaving the States was, 'to ask sympathy and co-operation for the three millions of slaves in America'. He added:

> ... the time was coming when liberty would be looked on as the inalienable right of every man, and that the inhabitants of this country would feel that, whether an oppressed being existed at home, on the broad peninsula of India, or on the continent of Africa, he was equally an object of sympathy.[27]

80 *Charles Lenox Remond (1810–1873)*

Before sitting down amid loud cheering, Remond said that he hoped that he would get another chance to address a Dublin audience. The reporter for the *Freeman's Journal* added a coda to his coverage of the meeting, informing the readers: 'From the sample Mr. Remond gave both of his oratorical power, and his earnestness on the subject, we would strongly recommend our fellow citizens to seize every opportunity of hearing him'.[28]

Like many other visiting abolitionists, Remond stayed at the home of Richard and Hannah Webb.[29] In total, Remond gave six lectures in Dublin, four in the Friends' Meeting House on Eustace Street and two in the 'Scotch' Church on Capel Street. Some of the meetings were so full that people had to be turned away.[30] Moreover, his message reached beyond the capital city. Several provincial papers reported on Remond's lectures, even as far away as Kerry, while the abolitionist *Nenagh Guardian* sent its own reporter to Dublin to attend some of the meetings.[31] Remond's lectures were praised both for their content and delivery:

> His style of speaking is remarkably clear, graphic, and forcible. He feels what he says. His face speaks, and his emotions are communicated undiminished to his auditors. When exhibiting the vast extent of degradation and misery experienced by so vast a population as nearly three millions his tone and his demeanour rise with his subject; and on those occasions we have heard from his lips some of the finest bursts of natural, trembling, heart-stirring eloquence it has ever been our lot to witness.[32]

Remond's physical appearance was occasionally described, 'His complexion is very dark, but not of the deepest African dye; his features are nearly European in their contour, and his figure is remarkably graceful and elegant'.[33]

Remond's final lecture in Dublin on 4 August was held in the Friends' Meeting House. As soon as it was over, the monthly meeting of the Hibernian Anti-Slavery Society was held in the Royal Exchange. It was chaired by Haughton. The main purpose of the second meeting was to introduce the Address to the public. The content had been drafted by Haughton and Richard Webb. Webb explained to the meeting that it was 'an address from the people of Ireland to the Irish in America, calling upon them to give their assistance to the abolitionists there, in overthrowing slavery'. He then read it in full.[34] Remond, who had joined the meeting towards the end, spoke about the Address with 'his head and heart'.[35] He thanked the audience for their enthusiasm and assured them:

> that one of the first subjects he would introduce to his countrymen, on his return to America, was the flattering reception he met with since his arrival in Ireland, and particularly the enthusiasm with which the cause of the poor slave was taken up by the vast masses of the people whom he had the honour to address since he came to this city.[36]

Remond concluded his well-received speech by saying:

> The cause of human freedom was going forward fast, and he hoped that the struggle of the Irish people would make them entitled to the gratitude of the entire world, and he felt that no persons would be more grateful to them than the very slaveholders themselves, from whose shoulders they would take such a vast mass of responsibility and guilt.[37]

Following his speech, several members of the audience made donations to help cover the expense of the Address.[38]

Remond left Dublin on 8 August, accompanied by Webb. His intention was to continue to lecture on slavery, and to promote the Address. His schedule had not been planned in advance, but was impromptu, he responding to local interest. Many of Remond's hosts were Quakers, often relations of Webb. Remond's tour of the south was heralded by the *Nenagh Guardian*, an outspoken champion of abolition:

> The wretched system which flourishes in America under the march of republicanism, degrading three millions of the United States' citizens into mere chattels, into down-trodden manacled slaves, has received a merited castigation in the metropolis by a very talented gentleman who has lately arrived in Ireland, and is now engaged in a tour southerly, Mr. Charles Lenox Remond. This individual is, we are informed, of the proscribed class in America, viz. a dark Mulatto, having African blood in his veins—an unpardonable circumstance to our *transatlantic lovers of liberty*. He is nevertheless highly educated, very talented, and has delivered a splendid series *of lectures* at the 'Scots Church and Friend's Meeting-house' in Dublin.[39]

Remond, accompanied by James and Richard Webb, first travelled to Wexford, where he held three 'crowded' meetings. They were hosted by relatives of the Webbs. In a long letter to Garrison, Webb described the local abolitionists as having 'zeal as well as knowledge', but admitted some pro-slavery supporters attended the meetings.[40] On 12 August, Remond arrived in Waterford and, within half an hour of getting there, lectured in the local Town Hall. Despite the city having a reputation for being apathetic on the issue, the venue was full and included a large number of women. Due to the success of this lecture, a further four were held, but a larger venue had to be secured and a small charge made to cover costs. In the middle of this schedule, Webb and Remond visited New Ross, where Remond gave one lecture. The two men also visited some of the local beauty spots, including the seaside village of Tramore. Again, Webb said that there was some resistance to Remond before his arrival, largely because of his association with Garrison and his support for women's rights and non-violence, but Remond charmed and reassured all doubters, by his 'modest, yet fearless' approach to the topic.[41]

Remond and Richard Webb then travelled to Limerick where they were 'kindly received' by Benjamin Clarke Fisher, a local merchant, and his family.

82   *Charles Lenox Remond (1810–1873)*

Fisher's daughters, Susanna, Rebecca and Charlotte, were active in the Limerick Anti-Slavery Society, which was affiliated with the Hibernian Society, and thus favoured Garrison. A few years later, the family would host Frederick Douglass. The city of Limerick had a small but vibrant Quaker community with an established history of anti-slavery. Fisher, a relative of Webb by marriage, had been active in the movement for decades. At a Quaker meeting in Limerick in 1821, he had been selected alongside William Alexander to collect subscriptions in support of the 'total abolition of the slave trade'. The subscriptions collected by Fisher and Alexander were forwarded to another Irish abolitionist, Joseph Bewley of Dublin.[42] More recently, Limerick had been at the centre of the struggle against the Jamaican Emigration Scheme with a number of ships departing from the port. In 1840, the Hibernian Anti-Slavery Society had appealed to the people of Limerick:

> Let our people go wherever they may better their condition ... but we protest against Ireland being made a new station for the enaction of the slave trade tragedy of the West India planters, now they can no longer set their feet on the neck of the black man.[43]

Charles Lenox Remond's first lecture in Limerick was held on 23 August in the Quaker's meeting house, on Cecil Street. The meeting was chaired by Samuel Evans, Secretary of the Limerick Auxiliary Anti-Slavery Society, which was affiliated to the British and Foreign Anti-Slavery Society, rather than to Garrison.[44] Those present were described as, 'a highly respectable audience, comprising ladies and gentlemen of different religious persuasions and political opinions'.[45] A journalist with the *Limerick Reporter* attended. The newspaper's stance was Catholic, pro-repeal, pro-O'Connell and anti-slavery. The journalist described Remond as a 'young man of colour' who lectured on 'the cruelties, injustice, horrors, and iniquities of American slavery'.[46] He also praised him fulsomely:

> Mr. Remond's address, manner, accent, and delivery are impressive, and calculated to bespeak the feelings of an educated audience. He is possessed of considerable fluency of language—great force in declamation—a nice choice of words—and an energetic power of logical development, laying down his arguments lucidly and strongly, and working them out with surprising ease and skill.[47]

Because more space was required, Remond's next two lectures were held at the Independent Congregationalist Chapel on Bedford Row on 25 and 27 August. The minister was Rev. Charles Gostling Townley, who would also host Douglass at the same location in 1845. When not hosting abolitionists or preaching, Townley, who was originally from England, spent his time 'translating large portions of the Scriptures into the Irish language'.[48] On 25 August, Remond spoke for about 90 minutes. He focused on the hypocrisy of the United States for the 'propping up of this inhumanising and unchristianising evil, which stands out in atrocious relief as the ugliest blot on the history of nations'. In what was a crowd-pleasing moment, he praised O'Connell, for his attempts 'to put an end to this cruelty by the thrilling power of his unmatched eloquence'.[49]

Webb described this lecture as being the most crowded and attentive audience he had ever seen.[50] He believed that this was because Irish people, whatever their religion or politics, supported Remond's 'mission of humanity' and 'their natural sympathies are in favour of the oppressed and unhappy'.[51] The *Reporter* agreed with Webb's analysis, writing of Remond's second lecture:

> The audience was far more numerous than on Monday. The house was thronged in every part. Even the stairs leading to the galleries, and the avenues to the body of the house were crowded with anxious groups, impatient to hear from the gifted tongue of this interesting person.[52]

Again, the writer was fulsome in his praise of Remond describing him as 'a sort of phenomenon in the intellectual world'. Inserting himself into the narrative, the reporter concluded by opining:

> As the avowed and uncompromising foes of despotism under every form and hue—whether in the monarchy, the republic, or the mixed government, at home or abroad—we think that we should be wanting in our duty if we did not give every encouragement to this lecturer, who, as far as he has gone, has shown himself eminently deserving of the patronage that has been hitherto bestowed upon his endeavors at the hands of the enlightened and liberal citizens of Limerick of all classes and persuasions. The parallel between the white slaves in Ireland and the black slaves beyond the Atlantic is so broad and obvious, that it requires little stretch of the imagination to fancy that, whilst depicting the wrongs of the one, Mr. Remond has an eye to the oppressions of the other. The only difference between them is, that the Irish slave is nominally a free subject—whilst the American is supposed to be chattel property—but the reeking lash, laid on the bare limbs of the latter, is not so excruciating as the caprice which consigns the former to the desert bleak of a callous world, or to the pangs of slow or immediate starvation and death— to extermination, in fact, in its most hideous form.[53]

At the end of an intense week, Remond, Webb and four fellow abolitionists took a holiday in County Clare. During this time, the six men went on walking excursions, travelling as far as the Lakes of Killarney and climbing Mount Brandon in Kerry. On visiting Loop Head, they were joined by an unnamed lady and a musician with Highland bagpipes. Readers of the *Liberator* would have been charmed by Webb's description of such an unusual grouping:

> Such a wild halloo as his music and Remond's aspect set up in the primitive district we travelled, nobody could conceive. Men, women and children followed us along the cliffs, along the roads, and into the cabins ... how the

84   *Charles Lenox Remond (1810–1873)*

music got them going. They ran, and jumped, and laughed, and showed their fine white teeth ... they crowded around us, stared and chatted in Irish.

For Remond, it must have been a memorable experience. While noting the extreme poverty of the people and their dependence on potatoes, he was also enchanted by them. He informed Webb that he had never encountered more pleasant faces than he met on that day.[54]

Webb and Remond then returned to Limerick for two more lectures; on 3 September and 7 September.[55] Each one was more crowded than the preceding one. Remond's 3 September meeting was reported on in detail by the *Limerick Chronicle*, which described attendance as 'overflowing', adding:

This tells well for the people of Limerick, as it proves that every class and persuasion sympathise with the wretched Slave, and entertain no other feelings than those of horror and execration towards the supporters of the most accursed and unchristian system that ever degraded and disgraced this country with inhabitants claiming to be ranked among free and civilized communities.

The paper also praised the lecturer:

In Mr. Remond we have full proof, if, indeed, proof could be necessary, that the mere accident of colour exerts no influence on the mind. No one could listen to the most popular lecturer without being impressed with the conviction that, together with a fluency of expression which could scarcely be surpassed, he has been gifted by nature with intellectual powers of the first order, and which evidently appear to have been subjected to a system of careful and judicious cultivation.[56]

Remond's theme was different to that of previous lectures, he explaining how slavery brutalized everybody, because the,

natural consequence of being permitted to practice oppression with impunity, was the engendering of a spirit so tyrannical among the Slave-owners, that even their dealings and intercourse, among themselves and with others, are regulated and characterized by principles of the most barbarous nature.

In what was a common trope in anti-slavery lectures, he read several reports from America as evidence. Remond's lecture lasted for two hours and was 'listened to throughout with the most marked attention'.[57]

Remond's final lecture in Limerick was described as 'a clear and powerful exposition of the horrors of that inhuman system'. Remond assured his audience that progress was being made on the issue as a result of public opinion. He also pointed out how former slaves conducted themselves in the West Indies and

Charles Lenox Remond (1810–1873)   85

Canada as proof that nobody needed to fear emancipation. Remond concluded his farewell Limerick lecture by appealing to the women present to get involved. He also asked that people sign the Address. He sat down, 'amid loud and repeated cheers'. Commenting on the lectures, the *Limerick Chronicle* opined:

> We cannot comprehend the principle on which the American slave-owner would advocate freedom for himself, and yet deny it to him, whose only crime has been to differ with him in colour ... What, however, can be the plea of the slave-owner, when proof unquestionable can be produced, that the Negro, when properly treated, is his equal in intellect, and much his superior in the exalted feelings of our nature.[58]

Remond's four lectures in Limerick received extensive coverage in both the *Limerick Reporter* and the *Limerick Chronicle* newspapers. At one point, a difference had arisen between the Hibernian Anti-Slavery Society and the *Chronicle*, the former accusing the paper of supporting emigration to Jamaica and Texas. The paper responded that:

> So far from the *Limerick Chronicle* being in the remotest degree the advocate of slavery, we can point to the fact that it was the only paper in Limerick that gave a full report of Mr. Remond's lectures, which were lately delivered in this city.[59]

In a long response, Richard Allen on behalf of the Hibernian Anti-Slavery Society, explained:

> They most willingly accept the avowal to the contrary—acknowledge the services the Chronicle conferred on the Anti-Slavery cause, in reporting so ably the lectures of Chas. Lenox Remond, and are prepared cordially to acknowledge it from henceforth as a firm ally, in the great cause of the abolition of slavery, which they are banded together to achieve.[60]

After Clare, Remond and Webb travelled to Cork, arriving in mid-September. Like other urban centres in Ireland, the city had a long tradition of anti-slavery activities, dating back to the later part of the eighteenth century. As was the case generally, many of these activities were spearheaded by the Society of Friends.[61] As early as 1789, a wealthy Quaker merchant, Cooper Penrose, had drawn up an anti-slavery petition.[62] Concurrent with this, however, merchants in Cork and other parts of Ireland had benefited from a Black Atlantic economy, specifically, trade with the West Indies.[63] Interest in abolition had revived in the 1820s, largely associated with Quaker, Joshua Beale, who had formed the Cork Anti-Slavery Society in 1826.

After giving a number of lectures in small locations, Remond held a large public meeting in the County Court House, the purpose being, 'to solicit the Citizens of Cork and others generally to participate in an Address that has already

86 *Charles Lenox Remond (1810–1873)*

been adopted in Dublin and elsewhere, to the American Congress, praying for the emancipation from Slavery of the Negroes in that Country'.[64] He asked his audience if 'the Citizens of this, as well as other parts of Ireland, would be willing to hear, as well as aid in, any proposition for the emancipation from such revolting bondage of their fellow men', which promoted cries of 'hear, hear, and cheers'. He also thanked them 'for their unanimous adoption of the Address that he would that day have the honour of laying before them for their approval and signature'. Unusually, Remond delved into Irish politics, saying:

> In this country he was aware that many and conflicting opinions existed amongst the people upon religion and politics, but his object presenting himself before Irishmen was to tell them that he was the ardent though humble advocate of men who sought emancipation from thraldom the most degrading known to human nature, and he, therefore, hoped to connect and combine every religious denomination, every sect and creed, and every political party, in aid of his mission.

He concluded by reading the Address, which was unanimously adopted by the meeting.[65]

As had proved to be the case elsewhere, Remond's lectures in Cork prompted a revival in anti-slavery activity amongst both men and women, with many newspapers commenting on the large attendance by females.[66] At a meeting of the Anti-Slavery Society hosted by the Mayor on 21 September, they praised Remond's activities and it was recognized that the city of Cork, which adjoined the port of Cobh, had a special role to play:

> The lectures of Mr. Chas. Lenox Remonde [sic], an exposition of the mischievous results of Slavery in America, which must be useful to the progress of the Anti-Slavery cause generally, but especially important to us in this locality, whence hundreds of our fellow-countrymen annually Emigrate, to put them on their guard against the seductions of Slave-holding cupidity; we recognise them as an effective demonstration of the fact, that humanity, justice, and advancing civilization, are incompatible with the brutalizing tendencies of American Slavery.[67]

At a follow-up meeting of Cork Anti-Slavery Society, they explained the significance of Remond's visit:

> To call us into action for such results Mr. Remond has lectured to instructed and gratified audiences. And, Sir, before I close, I must say that it would be ingratitude not to add our thanks to Wm. Martin, who was the principle means of procuring to us the advantages of having heard the learned American, whose advocacy has renewed our anti-slavery call. It would hurt the feelings of Mr. Martin to speak of his zeal and hospitality; nor shall I do more than put his name forward in company of that which is

Charles Lenox Remond (1810–1873)   87

the first object of our congratulation, and say that it is honoured by being associated with every useful exertion which belongs to the emancipation and moral advancement of the slave.[68]

Overall, Remond's trip to the south of Ireland was a triumph. It was even commented on by a small regional newspaper in England, which praised the re-energized anti-slavery activities in Ireland, including the Address, adding, 'Mr. C. L. Remond, likewise, is pursuing an anti-slavery tour in the south of Ireland, with unprecedented success'.[69] Remond was personally pleased. Writing from the home of Richard Allen in Dublin at the beginning of October, he informed Garrison that he had 'served our cause in Ireland as far south as the city of Cork [and] if I do nothing more I shall not regret my visit'. He also reassured Garrison that 'our cause is fast becoming valuable, its dimensions are being better known [and] appreciated'. He told him not to be discouraged as 'the New Organization has lost much of its charm and truth and reason and justice is fast superseding and again I say if we remain true, victory is ours'. Remond said that he would bring the Irish Address and goods for the bazaar safely back to Boston, asking Garrison to tell Mrs. Chapman that, 'the Bazaar Box from Ireland will be a good one'.[70]

If the public Remond was buoyant, the private Remond suffered from periods of despondency. In a long and frank letter to Garrison sent from the holiday home in Kilkee, which was published in the *Liberator*, Webb described Remond's time in Ireland as 'triumphant'. Yet, regardless of the success of Remond's public appearances in Ireland, privately, he seemed to have doubts about how he was perceived. Webb confided that although prejudice did exist in Ireland, Remond had not encountered it and therefore had 'no battle to meet in Ireland—neither unkindness nor persecution, not anything of the kind', yet he allowed himself to be troubled by the possibility he would be. Webb hoped, 'I wish he would let the day take care for itself, and he need not be so depressed as I see him at home'.[71] Webb's comments provide an insight into the stresses and strains of being constantly on the public circuit and in public view experienced by visiting abolitionists. Inevitably, they also felt homesickness at being away from their families for so long.

Remond returned to Dublin in early October. Like many abolitionists, he supported the temperance movement and he attended a meeting on this topic in the Royal Exchange on 7 October. Interestingly, one of the platform party was 'Monsieur L'Instant, a native of Hayti'.[72] Haiti, the first black republic in the world, was still under embargoes by the United States, while being forced to pay reparations to France. Remond gave one final lecture in the Music Hall. It was the largest venue in which Remond had spoken. Unusually, there was a charge.[73] The advertisement explained, 'In order to convenience all classes, and to cover the unavoidable expense of the Meeting, the following charges will be made:— Boxes, 4d.; Pit, 2d.; Gallery free'.[74] The meeting was chaired by Richard Madden who had just returned from Africa where he had carried out a fact-finding mission on behalf of the British government. The audience was described as, 'crowded and highly respectable'.[75] During his speech, Remond made it clear

88   *Charles Lenox Remond (1810–1873)*

that his approach to oppression was universal and inclusive, 'my words are designed to have a general and unbounded application to all who suffer under persecution or sorrow, under the bondage of the enthraller'.[76] Following on from this, he condemned slavery in British India. Additionally, Remond pledged his support to the cause of Irish liberty, promising, 'Nor do I pretend to ask from any Irishman that which I could not always most willingly and delightfully concede to him, if the occasion should ever arise'.[77] He endorsed the call of the Hibernian Anti-Slavery Society for the removal of Andrew Stevenson, the American Ambassador to Britain since 1836. As usual, Remond was warmly applauded throughout. He, in turn, praised the audience: 'My bosom swells with pride and pleasure, when I reflect that I am standing before Irishmen—men who in the year 1841, have the name of philanthropists (hear, hear, and loud cheers)'. This was coupled with an appeal:

> I call upon you, Irishmen, to extend to the oppressed and enthralled man, under whatsoever sun he may be found, that aid and cooperation, that sympathy and affection, which you would wish, were you in similar circumstances, should be extended to yourselves. (Cheers.) When Mr. O'Connell—and now, that I have mentioned his name, let me take occasion to say how deeply I venerate that good and mighty man, who has put himself forth as the undaunted and fearless champion of liberty and the rights of man in every clime the sun adorns. (A peal of applause here burst from the whole assembly which almost made the walls to shake, and which continued for several minutes.)[78]

It was Remond's final public meeting in Dublin and, yet again, it proved to be a masterful wide-ranging performance.

After Dublin, Remond travelled north to Belfast, a predominantly Protestant town. Belfast had a tradition of anti-slavery, although the local society's sympathies were with the British and Foreign Anti-Slavery Society rather than Garrison, they having joined the former in 1840. Unusually, therefore, Remond's hosts were not part of the Quaker network. Several of the leading abolitionists in Belfast belonged to the Presbyterian or Anglican churches and, in the case of the Rev. Thomas Drew, they were openly anti-Catholic.[79] Remond proved skillful at negotiated these divisions. In a town riven by sectarian divisions, slavery provided a middle ground on which all religious traditions could join in the condemnation.[80] One of Remond's hosts was a veteran activist, James Standfield. In 1833, Standfield had been part of a deputation that delivered a petition calling for the total and immediate end to slavery.[81] Not long before Remond's visit, Standfield had spoken out against the Jamaican emigration scheme, writing to the *News-Letter*:

> It is to be hoped that no Irishman will lend himself to West India Planters, who are anxious to introduce a new system of slavery, under the guise of apprenticeship, and are using all their influence to beguile our poor

Charles Lenox Remond (1810–1873)   89

countrymen to Jamaica, in order to coerce the black population, whom, if in their power, they would still hold in cruel bondage.[82]

Prior to arriving in the northern town, Remond's Dublin lectures and information concerning the Address had been reported in the *Belfast Commercial Chronicle*, so readers would have been aware of his history and purpose.[83] Local newspapers, when advertising his visit, had referred to him as, 'a gentleman of colour, from Rhode Island in the United States'.[84] Remond gave his first lecture in Belfast on the evening of 13 October in the Assembly Room in the Commercial Buildings.[85] The audience was described as, 'crowded and fashionable'.[86] He spoke 'at considerable length, and with much eloquence' on slavery in America, which he likened to 'an asp in a basket of flowers'.[87] Remond concluded by saying that it was such a large topic that he needed to give a second lecture. Standfield informed the audience that because the venue had proved to be too small, the next lecture would be at the meeting house of Dr John Edgar, a Presbyterian minister.[88] A number of local newspapers covered the meeting, including the *News-Letter*. The tone of their coverage was acerbic, referring to Standfield as the 'long-tried, faithful, and persevering advocate of the poor "n——"'. In marked contrast, the *Belfast Commercial Chronicle* referred to Standfield as 'the warm and untiring friend of the bondman, in every clime'.[89] The *News-Letter* also criticized the choice of venue, observing,

> The room, in fact, was literally crammed, and, indeed, the Committee, in selecting such a room, seemed to have but little idea of the interest which the Belfast public in general take in the rights and liberties of the poor slave.[90]

However, they were more favourable when commenting on Remond's lecture saying that he 'was listened to throughout with marked attention, and the applause which at intervals was bestowed upon him, manifested the general concurrence of the meeting in the several arguments which the speaker advanced'.[91]

Remond's second lecture, held at the Rev. John Edgar's Meeting House, was full, even though the newly built church could hold 700 people.[92] One paper reported that, 'the house was crowded to overflowing, and we have not seen on any occasion for any length of time so large and respectable an audience'.[93] Once more, Remond focused on the cruelty of the system, reading extracts of American newspapers that were pro-slavery. He asked his audience whether 'they should be at rest while a system that murdered so many human beings annually was in operation!', and answering, 'They should not keep quiet until the slave had *his* rights which came to him from God and nature'. Again, Remond was praised by the *News-Letter*, which commented:

> It was pleasing to observe the marked attention which was paid to the lecturer throughout his beautiful and most interesting discourse; and we are assured that the members of the Anti-Slavery Society, and the advocates of the cause in general, must feel that their labours have, to a certain extent,

90   *Charles Lenox Remond (1810–1873)*

been rewarded by the sympathy which is daily increasing throughout Great Britain on the subject.[94]

At the end of the meeting, Standfield announced that the next lecture would be held in the Independent Meeting House on Donegall Street, the following Tuesday. Several people responded by shouting 'Not large enough'. The ever-gracious Remond thanked the audience for their ongoing interest, and said, if the place turned out to be too small, he would delay his departure from Belfast for a few days.[95]

On 19 October, Remond lectured for the third time in Belfast. As had been predicted, the venue turned out to be too small. Even though extra benches had been set up in the aisles of the church, large numbers were sent away, greatly disappointed. A reporter from a local newspaper observed, 'Those who were fortunate as to obtain seats must have been highly satisfied, as the lecture throughout was one of the most spirit-stirring we ever had the pleasure of hearing'.[96] A large part of Remond's talk was devoted to showing how the churches in America were sustaining slavery through their support for it. He was especially critical of the Methodist Church, the largest church in America. He then explained how even in the free states there existed prejudice against people of colour. When talking about segregation in transport, Remond shared his own story of the voyage across the Atlantic, explaining:

> When he took his passage for this country, he could not get into the cabin, but had to take a berth below the deck and when he was only a few days at sea, and had got sea-sick, he was ordered out of the berth for which he was paying, by the mate of the vessel, and had to leave it; and, when he offered the Captain any sum he would require, to give him a place where he would be comfortable, it was denied him. Some might ask, why he left his native land, to put up with this treatment? It was, that he might breathe the air of heaven a freeman before he left this world.

Remond's final sentence was followed by 'a loud burst of applause, which lasted for some time'.[97]

On the following evening, Remond delivered his fourth lecture, in Dr. Hanna's Meeting House on Rosemary Street. The congregation had a long tradition of being involved with radical movements dating back to the 1790s. Unusually, Remond commenced his lecture by reading from the Bible—a portion of the writings of St. Matthew.[98] Remond also made a rare foray into Irish politics, referring to O'Connell and his contretemps with the American Ambassador, Stevenson. Remond urged his audience to sign petitions for Stevenson's removal.[99] Following his lecture, Remond was presented with a silver fruit-knife, with his initials engraved on it, by 'three very young ladies from Ballymacarrett'. It was accompanied by a letter, 'in admiration of his advocacy in favour of his brethren in slavery, in America'. Remond 'heartily thanked them for that unexpected token of friendship and promised to take their juvenile letter with him to the United States'.[100]

Remond's fifth lecture was held on the following evening in an even larger venue, Fisherwick Place Presbyterian Church in the centre of Belfast.[101] The focus of this lecture was not only on the cruelties of slavery, but the prejudice that existed in America, even towards free black people. The Rev. Daniel McAfee spoke after Remond and claimed that, 'He would rather have the intellect and the features of such a man as Mr. Remond, than those of hundreds of white men calling themselves Christians'.[102] Before giving his final lecture, Remond was given a soirée in his honour:

a number of the friends and admirers of Mr. Remond entertained him at a select tea party, in Mrs. Moreland's Victoria Temperance Hotel, for the purpose of testifying their admiration for his personal worth as a gentleman, as well as for the noble and humane cause he has so warmly advocated throughout Great Britain, and more especially in this town, during the past week.[103]

Those who attended included Monsieur L'Instant from Haiti, who was described as Remond's friend.[104] Remond was asked to speak more about slavery, after which fruit was served. Then, the 'remaining portion of the evening was spent in similar conversations, and altogether in a very happy and sociable manner'. One of the issues discussed was Irish emigrants to the States. The Rev. McAfee said, 'they should endeavour to instill into the minds of emigrants a hatred of slavery'. He had been in the habit of giving certificates to members of his church when they were going out to America, 'and he now pledged himself that he would never give another without writing a protest against slavery at the bottom of it'.[105]

At the soirée, it had been also announced that Remond had agreed to deliver one more lecture before leaving Belfast, on the topic of 'The Remedy for the Evils of Slavery in America'.[106] Remond's sixth and final lecture in Belfast was in Dr Cooke's Meeting House. Rev. Henry Cooke was an outspoken Presbyterian minister known for his opposition to Irish nationalism. He was associated with a traditional Calvinism that was uncompromising, especially in its attitude to Catholicism. O'Connell represented everything he disliked.[107] The personal, political and religious antipathy between the two men was particularly heightened at the time of Remond's visit to the town as, towards the end of 1840, local Repealers had issued an invitation to O'Connell. Cooke had challenged O'Connell to a public debate. The latter declined, but Cooke used the incident to label O'Connell, 'the invader of the north', while the Liberator responded by referring to the minister as 'Bully Cooke, the cock of the north'.[108] Despite the visceral antipathy between the two men, they found common ground when it came to opposing slavery.

Remond's final lecture was a success. One newspaper reporting, 'The interest excited by his lectures continues to increase. At no former meeting was there such a large attendance'.[109] Before talking about slavery, Remond informed his audience about the success of the anti-slavery cause, explaining, 'In 1830 there was not an anti-slavery society in America; there are at present between one

92 *Charles Lenox Remond (1810–1873)*

and two thousand abolition societies, containing about two hundred thousand members'. He recommended that a way to bring American slavery to an end was to encourage cotton growth in India, based on free labour. Remond then denounced 'with infinite energy', the demoralizing effects of slavery. Irishmen in the States could play their part by electing anti-slavery candidates to Congress. In an appeal to the women of Belfast, he asked them to support the upcoming bazaar in Boston. At the conclusion of the meeting, Standfield told the audience that copies of the Address could be signed when they left the meeting. He also paid tribute to Remond.[110] Tellingly, at his final lecture in Ireland, Remond paid tribute to Irish people, speaking of the kindness he had received in the country and stating that during this time he had 'not received any insult'. He thanked the people of Belfast for their attendance and sympathy.[111]

Remond's time in Ireland was an overwhelming triumph. He had attracted large audiences who were thrilled by his oratory, the word 'eloquent' frequently being used to describe him.[112] Attendance at most of Remond's lectures had been free, the organizers making it clear that his object in coming to Ireland had not been to collect money.[113] His presence encouraged both men and women to rekindle their interest in abolition. When lecturing, Remond had urged his audiences to carry on opposing slavery long after he had left the country. His impact on women was particularly visible in terms of the links with the bazaar in Boston. The Cork Ladies' Anti-Slavery Society took this message to heart, issuing an 'Appeal to their Fellow Countrywomen and Countrymen' in September 1842. The Cork women sent items to the bazaar in Boston, for which they were thanked by both Remond and Maria Weston Chapman. The donations included the autographs of 'Thomas Moore and Thomas Campbell, Elizabeth Fry, Dr. Madden and Father Mathew, Lord Morpeth, George Thompson, Thomas Clarkson and O'Connell', a tapestry, portraits and small boxes of wafer biscuits. The women of Ireland were praised by the Boston women:

> Most of the rich offerings of Ireland are yet unmentioned; and as we look upon their beauty, and see how much taste, and thought, and industry have been lavished upon them by the friends in Dublin, Limerick, Cork, Cove, Tralee, Clonmel, Waterford, Wexford, Bandon, Mallow, Athlone, Youghal, it is no wonder that we lose, for a moment, our New England exactitude of manner, (stiffness, as Frenchmen and Southerners call it), and exclaim our enthusiasm—*'Erin mavourneen ! Erin bragh'*.[114]

Women in the north of the country were similarly inspired by Remond. This was evident from an advertisement in the *Northern Whig* on 4 November saying:

> Those Ladies anxious to contribute to the AMERICAN ANTI-SLAVERY BAZAAR, to which allusion was made at Mr. Remond's last Lecture, are informed, that, by sending, on or before MONDAY, the instant, articles prepared for that purpose, to Mrs. GREER, Fisherwick-Place, or Mrs. WEBB, 119, York- Street, they will be packed and forwarded to Liverpool, to meet

Mr. REMOND, previous to his embarking for his native Country. The Bazaar is to open all Christmas. It is necessary, that whatever is contributed should be packed as would bear carriage, without danger of being injured by close packing.[115]

After Ireland, Remond returned to England where he delivered more lectures, including seven in Manchester in the space of a fortnight.[116] He returned to the States at the end of 1841, having lectured for 18 months to universal acclaim.

The address to Irish Americans

Outside of lecturing, the most important aspect of Remond's time in Ireland had been his role in collecting signatures in support of anti-slavery, officially named the 'Address from the people of Ireland to their countrymen and countrywomen in America'. This Address, which was drafted by Richard D. Webb and James Haughton, was eventually signed by over 60,000 Irish people, the majority of whom were Catholic. The list was headed by Daniel O'Connell, Fr. Theobald Mathew and the celebrated Dr. R. R. Madden—all three of whom were Catholic. Aligning anti-slavery with the demand for Irish independence, O'Connell had allowed his Repeal agents to gather signatures at their political rallies, while others had made door-to-door collections, consequently merging nationalist politics with anti-slavery.

When Remond arrived back in Boston in December 1841, however, he brought with him not only the Address, but boxes of goods from Irish women for the upcoming bazaar. Regarding the latter, Remond wrote:

I found the Boston friends on tiptoe for me, and I told them it was difficult for me to decide whether it was me or the bazaar boxes they most desired to see safely landed. It was, to be sure, a narrow escape. I landed on Tuesday at noon—the bazaar opened the next (Wednesday) morning. I have attended the bazaar very much of the time, and every lady and gentleman interested was delighted at the *Irish* contributions; and, when the boxes were opened, the beauty of the articles, especially the bags and worsted-work, created quite a sensation, and in no one more so than Lord Morpeth, who spent much time at the Fair over several days.

The goods from Ireland raised £500.[117] However, Remond's joy at being home was short-lived as, the morning after his arrival, he encountered prejudice when travelling to the bazaar. He explained to a friend in Ireland:

On going to the rail-road station I met my good friend William Bassett, of Lynn, and Mr. Hayward, of Salem; and, being anxious to talk with me in the carriage set apart for persons of color; they had barely taken their seats when the conductor ordered them both out; upon which contemptible demand, friend Bassett asked the conductor if he would not permit him to

94   *Charles Lenox Remond (1810–1873)*

ride with his friend, who had been long absent in another country; but it proved of little avail, as they were compelled to get out.

This incident led Remond to reflect:

> Can it be possible such transactions occur in a civilized country? Never, never did the conduct of my countrymen appear so uncivilized, so unchristian, so inhuman, so degrading and debasing, so trying and disheartening! and I ask, why was I born in such a land?

Remond added that, 'Was it not that I have a dear father, mother, sisters, and brothers, before another month could elapse, I would turn my back for ever on the land of my nativity'. It was in stark contrast to the respect he had been shown in Ireland and Britain, and a brutal reminder of his status within the land of his birth.[118] Remond's outrage was shared by the Irish press, the *Nenagh Guardian* expressing its disgust that 'the bearer of the Irish Address—a gentleman of education, who was received in terms of perfect equality into the houses of some of our most respectable citizens', was treated in such a way.[119]

The closing of the bazaar was immediately followed by the unveiling of the Address, on 28 January 1842, the final day of the tenth annual meeting of the Massachusetts Anti-Slavery Society.[120] For this purpose, a meeting had been convened in Faneuil Hall in Boston. It must have provided some satisfaction to the organizers that, only five years earlier, this building had hosted a meeting, attended by over 1,500 people, to condemn abolitionists and their 'incitement' of slaves. Present at the unveiling was a relative newcomer to the lecturing circuit, Frederick Douglass. Douglass was included in the platform party of those who made a speech.[121] Having a former slave in such a prominent position was remarkable, as one paper pointed out:

> ... the meeting was addressed by Wendell Phillips and Edmund Quincy—old revolutionary blood courses there! And Charles Lenox Remond, a BLACK man—Frederick DOUGLAS, a RUNAWAY SLAVE!!! Think of that, ye miserable flesh-mongers that are trying to excommunicate the venerable John Quincy Adams from your infamous Congress—a fugitive playing the Sam Adams before a Boston audience in Faneuil Hall ...[122]

At the Boston meeting, Garrison—not Remond—read the Address out loud. Remond did speak, however, in support of the resolution and his 'eloquent and thrilling speeches were constantly interrupted by loud and enthusiastic bursts of applause'.[123] An estimated 2,000 were present (some estimates calculated 5,000), the great majority of whom were Irish. A number of the speeches and resolutions paid tribute to Ireland and to O'Connell:

> The following resolution was offered by GEORGE BRADBURN, and adopted with great enthusiasm:

Charles Lenox Remond (1810–1873)   95

Resolved, That this meeting most cordially wishes Old Ireland success, in all her righteous efforts to redeem the Emerald Isle from every species of British oppression, and especially in the grand movement of DANIEL O'CONNELL, for the repeal of the fraudulent act of Union between his country and England.

On the motion of EDMUND QUINCY,

Voted, That the proceedings of this meeting be printed, and signed by the officers of this meeting, and copies transmitted to Daniel O'Connell and Theobald Mathew, and to our Senators and Representatives in Congress, with a request that they be laid before that body—also, that they be published in the papers of this city.[124]

The abolitionist *Herald of Freedom*, although they had no reporter present at the meeting, wrote about it in euphoric terms, exclaiming, 'God bless the Irish heart everywhere! It always sympathizes with the wronged. We wish we had been there, to have shouted for Liberty with them'.[125] Within Ireland, news of the meeting was greeted with joy, one paper opining:

We are not wrong, then, we think, in saying that Ireland may do great things for the freeing of the American slave; but, then, let it be recollected that it must be by upholding a high standard. There must be no compromise—no shaking hands with the slaveholders … until he washes his hands forever of all participation in the guilt of robbing his fellow-men.[126]

The early jubilation was misplaced. Irish America did not respond to the rally call, as forces opposed to the Address emerged. Two further meetings were held in Boston, both in the Marlboro Chapel, where the Address was displayed to prove its authenticity. No Irish attended.[127] Moreover, the hope that Remond would present the petition to Congress was stymied by the gagging order regarding presenting petitions on slavery, which remained in place from 1836 to 1844.[128] Nonetheless, the existence of the Address was clearly an irritant to some American politicians. In 1842, Congressman Henry Wise—a fervent supporter of slavery—named and condemned O'Connell for 'issuing his mandates to every Irish man in America' to support abolition'.[129]

Opposition was not confined to Congress. The initial warm welcome proved to be short-lived as both the Irish American press led by Boston *Pilot*, and the Catholic Church led by Bishop Hughes of New York, condemned the Address openly. The influential *Pilot* was a barometer of attitudes within Irish America. In recognition of this, experienced abolitionist John A. Collins had met with the editor, Patrick Donahoe.[130] Although Irish-born Donahoe supported O'Connell and Repeal, and was personally opposed to slavery, he did not endorse the Address. As he explained, opposing slavery and supporting abolition were, in the context of the United States, very different things, leading Donahoe to state, 'It would not do for them [Irish immigrants] to take hold of the question of abolition'. Another critic of the Address was Walt Whitman, editor of the

96   *Charles Lenox Remond (1810–1873)*

New York based, *Aurora*. In an editorial entitled 'Black and White Slaves' he juxtaposed poverty in England with 'domestic life at the south. A gentleman and lady, with two children, come to pay a call at the shanty of a family of their slaves. Everything bears the impress of cheerfulness and content'. He admonished, 'Let our transatlantic neighbors take the beam out of their own eyes—and then they can reasonably find fault with the mote in ours'.[131] These criticisms were mirrored within Irish communities. For example, a large meeting in Pottsville in Pennsylvania issued a long rejection of the Address, which echoed Bishop Hughes' claim that it was 'a vile fabrication'. They went further by challenging the premise on which the Address had been issued:

> we do not form a distinct class of the community, but consider ourselves in every respect as citizens of this great and glorious republic—that we look upon every attempt to address us otherwise upon the subject of the abolition of negro slavery or any subject whatever as base and iniquitous, no matter from what quarter it may proceed.

A pro-slavery, English-language newspaper, published in Paris, took delight in pointing out to the 'Pottsville Paddies' that the Address and O'Connell's signature were authentic, adding, 'the mock importance of these worthies must make this shrewd American smile'.[132]

News of the Boston meeting was reported in some of the Irish press, initially optimistically.[133] Unfortunately, the dilemma for Irish Americans was not understood by their compatriots 3,000 miles away. Nor did it garner any sympathy from abolitionists in America.[134] The opposition led Garrison to lament the fact that the Irish were controlled by 'a crafty priesthood and unprincipled political demagogues'.[135] He was especially critical of Irishmen who seemed indifferent to, or antagonistic towards, the Address, referring to them as 'bastard Irishmen (for they cannot have a drop of genuine Irish blood running in their veins) … Let no man claim to be the friend of O'Connell or of Ireland who is not an abolitionist'.[136] Garrison described the criticisms that appeared in the *Argos*, a supporter of the pro-slavery Democratic Party, as 'effrontery and folly' and he promised to accompany Remond to Albany in late April, the location chosen as 'there is a pretty large Irish population in Albany, and an Irish Repeal Association'.[137] Significantly, they planned to take the Address with them, as a way of proving its authenticity.[138]

Was the failure of the Address inevitable? Even before Remond had left Ireland, a note of disquiet had been sounded about the wisdom of reaching out to Irish Americans. The *Freeman's Journal* had published a letter, purporting to be from a member of the Society of Friends, sent to a Cork journal, condemning a great portion of the Address and saying it would do more harm than good.[139] These words were prescient. The reception of the Address by the Irish in America, and the strong opposition by the Catholic Church hierarchy and the press, disappointed abolitionists on both sides of the Atlantic.[140] Clearly, in an age of nativism and overt anti-Irish sentiment, it was difficult to ask immigrants to criticize a country that had given them a home, and an institution that was legal

Charles Lenox Remond (1810–1873) 97

and accepted by most politicians. Moreover, the abolitionists' radical stand on a number of issues—ranging from women's rights to Sabbatarianism—placed it on the extreme end of everyday politics. The condemnation of the Catholic Church and the pro-slavery Democratic Party were a final death knell for the Address. By the middle of 1842, however, Garrison had embarked on a new crusade—Disunion of the Union—and it had been inspired by O'Connell's campaign for a repeal of the Act of Union.[141] The Address had failed, but Ireland continued to influence American Abolition.

Later life

Despite the disappointing reception to the Address, Remond returned to the United States as probably the most well-known and celebrated black abolitionist in America. Breaking another barrier, in February 1842, he became the first black man to testify before the Legislative Committee of the Massachusetts House of Representatives.[142] In early 1842, he was joined by a new recruit to the lecturing circuit, Frederick Douglass. Douglass initially was mentored by Remond, but his compelling life story, having spent 20 years enslaved, gave him a perspective that was unique amongst abolitionist lecturers. During the next two years, Remond frequently lectured with Douglass and occasionally with Henry Garnet—both of whom could speak from first-hand experience of slavery. In contrast, Remond could only speak in the abstract. Their topics reflected this, Douglass often lecturing on the theme of 'Slavery, as actually existing at the South', whereas Remond's favourite topic was 'Prejudice against Color'.[143]

As agents of the American Anti-Slavery Society, Remond and Douglass endured a punishing schedule, travelling thousands of miles and sometimes speaking twice a day.[144] Those who heard them speak together were moved by the experience:

the deep, holy, burning indignation of Remond, or the keen, withering satire, the ineffably scalding, soul-shrivelling sarcasms of Douglass—all poured forth, too, from the fullness of hearts overflowing with universal benevolence —the being, I say, who could stand unmoved under this, must be less, infinitely less than man. What a loathsome, soul-sickening, ineffably contemptible thing is this American prejudice against color. Charles Lenox Remond and Frederick Douglass![145]

One report from Pittsburgh suggested that the two men were having a positive impact on the anti-slavery movement, claiming, 'We have heard of *many*, very many converts already made, and are assured that hundreds, if not *thousands*, have been awakened by the appeals of these orators—these eloquent pleaders for *their rights*'. It added:

We may say, without fear of contradiction, that more has been done during the past week, and almost solely by *Douglass* and *Remond* to push forward

98   *Charles Lenox Remond (1810–1873)*

the great and glorious cause, than could have been hoped for in months, by any other instrumentality.[146]

Remond's intense schedule may explain why, after he left Ireland, he failed to stay in contact with those who had hosted him. Webb shared his disappointment at not hearing from Remond with white abolitionist Maria Weston Chapman in Boston, writing: 'The Belfast people wonder that Remond never writes to them—they were very kind and generous to him and he made such protestations but eloquence and not gratitude are Remond's forte'.[147] It was a harsh evaluation, but not dissimilar to judgements that they would pass on Douglass a few years later.

At the end of 1842, Douglass's charisma and compelling life story led one newspaper to pose the question, 'If there is any jealousy or rivalry between Messrs. Douglass and Remond?' Remond felt he should answer this in the form of a letter to Garrison, which he asked him to publish. He explained:

> With all who are in the least acquainted with Mr. Douglass and myself, to have asked the question would have been to answer it, inasmuch as I unhesitatingly assert, that a more intimate, confiding and affectionate feeling and association does not exist, than between Frederick Douglass and myself, on matters of expediency, compliments or rejoicing, we frequently kindly differ, but on principles, never; that I sometimes think my good friend Douglass, in the fulness of his heart, is undeservedly lavish in his eulogiums, and on such occasions I always feel free to express my dissent, and I have the vanity to believe he never thinks the less of me.[148]

Throughout 1843, the men continued to lecture together and to win praise for their eloquence. By the end of the year a subtle change had occurred though, with the *Liberator* now referring to them as Douglass and Remond, possibly suggesting a change in ranking.[149] However, Douglass's third and youngest son, born in October 1844, was named Charles Remond Douglass in honour of their friendship.[150] A year later, Douglass would be in Ireland, retracing many of the steps taken by Remond four years earlier.

When Douglass returned from the United Kingdom in April 1847, he physically and ideologically moved away from Garrison. Remond remained loyal but, by the end of 1840s, he too was rejecting some of Garrison's ideas, although he remained loyal to the man. Remond increasingly believed that political organization was necessary to end slavery. Also, following the passage of the Fugitive Slave Act in 1850, he wondered whether moral force alone was sufficient. Regardless of his changing perspectives, Remond remained in the American Anti-Slavery Society, his focus being Disunion and the need to fight prejudice.[151] Remond and Douglass no longer lectured together and, after 1852, when Douglass officially broke with Garrison, opposed each other publicly. Remond's poor health—he suffering from tuberculosis—prevented him from lecturing for long periods of time.[152] In the late 1850s, however, he appeared with a new rising star, his sister, Sarah.[153] During the Civil War, Remond helped to recruit officers for the all-black 54th Massachusetts Infantry. However, he was critical of the 1863 Emancipation Proclamation, arguing, as he had repeatedly argued, that emancipation was meaningless without equality.[154] After the War, Remond campaigned for black male suffrage, attending the first Equal Rights Convention in 1867. Following this, he retired from regular public appearances, largely due to ill health.[155] Remond died in December 1873, aged 63. For 18 months he had suffered from consumption. Garrison, John T. Sargent and Wendell Phillips conducted the service.[156] Sarah did not attend, as she now living in Italy where she had qualified as a doctor.

Conclusion

Charles Lenox Remond—genteel, measured and cultured—was the first black man to be a regular lecturer for a major anti-slavery society and, by doing so, paved the way for those who came later. Moreover, his view of abolition was not a narrow one, he placing it in the context of the wider demand for justice. Remond also realized that ending slavery needed to be combined with ending prejudice and discrimination. Regardless of his talents and ground-breaking achievements, the historian Carter Woodson has suggested, 'On account of the unusual career of Frederick Douglass, Charles Lenox Remond has been all but forgotten as an anti-slavery orator'.[157] Stacy Kinlock Sewell has argued that, 'his proximity to the predominantly white Garrisonians isolated him from other black abolitionists [and] as a black man who had never been a slave, his appeal and value to the anti-slavery movement were limited'.[158] The latter comment suggests little appreciation of Remond's substantial contributions to both American and transatlantic abolition.

What was the impact on those who heard this eloquent black American in Ireland? For Woodson, Remond made some of his finest speeches while in Ireland. Moreover, they 'showed such an exact knowledge of slavery in all its international bearings that it is little wonder that the orator made a favourable impression'.[159] This sentiment was echoed in contemporary reports. As one Belfast newspaper reported, 'Mr. R. has been lecturing in various parts of Ireland, and from his thorough conversancy with the subject, and his energetic and eloquent expositions of the abominable iniquities of the system, has attracted considerable attention'.[160] Remond's presence in the country clearly re-energized the abolition movement. Moreover, by condemning slavery in British India, he demonstrated that his views of social justice were not narrow and that his concerns for enslaved people extended beyond the Atlantic.

Unwittingly, Remond's tour created a road map that was followed by Douglass four years later with great success, and that other black abolitionists subsequently followed with varying degrees of success. Both Douglass and Sarah Remond must have visited Ireland with a sense of how welcome they would be. Moreover, many of Remond's activities were printed in the *Liberator* and in other American newspapers, the former opining, 'It does him great credit'.[161] At a time when the New Organization appeared to be gaining

100 *Charles Lenox Remond (1810–1873)*

ground on both sides of the Atlantic, Remond had given the Garrisonian cause a much-needed boost. When Remond returned to the States, he was the most celebrated abolitionist on both sides of the Atlantic. Like all other black abolitionists though, he was to be overshadowed, both in his lifetime and in historical memory, by the meteoric rise and success of his friend and protégé, Frederick Douglass. Nonetheless, the achievements of this modest, talented man were remarkable.

Notes

1 Les Wallace, 'Charles Lenox Remond: The Lost Prince of Abolitionism', in *Negro History Bulletin*, vol. 40, no. 3 (May–June 1977), pp. 696–701.
   Wallace refers to Remond's time in the United Kingdom as his 'English tour'.
2 Ibid.
3 Richard W. Leeman, *African-American Orators: A Bio-critical Sourcebook* (Westport, CT: Greenwood Press, 1996), p. 302.
4 Ibid., p. 304.
5 Charles Remond, London, to Charles Bennet Ray, 30 June 1840, reprinted in the *Liberator*, 16 October 1840.
6 Garrison to Helen Garrison, 17 May 1840, William Lloyd Garrison, *The Letters of William Lloyd Garrison. A House Dividing against Itself*, vol. 2 (Cambridge, MA: Harvard University Press, 1971), p. 612.
7 'Letter from Charles L. Remond, London', *The Colored American*, 30 June 1840, reprinted in the *Liberator*, 16 October 1840.
8 *Proceedings of the World Anti-Slavery Convention* (London: British and Foreign Anti-Slavery Society, 1841), p. 15. Amongst other issues, O'Connell spoke out against salt tax and the enforced growing of opium, *Proceedings*, pp. 35–6.
9 Ibid., p. 11.
10 Ibid., pp. 13, 30.
11 *Letters of Garrison*, vol. 2, p. 654.
12 'Letter from Charles L. Remond, London', *The Colored American*, 30 June 1840, reprinted in the *Liberator*, 16 October 1840.
13 Lucretia Mott, *Slavery and 'The Woman Question'. Lucretia Mott's Diary of Her Visit to Great Britain to Attend the World's Anti-Slavery Convention of 1840*, ed. Frederick B. Tolles (PA: Friends' Historical Association & Friends' Historical Society, 1952), pp. 19–20.
14 *Proceedings*, p. 13.
15 Douglas H. Maynard, 'The World's Anti-Slavery Convention of 1840', in *The Mississippi Valley Historical Review*, vol. 47, no. 3 (Dec. 1960), 452–71, p. 463.
16 *Proceedings*, p. 13.
17 'Letter from Charles L. Remond, London', *The Colored American*, 30 June 1840, reprinted in the *Liberator*, 16 October 1840.
18 'Letter from C. L. Remond, EDINBURGH, 21 September 1840', the *Liberator*, 23 October 1840.
19 Within weeks of being in England, Remond wrote to his friend, Ray, 'prejudice … this hydra-headed personage, thanks be to God, has but few advocates in this country; if any, I have it to learn', *The Colored American*, 30 June 1840.
20 *Proceedings of a Public Meeting for the formation of The Northern Central British India Society held in the Corn Exchange, Manchester, on Wednesday evening, 26 August 1840* (Manchester, printed at Society's office, 1840), p. 1.
21 'Important Anti-Slavery meeting at Ipswich', *The Suffolk Chronicle; or Weekly General Advertiser & County Express*, 2 January 1841.

Charles Lenox Remond (1810–1873) 101

22 'Letter from C.L. Remond. EDINBURGH, 21 September 1840', the *Liberator*, 23 October 1840.

23 The proceedings appeared in *The British and Foreign Anti-Slavery Reporter*, 19 May 1841, xxxvii, vol. 2, no. 10; 'Charles Lenox Remond, "Slavery as It Concerns the British"', was reprinted in the *Liberator*, 9 July 1841.

24 'Letter from Charles L. Remond', *Liberator*, 21 May 1841.

25 Samuel Haughton, *Memoir of James Haughton: With Extracts from His Private and Published Letters* (Dublin: E. Ponsonby, 1877), p. 294.

26 'British India', *Freeman's Journal*, 22 July 1841.

27 Ibid.

28 Ibid.

29 Garrison had also stayed there in 1840.

30 'Anti-Slavery Meetings', *Freeman's Journal*, 5 August 1841.

31 For example, 'ANTI-SLAVERY MEETINGS', *Kerry Examiner*, 10 August 10, 1841, this paper was a supporter of abolition; 'Hibernian Anti-Slavery Society', *Nenagh Guardian*, 14 August 1841.

32 'Anti-Slavery Meetings', *Freeman's Journal*, 5 August 1841.

33 Ibid.

34 'The Anti-Slavery Cause. Slavery in America', *Nenagh Guardian*, 11 August 1841.

35 'Hibernian Anti -Slavery Society', *Dublin Morning Register*, 9 August 1841.

36 'The Anti-Slavery Cause. Slavery in America', *Nenagh Guardian*, 11 August 1841.

37 Ibid.

38 Ibid.

39 Ibid.

40 'Remond in Ireland', Letter from Richard Webb, Kilkee, to Garrison, 28 August 1841, reprinted in the *Liberator*, 24 September 1841.

41 Ibid.

42 Liam Hogan, 'Treat the Coloured People as Your Equals': Charles Lenox Remond in Limerick and the Failure of the Anti-Slavery Irish Address'. Available at:https://hcommons.org/members/liamhogan/.

43 'Slavery. An Irish Question Indeed', *Tuam Herald*, 12 December 1840. Handbills urging emigration were distributed in the city, 'Is Ireland to be Made a Slave Market?', *Freeman's Journal*, 9 December 1840.

44 Richard S. Harrison, 'Irish Quaker Perspectives on the Anti-Slavery Movement', in *The Journal of the Friends Historical Society*, vol. 56, no. 2 (1991), p. 117. Available at: https://journals.sas.ac.uk/index.php/fhs/article/view/3542.

45 'From the *Limerick (Irish) Reporter* of Aug. 24. Slavery in America', the *Liberator*, 24 September 1841.

46 Ibid.

47 Ibid.

48 Edward E. Cleal, *The Story of Congregationalism in Surrey* (London: James Clarke & Co., 13 & 14 Fleet Street, 1908), p. 197. Townley retired in 1846, but, according to his obituary, returned to distribute 'English bounty' during the Famine, *The Evangelical Magazine and Missionary Chronicle*, vol. 34 (1856), p. 654.

49 'Mr. Charles Lenox Remond', *Limerick Reporter*, 27 August 1841.

50 'Letter from Webb', the *Liberator*, 24 September 1841.

51 Ibid.

52 'Mr. Charles Lenox Remond', *Limerick Reporter*, 27 August 1841.

53 Ibid.

54 'Letter from Webb', *Liberator*, 24 September 1841.

55 https://medium.com/@Limerick1914/treat-the-coloured-people-as-your-equals-charles-lenox-remond-in-limerick-and-the-failure-of-e9e30ec87ec8.

56 'Negro Slavery', *Limerick Chronicle*, 8 September 1841.

102 *Charles Lenox Remond (1810–1873)*

57 Ibid.
58 Ibid., No title, 11 September 1841.
59 'THE ANTI SLAVERY CAUSE: Emigration TO TEXAS', *Limerick Chronicle*, 24 November 1841.
60 Ibid.
61 Harisson, 'Irish Quaker Perspectives', pp. 106–25.
62 Ibid., p. 107.
63 Nini Rodgers, 'Ireland and the Black Atlantic in the Eighteenth Century', in *Irish Historical Studies*, vol. 32, no. 126 (Nov. 2000), pp. 174–92.
64 'Anti-Slavery Lectures', *Southern Reporter and Cork Commercial Courier*, 28 September 1841. During his lecture, Remond referred to Haiti—the first Black Republic—in positive terms. While in Britain and Ireland, he sometimes lectured alongside a M. L'Instant from 'Hayti', who was described as Remond's friend. L'Instant de Pradine had written a prize-winning essay, 'Sur les moyens d'extirper les Préjugés des Blancs contre la coleur des Africaines et des Sang-melés'. In 1857, he (now Baron Pradine) was appointed Minister to London. There, he continued with his anti-slavery activities.
65 'Anti-Slavery Lectures', *Southern Reporter and Cork Commercial Courier*, 28 September 1841. The meeting was held in the Court House.
66 Ibid.
67 Ibid.
68 Ibid., 'CORK ANTI-SLAVERY SOCIETY', 14 October 1841.
69 'Anti-Slavery Movements Ireland', *Kendal Mercury*, 2 October 1841.
70 Remond, Dublin, to Garrison, 2 October 1841.
71 *Liberator*, 24 September 1841.
72 'Temperance Union', *Dublin Evening Post*, 9 October 1841.
73 'HIBERNIAN ANTI-SLAVERY SOCIETY', *Nenagh Guardian*, 16 October 1841.
74 'HIBERNIAN ANTI-SLAVERY SOCIETY', *Freeman's Journal*, 9 October 1841, 11 October 1841.
75 'HIBERNIAN ANTI-SLAVERY SOCIETY', *Statesman and Dublin Christian Record*, 12 October 1841.
76 'IRELAND. Hibernian Anti-Slavery Society', Redmond's speech was reprinted in the *Liberator*, 19 November 1841.
77 Ibid.
78 'Hibernian Anti-Slavery Society', *Nenagh Guardian*, 16 October 1841.
79 Sean Farrell, 'Going to Extremes: Anti-Catholicism and Anti-Slavery in Early Victorian Belfast', in *European Romantic Review*, vol. 28, no. 4 (2017), pp. 461–72.
80 His first lecture took place on 13 October, in a secular venue, and was reported by the Catholic pro-O'Connell *Vindicator* on 16 October 1841. The remainder of his lectures were in Protestant churches.
81 Daniel Ritchie, *Isaac Nelson: Radical Abolitionist, Evangelical Presbyterian, and Irish Nationalist* (Liverpool University Press, 2018), p. 55.
82 'To editor of the *News-Letter*', Belfast *News-Letter*, 25 December 1840.
83 'Hibernian Anti-Slavery Society', *Belfast Commercial Chronicle*, 14 August 1841.
84 'Lecture on Slavery', advertisement, *Northern Whig*, 12 October 1841.
85 Advertisement, Belfast *News-Letter*, 12 October 1841.
86 Ibid., MR. REMOND's LECTURE ON SLAVERY', 15 October 1841.
87 Ibid.
88 'Anti-Slavery Lecture', *Northern Whig*, 14 October 1841.
89 'Anti-Slavery Lecture', *Belfast Commercial Chronicle*, 16 October 1841.
90 'MR. REMOND's LECTURE ON SLAVERY', Belfast *News-Letter*, 15 October 1841.
91 Ibid.

Charles Lenox Remond (1810–1873)   103

92 Probably the Meeting House on Alfred Street. It had cellars for the stabling of horses. Edgar (1798–1866) was a Presbyterian minister and a social activist. He is sometimes attributed with being the original founder of the temperance movement in Ireland, pre-dating the better-known Father Mathew by ten years. See: *Dictionary of Ulster Biography*: www.newulsterbiography.co.uk/index.php/home/viewPerson/2007.

93 'ON SLAVERY', *Belfast Commercial Chronicle*, 16 October 1841.

94 'MR REMOND'S SECOND LECTURE ON SLAVERY IN AMERICA', Belfast *News-Letter*, 19 October 1841.

95 Ibid.

96 'Lecture on American Slavery', *Belfast Commercial Chronicle*, 20 October 1841.

97 'LECTURES on AMERICAN SLAVERY', *Northern Whig*, 21 October 1841.

98 'American Slavery', *Belfast Commercial Chronicle*, 23 October 1841.

99 'Lectures on American Slavery', *Northern Whig*, 21 October 1841. It is possible that Remond did mention O'Connell on other occasions but that the Protestant press did not report these comments.

100 'American Slavery', from the *Ulster Times*, reprinted in the *Northern Whig*, 23 October 1841: Anti-Slavery Collection in Boston Public Library, Digital copy at: www.digitalcommonwealth.org/search/commonwealth:2v23x021t.

101 This lecture took place on 21 October 1841.

102 'American slavery', *Northern Whig*, 23 October 1841.

103 'Soiree: TO Mr. REMOND', Belfast *News-Letter*, 26 October 1841.

104 No title, *Waterford Mail*, 27 October 1841.

105 'ANTI SLAVERY SOIREE', *Belfast Commercial Chronicle*, 23 October 1841.

106 'Soiree: TO Mr. REMOND', Belfast *News-Letter*, 26 October 1841.

107 Fergus O'Ferrall, 'Daniel O'Connell and Henry Cooke: The Conflict of Civil and Religious Liberty in Modern Ireland', in *The Irish Review*, no. 1 (1986), pp. 20–7, 25.

108 See, Christine Kinealy (ed.), *Lives of Victorian Political Figures: Daniel O'Connell* (London: Pickering and Chatto, 2007), pp. 119–21, 127–56; Henry Cooke, *The Repealer Repulsed. A Correct Narrative of the Rise and Progress of the Repeal Invasion of Ulster* (Belfast: William McComb, 1841).

109 'MR. REMOND'S FIFTH AND LAST LECTURE ON AMERICAN SLAVERY', Belfast *News-Letter*, 29 October 1841. It was actually his sixth lecture in Belfast and took place on Tuesday, 26 October.

110 Ibid.

111 Ibid.

112 'Hibernian Anti-Slavery Society', *Warder and Dublin Weekly Mail*, 16 October 1841.

113 "Charles Lenox Remond', 'Anti-Slavery Lectures in Waterford', from a Waterford paper, the *Liberator*, 17 September 1841.

114 'ADDRESS OF THE CORK LADIES' ANTI-SLAVERY SOCIETY TO THEIR FELLOW COUNTRY-WOMEN & COUNTRYMEN', *Cork Examiner*, 14 September 1842.

115 'Anti-Slavery Bazaar', *Northern Whig*, 4 November 1841.

116 'American Slavery and Prejudice against Colour', *Manchester Times*, 27 November 1841.

117 'Arrival of the Irish Remonstrance against Slavery, with its 60,000 Signatures, in Boston', quoted in *Nenagh Guardian*, reprinted in the *Liberator*, 1 April 1842.

118 Ibid.

119 Ibid.

120 'NOTICES. TENTH ANNUAL MEETING OF THE MASSACHUSETTS A.S. SOCIETY', the *Liberator*, 21 January 1842.

121 Ibid., 'From the *Herald of Freedom*, of the 4th instant', 18 February 1842.

122 Ibid.

104 *Charles Lenox Remond (1810–1873)*

123 Ibid., 'GREAT MEETING IN FANEUIL HALL', 4 February 1842.

124 Ibid.

125 Ibid., 'From the *Herald of Freedom*, of the 4th instant', 18 February 1842.

126 Ibid., 'Arrival of the Irish Remonstrance against Slavery, with its 60,000 Signatures, in Boston', quoted in *Nenagh Guardian*, reprinted in the *Liberator*, 1 April 1842.

127 Ibid.

128 'The House "Gag Rule"', United States House of Representatives: https://history. house.gov/Historical-Highlights/1800-1850/The-House-of-Representatives.

129 W. Caleb McDaniel, 'Repealing Unions: American Abolitionists, Irish Repeal, and the Origins of Garrisonian Disunionism', in *Journal of the Early Republic*, vol. 28, no. 2 (Summer, 2008), pp. 243–69, 265–6.

130 John Collins' birth and death dates are unknown. In abolition history, he is regarded as something of a maverick, he shortly after this becoming a socialist who promoted free love and communal living. Douglass complained about having to work with him in 1843: https://freethought-trail.org/profiles/profile:collins-john-anderson/.

131 Joann P. Krieg, 'Walt Whitman and the Irish'. The Walt Whitman Archive at: https://whitmanarchive.org/criticism/current/anc.00160.html.

132 The French newspaper was *Galignani's Messenger*. Reported in 'American Slavery', *Nenagh Guardian*, editorial, 16 April 1842.

133 'Slavery in America. Arrival of the Irish Remonstrance against Slavery', *Nenagh Guardian*, 26 February 1842.

134 Christine Kinealy, *Daniel O'Connell and Anti-Slavery. The Saddest People the Sun Sees* (London: Routledge, 2011), p. 97.

135 Garrison to Richard Allen, 2 July 1842, *Letters of Garrison* (vol. iii), p. 92.

136 Ibid., Garrison to Abel Brown, 18 March 1842, p. 56.

137 Ibid., Garrison to George Benson, 22 March 1842, p. 61.

138 'GRAND MEETING IN ALBANY', the *Liberator*, 25 March 1842.

139 'AMERICAN SLAVERY', *Freeman's Journal*, 15 October 1841.

140 Garrison to Richard Allen, 2 July 1842, *Letters of Garrison* (vol. iii), p. 92.

141 McDaniel, 'Repealing Unions', pp. 243–69.

142 'The Rights of Colored Citizens when Travelling', *Speech to the Legislative Committee of the Mass. House of Representatives*, 22 February 1842, quoted in *Liberator*, 25 February 1842.

143 'NOTICES. ANTI-SLAVERY LECTURES, AT AMORY HALL', the *Liberator*, 3 February 1843.

144 Ibid., 'Letter from Charles Lenox Remond', 22 September 1843.

145 Ibid., 'Letter to the editor of the Liberator', 'Prejudice against Color', from the *Clinton (Ohio) Republican*, 13 October 1843.

146 Ibid., 'DOUGLASS AND REMOND', 'Glorious Doings', from the Pittsburgh *Spirit of Liberty*, 24 November 1843.

147 Partial letter from Richard Davis Webb to Maria Weston Chapman, Anti-Slavery Collection, BPL, Available at: www.digitalcommonwealth.org/search/common wealth:qz20v631d.

148 The question was posed in the *Daily Bee*, 'MY DEAR FRIEND, W.L. GAR-RISON', the *Liberator*, 2 December 1842.

149 Ibid., 'Glorious Doings', from the Pittsburgh *Spirit of Liberty*, 24 November 1843.

150 Martin Delaney named his second son, Chares Lenox Remond (his first son was Toussaint L'Ouverture), William J. Simmons, *Men of Mark: Eminent, Progressive and Rising* (Cleveland, Ohio: Geo. M. Rewell & Co., 1887), p. 1008.

151 'TWENTY-FIRST ANNIVERSARY', *National Anti-Slavery Standard*, 20 May 1854.

152 Henry Louis Gates, Jr. and Evelyn Brooks Higginbotham (eds.), *African American Lives* (Oxford University Press, 2004), p. 708.

Charles Lenox Remond (1810–1873)   105

153 'APPOINTMENTS. SUSAN B. ANTHONY, of Rochester', the *Liberator*, 14 November 1856; Ibid., 'GRATIFYING TESTIMONY', 20 February 1857; Ibid., 'SALLIE HOLLEY, an Agent of the American Anti-Slavery', 4 June 1858.
154 Patrick G. Wheaton and Celeste M. Condit, 'Charles Lenox Remond (1810–1873), Abolitionist, Reform Activist', in *African-American Orators: a Bio-critical Sourcebook*, ed. Richard W. Leeman (Westport, CT: Greenwood Press, 1996), p. 303.
155 Ibid.
156 Wendell Phillips Garrison, Francis Jackson, *William Lloyd Garrison, 1805–1879: The Story of His Life Told by His Children* (New York: Century Co., 1885), pp. 253–54.
157 Carter G. Woodson, *Negro Orators and Their Orations* (New York: Simon and Schuster, 2016), p. 126.
158 Gates, *African American Lives*, p. 708.
159 Woodson reprinted the whole of Remond's 'eloquent appeal' on behalf of enslaved people, made before the Hibernian Anti-Slavery Society in Dublin. Woodson suggests it took place on 19 November 1841, which was the date it was reprinted in the *Liberator*. The meeting took place in Dublin on 11 October 1841, p. 130.
160 'Lecture on slavery', *Belfast Commercial Chronicle*, 13 October 1841.
161 'Ireland. Hibernian Anti-Slavery Society', the *Liberator*, 19 November 1841.

4 Frederick Douglass (1818–1895)

'Agitate, Agitate, Agitate!'

When Frederick Douglass, a 27-year-old fugitive slave, arrived in Dublin in August 1845, he did not anticipate that within four months he would feel transformed, having spent the happiest time of his life in the company of Irish abolitionists. Nor could he have known that his time in Ireland would prove to be an important step to his becoming an international champion of human rights. The success of Douglass's tour in Ireland, and the lessons he learned there, meant that on his return to the United States, Douglass became one of the most respected and renowned transatlantic abolitionists. Moreover, he became the black abolitionist against whom all others who crossed the Atlantic would be measured.

Early life

Douglass had been born into enslavement in Maryland, with the given name of Frederick Augustus Washington Bailey. He did not know his precise date of birth, calculating that he had been born in 1817 or 1818. He never knew who his father was, although he suspected it was the 'owner' of his mother, Harriet. Young Frederick was raised by his grandmother, only seeing his mother occasionally, she dying in 1825 or 1826. In 1827, he became the property and companion of a young boy, Thomas Auld. Around this time, he was taught the rudiments of reading by Thomas's mother, Sophia.[1] Teaching slaves to read was illegal and Sophia stopped at her husband's insistence, Hugh Auld, warning that if a slave could read and write:

> … there would be no keeping him. It would forever unfit him to be a slave. He would at once become unmanageable, and of no value to his master. As to himself, it could do him no good, but a great deal of harm. It would make him discontented and unhappy.[2]

Frederick realized that literacy would provide a pathway to self-liberation and so he surreptitiously persisted in learning to read. Aged about 12, he came across a copy of the *Columbian Orator*, a standard text in schools and one that included some of the greatest speeches ever made. One that particularly impressed Frederick

Frederick Douglass (1818–1895)   107

was by an Irish patriot, Richard Brinsley Sheridan, which had provided 'a bold denunciation of slavery, and a powerful vindication of human rights'.[3] To Frederick, it was an early insight into the struggles that Irish people were facing in trying to achieve their independence while concurrently demanding social justice for all oppressed peoples. Despite the risks, Frederick knew that he could not remain enslaved as 'The silver trumpet of freedom had roused my soul to eternal wakefulness'.[4] His determination was strengthened by an encounter with some Irish men, when Frederick was working on the docks in Baltimore:

> one of them came to me and asked me if I were a slave. I told him I was. He asked, 'Are ye a slave for life?' I told him that I was. The good Irishman seemed to be deeply affected by the statement. He said to the other that it was a pity so fine a little fellow as myself should be a slave for life. He said it was a shame to hold me. They both advised me to run away to the north; that I should find friends there, and that I should be free.[5]

In 1836, Frederick, with five other slaves, plotted to escape north to the free states, but the plan was uncovered and they were jailed briefly. A further attempt in 1838, assisted by a free black woman, Anna Murray, was successful. Frederick arrived in New York in September. He sent for Anna so that they could be married and he then changed his surname to Douglass.[6] Douglass would subsequently claim that his determination to escape had been inspired by his encounters with different Irishmen.[7]

The newly married couple moved to New Bedford, a largely Quaker community, where Douglass found work on the docks. There, he started to read the *Liberator*, the abolitionist paper founded by William Lloyd Garrison in Boston in 1831, and:

> I got a pretty correct idea of the principles, measures and spirit of the anti-slavery reform. I took right hold of the cause. I could do but little; but what I could, I did with a joyful heart, and never felt happier than when in an anti-slavery meeting.[8]

Douglass was persuaded to attend and speak at a large anti-slavery meeting to be held in Nantucket in August 1841, but did so reluctantly as, 'I felt myself a slave, and the idea of speaking to white people weighed me down'.[9] Douglass's compelling life-story and style of speaking mesmerized the audience, which included Garrison. Parker Pillsbury, a radical abolitionist minister, was also present and confirmed that Douglass started off nervously, becoming more confident as he spoke. The 'enchantment' felt by the audience, including Garrison, arose because:

> Before us stood one trophy, self-delivered, self-redeemed from our chattel slave system, then seething with all the terrors of the second death. And why should not we have rejoiced then and there? For that proved none other than the baptismal, the consecrating service of Frederick Douglass into the life-work and ministry which he has since so wondrously fulfilled.[10]

108 *Frederick Douglass (1818–1895)*

Garrison invited Douglass to lecture on behalf of the American Anti-Slavery Society for a trial period of a few months, but this soon became permanent. He was the first fugitive slave to hold such a position. Charles Lenox Remond was the only other black lecturer employed by the Anti-Slavery Society and the two men quickly became friends. Remond had recently returned from Ireland with a petition signed by almost 70,000 Irish men and women on behalf of abolition, and Douglass had been present in Faneuil Hall at its unveiling.[11] Regardless of Douglass's inexperience, he quickly rose to become one of the stars of the abolition circuit. The experienced abolitionist Nathaniel Peabody Rogers, who heard Douglass speak shortly after his appointment, was effusive in his praise:

> This is an extraordinary man. He was cut out for a hero. In a rising for Liberty he would have been a Toussaint or a Hamilton … A commanding person— over six feet, we should say, in height, and of most manly proportions. His head would strike a phrenologist amid a sea of them at Exeter Hall, and his voice would ring like a trumpet in the field. Let the South congratulate herself that he is a *fugitive*. It would not have been safe for her if he had hung around the plantations a year or two longer … As a speaker he has few equals. It is not declamation—but oratory, power of debate … He has wit, argument, sarcasm, pathos—all that first-rate men show in their master efforts. His voice is highly melodious and rich, and his enunciation quite elegant, and yet he has been but two or three years out of the house of bondage.[12]

Douglass proved to be so articulate that doubts were raised concerning the authenticity of his life story, especially as he avoided providing precise names or places as a way of protecting his identity. To counter such accusations, Douglass decided to write his autobiography, complete with names and places. The publication of Douglass's *Narrative* in May 1845 propelled him to the forefront of abolitionist debate. It also put him in danger of being recaptured under the Fugitive Slave Act of 1793. For his safety, he was persuaded to travel to the United Kingdom, leaving his family and friends behind. For Douglass's mentor, Garrison, a positive benefit would be that the new star of the abolitionist movement would re-energize the transatlantic links that he regarded as necessary for success.

Ireland

On 16 August 1845, Douglass sailed from Boston, bound for Liverpool aboard the *Cambria*. He was accompanied by James Buffum, an abolitionist from Massachusetts.[13] Buffum, a friend of Garrison since 1831, had physically defended Douglass when he had been grabbed off a railway carriage and attacked by a mob in 1841.[14] Buffum had also raised most of the money for Douglass's fare, the remainder coming from sales of the *Narrative*.[15] After only two days spent in the bustling port of Liverpool, the two men sailed to Dublin. Douglass's reason for travelling to Ireland was that a Dublin abolitionist printer, Richard Davis Webb, had agreed to publish an Irish version of the *Narrative*, as a way of providing Douglass with funds during his stay.[16] But what had started as a pragmatic reason for travelling to Ireland quickly became more personal, when Douglass encountered the ardency of Irish abolitionism. Unexpectedly also, for the first time in his life, he felt safe and the equal of white men. When he left Ireland in January 1846, during his four months in the country, and as part of his own private journey, he realized 'the chattel had become a man'.[17]

The day after he arrived in Dublin, Douglass wrote to Garrison saying that he was now 'safe in old Ireland'.[18] Douglass's reaction was not unusual amongst American abolitionists for whom Ireland held a special place in the anti-slavery struggle. Despite not being affiliated to any anti-slavery society, Irish abolition was indelibly linked with the charismatic Daniel O'Connell. O'Connell had won international attention when, in 1829, he had been successful in achieving Catholic Emancipation, that is, in forcing the British government to agree to allow Catholics to be Members of the British Parliament. This achievement won him the title, the 'Liberator'. Since 1824, O'Connell had also been a vociferous supporter of abolition, favouring an immediate and total ending to slavery throughout the world.[19] Following his own election to the House of Commons in 1829, he became a powerful parliamentary advocate for the complete abolition of slavery. In 1832, when asked by a pro-slavery group of merchants and politicians to remain silent on this issue in return for their support on Irish issues, he had responded:

> Gentlemen, God knows that I speak for the saddest people the sun sees, but may my right hand forget its cunning and may my tongue cleave to the roof of my mouth before, to help Ireland, I keep silent on the negro question.[20]

Both Douglass and Garrison were admirers of the Irish man. Douglass claimed that he had first become aware of O'Connell in 1838 when the Liberator had refused to shake the hand of the American Ambassador to Britain, on the grounds that he was a slave 'breeder'.[21] Garrison frequently reprinted O'Connell's denunciations of slavery in the columns of his paper. In March 1842, the *Liberator* published a ten-year retrospective of O'Connell's speeches, with the prediction, 'They will scathe like lightening and smite like thunderbolts. No man in the wide world has spoken so strongly against the soul-drivers of this land as O'Connell'.[22] In the Preface to the first edition of Douglass's *Narrative*, Garrison wrote, 'DANIEL O'CONNELL, the distinguished advocate of universal emancipation, and the mightiest champion of prostrate, but not conquered Ireland'.[23]

In Dublin, Douglass was welcomed by supporters of Garrison. Consequently, he had extensive contact with James Haughton, of whom Douglass said, 'there is not to be found a truer, or more devoted, vigilant, hard-working, persevering abolitionist on this side the Atlantic'.[24] Haughton was President of the Hibernian Anti-Slavery Society, which he had founded, together with Richard Webb and Richard Allen, in 1837.[25] Allen was its Secretary.[26] The Hibernian Society was closer to Garrison's American Anti-Slavery Society than to the more moderate British and Foreign Anti-Slavery Society. As so many visitors were to do,

110 *Frederick Douglass (1818–1895)*

Douglass and Buffum stayed at the home of Richard Davis Webb and his wife, Hannah Waring Webb.[27] The former, according to Douglass, was, 'the very impersonation of old-fashioned, thorough-going anti-slavery'.[28] Over two decades, the Webbs would open their home to many American abolitionists, including Garrison, Lucretia and James Mott, Henry Wright, William Wells Brown, and Charles and Sarah Remond. The Webbs were Quakers who were committed to many progressive causes, including abolition. The Dublin abolitionists were at the radical end of various reform movements, many of them also supporting world peace, temperance, ending enslavement in British India, women's suffrage and animals' rights. They were opposed to all wars, including the recent Opium War.[29] Their overt commitment to international social justice must have provided Douglass with a sense of comfort as he settled into his life as an exile. After only two weeks in Ireland, Douglass wrote to Garrison, informing him that 'I find myself not treated as a *color*, but as a *man*—not as a thing, but as a child of the common Father of us all'.[30] It was an empowering feeling.

Although Douglass had intended to spend only a few days in Dublin to oversee the publication of the *Narrative* and not to lecture, he accepted an invitation to speak at an abolition meeting. His first public lecture took place on Wednesday, 3 September 1845, when he spoke at the monthly meeting of the Hibernian Anti-Slavery Society in the prestigious Royal Exchange in the centre of Dublin.[31] It was well attended, with local newspapers reporting that the venue was 'crowded to excess', with many people being turned away.[32] Douglass spoke for about forty-five minutes, and was judged to be overwhelmingly successful. He praised Daniel O'Connell's role in the abolition movement, which clearly pleased the audience. The local newspapers provided detailed physical descriptions of the 27-year-old visitor, his demeanour and his oratory powers.[33] Other lectures followed as Douglass extended his stay in Ireland. On 9 and 12 September, he spoke at the Quaker Friends' Meeting House in Dublin.[34] Douglass was especially pleased as he would not have been allowed to speak at a religious venue in the United States. However, his elation was short lived. Douglass's criticism of some of the churches in America—in particular, the Methodist Church—for refusing to speak out against slavery, was regarded as being inappropriate in a place of worship, and so he was not allowed to use this venue again, much to the annoyance of Richard Webb.[35] As a consequence of this decision, Douglass's next lecture on 17 September was held in a new location, the Music Hall in Abbey Street, which could accommodate up to 3,000 people. To defray the expenses, there was an admission fee; 4*d*. for the body of the house, and 2*d*. for the gallery.[36] At Douglass's second lecture in the Music Hall, the Lord Mayor of Dublin, John Arabin, was the Chairperson. Both Douglass and Buffum were subsequently invited to dine with Arabin at his official residence, the Mansion House.[37] Despite the early controversy, Douglass the lecturer had been an overwhelming success in Dublin.

While Douglass was staying in Dublin, Daniel O'Connell returned from his family home in County Kerry. For many American abolitionists, O'Connell was a source of inspiration. Although he had never visited the United States (and refused to do so while slavery continued), engravings of him were sold at the

Frederick Douglass (1818–1895)   111

fund-raising bazaars and his speeches were reported in American newspapers, on each side of the slavery divide.[38] Now aged 70, O'Connell's health was deteriorating, but he continued to agitate for a repeal of the political union with Great Britain and for an ending to slavery. On 29 September, Douglass attended a repeal meeting, to hear his hero speak. Because the hall was so full, Douglass could only observe the proceedings from the back. Nonetheless, he was mesmerized and full of praise for the older man's oratorical skills:

> It seems to me that the voice of O'Connell is enough to calm the most violent passion, even though it were already manifesting itself in a mob. There is a sweet persuasiveness in it, beyond any voice I ever heard. His power over an audience is perfect.[39]

During his lecture, as was his habit, O'Connell spoke at length about American slavery, averring:

> While the canker of negro slavery eats the heart's core of America, she can never be strong; while that remains a plague spot on her institutions, Heaven forbids that any country should prosper which was tainted with that infernal system.[40]

Following O'Connell's speech, the hall had emptied, enabling Douglass to move to the front, where he was introduced to John O'Connell, Daniel's son. John, in turn, introduced him to his father, who invited Douglass on stage to say a few words. Douglass made an impromptu speech that was one of the shortest, but finest, that he made in Ireland. He commenced by saying that one of the reasons he had lingered in Dublin for so long was in the hope of hearing O'Connell speak. He added that:

> he felt bound to say that the expressions of sympathy which he had just heard for his enslaved countrymen, had stirred feelings within him which he could not express. He had often heard of the Liberator when he was a slave in a way that was dear to his heart; he had heard of him in the curses of his masters, and thus he was taught to love him (loud cheers). O'Connell was denounced by the slaveholders in America, as he was denounced by those in this country who hated Repeal. The poor trampled slave of Carolina had heard the name of the Liberator with joy and hope, and he himself had heard the wish that some black O'Connell would yet rise up amongst his countrymen, and cry 'Agitate, agitate, agitate'.[41]

The final three words were a frequent rallying call used by O'Connell, but Douglass made them his own, infusing them with a new and special meaning. Despite subsequent suggestions to the contrary, this was probably the only time that the two men, 27-year-old Douglass and 70-year-old O'Connell, were to meet. At this stage, O'Connell was in the twilight days of his career, with the Repeal

112 *Frederick Douglass (1818–1895)*

movement about to splinter into two opposing factions. Nevertheless, as his speech in Conciliation Hall proved, his passion and eloquence on the issue of anti-slavery remained absolute, and his words continued to resonate and to inspire Douglass, long after he had left Ireland.

Douglass, accompanied by Buffum, left Dublin on 7 October 1845. Although over the succeeding twelve months they returned to Dublin on at least two occasions, Douglass did not give any more public lectures in the city. Assisted by introductions from the Webb family, the two men had been invited to lecture in several other Irish towns and cities. They were initially heading to the city of Cork. As they travelled south, they were accompanied by Richard Webb and Maria Waring, sister of Hannah Webb, and Richard's sister-in-law.[42] The group stopped in Wexford and Waterford to give some impromptu lectures. Each location had an established Quaker community and the Waring sisters had family connections in both places, thus facilitating the Americans' visit.[43] Douglass was well received in both places. A newspaper in Waterford reported:

> Notwithstanding the unfavourable state of the weather, and the short notice which the public had received of the intended meeting, Mr. Douglass, whose manner is highly prepossessing, delivered himself with energy and feeling, and was listened to with marked attention by his auditory, whose sympathies he excited by his faithful recital of the black man's sufferings, and the black man's wrongs. We regret being unable to give any portion of the able lecture of Mr. Douglass. The cause he so ably advocates deserves the support of every friend to humanity—of every Christian, no matter of what denomination.[44]

In Wexford, Douglass praised O'Connell, saying he loved him 'because Mr. O'Connell befriended him when in the grasp of his tyrant slaveholders'.[45]

Douglass then headed to Cork, following the route taken by his friend, Charles Remond, four years earlier. There, he stayed with Thomas and Ann Jennings and their eight children for a month, at their fashionable home and business premises on Brown Street, close to the River Lee.[46] Thomas, an Anglican, was the manufacturer of 'non-intoxicating' soda water and vinegar.[47] During his stay, Douglass became a close friend of one of his daughters, Isabel Jennings, who was Secretary of the Cork Ladies' Anti-Slavery Society. They continued to correspond for many years after Douglass had departed from Ireland.[48] While in the city, Douglass met Father Mathew, 'the apostle of temperance'. Douglass, himself a champion of temperance, was invited to the priest's home for breakfast. Douglass admitted to being surprised by how simply the priest lived, observing privately he believed it was, 'rather too plain, I thought, for so great a man'.[49] Sadly, the men's friendship proved to be short-lived. In 1849, Douglass attacked Father Mathew for not speaking out against slavery during the priest's visit to America.[50]

While staying in Cork, Douglass visited Youghal, a small fishing village north of the city. No newspaper account of his visit appears to have survived, but a Cork abolitionist wrote that:

Frederick Douglass (1818–1895)   113

In company with Mr. William Martin, of this city, Frederick Douglass visited Youghall [sic]. They had an overflowing meeting. When Frederick Douglass had concluded his address, a vote of thanks was proposed to him, and carried by acclamation.[51]

During his stay in Cork, Douglass gave at least 13 lectures on abolition and on temperance, which were delivered in a mixture of secular and religious venues. His time there was not without controversy. As in Dublin, Douglass had criticized some of the Protestant churches in America for their stance on slavery and their failure to condemn slave holders. He accused several of them of enabling and supporting 'the corrupting influences of slavery'.[52] In turn, several ministers who were present attacked Douglass, accusing him of pandering to a largely Roman Catholic audience, while the Rev. Mackay said that he 'felt offended at the language used by Mr. Douglass'.[53] It was a reminder that even in the relatively safe haven of Ireland, there were deep-rooted sensitivities on the abolition question. In October 1845, while he was in Cork, Douglass learned that he had been 'sold' by his former master, Thomas Auld, to his brother, Hugh Auld, perhaps in response to his new-found notoriety and popularity. The sale price was $100.[54] Regardless of his success in Ireland and his new sense of freedom, 3,000 miles away, Douglass remained enslaved. Moreover, there was a price on his head and, under American law, he remained the property of another man.

Despite some criticisms, Douglass's time in Cork was an overwhelming success, he having made a deep impression on all those he met. Before he left the city, local abolitionists held a soirée in his honour. Placards decorated the room, including one that said, 'Cead mille failte'. They were later sent to Anna, Douglass's wife, as a gift from the women of Cork.[55] Moreover, the Mayor of the city, Richard Dowden, sent him a ring—the first ring that Douglass had ever owned. In a letter thanking Dowden, Douglass described the gift as 'representative of the holy feelings with which you espoused and advocated my humble cause'. He added, 'I shall ever think of my visit with pleasure'. Douglass took to wearing the ring on the little finger of his right hand.[56]

From Cork, Douglass travelled to Limerick, on the west coast. Previously, Douglass had been accompanied by Buffum, but they had parted ways in Cork, under tense circumstances.[57] Despite the older man being the more experienced lecturer, the newspapers accounts made it clear that the former slave overshadowed the white abolitionist in terms of popular appeal. Douglass was aware of this fact, admitting to a friend in America, 'My old friend Buffum finds the tables turned on him completely—the people lavish nearly all of their attention on the negro'.[58] Consequently, Douglass travelled to Limerick alone. He spent over three weeks there, staying with the Fisher family. The Fishers, who were Quakers, were related to Richard Webb. Benjamin Clark Fisher was a successful linen draper and a founding member of the Limerick Anti-Slavery Society. Benjamin had eleven daughters and one son. Douglass struck up a lifelong friendship with Rebecca and Susanna Fisher, who were also fervent abolitionists.[59] Douglass gave only three public lectures in the city. In addition to talking about his own

114   *Frederick Douglass (1818–1895)*

story, he spoke about the current political situation, especially regarding the Annexation of Texas and the Oregon Question.[60]

In Limerick, Douglass unwittingly courted controversy for criticizing a theatre act that had recently been staged in the city—a 'blackface' minstrel act performed by a Mr. Bateman.[61] Bateman's origins were uncertain, with one Irish newspaper referring to him as an American comedian who was touring Ireland, although elsewhere he was referred to as Irish.[62] Another, however, referred to him as the '*n—r* Comedian'.[63] Douglass had taken offence at the minstrel part of his programme. In turn, an editorial in the *Limerick Reporter* criticized Douglass for attacking Bateman 'so bitterly'.[64] Douglass was unrepentant, believing that Bateman and other minstrel performers were presenting an inauthentic view of slavery, in contrast to his attempts to present the authentic version.[65] To emphasize his point, Douglass showed his audience in Limerick a number of instruments that were used to torture slaves.[66]

In both Cork and Limerick, Douglass confronted an issue that clearly bothered him and concerned other visitors who had been enslaved. It was the question of whether the Irish were slaves, the expression being used frequently by nationalists. Douglass explained to an audience in Cork that he regarded himself as,

> A slave, not in the ordinary sense of the term, not in a political sense, but in its real and intrinsic meaning … By the laws of the country whence I came, I was deprived of myself—of my own body, soul, and spirit.[67]

Richard Dowden, the Mayor, further expanded on the difference between the situation of the Irish in Ireland and slaves in America, stating, 'They had many things to do to elevate their own country, but they had not to get rid of the lash, and the privilege they enjoyed of personal freedom they should strive to extend to all mankind'.[68] In his first lecture in Limerick, Douglass returned to the question of Irish 'slavery', challenging the usage of this word by some Irish people. He informed his audience:

> He had been met with the objection that slavery existed in Ireland, and that therefore there was no necessity for describing its character as found in another country (hear, hear). His answer was, that if slavery existed here, it ought to be put down, and the generous in the land ought to rise and scatter its fragments to the winds (loud cheers).—But there was nothing like American slavery on the soil on which he now stood. Negro-slavery consisted not in taking away a man's property, but in making property of him, and in destroying his identity—in treating him as the beasts and creeping things.[69]

From Limerick, Douglass returned to Dublin, again to the Webbs. After a brief stay in the capital city, where he made no public appearances, he travelled to Belfast, in the north of the country. Belfast had a long tradition of involvement with anti-slavery. In 1791, the republican group, the United Irishmen,[70] had welcomed Olaudah Equiano to the town.[71] Unlike the other places that

Frederick Douglass (1818–1895)   115

Douglass had lectured in, where the population had been largely Catholic, the town of Belfast was overwhelming Presbyterian.[72] A further difference was that while anti-slavery societies in the south largely allied with Garrison and the American Anti-Slavery Society, the majority of abolitionists in Belfast were supporters of the British and Foreign Anti-Slavery Society, which was aligned with the American and Foreign Anti-Slavery Society. Douglass skillfully negotiated this divide—perhaps too skillfully for those watching his progress from Boston. However, as Douglass's visit showed (and Remond's and Wright's before his), the Belfast abolitionists were willing to work with Garrisonians.

Douglass left Dublin on 4 December, travelling to Belfast by horse and carriage, as bad weather meant that he had missed his train connection. Before he arrived, notices had been placed around the town and in the local papers announcing his lectures, stating that he had lectured in other parts of Ireland, 'to large assemblies, who were delighted at the powerful eloquence displayed by the talented Lecturer'.[73] Douglass's hosts were two leading members of the Belfast Anti-Slavery Society, James Standfield and Francis Calder.[74] Of Standfield, Douglass wrote, 'I was much pleased with his face and more so with his conversation. I observed a heartiness about him, a little uncommon to those of his age', which he tempered with the comment, 'He was somewhat fearful I might disappoint them'.[75] The Society paid for Douglass to stay at the Victoria Hotel. Staying in a public venue as opposed to a private home was not as pleasant as Douglass might have anticipated. He confided in Webb that his lodgings were 'comfortable', but:

> The friends have placed me here they say to make me accessible to everyone that wishes to see me. They have gained their purpose thus far 'still they come'. I can thus far truly say that everyone that hears me seems to think that he has a special claim on my time to listen to his opinion of me, to tell me just how much he condemned and how much he approved—very well, let them come. I am ready for them although it is not the most agreeable.[76]

Douglass also informed Webb privately that:

> here as elsewhere the enemies of anti-slavery have been busy in creating prejudice against me on the grounds of my heterodoxy. From what I can learn, the Methodist minister in Cork as well as Dublin have written here against me. Do you see mine will be no bed of roses?[77]

Fearing that religious venues might be closed against him as they had been in Dublin, he was particularly pleased to find that he was allowed to lecture in a number of Protestant churches: on the first night, he spoke in an Independent Presbyterian Church, the second lecture took place in the Wesleyan Methodist Chapel, Donegall Square, the third, in the Presbyterian Meeting House, Donegall Street, and the fourth in the Presbyterian Church on Rosemary Street. By occupying these spaces, Douglass believed that he was striking a direct blow at American Protestant churches who supported slavery.[78]

116   *Frederick Douglass (1818–1895)*

Douglass's first lecture in Belfast took place on 5 December. He started off with his hallmark humility, saying 'He felt considerable embarrassment in thus standing before intelligent people, for the purpose of instructing them'.[79] He then explained to his audience why their involvement was so important:

> It will pain the conscience and anguish the heart of the slaveholder, to hear that, in the sacred soil of the Emerald Isle, the inhabitants of the Irish Athens, the emporium of commerce and seat of enterprise, interested themselves on behalf of the poor persecuted negro.[80]

He finished with a blistering attack on the country of his birth, perhaps the most damning that he had so far made:

> Let the Americans, when they come here, feel that they are not looked upon as Christians, while they continue to trade so largely in the bodies of their fellowmen. He wanted the people here, and everywhere, to rise up, in indignant remonstrance, to tell the Americans to tear down their star—spangled banner, and, with its folds, bind up the bleeding wounds of the lacerated slaves. (Great cheering).[81]

As had been the case in other venues, the Mayor of the town, Andrew Mulholland, chaired some of the lectures. Douglass's success in Belfast also extended to book sales, he informing Webb, 'Well all my books went last night at one blow. I want more. I want more'.[82] Writing the next day, Douglass predicted that he could sell over 100 books in one evening.[83] Douglass's visit was not without some issues. He was disappointed to find that his reception in the town was not as unreservedly open as it had been elsewhere in Ireland. Douglass made a public allusion to this treatment in the course of his lecture on 23 December, when he claimed that for the first time, he had been asked to provide credentials. Additionally, rumours were circulating that he was an imposter.[84] This skepticism was in strong contrast to the warm welcomes that he had received in other parts of the country and must have been a reminder to Douglass of the initial reason for writing his *Narrative*.

In Belfast, Douglass became caught up in the controversy regarding the Free Church of Scotland's acceptance of money from American slave-holders. The 'Send back the Money' campaign was to become a major part of Douglass's mission over the next year and would polarize the British and Irish abolition movements. Only a few weeks earlier, Douglass had stated that he did not want to be involved in this issue. The reason why he had changed his mind appeared to be rooted in the town's strong Presbyterian links. Immediately on Douglass's arrival in Belfast, Calder had given him leaflets about the Free Church, leading Douglass to the realization, 'It will be necessary to say much about them here'.[85] Two days later, he wrote to Webb that Belfast:

> is the very hot bed of Presbyterianism and free churchism, [and] a blow can be struck here, more effectively than in any other part of Ireland. One nail drove in a sure place is better than a dozen driven at random.

Frederick Douglass (1818–1895) 117

On these grounds, he explained 'I think it will be of the utmost importance that I remain here a much longer time than that allotted in the first instance'.[86] Douglass's uncompromising stand on the 'Send back the money' debate increasingly dominated his public appearances, but it undermined support for him, especially amongst Presbyterians in Belfast. While the local press continued to give extensive coverage to his lectures, the *Banner of Ulster* and the *News-Letter* accused Douglass of damaging the cause of abolition by his attacks on the Free Church.[87] Douglass responded to the criticism by saying: 'It was for her salvation he did it—it was for her purification he did it—it was for the redemption and disenthralment of his race from the chains of slavery he did it'. He also refuted claims that he was opposed to religion, a charge often leveled at followers of Garrison.[88]

In early January 1846, Douglass was joined in Belfast by Buffum, the men having reconciled. Douglass's final anti-slavery event in the town took place on 6 January, when he was honoured with a farewell breakfast by William Sharman Crawford, a progressive member of the British parliament.[89] Several female abolitionists were present and, inspired by Douglass's visit, they formally incorporated themselves into the Belfast Auxiliary Female Anti-Slavery Society. Mary Ann McCracken, sister of United Irishman Henry Joy, who had hosted Equiano in the 1790s, was one of the founding members. During the breakfast, Douglass was presented with a pocket Bible, bound with gold and inscribed, 'Presented by the Belfast Auxiliary to the British and Foreign Anti-Slavery Society'. Despite the controversy that he had courted in the town, Douglass was moved by this gesture, saying 'Wherever else I feel myself a stranger, I will remember I have a home in Belfast'.[90] It was a poignant reminder that the young traveller was a fugitive in his country of birth and denied citizenship there. There was no place that Douglass could call home and his family were 3,000 miles away.

Douglass left Ireland on 10 January, travelling to Scotland where he planned to continue with the 'Send back the money' campaign. He had spent four months in Ireland during which time he had experienced a number of highs and lows. Overall, it had been positive. Douglass had been warmly greeted wherever he went, telling an audience in Cork that 'he had not contemplated such respect at the hands of the Irish people as he received since he landed in this country'.[91] Regardless of any disagreements that had arisen, the telling of his life story and his message about abolition had been overwhelmingly well received. As a writer and a lecturer, he had been praised. Just as importantly, wherever he visited, he had walked the streets in the company of white men and white women, without ever being accosted or insulted. Before departing Ireland, Douglass wrote his fifth letter to Garrison in which he reflected on his time in the 'Emerald Isle'. Regardless of any slights or setbacks, his sense of liberation was palpable, summed up in his phrase, 'I breathe and lo! The chattel becomes a man'.[92] For Douglass, acquiring a sense of identity and of self-worth must have been particularly satisfying because, in so many ways, he defied easy categorization: he was no longer a slave, but he was not free; he was neither fully black nor fully white; he was a husband and a father, but living a solitary existence; he was a public celebrity, but his finances were always precarious.

118   *Frederick Douglass (1818–1895)*

Regardless of these contradictions, in Ireland, Douglass for the first time felt like a man—and that appeared to make all other ambiguities bearable.

For Douglass, his four months in Ireland had been overwhelmingly affirmative. On the eve of his departure from Belfast, however, he reflected on his isolation:

> ... as to nation, I belong to none ... The land of my birth welcomes me to her shores only as a slave, and spurns with contempt the idea of treating me differently. So I am an outcast from the society of my childhood, and an outlaw in the land of my birth.
> **
> I can truly say, I have spent some of the happiest moments of my life since landing in this country ... the entire absence of everything that looked like prejudice against me, on account of the color of my skin—contrasted so strongly with my long and bitter experience in the United States, that I look with wonder and amazement on the transition.[93]

Douglass's new-found independence was perhaps most evident in his handling of the re-publication of the *Narrative*. His initial purpose in travelling to Ireland had been to oversee the first non-American version of the memoir. Only weeks after his arrival, a new edition had been produced, which had quickly sold out, making a second Irish edition necessary. While the first Irish edition of the *Narrative* had been largely a replica of the Boston publication, Douglass, now in Scotland, intervened to ensure that the version produced in 1846 reflected his own interests. The flyleaf of the later edition included a resolution of the Hibernian Anti-Slavery Society welcoming Douglass to Ireland. This was followed by a new image of Douglass and a poem by John Greenleaf Whittier. His other interventions were more substantive, with Douglass effectively taking editorial control of the contents, signifying his sense of independence and determination to control his life story. Both the Boston and first Irish edition had opened with a Preface written by Garrison and a letter of endorsement written by Wendell Phillips—two white abolitionists. This was not unusual because, 'Even though it was desirable for ex-slaves to write their stories, dominant racist doctrine still mandated that relationship be established whereby whites functioned as those who sanctioned black voices.'[94] The pieces by Garrison and Phillips remained but their position was usurped by the inclusion of a Preface written by Douglass himself. In it he proclaimed, 'I am an American slave, who has given my tyrant the slip. I am in the land of liberty, with no man to make me afraid'.[95] More controversially, Douglass wanted to include in the appendix two endorsements praising him by Protestant ministers, Dr Nelson and Dr Drew, who had hosted Douglass when he was in Belfast.[96] Webb advised against this, on the grounds that it might add a sectarian dimension to the *Narrative*, but Douglass prevailed.[97] Shortly afterwards, these two ministers would also add their endorsements to a biography of Benjamin Benson, although neither man had met Benson.[98] All of these changes were indicative that a more confident and independent Douglass had emerged.

Frederick Douglass (1818–1895)   119

Douglass's time in Scotland did not go as smoothly as he had hoped, with the campaign against the Free Church proving divisive. Moreover, being away from his family for so long was taking its toll on his health. Although in his public letters Douglass appeared pleased with his progress, his private letters suggested otherwise. Writing to Garrison in mid-April, in a letter not meant for publication, he admitted 'I long to be at home ... Be it ever so humble, there is no place like home'.[99] In a letter to his 'sister', Harriet Bailey,[100] dated May 1846, he admitted that he had been feeling ill and out of sorts:

> My underlip hung like that of a motherless colt[.] I looked so ugly that I hated to see myself in a glass.
> There was no living for me. I was snappish. I would have kicked my old grans 'dadda'! I was in a terrible mood—'dats a fact! old missus—is you got any ting for a poor n——r to eat!!![101]

Douglass broke his despondent mood by purchasing a second-hand fiddle and 'I had not played ten minutes before I began to feel better ... as lively as a crikit [sic] and as loving as a lamb'.[102] Douglass included in his correspondence to Harriet a letter for his wife, 'Dear Anna'. Anna could not read or write, so he requested Harriet to read it 'over and over again till she can fully understand its contents'.[103]

Douglass, together with James Buffum, returned to Belfast to give a lecture in mid-June. While the two men were warmly received by their abolitionist friends, they were not totally welcomed. The *News-Letter* noted that: 'We perceive by placards posted through the town that Mr. Frederick Douglass has returned to Belfast, after his anti-slavery agitation tour in Scotland, and is about to deliver a public lecture on his favorite theme'.[104] Douglass gave only one lecture in the town.[105] From Belfast, the two men visited Dublin as Buffum, who was about to return home, wanted to say goodbye to his Irish friends. They gave no public lectures in Ireland's capital city, Webb explaining, 'their object being to rest a while after their stormy campaign in Scotland'.[106] From Dublin, Douglass returned to Britain. Without Buffum, his travelling companion for almost year, he was truly alone. In London, Douglass lectured on behalf of the British and Foreign Anti-Slavery Society on several occasions. For Garrison, watching from Boston, the fact that Douglass was consorting with his rival abolitionists was alarming. A public rebuke appeared in the columns of the *Liberator*,

> Considering the hostile position of the London Committee to the American A.S. Society, we are not a little surprised that Douglass should have complied with their invitation to make a speech at the meeting of the British and Foreign Anti-Slavery Society.[107]

Shortly afterwards, Garrison announced that he would be joining Douglass in Britain—ostensibly to accept an invitation to lecture by the Glasgow Anti-Slavery Society. Garrison left Boston on 16 July 1846.[108]

120 *Frederick Douglass (1818–1895)*

As Garrison was making his way across the Atlantic, Douglass returned to Belfast, his visit being timed to coincide with the annual meeting of General Assembly of the Presbyterian Church in Ireland.[109] Only days prior to this, 'after a warm discussion', the General Assembly of the Free Church of Scotland had decided **not** to send back the money.[110] A large part of the Assembly's discussion in Ireland was concerned with slavery, with a committee being appointed to examine the issue in more depth. A local newspaper observed Douglass unobtrusively attending the meetings of the General Assembly, sitting in the public gallery.[111] During his stay, Douglass gave several lectures in the town and its vicinity.[112] Sharman Crawford attended Douglass's lecture in Bangor on 13 July, demonstrating that the visitor still had the support of influential people within Ireland. Moreover, during his introduction, Sharman Crawford referred to Douglass as his 'friend'.[113] At this point, it appeared that this was to be Douglass's final appearance in Belfast as he had no plans to return to Ireland.[114] The arrival of Garrison, however, would force Douglass to change his plans.

Garrison explained that he had agreed to go to Britain on the grounds that his visit would strengthen links between abolitionists on both sides of the Atlantic and so that he could add his voice to the 'Send back the money' campaign. The *Liberator* enlightened its readers further, saying 'From every side, the cry is ever coming up to him, to "come over and help us," with the native logic, the keen sagacity, and the earnest eloquence which mark his public speeches'.[115] An additional, if unspoken, motive was clearly to keep an eye on his protégé, who had been so warmly welcomed by English abolitionists, particularly Garrison's foes, the British and Foreign Anti-Slavery Association. The *Liberator* also announced that after Garrison had attended to business in London, he would tour with Douglass.[116] Garrison's return to British shores pleased his supporters in Dublin. Richard Webb travelled to Liverpool to be part of the group who welcomed him.[117] Following his arrival, Garrison went straight to London, where he stayed with the veteran abolitionist, George Thompson. There, Garrison announced that part of his mission was to found a new anti-slavery league, which would be transatlantic.[118] In London, Garrison was reunited with Douglass and they were joined by their Irish friends, Webb, James Haughton and Richard Allen.[119]

On 17 August 1846, leading British, Irish and American abolitionists met at the 'Crown and Anchor Tavern' in London. Garrison, Douglass, Webb and Haughton were present.[120] The main purpose of the gathering was to create a new transatlantic organization that would be an auxiliary to the American Anti-Slavery Society. Throughout the meeting, Garrison held centre stage, speaking a number of times. In contrast, Douglass was relegated to being a subsidiary speaker. This discrepancy was evident even in press coverage; an American abolitionist newspaper gave extensive coverage of Garrison's speech, followed by the brief observation that, 'Mr. Douglass succeeded him'.[121] To an observer or reader of the newspaper accounts, there could be no doubt that a pecking order had been re-established and that Douglass had been returned to his traditional, auxiliary position—namely, that of being in Garrison's shadow.

Garrison had planned to leave Liverpool on 20 October.[122] Prior to that, he hoped to visit Dublin and Cork, not to lecture, but to see friends in these cities.

Frederick Douglass (1818–1895) 121

At some stage, however, he changed his mind and delayed his return until 4 November.[123] During his extended stay, Garrison lectured with Douglass at venues in England and Scotland. In the latter, the focus on the 'Send back the money' campaign disappointed audiences who wanted to hear about slavery and abolition. As one newspaper pointed out, the gathering was 'technically called an anti-slavery meeting' but, 'the slavery question, of course, was never mooted'.[124] It was not just in Scotland where Douglass and his mentor were disappointing and alienating audiences by their almost exclusive focus on the failings of the Protestant churches. Garrison's visit to Belfast, accompanied by Douglass, proved to be one of the most controversial aspects of his whole visit, with even Douglass's loyal allies, Standfield and Nelson, seeking to create distance between themselves and Garrison. Douglass and Garrison reached Belfast at the beginning of October 1846. Even before the two men arrived in the town, several local newspapers expressed reservations about the visit. They were mostly concerned about Garrison's sustained and embittered attacks on many Protestant churches. The *News-Letter* was in the vanguard of criticizing Garrison, condemning him for his 'ceaseless enmity' to the Protestant evangelical churches.[125] Tellingly, Garrison's first talk in Ireland took place not in a religious building, but in the Belfast Music Hall.

On 3 October, Garrison, with Douglass at his side, gave a lunch-time lecture in the Music Hall. Attendance was low, with only an estimated 220 people present, many of who were female. Just as significant, there was only one minister on the platform party. Before the lecture took place, Garrison had been taunted by the editor of the *News-Letter* for his 'infidel' sympathies, and the fact that no church had offered him space to speak.[126] Throughout the meeting, Garrison took the lead, with Douglass simply introducing the older man. Following Douglass's opening speech (which was an extended panegyric to Garrison), a number of ministers were invited to join them on the platform. It was an uncomfortable moment and this clumsy gesture was an indication that the ministers were not comfortable in giving their endorsement to the American visitors. Overwhelmingly, the tone of the meeting was fractious. During Garrison's long speeches (he spoke twice), he attacked the editor of the *News-Letter*, who was sitting with other journalists. It provided another awkward moment for those who had come to hear a speech on abolition and it added to the general bad feeling of the meeting. Garrison's pointed attacks on the Free Church led to audible hissing from the audience. Garrison, however, claimed that he welcomed the hisses as sounding like, 'American music to his ears'.[127] Undaunted, he continued his attack on various American churches and on the newly created Evangelical Alliance, which had convened in London in the summer of 1846.[128] Garrison also made a number of *ad hominum* attacks on two leading members of the Alliance, the Rev. Samuel Cox and the Rev. Clarke.[129] Overall, Garrison's unequivocal criticisms proved divisive and unpopular, they being received with as many hisses as cheers.[130] The meeting was ended peremptorily when the Chairman, James Tennant, felt that he could no longer control it.[131] Although Garrison left Belfast the following day, the controversy continued.

122 *Frederick Douglass (1818–1895)*

His uncompromising comments resulted in copious correspondence to the local newspapers, much of it negative. One letter pointed out that, though advertized as an anti-slavery meeting, its sole focus had been to denounce religious ministers.[132] Garrison had spent only two days in Belfast and while there he had lectured for approximately two hours, but the American had left behind him an abolition movement that was more divided than ever before.

At the meeting in the Belfast Music Hall, it had been announced that although Garrison was leaving Belfast, Douglass would be staying and would lecture on the following Tuesday evening, 6 October. His audience for what was to be his final appearance in Belfast (and, indeed, in Ireland) was described as 'respectable'. According to the *News-Letter*, however, it was 'composed principally of ladies and little boys' and when Douglass came forward to speak he was, 'received without any demonstration of applause'.[133] The lecture itself lacked the humour and self-deprecation that had been a hallmark of Douglass's early lectures. In what was predominantly a negative tirade, Douglass expressed his frustration with the abolition movement in the United Kingdom, saying:

> on coming to this country, he expected to find but one opinion as to the conduct of the American slave-holders, that whatever feeling existed with reference to slaveholding in the United States, but one opinion was entertained of the [same] in this Christian land; but in that idea he had been sadly disappointed, for recent events had disclosed for what he could not have supposed existed in the minds of any Christians, in this country.[134]

Echoing Garrison's lecture, a large part of Douglass's speech was devoted to attacking the Evangelical Alliance. Slavery itself was no longer the focus, but the churches who worked with slave-holders were now the main enemy.[135] In the four months that he had spent in Ireland at the commencement of his exile, Douglass had honed his skills as a lecturer, but the 'Send back the money' campaign had lost him the support of those who had welcomed him to Ireland. Furthermore, his uncompromising attacks appeared to be having little impact on the actions of the Free Church. It was one of Douglass's few misjudgments while in the United Kingdom, but it was a serious one.[136] Douglass's final lecture proved to be an inglorious ending to a tour that had achieved so much in the cause of abolition.

Later life

When Douglass left Ireland in October 1846, he returned to what had become his 'lonely pilgrimage' lecturing in Britain. He was sometimes accompanied by Henry Wright and Robert Smith of the Anti-Slavery League, as they attempted to promote Garrison's new transatlantic association. Douglass was missing his family and anxious to return to his anti-slavery activities in America. On 12 December 1846, Douglass officially became a free man, a legal process that had been instigated by Anna Richardson of Newcastle in the north east of

Frederick Douglass (1818–1895)   123

England during the summer. Anna was related to Ann Jennings, who had hosted Douglass in Cork.[137] As with so much in his life, the purchase of Douglass's freedom proved to be bittersweet. The idea of 'purchasing' freedom proved unpalatable to some abolitionists, including Wright, who begged Douglass not to touch the 'Certificate of Freedom', warning that if he did so:

> You will lose the advantages of this truly manly, and to my view, sublime position; you will be shorn of your strength—you will sink in your own estimation, if you accept that detestable certificate of your freedom, that blasphemous forgery, that accursed bill of sale of your body and soul; or even, by your silence, acknowledge its validity.[138]

Douglass politely, but firmly, disagreed. As he succinctly explained, it was a means of 'restoring myself to myself'.[139] In the space of less than 30 years, Douglass had been categorized as a slave, a fugitive, an exile, and now, a free man. Although he could return home without fear of capture, he had promised Garrison that he would stay in Britain until the following summer.[140] In the event, Douglass only remained until April 1847, at which point he had been away from home for 20 months.

Before leaving London, Douglass gave a powerful farewell address in which he quoted O'Connell:

> America presents to the world an anomaly, such as no other nation ever did or can present before mankind. The people of the United States are the boldest in their pretensions to freedom, and the loudest in their profession of the love of liberty; yet no nation upon the face of the globe can exhibit a statute-book so full of all that is cruel, malicious, and infernal, as the American code of laws. Every page is red with the blood of the American slave. Their history is nothing but blood! blood!—blood in the morning, blood at noon, blood at night! They have had blood to drink; they have had their own blood shed.[141]

Douglass was to use a variation of this quote from O'Connell on many other occasions during his long career.[142]

Many receptions were held in honour of Douglass's return.[143] In New York, one function was hosted by 'coloured people' to pay tribute to him, with Garrison appearing during the event.[144] Although Douglass continued to lecture for the American Anti-Slavery Society, he asserted his new-found independence by moving his family to Rochester and there establishing his own newspaper, the *North Star*, both against Garrison's advice.[145] In other ways, the sense of freedom and equality that Douglass had experienced while overseas must have quickly dissipated. An early incident on board a river boat on the Hudson, when a female abolitionist had tried to secure a cabin place for Douglass, the reserve of whites only, resulted in inches of column space and frenzied opprobrium being heaped on him. Even the *Liberator* was critical of Douglass and his champion for trying to subvert the

124   *Frederick Douglass (1818–1895)*

rules, 'by stealth', averring, 'they must be conquered openly, and through much suffering'.[146] Moreover, Douglass's new sense of confidence and purpose were not appreciated by all who opposed slavery. An article in the *Northern Christian Advocate*, which opposed both slavery and Garrison, reported on a lecture by Douglass and Remond in the autumn of 1847. Regarding Douglass, they said:

> He is the same whose recent visit to England has made so much noise. He is an intelligent looking, youngerly mulatto. A fellow of strong native sense, quick wit, considerable theatrical address, more assurance, and unbounded powers of sarcastic mimicry ... In other respects, ... Douglass lacks the modesty which is becoming in all public speakers, and especially one in his circumstance ... He strengthens the prejudice of those who say, 'Allow the coloured class to arise at all in society and they will tread you underfoot'.[147]

Regardless of such insults, Douglass proved indefatigable in spreading his message, writing in October 1847:

> I am at home again. Since I left home, less than three months ago, I have travelled more than 8,000 miles—spoken to more than 60,000 persons—held 100 conventions, and delivered not fewer than 150 lectures—written numerous letters for the press—had a number of private interviews with friends— many stern debates with enemies—been mobbed once—experienced some rebuffs and many hardships; yet here I am, in the bosom of my dear family, the embodiment of health, and in the best of spirits, for all of which I desire to feel sincerely grateful to God, whose servant I trust I am.[148]

During his lectures, Douglass often spoke about his recent experiences in Ireland and Britain. When exhorting his audiences to overthrow slavery, 'he pointed to the triumphs of the efforts of O'Connell and others which had brought emancipation to the Catholics of Ireland'.[149] His recently declared commitment to equal rights for all was evident in 1848 when he was one of the few men to sign the declaration supporting the rights of women at the Seneca Falls Convention. Significantly also, he was the only black person present on this auspicious occasion, and spoke alongside Elizabeth Cady Stanton in favour of women's suffrage.[150]

Douglass's departure from the United Kingdom did not mark an end to his relationship with British or Irish abolitionists, a number of whom continued to correspond with him. Women in Ireland remained particularly active in supporting his work. Maria Webb in Dublin helped to raise money for the founding of the *North Star* newspaper.[151] Several of the Irish Ladies' Anti-Slavery Societies carried on donating goods to the Boston and Rochester bazaars. Inevitably, the Famine in Ireland in the late 1840s, had a negative impact on donations. Writing in December 1849, the committee of the Belfast Ladies' Anti-Slavery

Frederick Douglass (1818–1895) 125

Association apologized for not contributing any goods that year, explaining, 'This is chiefly owing to the distress amongst the poor of our own country'. They reassured Douglass that:

> lest you should imagine that our sympathy with the slave is extinct, I enclose you a copy of a monster petition we have prepared to present to Her Majesty on behalf of 'the Victims of the African Slave Trade'.

The petition had been signed by 6,000 people, including 118 Irish women. Its uncompromising language had been condemned by the Society of Friends and members of the Cork Anti-Slavery Society.[152] In 1855, Julia Griffiths, an English-born abolitionist and loyal friend to Douglass, returned to Britain to raise money for Douglass's struggling new newspaper. She appealed directly to women's anti-slavery societies. Her reach extended to Ireland, resulting in several donations, including £20 being sent to Douglass by the Clogher Ladies Anti-Slavery Society. A grateful Douglass responded that, 'owing to the very depressed condition of business and the general derangement of the money affairs of the country, your donation has almost a double value'.[153] In the same year, a new Ladies' Anti-Slavery Society was formed in Dublin for the purpose of supporting the abolitionists in Douglass's home town of Rochester.[154]

Throughout the 1850s, Douglass moved away from the principles of the American Anti-Slavery Society, especially in regard to their rejection of the Constitution. When asked about this change of heart he explained:

> When he went West, and came in contact with such men as Beriah Green, Wm. Goodell, Gerrit Smith, and the powerful Samuel R. Ward, and met them in debate, both public and private, he was introduced to a different set of ideas and was forced to submit his mind to a new training to defend his positions; and the end was, that from inquiry to inquiry, he, finally, in open conviction, came to believe in the anti-slavery character of the United States' Constitution.[155]

On several other occasions, he spoke about Ward's influence on his thinking.[156] Douglass also was influenced by his friend, John Brown, the two men disagreeing on the question of using physical force.[157] In the wake of Brown's unsuccessful uprising in 1859, Douglass returned to Britain, feeling it necessary to flee America. In advance of leaving, he wrote to his Irish friend, Maria Webb, defending Brown's actions and describing him as 'that brave, and I believe, good man'.[158] In Britain, Douglass was warmly received, with none of the rancour that had marred his final tour with Garrison 15 years earlier. He lectured on occasion with Sarah Parker Remond, sister of this long-time friend, Charles Remond.[159] In Scotland, Douglass received news that his 10-year-old daughter had died, which caused him considerable sadness.[160] Her death led him to curtail his tour and return to America unannounced.[161] He experienced more personal tragedy in 1882, when his wife Anna died, following some years of bad

126 *Frederick Douglass (1818–1895)*

health. Two years later, he re-married Helen Pitts. The fact that Helen was white proved to be controversial, leading Douglass to pen a defiant rebuttal entitled, 'What business has the world with the color of my wife?'[162]

Over the subsequent decades, Douglass fought for civil rights in all areas of life, arguing for black men to serve in the Union army, for equality in the Reconstruction Era and for an end to the racist Jim Crow laws. During his lifetime, he occupied many public positions. He also advised six American Presidents, including Abraham Lincoln.[163] Throughout, Douglass never lost his affection for Ireland. However, while his admiration for Irish abolitionists in general, and O'Connell in particular, did not diminish over the decades, it was tempered by his frustration with the Irish in America, many of whom continued to support the pro-slavery Democratic Party and oppose the abolition movement.[164] O'Connell had expressed similar frustrations in the 1840s.[165] Douglass's vexation continued after the end of the Civil War, but it was mitigated by his knowledge of Ireland's own tragic history. In a powerful speech made in Lincoln Hall in 1883, he stated:

> Perhaps no class of our fellow citizens has carried this prejudice against color to a point more extreme and dangerous than have our Catholic Irish fellow-citizens, and yet no people on the face of the earth have been more relentlessly persecuted and oppressed on account of race and religion than have the same Irish people … Fellow citizens! We want no Black Ireland in America.[166]

In 1886, Douglass and Helen undertook a year-long tour of Europe and North Africa. Unlike during his visit in 1845, Douglass now came as a citizen, with a passport, who travelled first class and did not need to lecture in order to survive. Because her mother became ill, Helen returned early to America, leaving her husband to continue alone. In 1887, Douglass made a brief, and final, trip to Ireland. He again visited the Webb family on Great Brunswick Street, but this time staying with Alfred, eldest son of Richard, who had died in 1872. James Haughton and Richard Allen were also dead. According to Alfred, Douglass came 'to renew old memories of the 40s'.[167] Douglass reminisced on his earlier journey to Ireland, under very different circumstances:

> In Dublin, the first city I then visited, I was kindly received by Mr. Richard Webb, Richard Allen, James Haughton, and others. They were now all gone, and except some of their children, I was among strangers. These received me in the same cordial spirit that distinguished their fathers and mothers. I did not visit dear old Cork, where in 1845 I was made welcome by the Jennings, the Warings, the Wrights, and their circle of friends, most of whom I learned had passed away. The same was true of the Neals, the Workmans, the McIntyres, and the Nelsons at Belfast. I had friends in Limerick, in Waterford, in Eniscorthy [sic], and other towns of Ireland, but I saw none of them during this visit. What was true of the mortality of my friends in Ireland, was equally true of those in England. Few who first received me in that country are now among the living … I missed the

Frederick Douglass (1818–1895) 127

presence of George Thompson, one of the most eloquent men who ever advocated the cause of the colored man, either in England or America. Joseph Sturge and most of his family had also passed away. But I will pursue this melancholy enumeration no further, except to say that, in meeting with the descendants of anti-slavery friends in England, Ireland and Scotland, it was good to have confirmed the scriptural saying, 'Train up a child in the way he should go and when he is old he will not depart from it'.[168]

Alfred Webb, Douglass's host, was a nationalist and a supporter of Irish Home Rule. Shortly following his return to the United States, Douglass spoke at a meeting in Washington to promote Irish independence. He was the only black person on the platform and was warmly greeted by the large crowd present.[169] Despite his advancing years, Douglass showed no signs of slowing down in his desire for justice. In 1889, Douglass served as Consul General to Haiti, falling out with his own government over their plans to re-colonize part of it. In 1893, he paid public tribute to the beleaguered country—the first black republic—referencing both Ireland and Daniel O'Connell in his speech:

> It was once said by the great Daniel O'Connell, that the history of Ireland might be traced, like a wounded man through a crowd, by the blood. The same can be said of the history of Haiti as a free state.[170]

Frederick Douglass died in February 1895. Appropriately, earlier that day he had attended a meeting for women's suffrage and received a standing ovation.[171] Douglass's remains were taken to Rochester, where he was buried alongside his first wife, Anna, in Mount Hope Cemetery.[172] His passing was noticed in Ireland; the Belfast *News-Letter*, for example, included a paragraph about his funeral, referring to him as 'the departed champion of freedom'.[173] It was a fitting tribute and a reminder that Ireland had played an important role in helping Douglass to find and hone his voice on behalf of the oppressed everywhere.

Conclusion

Douglass's time away from the United States, but most particularly the early months spent in Ireland, helped re-energize the transatlantic abolitionist movement. Amongst other things, it galvanized women within the movement on both sides of the Atlantic. It also threw an uncomfortable spotlight on the role of the churches in upholding slavery. Just as importantly, Douglass's four months in Ireland changed him in a number of ways. He was aware of these 'transformative' changes. Shortly after leaving the country at the beginning of 1846, Douglass explained to Garrison, that, as a result of the visit, he had come to see the crusade for abolition as part of much wider struggle for social justice:

> I see much here to remind me of my former condition, and I confess I should be ashamed to lift up my voice against American slavery, but that

128   *Frederick Douglass (1818–1895)*

I know the cause of humanity is one the world over. He who really and truly feels for the American slave, cannot steel his heart to the woes of others; and he who thinks himself an abolitionist, yet cannot enter into the wrongs of others, has yet to find a true foundation for his anti-slavery.[174]

Douglass's time in Ireland had freed him in another way; the self-emancipated slave, found other ways to emancipate himself. This was most evident in the writing of his own Preface to the second Irish edition of his *Narrative*, suggesting a new-found confidence in no longer relying on a white abolitionist to validate his life story. It was significant that on his return to America, he moved physically, and increasingly ideologically, away from Garrison.

Douglass's time in Ireland, when, for the first time, he felt like a man rather than a chattel, helped to consolidate his view that the struggle of enslaved black people was part of a wider crusade for justice. During his time in the country, he witnessed the political oppression of white people and observed extreme poverty and even the onset of a famine. These novel experiences provided a prism through which he could view suffering and oppression everywhere, and articulate the demand for abolition in the context of a wider desire for universal human rights. This inclusive approach remained pivotal to his subsequent political philosophy.

In 2011, the year that Barack Obama visited Ireland in search of his own Irish roots, the American President paid tribute to Ireland's role in Douglass's development. He singled out Daniel O'Connell, the 70-year-old venerated statesman who had invited the 27-year-old fugitive slave to share the stage with him in 1845, for special praise:

> For his part, Douglass drew inspiration from the Irishman's courage and intelligence, ultimately modeling his own struggle for justice on O'Connell's belief that change could be achieved peacefully through rule of law. The two men shared a universal desire for freedom—one that cannot be contained by language or culture or even the span of an ocean.[175]

As the President recognized, Douglass's brief time in Ireland transformed him into a fearless champion of international human rights, the legacy of which continued to provide inspiration long after his death.

Notes

1 Frederick Douglass, *Narrative of the Life of Frederick Douglass, an American Slave, written by Himself* (Boston, MA: Anti-Slavery Office, 1845), p. 32.
2 Ibid., p. 33.
3 Ibid., pp. 39–40. There is a possibility that Douglass confused Sheridan with another Irish patriot, Arthur O'Connor, a member of the United Irishmen, who had hosted Olaudah Equiano when he visited Ireland in the 1790s.
4 Ibid., p. 41.
5 Ibid., p. 42.

Frederick Douglass (1818–1895)   129

6 Ibid., p. 110. On the marriage certificate, Frederick's surname appears as Johnstone; shortly afterwards, he changed it to Douglass, in honour of a Scottish hero in 'Lady of the Lake', a narrative poem by Sir Walter Scott.

7 Douglass made these claims in his *Narrative* and during his speech in Conciliation Hall on 29 September. See, 'Repeal Association', *Dublin Evening Mail*, 1 October 1845.

8 Douglass, *Narrative*, p. 117.

9 Ibid.

10 Parker Pillsbury, *Acts of Anti-Slavery Apostles* (Boston, MA, 1884), pp. 327–8.

11 See chapter on Charles Lenox Remond.

12 Nathaniel Rogers, *Miscellaneous Writings of Nathaniel Rogers* (New Hampshire: W. H. Fisk, 1849), pp. 203–4.

13 James Needham Buffum (1807–1887) had been born in Maine. Originally a Quaker, he abandoned his religion when he became a devoted supporter of the radical abolitionist, William Lloyd Garrison.

14 See Buffum's Obituary, *New York Times*, 13 June 1887.

15 Douglass to Maria Weston Chapman, marked private, 29 March 1846, Kilmarnock, Scotland, in John R. McKivigan (ed.), *The Frederick Douglass Papers: 1842–1852*, series 3, Correspondence, vol. 1 (New Haven, CT: Yale University Press, 2009), p. 99.

16 Richard Davis Webb (1805–1872) was an Irish Quaker publisher and one of the three founders of the Hibernian Anti-Slavery Association in 1837. His brothers, James Henry and Thomas, were also abolitionists, as was his wife, Hannah Waring, a member of the Waterford Quakers. All four attended the Anti-Slavery Convention in London in 1840, where they met Garrison.

17 'BREAKFAST TO MR FREDERICK DOUGLASS', *Belfast Commercial Chronicle*, 6 January 1846. In his speech, the actual phrase used by Douglass was 'the chattel becomes a man'.

18 Douglass to Garrison, 1 September 1845, reprinted in Christine Kinealy, *Frederick Douglass. In His Own Words*, vol. 2 (London: Routledge, 2019), p. 62.

19 Christine Kinealy, *Daniel O'Connell and the Anti-Slavery Movement. The Saddest People the Sun Sees* (London: Routledge, 2011), pp. 21–2. O'Connell was persuaded to support anti-slavery by Liverpool abolitionist, James Cropper.

20 This story was retold by Wendell Phillips and others, Wendell Phillips, 'A Lecture Delivered at the Academy of Music, New York, 12 May 1868', in Wendell Phillips (ed.), *Lectures and Speeches* (New York and London: Street and Smith, 1902), pp. 188–9.

21 Kinealy, *Saddest People*, pp. 64–71. The Ambassador was Andrew Stevenson and the issue was widely reported in newspapers on both sides of the Atlantic and even discussed in Congress.

22 Garrison to George W. Benson, Boston, 22 March 1842, in William Lloyd Garrison, *The Letters of William Lloyd Garrison: No Union with the Slaveholders, 1841–1849* (Cambridge, MA: Harvard University Press, 1973), p. 63.

23 Douglass, *Narrative*, Preface to Boston edition.

24 *Liberator*, 10 October 1845.

25 One of their first actions was to arrange for English abolitionist, George Thompson (1804–1878), to speak in Dublin on 11 August 1837. Thompson was a friend of Garrison.

26 Richard Allen (1803–1886), a successful Dublin draper, was active in the abolition, temperance and peace movements. He was supported by his wife, Anne Webb.

27 Hannah Waring Webb (1809–1862) was married to Richard Webb. Hannah welcomed many abolitionists into her Dublin home. Together, they had four children, Alfred John Webb (1834–1908) later became a nationalist Member of the British Parliament and hosted Douglass when he visited the country again in 1887, his parents being dead.

28 *Liberator*, 10 October 1845.

130   *Frederick Douglass (1818–1895)*

29 The Opium War (1839–1842) was a conflict between Britain and China over the latter's sovereignty regarding the importation of the drug, opium. A second Opium War took place from 1856 to 1860.

30 Douglass to Garrison, 16 September 1845, published in the *Liberator*, 10 October 1845.

31 The Royal Exchange, now City Hall, was opened in 1779. Douglass, in a letter to Garrison, claimed that he spoke twice at this venue, but there is no newspaper account of the second meeting, so he may have been mistaken.

32 'Slavery', *Freeman's Journal*, 8 September 1845.

33 Ibid.

34 *Freeman's Journal*, 10 September 1845.

35 The letter was written on 17 September 1845, it was published in Garrison's *Liberator* on 24 October 1845.

36 *Freeman's Journal*, 16 September 1845.

37 Following this meeting, Mayor John Arabin invited Douglass to dine at his official residence, the Mansion House.

38 *Liberator*, 18 December 1845.

39 Douglass to Garrison, 29 September 1845, Kinealy, *Douglass*, pp. 66–8.

40 'THE REPEAL ASSOCIATION', *London Standard*, 1 October 1845.

41 'The Repeal Movement', *Dublin Evening Post*, 30 September 1845.

42 Maria Waring, sister-in-law to Richard Webb, belonged to a network of Irish women who were both feminists and abolitionists. She escorted Douglass to Wexford and was captivated by him, regarding him as the most impressive abolitionist she had ever met. They corresponded for many years.

43 The Waring family originally lived in Wexford but moved to Waterford when the sisters were young.

44 'Mr Douglass. Anti-Slavery Lecture', *Waterford Mail*, 11 October 1845.

45 'ANTI-SLAVERY MEETING IN WEXFORD', *Waterford Chronicle*, 11 October 1845.

46 The Jennings' premises were at 11 and 12 Brown Street, Cork. See, *The County and City of Cork Post Office General Directory for 1842–1843* (Cork: Jackson, 1843), p. 45.

47 Jennings also patented an improved stopper for mineral water bottles, see, *Reporatory of Patent Inventions, July to December 1854*, vol. xxiv (London: Macintosh, 1855), p. 284.

48 Cork Ladies' Anti-Slavery Society in *The County and City of Cork Almanac, Calculated & Adapted by C. Thompson* (Cork: Jackson, 1843), p. 79; Isabel also subscribed to the *North Star*, 'Receipts for The NORTH STAR, from the 17th to the 24th of October', *North Star*, 24 October 1845.

49 Douglass to Garrison, Letter Four, 28 October 1845, in Kinealy, *Douglass*, vol. 2, pp. 69–70.

50 'Father Mathew', *North Star*, 17 August 1849.

51 Ralph Varian to William Garrison, 10 November 1845, *Liberator*, 12 December 1845.

52 *Southern Reporter*, 18 October 1845.

53 *Cork Examiner*, 20 October 1845.

54 'The Anti-Slavery Standard', *National Anti-Slavery Standard*, 5 March 1846.

55 *Liberator*, 23 January 1846.

56 Douglass to Mayor Dowden, 4 November 1845, Dowden Papers, U140/L/029, Cork City and County Archives.

57 'American Slavery', *Limerick Reporter*, 11 November 1845.

58 Douglass to Francis Jackson, Holist Street, Boston, 29 January 1846, Anti-Slavery Collection, BPL, MS A. 1.2. v.16. p.13.

59 Liam Hogan, *Frederick Douglass's Journey from Slavery to Limerick* (1845). Available at: http://www.limerickcity.ie/media/olj%2049%202015%20p021%20to%20p026.pdf.

Frederick Douglass (1818–1895) 131

60 'American Slavery', *Limerick Reporter*, 11 November 1845.
61 The 'inimitable Bateman' was touring Ireland, *Freeman's Journal*, 12 September 1845.
62 'The Theatre', *Galway Mercury, and Connaught Weekly Advertiser*, 18 October 1845; *Clare Journal and Ennis Advertiser*, 30 October 1845.
63 'Ballinasloe Fair', *Galway Vindicator, and Connaught Advertiser*, 11 October 1845.
64 *Limerick Reporter*, 11 November 1845.
65 This point is made by Kathleen Gough, *Haptic Allegories: Kinship and Performance in the Black and Green Atlantic* (London: Routledge, 2013), p. 166.
66 *Limerick Reporter*, 11 November 1845.
67 Douglass speaking at City Court House, Cork, reported in 'INTERESTING NARRATIVE OF FUGITIVE SLAVE', *Southern Reporter and Cork Commercial Courier*, 16 October 1845.
68 Ibid., Speech by the Mayor of Cork.
69 *Limerick Reporter*, 11 November 1845.
70 Inspired by the revolutions in America and France, the Society of United Irishmen had been formed in late 1791. They appealed to Irish people to put aside their religious differences and work together for an Irish republic. The founder of the movement was a Protestant solicitor, Theobald Wolfe Tone, other leaders included Henry Joy McCracken, whose sister Mary Ann was a prominent abolitionist in Belfast and had met Douglass. Leading members of the United Irishmen hosted Equiano during his visit to Belfast in 1791.
71 Olaudah Equiano (c. 1745–1797). Also see, Nini Rodgers, 'Equiano in Belfast: A Study of the Anti-slavery Ethos in a Northern Town', in *Slavery & Abolition. A Journal of Slave and Post-Slave Studies*, vol. 18, no. 2 (1997), pp. 73–89.
72 In 1810, only around 25,000 people lived in Belfast; by 1841, this number had increased to 70,000.
73 'MR FREDERICK DOUGLASS', Belfast *Vindicator*, 29 November 1845.
74 Lieutenant Francis Anderson Calder (1787–1855) had served in the Royal Navy. Calder was an activist for animal rights. He continued to send Douglass the Annual Reports of the Belfast Society for the prevention of cruelty to animals, which Douglass included in his various newspapers. See, 'Our thanks are returned to our friend Calder of Belfast', *Frederick Douglass' Paper*, 17 June 1852.
75 Douglass to Webb, 5 December 1845, Anti-Slavery Collection, Boston Public Library, MS A. 1.2. v.15 p. 85.
76 Ibid., Douglass to Webb, Victoria Hotel, Belfast, 6 December 1845, MS A 1.2. v. 15, p. 86.
77 Ibid., Douglass to Webb, 5 December 1845, MS A. 1.2. v.15 p. 85.
78 Ibid., Douglass informed Webb about this victory, 'in the face of letters prejudicial to me both from Cork and Dublin', Douglass to Webb, 6 December 1845, MS A 1.2. v. 15, p. 86.
79 'MR. FREDERICK DOUGLASS'S ADDRESS', *Banner of Ulster*, 9 December 1845.
80 'BELFAST ANTI-SLAVERY MEETING', Belfast *Vindicator*, 10 December 1845.
81 'MR. FREDERICK DOUGLASS'S ADDRESS', *Banner of Ulster*, 9 December 1845.
82 Frederick Douglass to Richard Davis Webb, 6 December 1845, Anti-Slavery Collection, MS A.1.2.v.15. p. 86.
83 Ibid., Douglass to Webb, Belfast 7 December 1845, MS A. 1. 2. V. 15 p. 87.
84 Belfast *News-Letter*, 26 December 1845.
85 Douglass, Belfast, to Webb, 5 December 1845, Anti-Slavery Collection, BPL, MS A. 1.2. v.15 p. 85.
86 Ibid., Douglass, Belfast, to Webb, 6 December 1845, MS A.1.2.v.15. p. 86.
87 *Banner of Ulster*, 2 January 1845; Belfast *News-Letter*, 6 January 1845.
88 'AMERICAN SLAVERY', *Belfast Commercial Chronicle*, 27 December 1845.
89 Ibid., 'BREAKFAST TO MR FREDERICK DOUGLASS', 7 January 1846.

132 *Frederick Douglass (1818–1895)*

90 *Northern Whig*, 8 January 1846.
91 'ENTERTAINMENT TO FREDERICK DOUGLASS AT. PATRICK'S TEMPER-ANCE HALL', *Southern Reporter and Cork Commercial Courier*, 30 October 1845.
92 Douglass, Belfast to Garrison, 1 January 1846, the *Liberator*, 30 January 1846.
93 Ibid.
94 Patricia J. Ferreira, 'Frederick Douglass in Ireland: the Dublin Edition of his *Narrative*', in *New Hibernia Review*, vol. 5, no.1 (Earrach/Spring, 2001), 53–67, p. 62.
95 Douglass, *Narrative*, p. vi.
96 Speech by Rev. Isaac Nelson, Primitive Wesleyan Chapel, Donegall-Place, Belfast, 'Anti-Slavery Meeting', *Northern Whig*, 9 July 1846.
97 Frederick Douglass, *Narrative of the Life of Frederick Douglass, an American Slave, Written by Himself* ..., Second Dublin edition. [With a portrait.] (Dublin: Webb & Chapman, 1846). Fionnghuala Sweeney refers to a second stop-gap edition that appeared in March 1846 as the 'variant edition'. She points out that it gave 1845 as its publication date. The final version of the Irish edition appeared in May 1846. See Fionnghuala Sweeney, '"The republic of letters": Frederick Douglass, Ireland, and the Irish *Narratives*', in *Éire-Ireland*, vol. 36, no. 1 & 2 (*Earrach/Samhradh* Spring/Summer 2001), 47–65.
98 See chapter on Benjamin Benson.
99 Douglass, Glasgow, to Garrison, 16 April 1846, reprinted in McKivigen, *Frederick Douglass Papers*, vol. 1, p. 108.
100 Harriet Bailey (1818–1900), whose slave name had been Ruth Cox, had also grown up in Talbot County in Maryland. She had escaped in 1842. Douglas mistakenly believed that she was his younger sister.
101 In the letter, Douglass uses the *n*—word.
102 Douglass to Harriet Bailey, 16 May 1846, Frederick Douglass Collection, Library of Congress: www.loc.gov/collections/frederick-douglass-papers/about-this-collection/.
103 Ibid.
104 'Frederick Douglass', Belfast *News-Letter*, 16 June 1846.
105 'American Slavery', Belfast *News-Letter*, 19 June 1846.
106 Richard Webb to *National Anti-Slavery Standard*, 30 July 1846.
107 'RECEPTION OF DOUGLASS IN LONDON', the *Liberator*, 26 June 1846.
108 Ibid., 'MR. GARRISON'S MISSION TO THE BRITISH ISLANDS', 24 July 1846.
109 *Belfast Vindicator*, 16 June 1846.
110 No title, *Tyrone Constitution*, 3 July 1846.
111 Douglass was spotted sitting in a gallery seat, *Banner of Ulster*, 10 July 1846.
112 *Northern Whig*, 9 July 1846.
113 Ibid.,18 July 1846.
114 'Temperance Meeting', *Belfast Commercial Chronicle*, 22 July 1846.
115 *Liberator*, 24 July 1846.
116 Ibid.
117 Garrison, *The Letters of William Lloyd Garrison*, p. 359.
118 'Mr. Garrison in England', *National Anti-Slavery Standard*, 10 September 1846.
119 *Proceedings*, Day One, p. 21.
120 Richard Webb sent a full account of the meeting to the paper, which described him as their 'Dublin Correspondent', *National Anti-Slavery Standard*, 10 September 1846.
121 *National Anti-Slavery Standard*, 10 September 1846.
122 Garrison to Richard Webb, Edinburgh, 25 September 1846, Garrison, *Letters of William Lloyd Garrison*, p. 428.
123 Letter from William Lloyd Garrison, Liverpool [England], to Elizabeth Pease Nichol, 12 October 1846, Anti-Slavery Collection, BPL: https://www.digitalcommonwealth.org/.
124 'American Slavery', *Dumfries and Galloway Standard*, 28 October 1846.

Frederick Douglass (1818–1895) 133

125 'American Anti-Slavery Agitators', Belfast *News-Letter*, 2 October 1846, 20 October 1846.
126 Ibid.
127 Ibid., 'Anti-Slavery Meeting', 6 October 1846.
128 About 900 Protestant churchmen, mostly from Britain and America had convened on London in the summer of 1846 for the purpose of forming an international Protestant Union. See, J. F. Maclear, 'The Evangelical Alliance and the Antislavery Crusade', in *Huntington Library Quarterly*, vol. 42, no. 2 (Spring 1979), pp. 141–64.
129 'Anti-Slavery Meeting', Belfast *News-Letter*, 6 October 1846.
130 For example, the meeting of 3 October 1846 was hurriedly ended by the chairman, see Belfast *News-Letter*, 6 October 1846.
131 'ANTI-SLAVERY MEETING', *Belfast Commercial Chronicle*, 5 October 1846; 'Anti-Slavery Meeting—William Lloyd Garrison', Belfast *News-Letter*, 6 October 1846.
132 Ibid., I. Steed, Belfast to Editor of *News-Letter*, 6 October 1846.
133 Ibid., 9 October 1846.
134 'Anti-Slavery Meeting', *Belfast Commercial Chronicle*, 10 October 1846.
135 'The Rev Daniel M'Afee on the Late Anti-Slavery meetings in Belfast', *Belfast Protestant Journal*, 10 October 1846. M'Afee was a Methodist minister.
136 Iain Whyte, *Send Back the Money! The Free Church of Scotland and American Slavery* (Cambridge: James Clarke & Co, 2012), p. 127.
137 L.M. Jenkins, 'Beyond the Pale: Frederick Douglass in Cork', *Irish Review*, no. 24 (Autumn 1999), pp. 80–95, 91.
138 Wright to Douglass, Doncaster, 12 December 1846, in McKivigan, *Douglass Papers*, pp. 179–81.
139 'Our London Letter', *Dundee Courier*, 20 October 1886.
140 Douglass to Garrison, Carlisle, 2 January 1847, McKivigan, *Douglass Papers*, pp. 190–1.
141 FAREWELL SPEECH TO THE BRITISH PEOPLE, at London Tavern, London, England, 30 March 1847, *Farewell Speech of Mr. Frederick Douglass Upon His Return to America, Delivered at the Valedictory Soiree Given to Him at the London Tavern on March 30, 1847* (London: R. Yorke, Clarke and Co., 1847).
142 For example, Douglas quoted O'Connell at a speech in Philadelphia: 'FREDERICK DOUGLASS IN PHILADELPHIA', *Frederick Douglass' Paper*, 6 April 1855.
143 'FREDERICK DOUGLASS', the *Liberator*, 7 May 1847; Ibid., 'RECEPTION OF FREDERICK DOUGLASS AT THE BELKNAP-STREET CHURCH, BOSTON', 21 May 1847.
144 Ibid., 'Reception of Frederick Douglass by the Colored People', 21 May 1847.
145 It was first published in December 1847.
146 'American Colorphobia', the *Liberator*, 11 June 1847. A similar attack took place in 1849, which was reported in the British press, 'Treatment of Frederick Douglass by his American brethren—badly treated on a steamer', *Leicester Chronicle*, 30 June 1849.
147 Reprinted in the *Liberator*, 22 October 1847.
148 Letter from Douglass, dated Lynn, Mass, 13 October 1847, 'Last Campaign of Frederick Douglass', *Essex Standard*, 28 January 1848.
149 'Anti-Slavery Convention', the *Liberator*, 25 June 1847.
150 Ta-Nehisi Coates, 'Frederick Douglass: A Women's Rights Man', *The Atlantic*, 30 September 2011.
151 Scrapbook of Maria Webb c. 1840–1890, Gilder Lehrman Collection, New York City, GLC08360, 1 v. See: http://ap.gilderlehrman.org/history-by-era/failure-compromise/essays/admiration-and-ambivalence-frederick-douglass-and-john-brow.
152 'Petition against the Slave Trade', *North Star*, 25 January 1850.

134   *Frederick Douglass (1818–1895)*

153 Douglass, Rochester to Mrs Maxwell, Treasurer of Clogher Anti-Slavery Society, 10 October 1857, in *Anti-Slavery Reporter*, 1 December 1857, p. 279.

154 Ibid., p. 240.

155 'FREDERICK DOUGLASS IN PHILADELPHIA', *Frederick Douglass' Paper*, 6 April 1855.

156 'Maine on the Slavery Question', *National Anti-Slavery Standard*, 31 March 1855; See also chapter on Samuel Ward.

157 John Brown (1800–1859) was a white abolitionist who believed an armed insurrection was necessary to end slavery. To this end, he led a raid on a federal armory in Harper's Ferry in October 1859, for which he was hanged. Douglass and Brown had met in 1847 and in 1858, Brown had stayed for one month at Douglass's home.

158 Douglass to Maria, 31 November 1859, Scrapbook of Maria Webb c. 1840–1890, Gilder Lehrman Collection, New York City, GLC08360, 1 v. See: http://ap.gilder lehrman.org/history-by-era/failure-compromise/essays/admiration-and-ambivalence-frederick-douglass-and-john-brow.

159 See chapter on Sarah Parker Remond.

160 'Mr Douglass in Ayr', *Paisley Herald and Renfrewshire Advertiser*, 31 March 1860.

161 'Frederick Douglass', *Newcastle Daily Chronicle*, 29 June 1860.

162 James O. Horton, '"What Business Has the World with the Color of My Wife?" A Letter from Frederick Douglass', in *Magazine of History*, vol. 19, no. 1 (Jan. 2005), pp. 52–5.

163 'When Douglass Met Lincoln', *New York Times*, 9 August 2013.

164 'Annual Meeting of Association', *Pennsylvania National Anti-Slavery Standard*, 7 October 1854.

165 See Kinealy, *O'Connell and Anti-Slavery*, passim.

166 Frederick Douglass, *Life and Times of Frederick Douglass, Written by Himself* (Boston, MA: De Wolfe & Fiske, 1892), p. 973.

167 Alfred Webb, Marie-Louise Kegge (ed.), *The Autobiography of a Quaker Nationalist* (Cork University Press, 1999), p. 66.

168 Douglass, *Life and Times*, pp. 668–9.

169 Tom Chaffin, *Giant's Causeway: Frederick Douglass's Irish Odyssey and the Making of an American Visionary* (Charlottesville: University of Virginia Press, 2014).

170 Douglass, 'Lecture on Haiti, World's Fair' (Chicago, IL: Violet Agents, 1893).

171 'OBITUARY. Death of Fred Douglass', *New York Times*, 21 February 1895.

172 When Helen died in 1903, she was buried in an adjoining plot.

173 Belfast *News-Letter*, 26 February 1895.

174 Frederick Douglass, Scotland, to Garrison, 26 February 1846, reprinted in the *Liberator*, 27 March 1846.

175 'Remarks by President Obama, Vice President Biden, and Prime Minister Enda Kenny of Ireland at a St. Patrick's Day Reception', *Press Release*, White House, 17 March 2011.

5 William Wells Brown (c.1814–1884)

'A cultivated fugitive'

In 2014, historian Ezra Greenspan published a book on William Wells Brown that, amongst other things, sought to recover the memory of the abolitionist from historical oblivion. In it, he suggested that Wells Brown was 'the most pioneering and accomplished African American writer and cultural impresario of the nineteenth century'.[1] Even amongst a generation that produced so many brilliant abolitionists who had been formerly enslaved, Wells Brown's little-known life story is extraordinary and deserves to be better known.

Just as Wells Brown had been largely forgotten, so was his relationship with Ireland. As was the case with several of his contemporaries, Wells Brown's time in the country was subsequently ignored or marginalized by biographers. However, like Frederick Douglass, Wells Brown's first weeks in Europe were spent in Ireland, hosted by the Hibernian Anti-Slavery Society. It was in Dublin that both men first lectured outside of the United States and where the first non-American versions of their life stories were published. Copies of both *Narratives* were reprinted by Richard Davis Webb, Quaker printer and ardent abolitionist. Similarly, the two 'fugitive' slaves found being in the United Kingdom a liberating experience, because, as they liked to remind those who heard them, there was no place in the United States where they were free and protected by law. In turn, audiences in Ireland and Britain were entranced by the oratory of both men, and Wells Brown, like Douglass, frequently referred to the fact that they had never had a formal day's schooling in their lives, but were self-educated.[2] Nevertheless, Wells Brown, like a number of other visiting black abolitionists, proved to be an extremely gifted orator and writer.[3] His literary talents extended to fiction; in 1853, he published a novel, *Clotel: or, the President's Daughter*, in the same year that Douglass penned his only work of fiction, *The Heroic Slave*.[4] Wells Brown was also producing works relating to travel writing, history, abolition, as well as on music and drama.[5] Regardless of a suggestion that some of Wells Brown's writings were derivative or plagiarized, it was an incredible output by a man who was self-taught and self-financing.[6] For five years, Wells Brown lectured extensively in Britain and Ireland, finally returning to the United States in 1854, following the 'purchase' of his freedom by English women abolitionists. Like Douglass, Wells Brown remained a prominent spokesperson for his people until his death. As abolitionists and champions of equality, it was in Ireland that both men experienced, for the first time in their lives, the feeling of being equal.

136 *William Wells Brown (c.1814–1884)*

Early life

Wells Brown was born in Lexington in Kentucky, probably in 1814. At birth, he was simply given the name 'William'. At some stage, it was casually changed to Sanford or Sandy by one of his 'owners'—a pointed reminder that enslaved people did not even own their names.[7] His mother was enslaved and of 'mixed blood', she having been kidnapped by a rich slaveholder, while his father was a 'well connected' white man.[8] Wells Brown later wrote:

> One of his first bitter experiences of the cruelties of slavery, was his witnessing the infliction of ten lashes upon the bare back of his mother, for being a few minutes behind her time at the field—a punishment inflicted with one of those peculiar whips in the construction of which, so as to produce the greatest amount of torture.[9]

When visiting Dublin in 1849, Wells Brown informed his audience that 'When a slave, he had an ardent thirst for learning'. Denied an education like other enslaved people, he had to scheme in order to acquire the skills to read and write. To this end:

> He contrived to purchase an old spelling book, and ... got his master's sons to teach him the rudiments at night by the light of a purchased candle, and through the bribe to his young teachers of a piece of sugar-stick for each hour's tuition.[10]

Self-education provided a pathway to self-emancipation. William escaped when he was aged about 20. Following this, he changed his name, reverting to William, but adding Wells Brown to it, in honour of a Quaker, 'my first white friend', who helped him to reach Canada.[11] Shortly afterwards, he married Elizabeth Schooner, a freeborn coloured woman.[12] In 1836, the couple relocated to Buffalo in New York, a free state and close to the Canadian border. There, they both engaged in anti-slavery activities. By 1843, Wells Brown was employed as a full-time agent for the Western New York Anti-Slavery Society. His multiple abilities meant that he soon became a renowned abolitionist. He combined this activity with being a supporter of temperance, women's rights and pacifism. In 1847, Wells Brown produced a narrative of his life, which was published by William Lloyd Garrison's anti-slavery press.[13] It was inspired by Douglass's publication of his life story two years earlier, Wells Brown writing that:

> the narrative of his life, published in 1845, gave a new impetus to the black man's literature. All other stories of fugitive slaves faded away before the beautifully written, highly descriptive, memoir of Frederick Douglass.[14]

Wells Brown's life story was a success, with four American and five Irish/British editions appearing before 1850, making it second in popularity only to Douglass's *Narrative*.[15]

William Wells Brown (c.1814–1884) 137

In 1848, Wells Brown's 'owner' offered to allow him to purchase his freedom, to which he responded,

> I cannot accept of Mr. Price's offer to become a purchaser of my body and soul. God made me as free as he did Enoch Price, and Mr. Price shall never receive a dollar from me or my friends with my consent.[16]

Wells Brown's defiant words put him at increased risk of being recaptured, a threat that would intensify with the imminent introduction of a more draconian Fugitive Slave Law in 1850. Garrison, partly out of self-interest, encouraged Wells Brown to follow the route undertaken by both Remond and Douglass. The impact of Douglass's visit had encouraged Garrison to believe:

> It was thought desirable always to have in England some talented man of colour who should be a living lie to the doctrine of the inferiority of the African race: and it was moreover felt that none could so powerfully advocate the cause of 'those in bonds' as one who had actually been 'bound with them'.[17]

Moreover, the American Anti-Slavery Society wanted representation at the upcoming Peace Conference in Paris. On 16 July, two days before he left, a large meeting 'of coloured citizens' was held in Boston to wish Wells Brown farewell. On 18 July, he sailed to England on board the *Canada*, a new transatlantic steamship owned by Cunard. Wells Brown's friends, William and Ellen Craft, also escaped slaves, were among the small group that came to see him off. The Captain was Charles Judkins, who had previously commanded the *Cambria* and had defended Douglass against pro-slavery passengers.[18] Wells Brown's reading during the journey included Macaulay's *History of England* and *Jane Eyre*. The first sighting of land in Europe was 'the grey hills of Ireland', to which Wells Brown responded, 'Yes! we were in sight of the land of Emmitt [sic] and O'Connell'.[19]

Wells Brown arrived in Liverpool in the north of England following a journey across the Atlantic of only nine days and 22 hours. Almost exactly four years earlier, Douglass had landed in the same bustling transatlantic port city. As was expected, Wells Brown carried letters of introduction, from Garrison and other leading members of the American Anti-Slavery Society.[20] At Liverpool, Wells Brown's suitcases were unpacked and examined by the Customs' officials:

> First one article was taken out, and then another, till an Iron Collar that had been worn by a female slave on the banks of the Mississippi, was hauled out, and this democratic instrument of torture became the centre of attraction; so much so, that instead of going on with the examination, all hands stopped to look at the 'Negro Collar'.[21]

Although the collar attracted much attention, Wells Brown was carrying other cargo to help bring his story to a wider audience. This included leg shackles

138   *William Wells Brown (c.1814–1884)*

given to him by a slave in Washington, DC, which were for display during his lecture tour. Additionally, Wells Brown had brought the plates from the 1847 American publication of his *Narrative*. Richard Webb, Irish Quaker printer and admirer of Garrison, had, reluctantly, offered to print copies of it in order to provide Brown with much-needed income during his travels.[22] In addition, Wells Brown's luggage included a number of 'scene-scapes', which he had commissioned from artists in Boston.[23] He intended to develop these into a panorama, depicting the cruelty of enslavement. By the 1840s, panoramas had become a viewing craze on both sides of the Atlantic. The abolition movement made full use of this resource, and, 'by utilizing this visual, the anti-slavery movement participated in the perception revolution under way in US culture' and the panorama was a central part of this revolution.[24] Wells Brown had first visited a panoramic exhibition in Boston in early 1847, which he believed portrayed slavery in a benign way. He believed that 'slavery has never been represented; Slavery never can be represented', so when he travelled to Europe, he wanted to incorporate a panorama into his programme.[25] Like Douglass, he understood the power of visual imagery, and so had developed his own panorama to provide a more realistic view of slavery.

In Liverpool, Wells Brown stayed at Brown's Temperance Hotel. His sense of liberation was immediate:

> … no sooner was I on British soil, than I was recognised as a man, and an equal. The very dogs in the streets appeared conscious of my manhood. Such is the difference, and such is the change that is brought about by a trip of nine days in an Atlantic steamer … For the first time in my life, I can say 'I am truly free'.[26]

Ireland

Following in Douglass's footsteps, Wells Brown did not linger in England but, after only two days, sailed from Liverpool to Dublin. There, he was 'warmly received by Mr. Haughton, Mr. Webb, and other friends of the slave, and publicly welcomed at a large meeting presided over by the first named gentleman'.[27] Like Remond and Douglass before him, Wells Brown stayed at the home of Richard and Hannah Webb on Great Brunswick Street, close to Trinity College. By doing so, he was thrust not only into the centre of life in Dublin, but into the heart of Ireland's vibrant anti-slavery movement.

Wells Brown's introduction to Ireland was gentle, but also challenging. Before lecturing, he spent almost two weeks exploring Dublin, writing favourably of the architecture of the Bank of Ireland (formerly the Irish parliament), the Custom House and the fashionable Upper Sackville Street (later renamed O'Connell Street). He was then taken to some of the poorer parts of the city and, just as Douglass had been, Wells Brown was also shocked that such poverty existed in what was regarded as the second city of the British Empire. Describing the people as 'the poorest of the poor', he explained:

William Wells Brown (c.1814–1884)   139

All the recollections of poverty which I had ever beheld, seemed to disappear in comparison with what was then before me. We passed a filthy and noisy market, where fruit and vegetable women were screaming and begging those passing by to purchase their commodities; while in and about the market-place were throngs of beggars fighting for rotten fruit, cabbage stalks, and even the very trimmings of vegetables. On the sidewalks, were great numbers hovering about the doors of the more wealthy, and following strangers, importuning them for 'pence to buy bread'. Sickly and emaciated-looking creatures, half naked, were at our heels at every turn. After passing through a half dozen, or more, of narrow and dirty streets, we returned to our lodgings, impressed with the idea that we had seen enough of the poor for one day.[28]

What Wells Brown may not have realized was that parts of Ireland were still undergoing a major famine and that port towns such as Dublin had seen wave after wave of starving poor arrive, hoping to find work or to emigrate. Douglass also had been shocked by the poverty that he witnessed in Ireland in 1845. However, four consecutive years of potato failures had added to the country's levels of poverty. For American visitors, especially black abolitionists, the idea that starvation and famine could exist at the heart of the British Empire—and amongst free white people—proved shocking.[29]

Wells Brown's excursions ended on a happy note as, on the way to his accommodation, he passed the birth place of the poet Thomas Moore, leading him to recall lines from 'So lowly the slave'—a favourite with many abolitionists.[30] He later elaborated on his admiration, writing:

of Ireland's sons, none stands higher in America than Thomas Moore, the Poet. The vigour of his sarcasm, the glow of his enthusiasm, the coruscations of his fancy, and the flashing of his wit, seem to be as well understood in the new world as the old; and the support which his pen has given to civil and religious liberty throughout the world, entitled the Minstrel of Erin to this elevated position.[31]

On the first Sunday of Wells Brown's stay, Queen Victoria arrived in Dublin on her first ever visit to the country. As all the trains were full, Wells Brown and the Webb family joined thousands of other people who walked five miles to Kingstown to catch a glimpse of the Queen's yacht.[32] The following day, he watched the royal entourage as it entered Dublin and partook of the illuminations provided in the evening.[33] He enjoyed the whole experience. Webb, writing in his capacity as Dublin Correspondent of the *National Anti-Slavery Society*, provided an account of the Queen being welcomed in Ireland, adding, 'We have another guest just now whose presence has been a much greater source of pleasure to our circle than the Queen's visit. I mean William Wells Brown'.[34] Despite playing the host to many visiting American abolitionists, Webb appeared particularly taken by Wells Brown, writing to a friend in Boston

140   *William Wells Brown (c.1814–1884)*

that, 'He is very intelligent and easy, full of anecdote and staunch to his colour'.[35] Writing for an abolitionist newspaper, Webb elaborated:

> We are greatly pleased with him. He is an upright, downright, straightforward fellow; intelligent, sagacious, gentlemanly, and self-respecting. He is excellent company, full of anecdote, has graphic and dramatic powers of no mean order, and a keen appreciation of character. His knowledge of the Cause and its advocates is extensive and discriminating, and it is quite a feast to listen to him. He not only has a good pair of eyes, but, which is not so common, he makes use of them, and this is a valuable tendency in a visitor to strange countries. Besides he will be likely to be a much more useful and intelligent labourer on behalf of the slave when he returns amongst you. He and I get on so pleasantly together, and he is so much beloved by my friends that I naturally look on him as a perfect rock of sense. Besides all this, he brings with him the highest recommendations. In short, I think he is sure to be beloved wherever he goes …

To reassure Garrison regarding his ongoing fear that his talented lecturers would defect to his abolitionist rivals, the 'New Organization', officially known as the American and Foreign Anti-Slavery Society, Webb added, 'I have no doubt he will continue true to the Cause and to its advocates, his late fellow-labourers in the United States'.[36]

Due to a combination of the Queen's visit to the country and the shortness of Wells Brown's visit to Ireland, there was only time for one public lecture. Wells Brown spoke in the Rotundo Rooms on 16 August 1849. The publicity described him as 'a self-emancipated slave', adding that his daring escape meant that he had achieved 'at last in his own person the triumph of perseverance in the cause of freedom'.[37] It was a pointed refutation of the term, 'fugitive'. The venue was a prestigious concert hall in the centre of Dublin, which Webb referred to as 'the most respectable place for the purpose'.[38] The hall filled up quickly with 'intelligent and respectable citizens' which, inevitably, included a large number of members of the Society of Friends and others 'distinguished for philanthropy and practical benevolence'.[39] Writing to American friends, however, Webb stated that a large portion of the audience were 'of the poorer sort, and … the name of O'Connell was very dear to a large part of the audience'.[40] However, not only were all the seats taken, but all standing room was used up, leading one newspaper to estimate 600 were present.[41] The platform party consisted of familiar faces in Irish anti-slavery and included Richard's brother, James Webb. Haughton was in the chair and introduced the speaker as, 'Mr. Brown, once the goaded and beaten slave of a hard taskmaster, now the graceful and energetic lecturer on the humiliations, sufferings, and injuries of his race to the enlightened audiences of Europe'. Wells Brown, in turn, responded to the warm welcome from the audience 'very gracefully and unaffectedly'.[42] Because parts of his life story had been printed in the British and Irish press, there existed, 'much of romance about the man and his story, and no small interest was excited in his appearance'.[43] Wells Brown's appearance was described as 'prepossessing', but it was refracted through a racial lens that added, 'he possesses little of the Nubian or negro cast of head and features.

William Wells Brown (c.1814–1884) 141

His forehead is good, and well developed in the frontal formation, and his figure erect and graceful'.[44] Wells Brown's speaking abilities (apart from his occasional use of 'American idioms') were particularly admired:

> His language is strictly grammatical, and his style correct and energetic ... his eloquence is that of a well-taught and unaffected speaker. He certainly seems to possess the rare faculty of keeping alive to the last word he uttered the undivided attention of his auditory.

Wells Brown's opening statements were a theme to which he would often refer—his lack of education, pointing out, 'It could not be otherwise, for twenty of his best and youngest years had been spent, not under the gentle guidance of a preceptor, but under the bitter lash of the taskmaster in hopeless and helpless slavery'.[45] After lambasting the lack of Christianity of those involved in slavery in America, Wells Brown turned to a local hero, 'Daniel O'Connell (loud and repeated cheers)'. Wells Brown then retold the story of O'Connell refusing to shake the hand of Andrew Stevenson, the American Ambassador to Britain, on the grounds he was a slaveholder.[46] It was a crowd pleaser, and a story that many American abolitionists liked to repeat. He also told of a family of slaves who preferred death to separation. Again, similar stories were repeated by other lecturers, but the Dublin audience were shocked and responded with 'sensation'. Demonstrating a skill for which he was famed, Wells Brown lifted the mood of the meeting by telling an amusing story regarding slaveowners in Philadelphia who attended a meeting to celebrate the revolution in France in 1848. While they were shouting 'Liberty', 700 of their slaves ran away, 'and the liberty spouters forgot all they had been preaching, and all ran to catch (if they could) the runaway slaves (laughter)'.[47] Wells Brown told a number of other anecdotes that oscillated between amusing and appalling his listeners. He explained the achievements of American Anti-Slavery Society as having:

> ... brought him (Mr. Brown) and others out of degradation, and placed them on the common platform of humanity. Next, through its instrumentality, the laws which formerly existed in Massachusetts and other States against persons of colour travelling in the same railway carriage with whites had been done away with. Previous to that event a separate carriage was provided for the former on every railway, called the Jim Crow Car.[48]

Wells Brown concluded his well-received lecture,

> with a forcible appeal to the Christian sympathies of Irishmen to use every effort, and to add the weight of their influence to the endeavours which were becoming every day more successful in putting an end forever to the vile system of human slavery.[49]

Wells Brown sat down amid 'loud cheering'. Webb told the audience that copies of his *Narrative* were available for sale, and a large number were purchased.[50] It

142   *William Wells Brown (c.1814–1884)*

was Wells Brown's only lecture in Ireland but it was a major success, confirming his abilities as an ambassador for American anti-slavery. Coverage in both Dublin and Irish provincial newspapers meant that his impact extended far beyond those who heard him speak.[51] Across the Atlantic, Wells Brown's movements were being followed. Douglass included news about Wells Brown's visit to Ireland in the *North Star*, which, in turn, was based on Irish newspaper reports. The story of Wells Brown's lecture in the Rotunda was given the headline, 'Wm. Brown in Dublin—No Colorphobia there'.[52] The *National Anti-Slavery Standard* also reported of Wells Brown's successful lecture.[53] The *Liberator* printed a letter from Haughton to Garrison, which opened with 'W.W. Brown has been here with us, and we all liked him very much'. It went on to describe him as 'a superior man' with 'considerable power as a speaker'.[54]

One of Wells Brown's main purposes in Ireland was to oversee the reprinting of his *Narrative*, which had first appeared in 1847. Within less than 18 months of its publication, 8,000 copies had sold, making it one of the fastest selling anti-slavery books to date.[55] He had brought with him the American stereotype plates, for Webb to utilize.[56] Despite its Dublin origins, the reprinted book was published under the imprint of London publisher Charles Gilpin, also a Quaker and a member of the British and Foreign Anti-Slavery Society.[57] Webb and Gilpin had also collaborating in publishing the narrative of Moses Grandy.[58] The advertisements for Wells Brown's book stated:

> The author of this narrative is a fugitive slave, similar in condition to Frederick Douglass, and like that noble specimen of the coloured race, he has visited this country to relate the horrors of American slavery and to promote the growing feeling against that infamous system.[59]

Favourable reviews of the publication, helped to keep its author in the public eye, while generating much needed income.[60]

Just as Douglass had done, Wells Brown inserted himself into the new Irish edition of his narrative. This included the verses of a song that he had written, which started, 'Fling out the anti-slavery flag'. The new Irish/British edition also included a 'Note to the Present Edition' written by Wells Brown while staying in Webb's home. He stated that his purpose in coming to Europe was two-fold, to attend the Peace Congress and to

> follow up the work of my friends and fellow-labourers, Charles Lenox Remond and Frederick Douglass, and to lay before the people of Great Britain and Ireland the wrongs that are still committed upon the slaves and the free coloured people of America.[61]

To this end, both the *Narrative* and Wells Brown's lectures were to counteract the influence of slavery 'and this can only be effected by the promulgation of truth, and the cultivation of a correct public sentiment at home and abroad'.[62]

For Wells Brown, Ireland had proved to be a land of paradoxes:

William Wells Brown (c.1814–1884)   143

How varied their aspect—how contradictory their character. Ireland, the land of genius and degradation—of great resources and unparalleled poverty—noble deeds and the most revolting crimes—the land of distinguished poets, splendid orators, and the bravest of soldiers—the land of ignorance and beggary! Dublin is a splendid city, but its splendour is that of chiseled marble rather than real life.[63]

Like others before and after him, he was impressed with the ardency of Irish abolitionists. Before arriving, he had been told about it, but 'the reception I met with on all hands while in public, satisfied me that what I had heard had not been exaggerated. To the Webbs, Allens, and Haughtons, of Dublin, the cause of the American slave is much indebted'. Although he only spent two months in the country, he wrote, 'I quitted Dublin with a feeling akin to leaving my native land'.[64] Although Wells Brown wrote in detail about his experiences in Ireland in his travel memoir, he did not mention the fact that during his stay there he lectured on anti-slavery. Moreover, it was his first lecture on European soil.

After Dublin, Wells Brown, in the company of Webb, returned to Liverpool, then onwards to London for 24 hours, before travelling to Paris where he was a delegate at the Peace Congress.[65] The Peace Congress ran from 22 to 24 August 1849. The French writer, Victor Hugo, was President.[66] Wells Brown was one of the platform party, as were fellow Americans, the Rev. James Pennington and Elihu Burritt. Wells Brown spoke about ending slavery, referring to France having done so in 1848.[67] Webb informed his friends in America that Wells Brown had been

> treated with marked respect and courtesy by many of the most eminent men present at the Congress. His presence on this occasion is likely to prove of great use to him, for he was introduced to some of the best people in England.[68]

Following the ending of the conference, the two men went sightseeing together in Paris, Wells Brown now referring to the Irish man as 'my friend'.[69] The longer-term friendship between Wells Brown and Webb, however, experienced some of the difficulties that had accompanied Webb's relationship with Douglass. By the end of 1849, when Wells Brown had long departed from Dublin, Webb admitted that he had been left with debts regarding the reissue of the *Narrative*, and that Wells Brown was not responding to him.[70] Regardless of the strains on their business relationship, their personal friendship continued and Webb, just as he had done for Douglass, helped to set up speaking engagements for Wells Brown when he arrived in Britain.[71]

Return to Britain

Wells Brown arrived back in London at the end of August. In France, he had been warmly welcomed and feted, but in London he now had to earn a living,

144 *William Wells Brown (c.1814–1884)*

while not offending either side of the anti-slavery divide. Wells Brown rented rooms at a boarding house on Cecil Street, near the fashionable Strand area, where he remained during his five-year stay in the country. After only five days in the capital, he gave his first English lecture in Croydon. Garrison's close friend, veteran abolitionist, George Thompson, travelled down to introduce him. Liverpool-born Thompson, an MP in the British parliament since 1847, had welcomed many visiting abolitionists to Britain. Wells Brown adopted a similar format to that of his Dublin lecture—apologizing for his lack of formal education followed by a selection of crowd-pleasing anecdotes. It was a success, and 50 copies of his newly available *Narrative* were sold.[72] It was an encouraging start.

Thompson was again involved in a large event to officially welcome Wells Brown to England. It took place on 27 September in London's Music Hall. In his speech, Thompson invoked the earlier visit by Douglass. He also informed the audience that Wells Brown had letters of recommendation from Garrison.[73] This public reassurance demonstrated the importance of patronage to travelling black abolitionists, no matter how talented they were. The meeting was featured in the *Liberator* and the *North Star*, with the by-line of 'Public Reception of Wm. W. Brown in the Metropolis of England'. According to the report in the *Liberator*:

> a public meeting was convened in the spacious and elegant concert-room in Store street, London, for the purpose of greeting W.W. Brown on his arrival in England, as the representative of the free persons of color in the United States, and to afford that gentleman an opportunity of giving information relative to the present position of the anti-slavery cause in his native land ... The hall was crowded in every part by a highly respectable audience.[74]

There was a pro-slavery heckler from Boston in the audience, who was invited to join the platform party. His presence made for an exceptionally lively meeting. Wells Brown, when recreating the encounter in a letter to Wendell Phillips, informed him that, 'G.T. skinned a proslavery Bostonian alive last night, all except the feet, and they say that I took the skin off them'.[75]

The auspicious commencement to Wells Brown's tour disguised the fact that his was a precarious existence, especially as he did not have the backing of the influential British and Foreign Anti-Slavery Society. At one point, he found himself on the streets of London with only a farthing in his pocket.[76] His isolation, homesickness and financial vulnerability were shared by other visiting black abolitionists. Sales of the *Narrative*, however, proved healthy with a second printing by Webb and Gilpin released at the beginning of 1850. Wells Brown also proved to be an indefatigable lecturer and self-promoter. The Quaker network, opened up to him by Webb, was invaluable, with the second edition of his *Narrative* giving his address as Newcastle, his base in the north of England and home of the Richardson family.[77] Like the Webbs in Dublin, the Quaker Richardson family opened their homes and their hearts to many visiting abolitionists.[78] Only six months later, a further Irish/British edition of the

Narrative was published.[79] To augment his income from book sales, Wells Brown also sold engravings depicting his friend and fellow fugitive slave, Ellen Craft.[80] He used his enjoyment at being a tourist as the basis for a new publication in 1852, entitled *Three Years in Europe*, which was based on his letters describing his experiences and observations in Ireland, Britain and France.[81] A number of the letters had already been published in Douglass's newspapers.[82] His daughter Josephine Brown later explained that the publication was motivated by the shortness of the lecture season that year, and her father's need to supplement his income.[83] It was published by Gilpin of London. The book was reviewed widely and when it was republished in 1855, with the new title, *The American Fugitive in Europe*, it included an Irish review:

> THREE YEARS IN EUROPE—The remarkable man who is the author of this work is not unknown to many of our readers. He was received with kindness in this city, and honored with various marks of respect by many eminent characters in the sister country. Since his arrival Mr. Brown has contributed much to the press; and the work before us, though small and unpretending, is of a high character, and evinces a superior and cultivated mind. Dublin General Advertiser, October 30, 1852.[84]

Wells Brown repeatedly demonstrated that he understood the power of spectacle. The slave collar and leg shackle that he had carried from America were frequently used as props to shock his audiences. Many other abolitionists used similar artefacts, but Wells Brown went one step further. In November 1849, he parcelled up these artefacts and sent them to the British Museum, suggesting that they display them. His offer was declined.[85] Pushing other boundaries, Wells Brown agitated to be given a passport—something that was unthinkable for a fugitive slave. Moreover, prior to sailing to Liverpool, his request for an American passport had been ignored—a tacit denial of Wells Brown's application.[86] Undeterred, towards the end of 1849, the American legation in London did issue him with a passport, thus enabling him to be a citizen of Europe, if not the United States.[87] The timing was judicious as the passage of the Fugitive Slave Law meant that Wells Brown's absence from home was likely to be a prolonged one.

Unlike most abolitionists who kept their personal life separate from their public one, Wells Brown's private life intruded in a way that was messy and damaging to his reputation. His estranged wife Elizabeth (Betsey) found an outlet for attacking her absent husband when the *New York Tribune* published her letter to the editor on 12 March 1850, under the heading, 'A Stray Husband'. Amidst claims of cruelty and abandonment, she claimed, 'Mr. Brown has become so popular among the Abolition ladies that he did not wish his sable wife any longer'.[88] The pro-slavery press and opponents of Brown on both sides of the Atlantic rejoiced. Wells Brown tackled the problem head on, writing 'To the Public', from London on 1 June, which appeared in the *Liberator* on 12 July. It commenced by casting aspersions on the moral character of members of Betsey's family, but stated that he loved her anyway. It then outlined, in

146 *William Wells Brown (c.1814–1884)*

painful detail, her relationship with another man, a former friend of Wells Brown. He ended by saying, 'I give this statement with great reluctance, but he felt that he had to break his silence'.[89] Only a few months later, in January 1851, while Wells Brown continued in exile, Betsey died in Buffalo.[90] The episode with Betsey was a painful public exposition of a failed marriage. It was also a reminder of the fine line that visiting abolitionists had to tread when seeking the support of women abolitionists.

In the years after 1850, Wells Brown continued to traverse England, giving his lectures and selling his books. Despite the success and impact of his appearances, none of his events were covered in the *British and Foreign Anti-Slavery Reporter*, a fact noted by supporters of Garrison in America.[91] In between travelling and lecturing, Wells Brown visited art galleries, museums, memorials, ancient sites of worship, history and heritage sites, while reading voraciously. Wells Brown, more than any other visiting abolitionist, absorbed European culture, writing about it in a way that distinguished him as urbane, sophisticated and cosmopolitan.[92] On Christmas evening 1851, Wells Brown lectured to a packed audience in the Cavendish Baptist church in Ramsgate.[93] The church could accommodate up to 1,500. Shortly afterwards, a minister in Kent, the Rev. Edward Hoare, wrote to Enoch Price, 'owner' of Wells Brown, offering him £50 if he would relinquish all claim to him and allow him to return to the States.[94] Price refused pointing out that 'the laws of the United States are materially changed' so he wanted £100 (or $500) in order to release Wells Brown.[95] It was an insight into how the 1850 Fugitive Slave Law had emboldened slaveholders. It also suggested that Wells Brown, who now wanted to return to the United States, was homesick.

The passage of the Fugitive Slave Law changed the focus of Wells Brown's lectures, with audiences wanting to know more about this topic. He had carried with him panoramic scenes that he hoped would form the basis for a show, but additional outlay was needed to make this happen. Despite solid book sales and other donations, Wells Brown needed to borrow money, appealing to supporters of Garrison who had befriended him, namely, the Estlin family in Bristol and the Richardsons in Newcastle.[96] In summer 1850, Wells Brown commissioned artists in London to create more oil-canvas panels for him. By October, 25 panels were complete and, acting on the advice of friends, the show opened in Newcastle. The northern town, a Garrisonian stronghold, was regarded as a safer option than London in terms of garnering favourable publicity.[97] The panorama was displayed twice a day and, given Wells Brown's limited resources, he did most of the work himself, including providing 'a descriptive account of the scenery' and supplying the musical accompaniment.[98] Only a few days later, Wells Brown and his panorama moved to nearby Durham where it was hoped that the show would be well received, with 'vast' numbers attending. The local press explained to its readers the importance of attending,

> From the excitement at present prevailing in the United States … in consequence of the late most iniquitous law relating to the coloured fugitives of

William Wells Brown (c.1814–1884)   147

the Southern States, and which has deeply stirred the feelings of the people of England on the slavery question.[99]

For Wells Brown, delivering this one-man show proved to be gruelling. Moreover, within only two weeks of his show opening, another fugitive slave, with the same surname, had landed in Liverpool, his arrival being widely noted in the press. Henry Boxer Brown, a fugitive slave from Richmond, Virginia, had dramatically fled from enslavement in 1849, standing upright in a box. He was now earning a living by showing a panorama depicting the horrors of slavery and the spectacle of his escape.[100] In this venture, Boxer Brown was accompanied by James Boxer Smith, a free black man. Their arrival meant that Wells Brown had competition.

More cheeringly, two of Wells Brown's friends, Ellen and William Craft, were also making their way across the Atlantic. For the second time in their short lives, the Crafts had dramatically escaped from capture and enslavement. The three former slaves had toured together in the United States and Wells Brown was happy to recreate this. By early 1851, Wells Brown was lecturing with the Crafts in Scotland, augmenting their talks with a panorama.[101] This venture initially proved to be successful and lucrative. Perhaps because there were a number of other black abolitionists on the circuit, Wells Brown did not always attract a full attendance. Unusually, when lecturing in Gloucester with Craft, they had a 'scant audience', leading a local newspaper to speculate that it was probably the worst reception they had ever had.[102] It was a further reminder that life on the road could be precarious. Wells Brown's hard work to ensure that he had a constant income enabled him to finally send for his daughters, Josephine and Clarissa, in 1851, his plan being for them to attend boarding school in France, with a view to becoming teachers.[103]

Rather than simply lecture and write, Wells Brown continued to demonstrate his gift for spectacle and drama, this time on the largest stage in the world—at the Great Exhibition, which ran in the Crystal Palace in London from May to October 1851.[104] Wells Brown and the Crafts chose to hold an anti-slavery demonstration on what was expected to be the busiest day of the Exhibition, 21 June, which was also the longest day of the year and the one when many American tourists would be present.[105] They were joined by fellow supporters of Garrison, including Richard and Hannah Webb and two of their children, who had travelled over from Dublin.[106] In a further act of defiance, Wells Brown walked around the Exhibition arm-in-arm with Jenny Thompson, daughter of George. He knew this simple demonstration of equality would shock American visitors. The group of abolitionists then positioned themselves in front of the much-visited and highly idealized white marble statue of 'The Greek Slave', the only work of art provided by the United States.[107] Standing next to the statue, Wells Brown held up a *Punch* image of a Virginian slave. He then placed the image next to the statue. Wells Brown and the Crafts attended the Crystal Palace on a number of other occasions to challenge American visitors on slavery.[108]

Only days following the publicity stunt, Wells Brown organized what he regarded as one of his major successes while overseas, namely, a meeting to celebrate the Emancipation of the British West Indies, to be held on 1 August

148   William Wells Brown (c.1814–1884)

in London.[109] A secondary purpose was to welcome George Thompson back from his recent visit to America. Despite an admission fee of one shilling, almost 1,000 men and women attended. Although the meeting had been Wells Brown's idea, it was publicized as being organized by 'fugitive slaves'.[110] In addition to the Wells Brown family, the platform party included former slave, Alexander Duval, Francis Anderson and the enigmatic Benjamin Benson.[111] Unusually, it was the black speakers who occupied the front row on the stage, with the white guests sitting behind them. The meeting, which was chaired by Wells Brown, unanimously adopted his 'An Appeal to the People of Great Britain and the World'. His daughters, Josephine and Clarissa, each spoke about the prejudice that they had encountered in their short lives. The meeting concluded with tributes being paid to Garrison.[112] The meeting, which was also reported in Ireland and America, was a triumph for Wells Brown, and for supporters of Garrison.[113] Wells Brown, it seemed, was fearless in the multiple ways that he challenged the system of slavery. In only two years in exile, he had changed the nature of debate in multiple ways. By showcasing the success of emancipation in the West Indies, he had energized the movement and given it a positive focus; moreover, a focus that foregrounded the skills and achievements of black people. By his words, images, music and charismatic presence, Wells Brown had deepened transatlantic cooperation at a time when pro-slavery forces seemed stronger than ever in the United States.

Although Wells Brown did not return to Ireland to lecture, his activities continued to be reported in the Irish press and extracts from his *Narrative* intermittently appeared.[114] Moreover, his relationship with Irish abolitionists continued. In 1852, Brown ventured into a new field, albeit in a junior way—helping, along with fellow Garrisonians, Richard Webb and John Estlin, to found an abolitionist journal, the *Anti-Slavery Advocate*.[115] In its ten-year existence, this monthly would provide an alternative news source to the British and Foreign Anti-Slavery Society's *Anti-Slavery Reporter*, for, 'the express purpose of circulating unprejudiced information about Garrison's wing of abolitionism'. It would fall to Webb and his Dublin-based printing operation to do the heavy lifting in terms of making it viable. While based in London, Wells Brown was a regular contributor with the paper also following his movements.[116] This collaboration between a Dublin Quaker printer, an English doctor and an American fugitive slave was an example of the cooperation that Garrison had so much desired. This partnership had another positive outcome. Largely due to the generosity of John Estlin, the two Crafts attended college in late 1851, where they acquired something that remained elusive to Brown—a formal education. Their change in circumstances meant that Wells Brown was alone again.

An unlooked-for aspect of the Fugitive Slave Law had been the pressure that it put on employment opportunities in Canada and England. The consequence of thousands of fugitive slaves fleeing from America to Canada had resulted in increased unemployment, which led several of them to continue onwards to England. Their presence and inability to support themselves worried Wells Brown, especially those who 'have set themselves up as lecturers, and who are in fact little less than beggars'. Wells Brown sent letters across the Atlantic, with the simple message, 'Don't come to England'.[117] His preferred solution was for runaway slaves to emigrate to Jamaica, where they would be free and where there were employment opportunities. Wells Brown even wrote to the London *Times* on this topic, suggesting that he felt confidence in his authority as a public spokesman for his people.[118] In a further demonstration of his self-assurance, he penned a criticism of the 'literary giant' and one of the most important social commentators of the time, Thomas Carlyle. Following one of their visits to Crystal Palace, he and the Crafts had found themselves sitting across from Carlyle on an omnibus. Wells Brown, previously an admirer, increasingly saw Carlyle as somebody who 'exists not by sympathy but by antipathy'.[119] In a written critique, Wells Brown accused the acerbic Scotsman of pretending to be the 'prince of reformers' while, in reality, 'scorning every-thing' including the poor and the black people in the West Indies.[120] The story was picked up by a number of Irish provincial newspapers. Under the title, 'Criticism by a Fugitive Slave', they sided with Wells Brown, averring that, 'We are not so sure that an Edinburgh reviewer would write so sensibly of the literary giant'.[121] A few years later, Sarah Parker Remond would express similar abhorrence at Carlyle's overt racism.[122]

The publication and success of *Uncle Tom's Cabin* in 1852, revived interest in anti-slavery, leading Wells Brown to extend his panorama show and incorporate the use of magic lantern slides. Using his new equipment and images, he under-took a successful tour in the winter and spring of 1852 and 1853. In early 1854, the question of purchasing Wells Brown's freedom was raised by his Richardson friends in Newcastle. Price, Wells Brown's owner, had now reduced the amount to £60 ($300), and so Ellen Richardson set herself the task of handling this deli-cate and complicated matter. As the process was taking place, Wells Brown did what he had done for the previous four winters, namely, lecturing throughout the country, usually alone, in order to keep his finances solvent.[123] In a biography of her father published in 1856, Josephine included some of the legal documents relating to the purchase, stating that they were 'a true copy of the bill of sale by which a democratic, Christian American sells his fellow-countryman for British gold'.[124] As Douglass's had been, the purchase was controversial, especially among several white abolitionists, but Sydney Howard Gay of the *Anti-Slavery Standard*, and Garrison defended Wells Brown's decision, the former writing:

> WILLIAM WELLS BROWN, the *Liberator* informs us, is about to return to the United States, his friends in England having kindly contributed the amount necessary to secure his ransom from bondage. He is expected to land in Boston within a few weeks. His labours in Great Britain have been highly useful, and the friends of our cause in the United States will hail his return with peculiar satisfaction.[125]

Wells Brown's final public appearance in Britain was in Manchester on 1 August 1854. Since his first lecture in Dublin in 1849, Brown estimated that

150 *William Wells Brown (c.1814–1884)*

he had given more than 1,000 talks and travelled 25,000 miles.[126] The Manchester meeting was to celebrate the twentieth anniversary of West Indian Emancipation. The platform party included Wells Brown's friend, George Thompson, and fellow fugitive slaves, Rev. Samuel Ward and a Mr North from South Carolina. One newspaper reported that the attendance was small, with only between 80 and 100 present.[127] During his lecture, Ward 'strongly advised Mr. Wm. Wells Brown not to return to the United States as his free papers might be easily, and would probably, be stolen from him'.[128] It was a worrying note on which to conclude a five-year successful lecture tour that had commenced in Ireland.

Later life

Wells Brown arrived in the port of Philadelphia on 26 September 1854, after 20 days at sea. He immediately encountered racism being told, when trying to board an omnibus, 'We don't allow n—s to ride in here'.[129] Wells Brown remained philosophical, writing:

> I had returned to the country for the express purpose of joining in the glorious battle against slavery, of which this Negrophobia is a legitimate offspring. And why not meet it in its stronghold? I might have remained in a country where my manhood was never denied; I might have remained in ease in other climes; but what was ease and comfort abroad, while more than three millions of my countrymen were groaning in the prison-house of slavery in the Southern States? Yes, I came to the land of my nativity, not to be a spectator, but a soldier—a soldier in this moral warfare against the most cruel system of oppression that ever blackened the character or hardened the heart of man.[130]

Back home, Wells Brown continued to work on behalf of the New England Anti-Slavery Society. He also continued to write in a variety of genres. Like many abolitionists, Wells Brown was an admirer of the black republic of Haiti. In 1854, he had lectured in London on this topic and, in 1855, he released, 'St. Domingo: its revolutions and its patriots. A lecture'.[131] Again, it was a groundbreaking discourse, the scholar Benjamin Fagan arguing that:

> In his 1854 lecture Brown presents a model for historicizing black revolution that forestalls attempts by white writers, many sympathetic to Brown's abolitionism, to assimilate successful black revolutionaries into a white revolutionary narrative.[132]

For Fagan, Haiti represented the start of an unfinished revolution, he seeing it, 'not as a singular, contained event, but instead as one part of a larger, unfinished struggle for black liberation'.[133] Wells Brown continued to write in a variety of genres. His other publications included *The American Fugitive in Europe* in 1855

William Wells Brown (c.1814–1884)   151

(which was his 1852 travelogue), and in 1858, he wrote what is regarded as the first play by an African American, *The Escape; or, A Leap for Freedom*. In 1863, Wells Brown published his study of African Americans, entitled, *The Black Man: his Antecedents, His Genius, and His Achievements*. In 1867, *The Negro in the American Rebellion* was published, which was the first history to focus on black soldiers. Wells Brown's final book was published in 1880, four years before his death, and it was called, *My Southern Home; or, The South and Its People*. It concerned the author's search for a place he could call home in a land where slavery and racism existed. Wells Brown's disenchantment was evident in other ways. His ongoing admiration for Haiti and disillusionment with the United States led him to advocate emigration to Haiti in 1861. The onset of war did not reassure Wells Brown that enslaved people would ever be treated fairly in the United States. Consequently, he initially opposed the conflict.[134] Like many other black abolitionists, Wells Brown was skeptical about President Lincoln's intentions regarding enslaved people. Even following the 1863 Proclamation, Wells Brown continued to speak on the need for 'Liberty for all'.[135] He did, however, assist in recruiting for the Black 54th Massachusetts Regiment, who distinguished themselves for their bravery during the War.[136]

In 1864, Wells Brown embarked on a rigorous lecture tour, during which he argued that freedom should also mean equality. By 1865, he was lecturing on the need for 'Negro Suffrage'.[137] Wells Brown also continued to publish his works including *The Black Man, a History of the Distinguished Individuals of the Race* (1863). As ever, Wells Brown was asserting his agency, now as a historian of his people.[138] During this time also, demonstrating his remarkable range of abilities and inspired by his relationship with Estlin while in England, Wells Brown started to practice homeopathic medicine.[139] In the postbellum decades, Wells Brown continued to be influential in many areas, including being a proponent of rejecting the term 'Negro' and replacing it with 'African'.[140] The post war segregation and lynchings resulted in Wells Brown returning to Britain in 1877, again to seek support from across the Atlantic, but this time, in support of temperance.[141] As he had done in 1849, he sailed from Boston to Liverpool, with his arrival being noted in some of the British press.[142] Once there, he attended numerous temperance meetings, arguing that sobriety was a key factor in achieving success and equality.[143] These arguments mirrored the ones made by Douglass in the mid-1840s. As part of his brief tour, Wells Brown did return to Dublin, speaking in the Rotunda on 18 July, where his first lecture in Europe had taken place 28 years earlier.[144] The following evening, he provided the formal address at a literary and musical concert in the same venue.[145] Both events had been organized by the Independent Order of Good Templars, a temperance organization.[146] Newspaper coverage was brief, with Wells Brown being simply described as 'a coloured man and ex-slave' from Boston.[147]

In his personal life, Wells Brown experienced both joy and tragedy. In 1860, he married Anna Elizabeth Gray from Massachusetts. They had two children but their son, William Wells Brown Jr., born in 1861, died as an infant of cholera, and his newborn daughter, Clotelle, died in 1862 of typhoid fever.[148]

152 *William Wells Brown (c.1814–1884)*

Josephine also predeceased her father, dying in tragic circumstances in 1874.[149] Wells Brown died in November 1884 at his home in Chelsea, Massachusetts. To the end, he was fighting for equal rights for his people, whether in the United States or further afield.[150] Wells Brown's death went largely unnoticed in the national press, which was ironic given that throughout his life he had proven to be an expert at creating a spectacle and a presence. The *Christian Recorder*, however, referring to him as Dr Brown, MD, opined, 'His services on behalf of this race have been of the highest order'.[151] Regardless of this tribute and Wells Brown's remarkable life and his multiple achievements, he was buried in an unmarked grave in the Cambridge Cemetery in Massachusetts.[152]

Conclusion

In a number of ways, the life of William Wells Brown mirrored that of the more famous Frederick Douglass. Sometime friends, at other times rivals, the two men's lives paralleled each other's.[153] Their early lives were spent in enslavement, they escaped and self-emancipated when aged 20, their dizzying amount of accomplishments, including publications, were remarkable especially given their lack of formal education. Wells Brown's literary achievements, and his ability to succeed in so many genres, were particularly impressive, especially, as he liked to remind his readers and audiences, 'the education he has acquired was by his own exertions, he never having had a day's schooling in his life'. A prolific publisher, he used his later books as a way of publicizing and praising his earlier publications. For Nell Irvin Painter, one of Wells Brown's unique strengths was that he was a 'fugitive slave, abolitionist, lecturer, travelogue writer, novelist and performer whose wide-ranging intelligence turned a gaze on white people (for a change)'.[154]

Even when compared with his formidable contemporaries, notably Douglass, Garnet and Ward, Wells Brown stands out as being special in terms of his multiple and diverse forms of self-expression, in each of which he excelled. In a field where there was tough opposition, he was a master of promotion and propaganda, using many more mediums than his colleagues, and never being afraid to innovate or change. His lectures were multimedia performances, using visuals (the panorama and magic lantern) and music (he loved to sing) to enhance his performances. And, just as Douglass had utilized photography to break down stereotypes, Wells Brown chose a different path to do so, using the new and popular medium of panoramas. Both men understood the powerful impact of visual imagery. Wells Brown's skills and vision meant that he quickly became a massive presence on the transatlantic stage. His intense lecturing programme and multiple and diverse publications were unrivalled. Although he was away for five years, his name was kept before American abolitionists through a stream of letters, a large portion of which were published by Douglass.

The timing of Brown's departure from the United States, only months before the Fugitive Slave Law was enacted, meant that his stay in United Kingdom was protracted. In total, he spent five years in exile, far longer than many other

William Wells Brown (c.1814–1884) 153

black abolitionists. His protracted stay meant that he was able to experience being overseas in ways other than simply as an anti-slavery activist. During his time in Europe, Wells Brown published *Three Years in Europe; or, Places I have Seen and People I have Met* (1852). In it, he approached his time in Europe through the lens of a tourist. As a consequence, he has been described as a 'cultivated fugitive', and, because he combined his lecturing and celebrity with being a sightseer, a 'fugitive tourist'.[155] Wells Brown's success, sophistication, sophistry and cultural aspirations, to which *Three Years* was a public testimony, at times may have appeared to overshadow his anti-slavery activism, and has led to unfounded accusations that he was 'a self-serving black bourgeois or elitist cultural tourist'.[156] While visiting museums and art galleries etc., Brown was challenging common-place stereotypes. Moreover, he continued to be indefatigable in speaking out against slavery.

While there are many parallels between Brown and Douglass, there are some differences as well. Charles Baraw has argued that while Douglass came as a fugitive slave, Brown arrived as a fugitive tourist:

> In contrast to his predecessor Frederick Douglass, who emphasizes the radically different meanings Great Britain held for him as a 'rude, uncultivated fugitive slave' and for 'American young gentlemen' in search of 'knowledge, ... pleasure,' and refinement of 'their rough democratic manners', William Wells Brown publicly adopts the role of a cultivated fugitive, integrating tourism and its representational strategies into his own antislavery discourse. With the publication of Three Years in Europe, Brown produces a new kind of 'fugitive tourism' that adopts key conventions of Anglo-American travel historical sightseeing, museum-going, literary pilgrimages, and the sentimental encounter with the Other—and transforms them into powerful counter-narratives that expose the instability of monumental histories of nation, empire, and race. 'Fugitive tourism' enabled Brown to represent slavery—and to represent himself as a fugitive slave—in ways that facilitated his career-long critique of the parochialism, historical myopia, and the barely concealed violence that sustained slavery in the United States. By embracing the conventions of Anglo-American tourism as no African American writer had before, Brown politicizes antebellum travel, further exposes the fallacies and hypocrisies of the slave-owning republic, and establishes for himself what his first biographer calls 'a position among literary men never before enjoyed by any colored American'.[157]

Like Douglass, Wells Brown spent the first weeks of his exile in Ireland overseeing the publication of his *Narrative*. Yet, Wells Brown's time in Ireland has been ignored. A recent 600-page biography, for example, devotes two long chapters to Brown's time overseas, but entitles them simply 'England'.[158] The significance of Ireland is that it was the first place Wells Brown visited in Europe, the first place where he lectured within the United Kingdom, the first country to arrange publication of his *Narrative* outside the United States, and

154   *William Wells Brown (c.1814–1884)*

the location where friendships that were formed that continued for the remainder of his stay in Europe and beyond those years. Ireland was the place where Wells Brown, just as Douglass had some years earlier, felt both safe and equal for the first time in his life. Similarly, they both witnessed, and were shocked by, white poverty. For both men, it was a transformative experience. When writing a biography of her father in 1856, Josephine referred to this visit in warm terms:

> FROM Liverpool, Mr. Brown went to Dublin, where he was warmly greeted by the Webbs, Haughtons, Allens, and others of the slave's friends in Ireland. Her Britannic Majesty was visiting her Irish subjects at that time, so the fugitive had an opportunity of witnessing Royalty in all its magnificence and regal splendor. The land of Burke, Sheridan and O'Connell would not permit the American to leave without giving him a public welcome. A large and enthusiastic meeting was held in the Rotunda, and presided over by JAMES HAUGHTON, Esq., and gave Mr. Brown the first reception which he had in the Old World.[159]

While both Wells Brown and Douglass had made Ireland their first venue while in the United Kingdom, their experiences were very different. Despite the warmth of the welcome, and spending almost five years based in London, Wells Brown did not return across the Irish Sea until he revisited Ireland as a promoter of temperance in 1877. In Dublin, he had praised Daniel O'Connell, but unlike Douglass, his admiration appeared transitory and with no lasting impact. Tellingly, in 1854, the year Wells Brown returned to the United States, one of his essays was included in the second edition of Julia Griffith's 'Autographs for Freedom'. It was a eulogy to a now dead, English abolitionist, entitled, 'Visit of a Fugitive Slave to the Grave of Wilberforce'.[160] The final sentence was,

> Let the name, the worth, the zeal, and other excellent qualifications of this noble man, ever live in our hearts, let his deeds ever be the theme of our praise, and let us teach our children to honor and love the name of William Wilberforce.[161]

It was an interesting choice; for Remond, Douglass and many other Garrisonians, O'Connell was the transatlantic hero of abolition, for Wells Brown, it was William Wilberforce.[162]

Back in the States, in 1855, Wells Brown reprinted his travelogue, with a different title. He also added a chapter reflecting fondly on his time overseas and those who had befriended him. He concluded the section by saying:

> I had spent hours at the hospitable firesides of Harriet Martineau, R. D. Webb, and other distinguished authors. You will not, reader, think it strange that my heart became sad at the thought of leaving all these dear friends, to return to a country in which I had spent some of the best days of my life as a slave, and where I knew that prejudice would greet me on my arrival.[163]

William Wells Brown (c.1814–1884) 155

Slave, abolitionist, autobiographer, orator, travel writer, cultural critic, performer, novelist, playwright, historian, equal rights activist, medical doctor, Wells Brown's life had been an incredible journey of discovery, defiance, self-definition and re-definition. Wells Brown, the self-emancipated slave, refused to be pigeon-holed or stereotyped, and any attempt to do so by others would do a dis-service to this brilliant, multi-faceted, pioneering champion of his people.

Notes

1 Ezra Greenspan, *William Wells Brown: An African American Life* (New York: Norton and Co., 2014), p. 2.
2 W. Wells Brown, *Three Years in Europe; or, Places I Have Seen and People I Have Met, by a Fugitive Slave, with a Memoir of the Author, by William Farmer, Esq.* (London: Charles Gilpin; Edinburgh: Oliver and Boyd, 1852), p. xxxii.
3 Richard W. Leeman included Wells Brown in his selection of great African American orators.
4 Frederick Douglass, William Wells Brown and Harriet E. Wilson, *Three Great African-American Novels* (New York: Dover Publications, 2008), pp. iii–iv.
5 For example, William Wells Brown, *Anti Slavery Harp: A Collection of Songs for Anti-Slavery Meetings* (Boston, MA: Bella Marsh, 1848). In a number of his writings, Geoffrey Sanborn has suggested that much of Wells Brown is plagiarized and that he probably wrote much of William Craft's narrative. See, Sanborn, 'The Plagiarist's Craft: Fugitivity and Theatricality in *Running a Thousand Miles for Freedom*', in *PMLA*, vol. 128, no. 4 (October 2013), pp. 907–22.
6 Ibid.
7 Preface, William W. Brown, *Narrative of William W. Brown, a Fugitive Slave. Written by Himself* (London: Charles Gilpin, 1849), pp. vii–viii.
8 'Rotundo-Slavery in the United States of America. A lecture by William Brown, a self-emancipated slave', *Freeman's Journal*, 17 August 1849.
9 Wells Brown, *Three Years in Europe*, p. x.
10 'Rotundo—Slavery in the United States of America. Lecture by William Brown, a self-emancipated slave', *Freeman's Journal*, 17 August 1849.
11 William W. Brown, *Narrative of William W. Brown, a Fugitive Slave. Written by Himself* (Boston, MA: Anti-Slavery Office, 1847), pp. 104–5.
12 The marriage was not happy and the couple was estranged, possibly divorced. Wells Brown had custody of their two daughters, Josephine and Clarissa. Elizabeth died in 1851 or 1852, while Brown was in England. In 1860, he remarried, to a woman almost 20 years younger.
13 Brown, *Narrative*, Boston, 1847.
14 William Wells Brown, *The Black Man, His Antecedents, His Genius, and His Achievements* (New York: Thomas Hamilton; Boston, MA: R.F. Wallcut, 1863), pp. 180–1.
15 Mary Alice Kirkpatrick, Summary of the *Narrative*: https://docsouth.unc.edu/neh/brown47/summary.html.
16 Farmer in Brown, *Narrative*, p. xxi.
17 Ibid., p. xxi.
18 Christine Kinealy, *Frederick Douglass. In His Own Words* (London: Routledge, 2018), see documents relating to the *Cambria* incident, pp. 111–41.
19 Wells Brown, *Three Years in Europe*, p. 4.
20 'AMERICA LATEST', *The Advocate: or, Irish Industrial Journal*, 22 August 1849. Dublin abolitionist James Haughton informed Garrison that this letter of introduction was not needed on the grounds that, 'I need hardly say, any friend of yours is

156   *William Wells Brown (c.1814–1884)*

welcome to me', Haughton to Garrison, Dublin, 10 September 1849, the *Liberator*, 12 October 1849.

21 Wells Brown, *Three Years in Europe*, p. 6.

22 He did so reluctantly because the reprinting of two editions (plus an interim edition) of Douglass's *Narrative* had left Webb out of pocket and had soured the relationship between the two men. Webb to an unnamed friend, 8 July 1849, Weston Papers, Boston Public Library (BPL), Anti-Slavery Collection.

23 Greenspan, *William Wells Brown*, p. 192.

24 Teresa A. Goddu, 'Visual Culture and Race', in *The Society for the Study of the Multi-Ethnic Literature of the United States*, vol. 39, no. 2 (Summer 2014), 12–41, p. 12.

25 This was part of his speech to the Salem Ladies' Anti-Slavery Society in mid-November 1847. See, Charles Baraw, 'William Wells Brown, Three Years in Europe, and Fugitive Tourism', in *African American Review*, vol. 44, no. 3 (Fall 2011), pp. 453–70.

26 Wells Brown, *Three Years in Europe*, pp. 7–9.

27 Farmer in Wells Brown, *Narrative*, p. 3.

28 Wells Brown, *Three Years in Europe*, pp. 12–13.

29 When in Scotland, Douglass sent Garrison a long letter in which he reflected on Irish poverty, describing the extent of, 'human misery, ignorance, degradation, filth and wretchedness'. At this stage, a temperance zealot, he attributed much of it to drinking alcohol. See Kinealy, *Frederick Douglass and Ireland. In His Own Words* (London: Routledge, 2018), vol. 2, pp. 79–82.

30 Wells Brown, *Three Years in Europe*, p. 13. Thomas Moore (1779–1852), also penned '*To the Lord Viscount Forbes from the City of Washington*' (1806). He frequently made the comparison between American slaves and the Irish peasantry. In his mid-20s, he had toured some of the southern states in America, an experience that consolidated his hatred of slavery.

31 Ibid., pp. 20–1.

32 Despite the continuation of famine in parts of Ireland, the arrival of the Queen and her family caused great excitement and for days people had been travelling to the harbour at Kingstown, on the outskirts of Dublin, in expectation of their arrival, 'The Royal Visit to Dublin', *Cork Examiner*, 8 August 1849.

33 Wells Brown, *Three Years in Europe*, pp. 16–20.

34 'Foreign Correspondence. From our Dublin Correspondent', *National Anti-Slavery Standard*, 13 September 1849. The letter was from Richard Webb, Dublin, 16 August 1849.

35 Webb to an unnamed friend, 3 August 1849, Weston Papers, BPL, A-SC.

36 'Foreign Correspondence. From our Dublin Correspondent', *National Anti-Slavery Standard*, 13 September 1849.

37 'Lecture by Mr William Brown, a self-emancipated slave', *Dublin Evening Packet and Correspondent*, 18 August 1849.

38 'Foreign Correspondence. From our Dublin Correspondent', *National Anti-Slavery Standard*, 13 September 1849.

39 'Rotundo—Slavery in the United States of America. Lecture by William Brown, a self-emancipated slave', *Freeman's Journal*, 17 August 1849.

40 'Foreign Correspondence. From our Dublin Correspondent', *National Anti-Slavery Standard*, 13 September 1849.

41 'Rotundo—Slavery in the United States of America. Lecture by William Brown, a self-emancipated slave', *Freeman's Journal*, 17 August 1849.

42 'Lecture by Mr William Brown, a self-emancipated slave', *Dublin Evening Packet and Correspondent*, 18 August 1849.

43 For example, a portion of the *Narrative* was reprinted in, 'The Slave Holders Present' *The [Dublin] Pilot*, 26 January 1849.

William Wells Brown (c.1814–1884)   157

44 'Rotundo—Slavery in the United States of America. Lecture by William Brown, a self-emancipated slave', *Freeman's Journal*, 17 August 1849.

45 'Lecture by Mr William Brown, a self-emancipated slave', *Dublin Evening Packet and Correspondent*, 18 August 1849.

46 'Rotundo—Slavery in the United States of America. Lecture by William Brown, a self-emancipated slave', *Freeman's Journal*, 17 August 1849.

47 'Lecture by Mr William Brown, a self-emancipated slave', *Dublin Evening Packet and Correspondent*, 18 August 1849.

48 'America Latest', *The Advocate: or, Irish Industrial Journal*, 22 August 1849.

49 'Rotundo—Slavery in the United States of America. Lecture by William Brown, a self-emancipated slave', *Freeman's Journal*, 17 August 1849.

50 'America Latest', *The Advocate: or, Irish Industrial Journal*, 22 August 1849.

51 *Athlone Sentinel*, 22 August 1849.

52 'Wm. Brown in Dublin. No Colorphobia there', *The North Star*, 14 September 1849, reprinted from the *Dublin Freeman's*.

53 'Slavery in the United States of America', *National Anti-Slavery Standard*, 13 September 1849.

54 Haughton to Garrison, Dublin, 10 September 1849, reprinted in *Liberator*, 12 October 1849.

55 'Note to the Fourth American Edition', William W. Brown, *Narrative* (London: Charles Gilpin, 1849), p. iii.

56 Although published under the Gilpin imprint, one of title pages stated, 'Printed, chiefly from the American Stereotype Plates, by Webb and Chapman, Great Brunswick-street, Dublin'.

57 Gilpin, who had opened his London business in 1842, was a nephew of Joseph Sturge, one of the founders of the BFASS. See, James Gregory, *Victorians against the Gallows: Capital Punishment and the Abolitionist Movement in Nineteenth Century Britain* (London: I. B. Taurus, 2011).

58 Moses Grandy, *Narrative of the Life of Moses Grandy; Late a Slave in the United States of America* (London: C. Gilpin, 5, Bishopsgate-Street, 1843), p. 71.

59 The Narrative appeared under the imprint of Charles Gilpin of London, who often collaborated with Webb. Its release was advertised in British and Irish newspapers: *North & South Shields Gazette and Newcastle Guardian and Tyne Mercury*, 8 December 1849.

60 A long and favourable review of this 'thrilling narrative' appeared in 'Literature', *Morning Advertiser*, 12 August 1851.

61 The Note is dated 14 August 1849 and sent from 176 Great Brunswick Street, Dublin. Wells Brown, *Narrative*, 1849, pp. iii–iv.

62 Ibid., p. iv.

63 Wells Brown, *Three Years in Europe*, pp. 19–20. Wells Brown variously said that he spent 15 days or three weeks in Ireland.

64 Ibid., p. 21.

65 Ibid., pp. 22–4. Like other black abolitionists, Wells Brown did not have a passport as he was not considered to be an American citizen. Because he was attending the Congress, this requirement was waived.

66 'The Peace Congress at Paris', *Norfolk News*, 1 September 1849.

67 'Peace Congress at Paris', *Northern Whig*, 30 August 1849.

68 'Foreign Correspondence. From our *Dublin* Correspondent', *National Anti-Slavery Standard*, 18 October 1849. Letter from Richard Webb, Dublin to Sydney Howard Gay, 21 September 1849.

69 The two men tried to find the house lived in by Robespierre. Wells Brown found it after Webb had left. Wm. Wells Brown, *The American Fugitive in Europe. Sketches of Places and People Abroad* (Boston, MA: John P. Jewett, 1855), p. 82.

158 *William Wells Brown (c.1814–1884)*

70 Webb to Mrs. Hateful Perkins, 11 December 1849, Weston Papers, BPL, A-SC.
71 William Wells Brown, edited by Ezra Greenspan, *William Wells Brown: A Reader* (University of Georgia Press, 2008), p. 163.
72 Ibid., p. 226.
73 'American Slavery', *Morning Advertiser*, 28 September 1849.
74 The *North Star*, 26 October 1849, reprinted from the *Liberator.*
75 Brown to Wendell Phillips, 28 September 1849, quoted in Greenspan, *Brown*, p. 227.
76 Wells Brown, *Three Years in Europe*, pp. 113–14.
77 The 'Note' by Brown at the beginning of this publication gave his address as being Newcastle-Upon-Tyne.
78 Matthew Scott & Nick Megoran, 'The Newcastle Upon Tyne Peace Society (1817–50)', in *Northern History*, vol. 54, no. 2 (2017), 211–27.
79 Mary Alice Kirkpatrick states that by the end of 1850, four American and five Irish/British editions had appeared. In regard to the latter, this seems high. But three had been printed in Brown's first year away from home. *Narrative*: https://doc south.unc.edu/neh/brown47/summary.html.
       The 1853 version of *Narrative* was published by William Tegg, a London publisher, however, it was unauthorized. In 1853, Partridge & Oakey: London, published *Clotel.*
80 Greenspan, *Brown*, p. 229.
81 In an article assessing Brown's book and his role as a 'sophisticated' fugitive tourist, Baraw makes no mention of Brown's time in Ireland and his observations there.
82 For example, 'A dark day in London', the *North Star*, 15 March 1850.
83 [Josephine Wells Brown], *Biography of an American Bondman, by His Daughter* (Boston, MA: R. F. Wallcut, 1856), p. 89.
84 Brown, *The American Fugitive in Europe*, p. 319.
85 Greenspan, *Brown*, pp. 228–9.
86 Elizabeth Stordeur Pryor, *Colored Travelers: Mobility and the Fight for Citizenship before the Civil War* (Chapel Hill: University of North Carolina Press, 2016), p. 103.
87 Greenspan, *Brown*, p. 231. The 1857 *Dred Scott* decision further complicated this issue by its ruling that no black person, whether free or enslaved, could claim U.S. citizenship.
88 Quoted in Greenspan, *Brown*, p. 233.
89 'To the Public', the *Liberator*, 12 July 1850.
90 The date is sometimes given as 1852.
91 'Foreign Correspondence. From our Dublin Correspondent', *National Anti-Slavery Standard*, 20 March 1851.
92 Brown, *The American Fugitive in Europe*.
93 'Ramsgate', *South Eastern Gazette*, 30 December 1851.
94 In the 'Sketch', in *Clotel*, Brown refers to the minister as Rev. Hore of Ramsgate.
95 The letter from Enoch Price was from 'St. Louis, Feb. 16th, 1852', Introduction, *Clotel*, pp. 51–2.
96 The Richardson family consisted of Anna, her husband, Henry and her sister in law, Ellen—all Quakers. Anna and Ellen had famously 'purchased' Douglass's freedom.
97 'American Slavery', *North and South Shields Gazette*, 8 November 1850; Greenspan, *Brown*, pp. 243–4. Garrison visited the town in 1867, where he was given a 'grand reception'. Newcastle did not become a city until 1882. For more on Newcastle's role, see: radicaltyneside.org/events/william-lloyd-garrison-visits-newcastle.
98 'Panorama of American Slavery', *Newcastle Guardian and Tyne Mercury*, 26 October 1850, opined, 'we have no doubt the visitor will be highly gratified and instructed'; 'A panorama', *Newcastle Journal*, 9 November 1850, said there were 20 slides, and whole show was 'highly interesting'.
99 'American Slavery', *Durham Chronicle*, 1 November 1850.

William Wells Brown (c.1814–1884) 159

100 'A Fugitive Slave in Liverpool', *Glasgow Herald*, 11 November 1850. The two men did not have the money to get the panorama through customs, so an appeal was made to 'benevolent friends'.
101 'Slavery in America', Belfast *News-Letter*, 10 January 1851.
102 *Gloucester Journal*, 24 May 1851.
103 'Sketch of the Author's Life', William W. Brown, *Clotel* (London: Partridge and Oakey, 1853), p. 51.
104 The Great Exhibition took place in London from May to October 1851 to showcase technological advances and culture from around the world, but with achievements in the British Empire, more particularly Britain, foregrounded.
105 In *The American Fugitive in Europe*, Wells Brown says that he visited the Great Exhibition on 15 days, but he is vague about the dates, and he does not mention the stunt or the presence of the Webbs, just mentioning that he and the Crafts were taken to the Exhibition by 'friends', p. xv.
106 'Letter to the *Liberator*', the *Liberator*, 18 July 1851. Letter from Mr Lenon and dated 20 June 1851: 'MY DEAR SIR: An interesting anti-slavery demonstration took place at the Great Exhibition on Saturday last week our friends here ...'.
107 Brown, *The American Fugitive in Europe*, p. 211.
108 'Fugitive Slaves at the Great Exhibition', letter from William Farmer, London, 26 June 1851, *National Anti-Slavery Standard*, 24 July 1851.
109 Greenspan, *Brown*, p. 260.
110 'Advertisement', *Morning Advertiser*, 1 August 1851.
111 See chapter on Benjamin Benson. The presence of the other three fugitive slaves is not mentioned in some accounts, see 'Anti-Slavery Soiree', *London Daily News*, 2 August 1851. The presence of Maria Weston Chapman, visiting from Boston, was mentioned.
112 'Anniversary of West Indian Negro Emancipation', *Morning Advertiser*, 2 August 1851.
113 'Anniversary of West Indian Negro Emancipation', *The Advocate: or, Irish Industrial Journal*, 6 August 1851; *Longford Journal*, 9 August 1851; the *Liberator*, 5 September 1851.
114 'W. W. Brown', *The Advocate: or, Irish Industrial Journal*, 6 August 1851; 'The Life and Escape of William Wells Brown', *Ulster General Advertiser, Herald of Business and General* Information, 20 September 1851; 'English Unitarians on American Slavery, *Belfast Mercury*, 1 July 1851, also in *The Advocate: or, Irish Industrial Journal*, 25 June 1851.
115 It cost one penny. Brown to Wendell Phillips, 1 September 1852, quoted in Greenspan, *Brown*, p. 281.
116 For example, *Anti-Slavery Advocate*, December 1852, March 1853.
117 'Don't Come to England', *Frederick Douglass' Paper*, 24 July 1851.
118 'William Wells Brown', *Wiltshire Independent*, 28 August 1851.
119 Brown, *Three Years*, p. 218.
120 No title, *Leeds Times*, 6 September 1851.
121 *Roscommon Journal, and Western Impartial Reporter*, 6 September 1851; *Kilkenny Journal, and Leinster Commercial and Literary* Advertiser, 6 September 1851.
122 See chapter on Sarah Parker Remond.
123 Greenspan, *Brown*, p. 309.
124 Josephine Brown, *American Bondman*, p. 99.
125 'William Wells Brown', *National Anti-Slavery Standard*, 17 June 1854.
126 *Liberator*, 15 December 1854.
127 'Anti-Slavery Conference and Meeting', *Sheffield Independent*, 5 August 1854.
128 'Anti-Slavery Conference in Manchester', *Manchester Times*, 2 August 1854. Pillsbury was one of the platform party.

160   *William Wells Brown (c.1814–1884)*

129 Brown, *The American Fugitive in Europe*, p. 312.
130 Ibid., pp. 314–15.
131 Boston, MA: Bela Marsh, 1855.
132 Ben Fagan, 'Reclaiming Revolution: William Wells Brown's Irreducible Haitian Heroes', in *Comparative American Studies. An International Journal*, vol. 5, no. 4 (2007), 367–83.
133 Ibid., p. 369.
134 Greenspan, *Brown*, pp. 367–8.
135 '*WILLIAM WELLS BROWN* will speak at Concord, N.H., on; "Liberty for all"', the *Liberator*, 20 May 1864; 'FREEDOM FOR ALL—*WILLIAM WELLS BROWN*', the *Liberator*, 24 June 1864.
136 '54th Regiment', *Encyclopeadia Britanica*: www.britannica.com/topic/54th-Massachusetts-Regiment.
137 'NEGRO SUFFRAGE', the *Liberator*, 21 July 1865.
138 Advance publicity said, 'Have you seen "THE BLACK MAN?" The new book for the times. JUST OUT!—Containing a history of the Negro, Past and Present, With Biographical Sketches of 50 Distinguished Individuals of the Race', *National Anti-Slavery Standard*, 20 February 1864. In 1867, Wells Brown gave a lecture on the 'Heroism of Colored Men in the Late War'; he was described as the 'able colored historian', 'Editorial Items', *The Christian Recorder*, 16 February 1867.
139 Greenspan, *Wells Brown: A Reader*, p. xxxiii.
140 'Who Are We?' by J.H. Scott, the *Christian Recorder*, 30 December 1880.
141 Ibid., 'DR. BROWN'S RECEPTION', 4 October 1877.
142 He arrived on 19 June 1877, *Liverpool Daily Post*, 20 June 1877; *Liverpool Mercury*, 20 June 1877; *Edinburgh Evening News*, 21 June 1877.
143 'Good Templar Conference', *The Scotsman*, 27 June 1877; *Edinburgh Evening News*, 26 June 1877; 'Temperance Meeting', *Burnley Gazette*, 11 August 1877. In addition to being described as an ex-slave, he was also referred to as 'the leader of the coloured population in the United States on the Good Templar question'.
144 The meeting was convened by the Independent Order of Good Templars, *Irish Times*, 18 July 1877; Ibid., 19 July 1877; *Dublin Daily Express*, 20 July 1877.
145 'Good Templar Concert', *Freeman's Journal*, 20 July 1877.
146 'Independent Order of Good Templars', *Dublin Daily Express*, 20 July 1877.
147 *Freeman's Journal*, 18 July 1877.
148 'Historic Missourians': https://historicmissourians.shsmo.org/historicmissourians/name/b/brownw/.
149 It is thought that Josephine died of TB, but Greenspan suggests that prior to her death, she had led a promiscuous life, which devastated her father.
150 'The Denial of Equal Rights', *Christian Recorder*, 9 August 1883.
151 Ibid., 'William Wells Brown, M.D.', 27 November 1884. The paper gave his age as 68.
152 See: www.findagrave.com/memorial/7234157/william-wells-brown.
153 They did lecture together—for example in 1867, Brown, Douglass and Remond were the key speakers at an event to celebrate the anniversary of the Proclamation, 'Our Boston Correspondence', *National Anti-Slavery Standard*, 12 January 1867.
154 Nell Irvin Painter in the *New York Times*, 14 November 2014.
155 Charles Baraw, 'William Wells Brown, Three Years in Europe, and Fugitive Tourism', in *African American Review*, vol. 44, no. 3 (Fall 2011), p. 453.
156 Greenspan, *Brown*, p. 279.
157 Baraw, 'Fugitive Tourism'.
158 'England', Greenspan, *Brown*, pp. 203–314.
159 Wells Brown, *American Bondman*, p. 62.
160 Wells Brown, 'Visit of a Fugitive Slave to the Grave of Wilberforce', in Brown, *Three Years in Europe*, pp. 70–6; William Wilberforce (1759–1833) was part of the

first wave of English abolitionists who sought to end the slave trade. In 1785, he had converted to evangelical Christianity. Due to ill health, Wilberforce retired from parliament in 1826. He died the same year that slavery was ended in the British Empire.

161 Wells Brown, 'Visit of a Fugitive Slave', p. 76.

162 In *The American Fugitive in Europe*, Wells Brown only refers to O'Connell in the context of being an effective 'agitator' on behalf of the Irish people, pp. 49–50.

163 Wells Brown, *The American Fugitive in Europe*, p. 305. Harriet Martineau (1802–1876) was an English-born writer who specialized in political economy. Following a visit to the United States in the mid-1830s, she became a committed abolitionist.

6   Henry Highland Garnet (1815–1882)
'A staunch new organizationist'[1]

Writing in 1928, historian W. M. Brewer lamented the fact that Henry Highland Garnet had largely been ignored in the historical record of abolition, arguing that he:

> ... represents a type of leadership during the anti-slavery and reconstruction periods that has not received due consideration ... little attention has been given to the role of Garnet who deserves front rank as the radical fore-runner of Frederick Douglass, the advocate of moral suasion rather than resistance ... Garnet truly blazed the way for Negro abolitionists and kept the flame of freedom burning.[2]

Almost 100 years' later, Garnet still remains largely unknown, or as an article written in February 2018 by historian Paul Ortiz suggested, 'Today, the Reverend Dr Henry Highland Garnet is the most famous African American you never learned about during Black History Month'.[3] Yet, Garnet was regarded by those who heard him speak as being 'equal in ability to Frederick Douglass especially excelling in logic and terse statement'.[4] Subsequent scholars have judged him to be 'an intellectual catalyst for Douglass'.[5] Yet, much like his second cousin, Samuel Ringgold Ward, he remains on the sidelines of abolitionist history, with his visits to Ireland being largely forgotten.

Early life

Garnet was born in 1815 into enslavement in Maryland to George and Henrietta Trusty. On his father's side, his grandfather had been a chief of the Mandingo tribe of West Africa, but had been imprisoned and sold by a rival chief.[6] On the death of his owner, Colonel Spencer, Garnet's father decided that the family should escape and take the surname Garnet. Garnet was then about 9 years old. His adult life, therefore, was spent in freedom, albeit with the status of being a 'fugitive'. On account of Garnet's age, he received a formal education. He attended the New York African Free School, whose pupils included Samuel Ringgold Ward, Dr James McCune Smith and the Rev. Alexander Crummell, each of whom went on to become acknowledged intellectuals of the movement. They also remained friends. As a young man, Garnet was subject to mob attacks

Henry Highland Garnet (1815–1882)   163

simply because of his colour: he and five other black students were driven out of Canaan Institute in New Hampshire when the local people objected to their presence.[7] He next attended Oneida Theological Institute, graduating in 1840, with honours. In the same year, he attended a meeting of the American Anti-Slavery Society in New York where he delivered his first speech on the topic.[8] It marked the launch of a remarkable career.

Possibly because so few opportunities were open to him, after finishing with his formal education, Garnet intermittently worked at sea.[9] During this period, he visited Cuba several times. Unfortunately, around this time, Garnet's sister was captured and returned to slavery, demonstrating the risk of even being in a free state.[10] Due to an injury, Garnet's lower leg was amputated in 1841. In the same year, Garnet married Julia Williams, whom he later described as a 'young and lovely coloured girl'.[11] She was much more. Like her husband, Williams had received a formal education, including at Noyes College, and she was a teacher and a fervent abolitionist.[12] They had three children together.

In 1841, Garnet was ordained a Presbyterian minister and became a pastor in Troy in New York.[13] Like his second cousin, Samuel Ringgold Ward, Garnet chose a religious prism for condemning slavery, but, unlike Ward, Garnet chose the Presbyterian Church. Garnet spent the 1840s alternating between his two passions: abolition and his ministry, while occasionally augmenting his income by teaching. He also published, contributing to a number of abolitionist newspapers, including *The National Watchman*, which had been founded by the free black abolitionist William G. Allen in 1842.[14] In 1843, Garnet received an annual stipend of $100 from the American Home Missionary Society for his work in promoting temperance, with a number of groups being named in his honour.[15] Regarding abolition, Garnet positioned himself at the radical end of the movement—too radical even for Garrison, at times. They disagreed on a variety of issues, including the need for slave resistance and disobedience, as opposed to Garrison's faith in 'moral suasion'. Also, Garnet did not support the Garrisonian principle of women being equal. The formal break came in 1840, shortly before the first international anti-slavery convention in London. Garnet helped to found the American and Foreign Anti-Slavery Society—with its all-male leadership.

Garnet's radicalism was most evident when, in August 1843, he delivered a 'Call to Rebellion' speech at the National Negro Convention in Buffalo in New York. In it, he suggested that enslaved people should revolt against their owners. This proposition was too extreme for many of his fellow abolitionists.[16] Regardless of its radical content, Garnet's delivery was said to have moved the audience to tears.[17] It also resulted in a public clash with Frederick Douglass, who took the side of his mentor, Garrison, in favouring the power of non-resistance and moral suasion. In 1843, Douglass was a relatively new voice on the abolitionist circuit. This was to change following the publication of his *Narrative* in 1845 and his extended exile in the United Kingdom. Following Douglass's return to the United States, the public rivalry between Garnet and Douglass increased.[18] In the 1847 Black Convention in Troy, the men clashed publicly as a result of Douglass's unequivocal denunciation of the American

164 *Henry Highland Garnet (1815–1882)*

churches, all of whom, he argued, were pro-slavery by default. Inevitably, Garnet, a Presbyterian minister, was offended, believing that not all churches were complicit in, or accepting of, slavery.[19] Despite their disagreement, Garnet praised the appearance of the *North Star* later in the same year, prompting Douglass to thank him for his unexpected 'manly commendation'.[20] In turn, Douglass promised to use his newspaper for all shades of opinion, even if they did not reflect his own.[21] This was evident when an article by Garnet, recommending that black people leave America and go to where they could find 'freedom and enfranchisement', a suggestion disliked by Douglass and other Garrisonians, was printed in the *North Star* in March 1849.[22]

Outside the columns of the paper, Garnet and Douglass continued to disagree publicly on several other occasions, revealing deep-seated personal differences—and possibly jealousies. Garnet wrote to Douglass in September 1849, in a letter that was published in the *North Star* and which was clearly an *ad hominin* attack, saying, 'the green-eyed monster has made you mad. Pardon me, when I tell you that you never imbibed a spirit so narrow from any dark son of our native Maryland, living or dead'.[23] The multiple public clashes between these two men took on a fresh intensity when Douglass overtook the more seasoned lecturer in becoming the most pre-eminent voice of abolition. These personal quarrels, however, were a microcosm of the deep divisions within the American abolition movement; divisions that migrated overseas to Ireland and Britain.

The United Kingdom

As controversies raged in America over the passing of a more stringent Fugitive Slave Act in 1850, Garnet followed the path of several black abolitionists by travelling to Europe. Like others in the mid-nineteenth century, and as a fugitive slave himself, he went seeking support, sanctuary and safety from his transatlantic sympathizers in the United Kingdom. Similar to many black abolitionists, even before he landed in England, Garnet was a fan of 'glorious Britannica', having praised the country when a student in 1839 for its role in freeing slaves in the West Indies.[24]

Garnet arrived in Liverpool in August 1850, and from there, he travelled to Newcastle to meet his sponsors, Anna and Henry Richardson. His visit to Britain had been at the invitation of Anna Richardson, the founder of the Free Produce Movement, which sought to end slavery by rejecting the use of products produced by slave labour. It was Richardson, an English Quaker abolitionist, who had been instrumental in purchasing Douglass's freedom four years earlier. From Newcastle, Garnet travelled to Frankfort to attend the World's Peace Congress as representative of the Pennsylvania Peace Society.[25] Garnet's first public appearance in Europe was at the Congress, which met from 22 to 24 August. He was one of 36 delegates from America, which included Elihu Burritt.[26] Garnet's contributions drew the attention of several German newspapers, who commented on his brilliance—and his blackness. Shortly afterwards, inspired by Garnet, a German Anti-Slavery Society was formed in Frankfurt.[27]

Henry Highland Garnet (1815–1882) 165

Following the Peace Congress, Garnet returned to Newcastle. He then undertook a demanding tour of England and, later, Scotland, during which he explained the horrors of slavery while promoting the use of Free Produce.[28] Occasionally, Garnet lectured with other visiting abolitionists, including Dr James Pennington, also a fugitive slave.[29] For the most part though, Garnet traversed the country alone, hosted by various abolitionist groups and by members of his church. As had been the case in the States, Garnet proved to be a popular lecturer, and his speaking style was widely praised. Apart from his intellect, Garnet cut an imposing figure physically. He was over six foot in height with 'a frank, manly way of dealing with everybody'.[30] Similar to Ward, the fact that Garnet was not mixed race was alluded to on several occasions. In an 1848 account, Garnet was described as 'a pure Black, about 32 years of age, and is scrupulously careful of his personal attire'.[31] However, as had proved to be the case with other black abolitionists, he was occasionally described through the prism of race, as the following newspaper report from Scotland showed:

> Though a thorough black man, he speaks the English language with the greatest precision and propriety, and had anyone entered the church during the address, without looking at the speaker, he could not have suspected that he was listening to a negro, but an eloquent home-minister.[32]

The early success of Garnet's mission was evident, as, by end of 1850, 26 Free Produce societies had been formed in Britain resulting from his efforts.[33] This may have affected Garnet's decision to remain overseas. His original intention had been to return to the United States in 1851 but the success of the tour and his fear of recapture, led him to stay in Britain. Instead, he asked his family to join him there.[34] This decision meant that Garnet was able to take his abolitionist message to Ireland.

Ireland

Like many other black abolitionists, Garnet visited Ireland where the abolition movement was strong, if divided. As a Presbyterian minister, it was to be expected that he would be hosted by his fellow ministers. Unusually though, and similar to the path that would be later taken by Ward, Garnet did not contact the Hibernian Anti-Slavery Society in Dublin, whose membership included many Catholics and Quakers. Instead, most of Garnet's time was spent addressing Protestant audiences in the north of Ireland.

At the beginning of 1851, Garnet sailed from Whitehaven in the north west of England to Belfast, arriving on 14 January. He was there at the invitation of the Belfast Anti-Slavery Society who hoped that his visit would re-energize the 'dormant AS' spirit'. They also hoped to build on the outrage that had resulted from the introduction of the 1850 Fugitive Slave Law.[35] At this stage, Garnet's only concrete plans were to visit a number of schools and to preach in the Donegall Street Presbyterian Church on the 19 of the month.[36] For his first few

166 *Henry Highland Garnet (1815–1882)*

days in Ireland, therefore, Garnet's meetings were with the local women and children: the day after arriving, he visited the Ragged School on Frederick Street, and a few days later, he spoke to the Ladies' Anti-Slavery Society on the topic of using free produce.[37] However, only days following his arrival, the Belfast Anti-Slavery Society placed advertisements in local newspapers publicizing Garnet's first lecture on anti-slavery. In them, he was described as 'a black gentleman, formerly a slave' or 'a man of colour and formerly a slave'.[38]

Belfast was a predominantly Presbyterian town and Garnet's first public lectures took place in the Presbyterian Church on Donegall Street. The minister was the Rev. Isaac Nelson, an ardent abolitionist. Nelson had not only welcomed Douglass to this venue five years earlier, but had provided an endorsement for the Irish reprint of Douglass's *Narrative*.[39] On the morning of 19 January, Garnet had preached at the church on behalf of the Home Mission of the Presbyterian Society.[40] The evening meeting was organized by James Standfield and Francis Calder of the Belfast Anti-Slavery Society, who had also hosted Douglass over five years earlier.[41] The church was so full that people were forced to stand in the aisles.[42] The subject of the meeting was the recently enacted Fugitive Slave Law. The meeting opened with a statement by Standfield condemning the legislation, which, he stated, 'dooms again to slavery, those who were formerly emancipated, and experienced the blessings of liberty'. Garnet spoke next and opened by saying that being in Ireland 'filled his heart with gratitude and delight', explaining that he now felt truly free. Praising his audience, he added:

> when he looked abroad upon that vast assembly, he was persuaded that his cause was appreciated and loved (cheers) and he was persuaded more than ever that the views he had entertained of this country were correct, and that in Ireland—a country so renowned in history for intensely interesting associations, and whose sons were so distinguished for eloquence—might be found a love for that principle which was the foundation of all true eloquence—he meant, an undying attachment to the principles of liberty.[43]

Garnet felt being in the country was especially significant because of the large number of emigrants from Ireland to America. Rather than criticize Irish Americans though, he appealed to their tradition of social justice:

> ... it was important that the sons and daughters of this country—which had done something for the cause of freedom—should, when they put their foot upon the soil of America, be in a position to let their first accents be shouts of freedom, and a cry to 'break off the yoke, and to let the oppressed go free'.[44]

Regarding the new fugitive law, Garnet said that it had had 'brought out slavery in its true colours'. Explaining how slavery made a mockery out of the Declaration of Independence, he outlined the cruelty of slaveholders and urged his audience to stop buying any of the produce of slavery as the best means of

Henry Highland Garnet (1815–1882) 167

putting an end to it. He promised that if the system was ended it would, 'make America what it professes to be, the land of liberty and freedom'. Significantly, he also criticized the northern states for propping up slavery and for being racist, thus perpetuating prejudice against black people everywhere.[45] His arguments were similar to those that had been made by Charles Remond a decade earlier. At the end of the meeting, 'a collection was taken up to defray expenses'.[46]

Three days later, Garnet lectured in the Townsend-Street Presbyterian Church. His topic was 'The position of the American Churches regarding Slavery'.[47] The publicity stated, 'The Ministers of every religious denomination are respectfully invited to the Meeting'.[48] The church was 'densely' crowded, and the audience listened with 'the deepest attention'.[49] Again, the event was sponsored by Standfield and Calder. A theme of Garnet's lecture was the complicity of some of the churches in America—a topic that had been explored by several visiting abolitionists, but one that was sometimes avoided by those who were themselves ministers. Garnet referred to denominations in the United States who had rejected slavery, including the Wesleyan Methodists, Free Will Baptists, Covenanters, Universalists, Unitarians, the Society of Friends and sections of the Presbyterian and Catholic churches, but added that 'there were only a few in the English or Episcopalian Church who were decided opponents to the holding of their fellow creatures in that state of degradation'. Garnet also named several leading churchmen who defended slavery and he drew laughter from the audience when he cited the writings of the Bishop Meade of Virginia,[50] who had advised:

Now, you (the slaves) must be bound to your master, for they are placed instead of God over you. If you are whipped, don't murmur, not even for a crime of which you may not be guilty, because there may be many crimes you have committed before, and were not punished, and so you are paying for it all at last.[51]

Garnet informed his audience that, 'Clergymen of that description must surely think that the slaves were not only black, but also exceedingly *green*, when they could believe such a doctrine'.[52] Garnet concluded with an 'eloquent appeal' to the ministers and people of Ireland, to exert themselves against slavery. He followed up his lecture by a visit to the Ulster Institute for the Deaf, the Dumb and the Blind on 27 January. His visit prompted one of inmates, a deaf and dumb orphan, to write to the local press praising Garnet and condemning slavery.[53]

On 28 January, Garnet lectured in the First Presbyterian Church in Newtownards, at a meeting convened by the Belfast Anti-Slavery Society. An estimated 2,000 people were present.[54] There were several other speakers whose speeches were 'short, comprehensive, and hearty'. Garnet, however, was referred to as 'the great attraction of the meeting'.[55] Unusually, this lecture was covered in detail by a nationalist newspaper in Dublin, the *Nation*. Furthermore, the report included details of the meeting that had been absent in the Belfast papers. In an article sub-titled, 'Black and white slavery', Garnet was praised:

168 *Henry Highland Garnet (1815–1882)*

... himself a Black and once a Slave, addressed the assemblage in a most lucid, affecting, and eloquent lecture for nearly two hours, depicting the iniquity of the recently enacted American Fugitive Slave Law, and the crimes and miseries of Slavery, so as alternately to move his audience to groans of indignation, and silent tears.[56]

The bulk of the article, however, was devoted to comments made by the Rev. Dr Coulter, a fellow Presbyterian minister, who had spoken on behalf of Irish tenants, whom, he believed, were also slaves.[57] Coulter had likened Negro slavery to tenant bondage in Ireland and he asked for the sympathy of the meeting for the rights of Irish tenants. He ended by requesting the Anti-Slavery delegation from Belfast and for Garnet to 'direct their attention to Black Slavery in America and White Slavery in Ireland', and to advocate for ending both. He further suggested that Garnet would continue to campaign against Irish slavery following his return to America. Garnet, seemingly taken aback by such a request, responded 'with becoming reserve and modesty', adding an anodyne promise that he would 'keep his eyes and ears open'.[58] The tone of his answer was in marked contrast to what had been described as, 'his accustomed forcible style'.[59] Garnet had come face to face with Irish nationalist politics and it had taken him out of his comfort zone.

The following day, Garnet lectured in a Presbyterian church in Ballymena, again on the topic of the Fugitive Slave Law. Although the meeting had been called at short notice, the attendance was 'numerous'. Standfield spoke first. Garnet then addressed the meeting for over an hour, 'in words of thrilling eloquence'. This included reading a poem called 'The Blind Slave Boy'.[60] The poem had first appeared in an 1848 collection of 'Songs for Anti-Slavery Meetings', collated by fellow black abolitionist, William Wells Brown.[61] Garnet called on the audience to avoid using anything produced by slave labour. The meeting concluded with speeches by local ministers followed by a benediction.[62]

On 30 January, Garnet lectured in the First Presbyterian Church on Rosemary Street in Belfast. This venue had welcomed many abolitionists to its pulpit. Again, Garnet attracted large crowds and 'The spacious building was crowded to suffocation, and several were obliged to go away'. Garnet did not disappoint his audience and his lecture:

> like those previously delivered by the same gentleman, contained many conclusive arguments against the system of slavery as practised in the United States, and abounded with amusing anecdotes, which frequently affected the risible faculties of the audience.[63]

Garnet then travelled to Ballymoney, which was almost 50 miles north of Belfast. It was an overwhelmingly Protestant town. Garnet's host was fellow Presbyterian minister, the Rev. John Rentoul, who provided 'an Irish welcome'.[64] Garnet gave two sermons in Rentoul's Trinity Presbyterian Church, the purpose also being to raise funds to help the church pay off an old debt. The following

Henry Highland Garnet (1815–1882) 169

evening, the ladies of the congregation held a soirée in honour of Garnet. It was attended by 600 people, including 10 Presbyterian ministers. Enjoyment was combined with more serious aspirations. During the evening, resolutions were passed condemning slavery.[65]

Garnet then returned to Belfast where he delivered a farewell lecture on 5 February in the Primitive Methodist Chapel on Donegall Place. Unusually, there was an entrance charge of three pence but, regardless, the church was full of both men and women. Garnet was greeted with loud applause when he commenced and concluded speaking. His topics were the unchristian nature of some of the churches in America, and American prejudice towards black people. Demanding immediate abolition, Garnet praised the actions of the British government in the West Indies. On a more personal note, Garnet also told his audience that abolitionists had been accused of being violent and only a few days earlier he had been asked if he was a violent man. Garnet admitted that he 'was somewhat proud to hear of this, for he had been in the habit of reproaching himself with being rather tame'.[66] He concluded by urging people to use the produce of free labour and then thanked everyone 'for the kindness shown to him since his arrival in this part of the country'.[67] Garnet's final meeting was interesting for two further reasons. The Rev. Rentoul of Ballymoney informed in the meeting that, like the Rev. Nelson, he believed that some ministers in Belfast were not doing enough to bring about the ending of slavery. He criticized them for not giving their support to Garnet on the grounds he was 'too violent'.[68] Rentoul's criticisms suggested divisions in the Presbyterian Church between the old and new guard, the latter represented by these two ministers. Moreover, the disagreement with the Free Church of Scotland, which had been inflamed by Douglass's campaign, was still relatively raw. Less divisively, Rentoul proposed that Garnet's wife and children be sent for 'and all should be kept in this country'. The proposal was greeted with much enthusiasm.[69] It was a fitting conclusion to a successful visit, which had helped to revive the anti-slavery cause in Belfast. Furthermore, despite their differences, Garnet's time in the north of Ireland received comprehensive coverage in Garrison's *Liberator*.[70]

The Belfast *News-Letter*, which had covered Garnet's lectures in detail, judged that, during his three-week stay in the north, he had 'met with the most cordial reception from the people of Belfast'.[71] Throughout his time in the north, Garnet had shown why he was so admired as a speaker: he had displayed charm, humour, knowledge and passion, and had always engaged his large audiences. However, unlike several other visiting abolitionists, his scope had been narrow. He had only visited Protestant venues and spoken mostly in Presbyterian churches. Overall, he had done little to reach out beyond his own Presbyterian circles. In the context of Ireland, it offered a narrow ground on which to build an inclusive transatlantic abolition movement.

From Belfast, Garnet travelled south to Dublin, where he lectured in a secular venue, the Rotundo. The advertisement stated that the purpose of the meeting was to bring 'before the Irish public the iniquities of the American Fugitive Slave Law, enacted last year', and it was to be addressed by 'HENRY H. GARNET, an

170 *Henry Highland Garnet (1815–1882)*

American coloured Gentleman, and other speakers'.[72] Present at the meeting were the stalwarts of the Hibernian Anti-Slavery Society—James Haughton, Richard Allen and brothers, Richard and William Webb. William P. Powell, a freeborn black American, was also present.[73] The Chair was taken by the Rev. Dr Urwick, a minister in the Congregationalist Church, who would welcome Ward, a fellow Congregational minister and former slave, to Ireland four years later.[74] Before Garnet spoke, Powell was introduced to the meeting as somebody who had come to the country to get an education for his children. Allen spoke next, describing the Fugitive Slave Law as the last gasp of slavery. When Garnet stood up to speak, he was greeted with cheers, and his opening comments were designed to please his audience:

> … he could scarcely give expression to his feelings on that occasion when he remembered he was for the first time enjoying the privilege of standing *before an Irish audience* in the capital of Ireland. He regarded their enthusiastic reception of him as a proof of sympathy in the welfare of his race (hear, hear). In coming before them he did not think he was much out of place in speaking upon American slavery, for he could bear testimony to a remark of the last speaker, that the Irish, above all people on the face of the earth, ought to be interested in the welfare of the United States of America (hear, hear).

Garnet concluded by saying that on Tuesday, 11 February, he would speak again on the use of free produce.[75]

Garnet's second Dublin meeting was described as having a 'large and respectable audience', which included many members of the Society of Friends and a large portion of women. Haughton was in the chair. Garnet was again greeted with cheers. He explained that:

> … he addressed himself to Irishmen, because he thought there was not on the face of the earth a people whose hearts beat more warmly in the cause of liberty, or who sympathized more fully with the oppressed and downtrodden, than the inhabitants of this beautiful island (loud cheers). He knew that he could not find a more congenial foil on which to disseminate the seeds of freedom than the land over which the glorious eloquence of Curran was shed, and in whose bosom reposed the remains of the immortal O'Connell (loud and prolonged cheering).[76]

Later in his speech, Garnet again referred to O'Connell, saying:

> Would there be any difficulty of understanding the distinction of robbing a man of his property? The late Daniel O'Connell, who knew how to understand the subject well, was once waited upon by an American gentleman desiring an introduction to him. Mr. O'Connell asked him, after a few questions, if he were a slaveholder; and he answered not, but that if he had the opportunity

of a conversation, he would convince him (Mr. O'C) that slavery was not so bad as supposed. Mr. O'Connell rang the bell, and desired the servant to show his American visitor downstairs, and, as he descended, cried out after him, 'I would as soon discuss the propriety of purse-stealing with you as discuss the propriety of man-stealing' (loud applause).[77]

Garnet repeatedly praised O'Connell, telling the audience that he and Powell had visited the Liberator's grave, adding:

No matter where the man suffered, whether in America, Asia, Africa or Europe, no matter whether he was white or black in colour, O'Connell's voice was ever raised on the tide of human freedom (hear, hear, and cheers). He (Mr. Garnett [sic]) remembered well when that mighty voice was heard across the ocean calling upon Irishmen not to disgrace their country by supporting slavery, the feelings of the slaves of that time; and when gazing upon the coffin containing his remains, he (Mr. G) raised his voice and thanked God that such men had lived in the world. He trusted Ireland might never see the day when she would want a patriot as bold and as uncompromising in her cause as the great O'Connell had been (loud cheers).[78]

Garnet's praise for O'Connell had been absent from his speeches in the north of Ireland, suggesting his familiarity with, and sensitivity to, local Irish politics. References to the Catholic and nationalist O'Connell would not have appealed to his predominantly Protestant audiences in the north-east.[79] Clearly, Garnet, the abolitionist, was also a pragmatist. After Dublin, Garnet returned to Britain where he continued to lecture.

Even after Garnet had left Ireland, interest in his life story continued. A number of newspapers published extracts from 'A Tribute for the Negro' which included extracts of Garnet's personal history.[80] This book had been published in England in 1848 and was the nearest that Garnet got to writing his own narrative.[81] Knowledge of Garnet's warm reception was not just confined to Ireland. Frederick Douglass gave his erstwhile rival coverage in his own two newspapers. Following the precedent set in the *North Star*, its successor, *Frederick Douglass' Paper*, covered Garnet's tour of the United Kingdom, reporting in March 1852 that,

We have much pleasure in stating that our valued friend, Henry H. Garnet, has satisfactorily concluded his labors in the North of Ireland, and after a short visit to Scotland, is now resident, with his wife and family, at 89, Blandford Street, Newcastle-on-Tyne.[82]

Not everybody, however, was impressed with Garnet. Even before the American had set foot on British or Irish soil, Richard Webb had written critically of him in the Garrisonian press:

172   *Henry Highland Garnet (1815–1882)*

> As Garnett [sic] is fiercely opposed to moral suasion, relies on physical force, and is a staunch new organizationist ... A Presbyterian man of color, in full union with all the churches, who is desirous to give Bibles to the slaves, he will be a perfect God-send to New Organization in England.[83]

Hearing Garnet speak in Dublin did not alter the Irish man's opinion. In February 1851, Webb wrote from Liverpool to Sydney Gay, editor of the *National Anti-Slavery Standard* in New York, that:

> Just before I left Dublin, I was present at an Anti-Slavery meeting, at which the Rev. Henry Highland Garnet made his appearance. You know him as a Liberty Party man, and a bitter enemy of the American Anti-Slavery Society in general, and of Frederick Douglass in particular. On general Anti-Slavery matters he spoke very well, and the meeting was well attended. He afterwards held a large meeting for the purpose of recommending the Free Labor Produce Panacea. This he recommends everywhere by request of an indefatigable lady in the North of England, who has the utmost faith in this nostrum, and has invited him over from the United States to be its apostle.[84] In my opinion, it is only a quack medicine—utterly inefficient to meet the evil, and calculated to turn the attention of well-intentioned people from the true remedy—the promulgation of purer principles and a noble morality. One man like Douglass is worth a hundred such priests as Garnet.[85]

Webb's dismissal of Garnet was clearly rooted in the visitor's shunning of the Garrisonian position on so many issues. Moreover, Garnet, unlike other visiting abolitionists, had shown little interest in working with the Hibernian Anti-Slavery Society. Webb was not alone in his criticisms. Parker Pillsbury, also an ally of Garrison, writing from Belfast, castigated Garnet, Ward, Pennington and other abolitionists who unashamedly used their situations to raise money, characterizing them as, 'all sorts of creatures travelling in the name of American Anti-Slavery, and picking people's pockets ... they are an outrage on all decency, and a scandal to the name of anti-slavery'.[86] Pillsbury's comments reveal that the differences extended beyond simply ideological ones. Moreover, the criticisms of the gifted and articulated Garnet reveal that despite the threat posed by the Fugitive Slave Law, the divisions within the abolition movement remained entrenched.

Return to the United Kingdom

Throughout summer, Garnet continued to lecture Britain. His prominence as an abolitionist speaker was evident when, in summer, he addressed the British and Foreign Anti-Slavery Society in Exeter Hall, along with the Rev. Pennington. Garnet's speech was praised on the grounds that 'it would have done honor to the most gifted of England's sons'.[87] In July, he was again a delegate to the World Peace Conference, which was held in London to coincide with the Great

Henry Highland Garnet (1815–1882)   173

Exhibition. Garnet was one of only three Americans to speak, the others being Burritt and the Rev. George Beckwith. According to one report, 'Mr. Garnett [sic] was received with decided favor'.[88] Garnet's public successes were not mirrored in his private life. His wife, Julia, together with their three children, had joined him in England. She was constantly struggling to make ends meet financially. In 1851, their 7-year old son, James Crummell Garnet, died. Both parents were devastated.[89]

Return to Ireland

Garnet returned to Ireland in early August 1851, this time with his family. On 13 August, he spoke to an audience of 1,200 persons at the First Presbyterian Church in Bangor.[90] The high turnout was in spite of the severe weather, leading one newspaper to suggest that the church was filled with, 'a dense mass of people whose earnestness of manner gave to the spectator a vivid conception of the deep and inextinguishable abhorrence of slavery that lives in the heart of every Irishman'.[91] The chairperson was William Sharman Crawford, a local landowner and a member of the British parliament. Crawford had also chaired several lectures by Douglass. Although Standfield was present, he explained that the meeting was not being hosted by the Belfast Anti-Slavery Society, but had been convened at the suggestion of the Rev. William Patteson.[92] Since 1829, Patteson had been the incumbent of the Presbyterian minister of the Second Presbyterian Church.[93] A number of ministers spoke at the meeting, condemning slavery. Garnet spoke about the Fugitive Slave Law, but before doing so, he praised the French Republic and their recent decision to end slavery. He then gave many individual examples showing the cruelty of the new Law. Garnet asked the audience to influence their American friends and all future Irish emigrants to remain on the side of freedom. Before sitting down, he recited what appeared to be his favourite poem, 'The Blind Boy'.[94] The *Banner of Ulster* described Garnet's lecture, which lasted over an hour, as 'most interesting and instructive', with 'harrowing' examples of the pain inflicted by the Fugitive Slave Law.[95]

Crawford concluded the meeting by praising the large audience turnout. He then praised Garnet:

> he had ever been the advocate of civil and religious liberty; and claimed it, not for his own country merely, but for the entire world. It was the right of man of every colour. In Christianity there were no distinctions of colour. The benefits of that salvation which provided for mankind were extended to all nations. Some said that men of colour were inferior to the white race. They had proof of the contrary that night. No white man could have acquitted himself more creditably than Mr. Garnet had done … It was creditable to their country to shew their desire for the emancipation of the negro race; and, though they were not American citizens, they had much influence in America; they had many friends there; and it was important that they should be stirred up against the diabolical system of slavery.[96]

The meeting ended with a benediction.

174 *Henry Highland Garnet (1815–1882)*

On 4 September, Garnet spoke in Lisburn. When publicizing the lecture, the Belfast *News-Letter* averred that the lectures were 'doing good everywhere' and that Garnet, 'having himself been a slave, is intimately acquainted with all its workings'.[97] As usual, Garnet gave 'a lucid and highly interesting statement regarding the condition of the slaves in the United States'. The meeting was held in the Presbyterian church in Lisburn, which was overflowing, despite it being one of the larger churches. The audience included ministers from various denominations and several members of the Society of Friends. Unusually, a man from New Orleans was present who admitted that he did not agree with Garnet, but that everything that the abolitionist said had been factual.[98]

In Ireland, Garnet combined his anti-slavery activities with his duties as a minister. However, his schedule was far less intense than during his visit earlier in the year, possible because of the presence of his family. On 7 September, Garnet gave two sermons—one in the morning and one in the evening—in the Second Presbyterian Church in Dromore. His purpose was to raise funds so that the Rev. McKee could pay off a debt for a gallery. The attendance was so large that extra seats had to be brought in. The *Banner of Ulster*, which had been founded in 1842 by the Rev. William Gibson to uphold orthodox Presbyterian values, reported that:

> All were perfectly delighted with the preacher's discourses. He has very much to recommend him in the pulpit, as well as in private life. He seems largely imbued with his Master's spirit, and his preaching is quite apostolic in its character, distinguished for earnestness and simplicity.[99]

A total of £42–12*s*. was raised from Garnet's sermons. The following evening, an anti-slavery meeting was held in the same church. The building was described as 'crammed' with Garnet delivering an 'eloquent and feeling address on the vile and abominable system of slavery existing in America'. Following speeches by a number of ministers, the meeting closed with a prayer.[100] On 14 September, Garnet preached at Cargygreevy Presbyterian Church near Lisburn. The attendance was 'large' and 'highly respectable' and Garnet delivered 'a lucid and impressive discourse'. The collection amounted to £10.[101]

In the weeks that followed, Garnet spoke about religion and slavery in Belfast, lecturing to the public and to the various Protestant Mission Stations in the town. Many of his events were full to overflowing, with people often having to stand. Garnet seemed pleased with this response; at one event in October, he stated that he had never had such an attentive audience.[102] On 20 October, Garnett attended a meeting to discuss the African Colonization Scheme in the Presbyterian Church in Donegall Street in Belfast. Opposition to various colonization schemes was something that Garnet and the Garrisonians agreed on. The meeting was publicized as being the last opportunity to hear Garnet speak in Belfast.[103] This news inevitably resulted in 'a large assemblage'. The advance publicity in a local newspaper averred that Garnett was

Henry Highland Garnet (1815–1882) 175

not only fully competent to undertake the task, but is duly qualified by a sad personal experience, to tear the veil from the monster iniquity and show in how far the American ministers can lay claim to Bible authority for its continuance.[104]

The meeting was chaired by the Rev. Coulter. When Garnet spoke, he was received with 'enthusiastic acclamation'. He gave a critical history of the Colonization Scheme, describing its aim being 'the extirpation of the free coloured population in order that slave property might be preserved'. Two more speakers, Dr Drew and the Rev. Nelson, also condemned the scheme. These two ministers were linked by their having provided character endorsements in Douglass's *Narrative*.[105] At the end of the meeting it was announced that Garnet would be thanked with a farewell soirée.[106] The meeting then ended with a prayer.[107]

A week later, on 28 October, the Belfast Ladies' Anti-Slavery Society hosted a gathering for Garnet, 'the indefatigable apostle of negro slavery', in the Wesleyan Methodist Chapel.[108] Following this event, Garnet and his family left Ireland and he resumed lecturing in Britain.[109] As had been the case with his first visit, during his return to the north of Ireland, Garnet had appeared in venues where his audiences would be overwhelmingly, if not exclusively, Presbyterian. Although his visits to the country occurred towards the conclusion of the Great Hunger, apart from brief references to O'Connell when in Dublin, Garnet avoided commenting on either Irish politics or Irish poverty. Moreover, unlike several other visiting abolitionists, he appeared unmoved by the social injustices that existed in Ireland.

Jamaica

In October 1852, the United Presbyterian Church in Scotland announced that they would be sending Garnet as a missionary to Jamaica. He was the first black minister to be employed in this capacity. Garnet's work there was to be subsidized by money from Presbyterian churches in England and Scotland.[110] News of the appointment was also carried by Irish newspapers.[111] The Garnet family sailed from Southampton to Jamaica at the beginning of November 1852.[112] They took with them Stella Weims, an escaped slave girl whom Garnet had adopted two years earlier.[113] Before departing, it was learned that Weims' family were being sold to another master and so, on the eve of their departure, Garnet made an appeal for subscriptions to buy their freedom, his letter appearing in many newspapers.[114] Interest in Garnet's travel was evident, with details of their journey to Jamaica, including being forced to take shelter in Madeira, being carried by newspapers in Ireland and Britain.[115] Clearly, Garnet had become a celebrity abolitionist whose movements were considered newsworthy. Garnet was soon to be replaced on the British abolitionist lecture circuit by the Rev. Samuel Ringgold Ward, a relative and a friend, who praised Garnet for being an example of both a black intellectual and a skilled theologian.[116]

For many abolitionists, the West Indies was held up as an example of how emancipation could be achieved without bloodshed or chaos. Being in Jamaica,

176   Henry Highland Garnet (1815–1882)

therefore, meant that Garnet could observe the impact of emancipation first-hand. It was also a way of promoting his ongoing commitment to the use of free produce labour. Once in Jamaica, Garnet lost no time in lecturing—he began speaking on the Fugitive Slave Law in Kingston on 19 December 1852.[117] His wife Julia taught at a female industrial school. Interest in his progress was still evident in Ireland. In April 1853, the *Northern Whig* published part of a letter that Garnet had written to friends in England. In it, he said that after years of wandering he now had a proper home, which reminded him of an English parsonage. Moreover, he stated, the local people were happy to have a black minister, some of them weeping tears of gratitude.[118] It appeared an idyllic ending to Garnet's three years of wandering. Yet, similar to Ward some years later, Garnet viewed the local people through a racialized prism, opining, 'The Creole is naturally indolent, and the climate and soil is so productive, that a livelihood can be secured without much exertion, and they seem destitute of sufficient physical energy to impel them to hard labour'. Garnet, once opposed to black emigration, now appealed to free black Americans to travel to Jamaica where they would find employment.[119] Garnet's happiness in being in Jamaica proved to be short-lived, and his trademark restless soon re-emerged. His adopted daughter Stella became ill and died and Garnet also became sick with fever. He asked the Presbyterian Church in Scotland for permission to leave Jamaica. It was granted and he left the island at the end of 1855.[120] Regardless of their many disagreements, Douglass welcomed Garnet's return to the United States as he believed that the coming battle to end slavery needed to be fought on American soil.[121]

Later life

Despite having left the United Kingdom in 1852, the Garnet family was not forgotten. Julia continued to correspond with Anna Richardson in Newcastle, even after the family was living in Jamaica.[122] At the same time, Garnet's own engagement with British abolitionists continued, usually, in the form of pleas for financial support. In 1857, Garnet issued an appeal, which was published by many newspapers, to purchase the freedom of his enslaved niece, Cordelia.[123] The funds were raised, largely due to the efforts of Richardson.[124] This news was reported widely in the British and Irish press.[125] It was a reminder of the cruelty of the Fugitive Slave Law and of Garnet's role in resisting it. It also suggested that Garnet's time in Britain and Ireland had had a lasting impact.

After leaving Jamaica, the Garnet family returned to New York where Garnet continued with his usual lecturing activities. His feud with Douglass persisted. Following John Brown's failed rising at Harpers Ferry in 1859, Douglass fled to Britain fearing—with good reason—that he was about to be arrested. Garnet criticized him for not staying and fighting it out but instead seeking the protection of 'the British lion'.[126] Like many black abolitionists, Garnet had been a critic of the American Colonization Society but, in later life, came to favour colonization. In 1858, he had founded the African Civilization Society, which promoted voluntary emigration to Africa and, he believed, would help to develop a black nationality.[127] Its purpose, however, was two-fold, and revealed much about

Henry Highland Garnet (1815–1882) 177

Garnet's deep evangelicalism. Unsurprisingly, the Society's Constitution was infused with religious language, its opening statement revealing that its key aim was to 'promote the civilization and Christianization of Africa, as well as the welfare of her children in all lands'.[128] Garnet also enthusiastically supported a scheme to encourage black Americans to emigrate to Haiti. In 1860, he even became an agent of the Haitian Emigration Bureau, which had headquarters in Boston.[129] Both Douglass and the Rev. Pennington were critical of this form of black separatism, seeing it as weakening the position of people of African descent in America.[130] At this stage, Douglass's views on Haiti were ambivalent, he, for a period, supporting American expansion into the Republic.[131]

At the beginning of 1861, an appeal appeared in several British newspapers for financial aid to support a new scheme by Garnet to help black people in America and Canada settle in Abeokuta, in the Niger Valley district. He explained that as the area was excellent for growing cotton, the project would also strike a blow at slavery in the United States. Garnet, who was referred to as 'a man known for piety', had agreed to travel with the first group of over 100 people from New York and, with his family, help them to establish the new communities.[132] Not unexpectedly, given Garnet's evangelical leanings, the article stated that only 'men of acknowledged Christian principles and character' were eligible to participate.[133] A number of towns and cities in Britain, including London and Manchester, established fundraising committees to assist the scheme.[134] It appeared that Garnet was finally taking his Christianizing mission to Africa.

Garnet did not, however, travel to Abeokuta. Instead he returned to Britain. He arrived in Liverpool in September 1861. Garnet claimed to be visiting in order to promote his emigration project.[135] Given that the Civil War had commenced in April 1861, it is not surprising that he primarily lectured on this topic. One newspaper reported that,

> The Rev. H. H. Garnet of New York, who revisits this country to lay the cause of his coloured brethren before their English friends, and to present to us the views of an intelligent American on the present war, addressed an assembly of our townsmen last night.[136]

His visit attracted attention for another reason—Garnet was travelling with a passport.[137] It was the first passport given to a black person since the Dred Scott decision in 1857, when the Supreme Court had ruled that black people— both slaves and free—could never be citizens of the United States. At Garnet's insistence, the word 'negro' had been included in the document.[138] Garnet did not travel to Ireland, but his lectures on the War in America did receive press coverage there.[139] He returned to the United States early in 1862.

The draft riots

On his return to the United States, similar to other black abolitionists, Garnet helped to recruit black men into the Union Army. In July 1863, he was in

178 *Henry Highland Garnet (1815–1882)*

New York during the disreputable Draft Riots, which had been instigated by Irish immigrants. Writing in 1865, Garnet's friend, McCune Smith, explained that:

> The Rev. Garnet was too prominently known to escape the attention of the July rioters: they rushed down Thirtieth Street where he resided, loudly calling him by name. By the lucky forethought of his daughter who wrenched off the door-plate with an axe, his house escaped.[140]

An alternative version of how he escaped appeared in Garnet's obituary, which claimed that his life had been saved by a 'friendly Irish man', a grocer, who helped him reach his home and then told the mob that the family had left the house.[141] Garnet himself also demonstrated less than total honesty when referring to the riots in 1864, at the National Convention of Colored Men held in Syracuse in New York. The two stars of the conference were also two long-term rivals—Henry Garnet and Frederick Douglass. At this stage in their lives, both men were powerful leaders who were confident in their abilities and their positions. Garnet spoke in support of the enlistment programme. He also talked about his long-standing plan for black emigration, basing it in his desire for 'negro nationality'.[142] He then referred to the recent Draft Riots in which Irish men had played such a disgraceful role in attacking the black population. Like many abolitionists before him, he lamented on the difference between the Irish in Ireland and once they landed in America, saying:

> He had travelled from Belfast to Cork, and from Dublin to the Giant's Causeway, and the treatment he received was universally one of kindness. He had stood in public beside the great O'Connell; and we know what his hatred of oppression was.[143]

Garnet attributed the change in the Irish people to the debasing influence of unprincipled American politicians.[144] More puzzling, however, was Garnet's claim that he had met O'Connell, which had no basis in fact. The Irish Liberator had died in May 1847, long before Garnet set foot on Irish or British soil. Why did he tell this untruth? Was it to outdo his erstwhile nemesis, Douglass—who had shared a stage with O'Connell in September 1845?[145] Or did Garnet hope that by mentioning O'Connell he would be drawing a distinction between the Irish in Ireland and the Irish in America? Or did he hope to curry favour with the audience, because, as the minutes recorded, 'The name of O'Connell was received with great applause'.[146] Taking this comment at its face value, Garnet's biographer, Joel Schor, repeated it in his biography.[147] Whatever Garnet's motivation, it was an act of blatant dishonesty, out of keeping with a man of the cloth or of the people. The assassination of President Lincoln in the following year brought Garnet and Douglass together again, but in an unusual way. Both men received walking canes from Mrs. Lincoln that had been owned by her husband.[148] It was a gentle reminder that these two former slaves, whatever their flaws and their differences, had advised a President of the United States.

Henry Highland Garnet (1815–1882) 179

In 1870, Garnet's wife Julia, an abolitionist in her own right, died.[149] In 1879, Garnet married Sarah Smith Tompkins, also a teacher and activist. In his later years, Garnet remained active both politically and in terms of his ministry. The former included supporting Cuban independence in its long struggle to be free of Spain and to end slavery.[150] Throughout his life, Garnet had expressed his desire to visit Africa. He was not to do so until he was an old man. In 1881, Garnet was appointed by President Garfield to serve as Minister to Liberia. Liberia had been formed by American slaves in the 1820s, but the project had been funded and organized by the American Colonization Society—a body that Garnet had initially criticized for denying black Americans of their birth right to be American.[151] Before departing for Liberia, Garnet said:

> How strange that the son of that conquered chieftain should now be sent to the very scene of his ancestor's defeat and degradation as the minister and Consul General of this great nation.[152]

Garnet died in Liberia in 1882, only two months after his arrival. He was buried in Monrovia, the capital city. Garnet had finally gone home. Because of his official position, the State Department in Washington had first been informed of his death. In his long obituary in *The New York Times*, his three years lecturing in Britain and Ireland was briefly mentioned.[153] A eulogium was delivered before the Union Literary and Historical Association in Washington on 4 May by Garnet's lifelong friend, Rev. Alexander Crummell.[154] His passing and remarkable achievements were acknowledged by all American abolitionists, including Douglass. For Cuban patriot, José Martí, Garnet was a 'Messiah' and a 'Moses', who had died 'beloved'.[155]

Conclusion

Garnet was one of a cluster of gifted black abolitionists who came to prominence in the 1840s and 1850s. He was unusual in that, despite being highly educated, he did not write a narrative. Although his private papers were destroyed by fire, many of his speeches survive and newspapers on both sides of the Atlantic covered his activities in great detail. In terms of historical significance, Garnet was one of the first abolitionists to advocate black militancy, something that shocked his fellow abolitionists in the 1840s. His heritage, being a black abolitionist of completely African descent, and being a former slave and then a fugitive slave, all meant that Garnet had a compelling story to tell. And he told it in a way that enthralled those who heard him speak.

Like his illustrious contemporaries, Garnet achieved a number of firsts, one of them being that he was the first African American minister to preach before Congress in February 1865, within days of Congress's adoption of the 13th Amendment banning slavery and involuntary servitude.[156] His sermon was entitled, *'Let the Monster Perish'*.[157] In his searing attack on slavery, he praised Irish lawyer, John Philpot Curran, and his speech in defence of James Somerset, a Jamaican

180 *Henry Highland Garnet (1815–1882)*

slave who declared his freedom upon being brought to Britain. Curran's speech was quoted frequently by abolitionists, including Douglass, as being an eloquent and powerful denouncement of enslavement. For Garnet:

> From the days of Balak to those of Isaiah and Jeremiah, up to the times of Paul, and through every age of the Christian Church, the sons of thunder have denounced the abominable thing. The heroes who stood in the shining ranks of the hosts of the friends of human progress, from Cicero to Chatham, and Burke, Sharp, Wilberforce, and Thomas Clarkson, and Curran, assaulted the citadel of despotism. The orators and statesmen of our own land, whether they belonged to the past, or to the present age, will live and shine in the annals of history, in proportion as they have dedicated their genius and talents to the defence of Justice and man's God-given rights.[158]

Inevitably, comparisons were sometimes drawn between black abolitionists, occasionally by other black abolitionists. Both during his lifetime and subsequently, Henry Garnet was often compared to Frederick Douglass in terms of the brilliance of his oratory and his skilful use of rhetoric. In a number of significant areas, the two men clashed on several key issues—resistance, political involvement, Haiti—although, increasingly, Douglass came to share Garnet's views as he moved away from Garrison.

During his life, Garnet was also frequently compared with Ward. A contemporary of both men, William G. Allen,[159] offered several interesting, if colourful, insights into their characters:

> Garnet, as an orator, is more polished than Ward, as well as more elaborate. He has more application as a student—is more consecutive in his thoughts and employs more method in their arrangement. He would, consequently, be more pleasing to a select audience; while a promiscuous one would be more easily swayed by Ward. His personal appearance is fine. He is about five feet and two inches tall,[160] erect of figure, and somewhat slender in build. He is as black as Ward, but of smoother texture of skin; has a fine eye, and prominent brow. He dresses in the best broadcloth, and with most scrupulous exactness; carries a cane, and altogether his presence impresses you with the fact, that, though somewhat aristocratic, he is, nevertheless, not only a well-bred man, but a most accomplished gentleman. He is a cousin of Ward, and is, as Ward is, a Southerner. Hot blood runs in his veins; and he would throttle the life out of a slaveholder with as little compunction of conscience as he would tread the life out of a snake.[161]

However, as both Garnet's and Ward's time in Ireland revealed, the two men shared a narrow and evangelical view of religion, which determined where and how they chose to lecture.

Writing in 1972, Earl Ofari praised Garnet for giving 'black nationalism a theoretical and political dimension, which it previously had lacked'. In regard

Henry Highland Garnet (1815–1882) 181

to Garnet's ideas on black freedom and colonization, Ofari was more critical, describing them as 'impractical, narrow, racist in their emphasis on Christian missionary activity, and elitist in favouring the creation of a ruling class'.[162] Schor, however, has defended Garnet from charges of elitism, saying 'while Garnet and Douglass were educated men well above the level of the black masses, it is not necessarily true that they were completely cut off from the aspirations of black Americans'.[163] Here, a comparison with Ward, not Douglass, might be more appropriate. In terms of Garnet's political philosophies and outlook, both he and Ward demonstrated an elitism and a coldness when it came to class and religion. Similarly, the two men had chosen the ministry as their profession, and it led them to careers in Jamaica, facilitated by patrons in Britain. When lecturing in Ireland, their choice of locations suggested a pro-Protestant agenda, which in Ward's case, was openly anti-Catholic. Schor has argued that Garnet made his greatest impact in Scotland and Wales, where 'the masses were more actively involved in the religious institutions'.[164] He went on to say, 'In England and Ireland, millions of workers did not attend any place of worship and were consequently cut off from the moral improvements of the age'. In saying this, Schor is quoting directly from Ward's narrative, which provided a self-serving and distorted view of religion, especially of Catholicism in Ireland.[165]

Although Garnet's travels in Britain and other parts of Europe are referred to often, Garnet's time in Ireland is rarely mentioned in biographies.[166] Yet, his time in the country revealed aspects of his character that defined his outlook and approach to abolition. Nonetheless, Garnet's undoubted abilities endeared him to all who heard him speak and, even though his time in Ireland was short and limited, his impact was powerful. Moreover, at a time when the country was slowly recovering from the devastating effects of the Famine, Irish abolitionists continued to express their concern and compassion for enslaved people 3,000 miles away. Visitors such as Garnet were crucial in consolidating these transatlantic bonds. Garnet may have been a flawed messenger, but his contribution in keeping the abolitionist flame alive, and as a distinguished and eloquent champion of enslaved people, was immense.

Notes

1 This is a reference to the divisions in the American anti-slavery movement, which took place in 1839 and 1840, when the Tappan brothers broke away from William Lloyd Garrison, ostensibly on the question of women's suffrage, but on a range of other issues including involvement in politics. The new group was named the American and Foreign Anti-Slavery Society, but their opponents referred to them as 'the new organization'. Those who remained loyal to Garrison were the 'old organization'.

2 W. M. Brewer, 'Henry Highland Garnet', in *The Journal of African American History*, vol. 13, no. 1 (Jan. 1928), 36–52, p. 36.

3 Professor Paul Ortiz, 'One of History's Foremost Anti-Slavery Organizers Is Often Left Out of the Black History Month Story', *Time*, 31 January 2018.

4 George Washington William quoted in Joel Schor, 'The Rivalry between Frederick Douglass and Henry Highland Garnet', in *The Journal of Negro History*, pp. 30–8, 30.

182   *Henry Highland Garnet (1815–1882)*

5   Joel Schor, *Henry Highland Garnet* (Westport, CT: Greenwood Press, 1977), p. 30.
6   William Armistead, *A Tribute for the Negro: Being a Vindication of the Moral, Intellectual, and Religious Capabilities of the Colored Portion of Mankind; with Particular Reference to the African Race* (Manchester and London: W. Irwin, 1848). In this publication, Garnet claimed that his great grandfather was the son of a stolen African chief.
7   Obituary in the *New York Times*, 11 March 1882.
8   'Henry Highland Garnet': www.encyclopedia.com/people/social-sciences-and-law/social-reformers/henry-highland-garnet.
9   Schor, *Garnet*, p. 7.
10   Timothy L. Hall, *American Religious Leaders* (New York: Infobase Publishing, 2014), p.141.
11   Armistead, *Tribute for the Negro*. The publication was dedicated to: '*James W. C. Pennington, Frederick Douglass, Alexander Crummell, and many other noble examples of elevated humanity in the negro; whom Fuller beautifully designates "the image of god cut in ebony": this volume, demonstrating, from facts and testimonies, that the white and dark coloured races of man are alike the children of one heavenly father, and in all respects equally endowed by him; is respectfully inscribed'*. The author was an English Quaker abolitionist from Leeds who welcomed many black abolitionists to his home and his city. The publication was 560 pages in length. In it, Garnet was spelled Garnett.
12   'Henry Highland Garnet': www.encyclopedia.com/people/social-sciences-and-law/social-reformers/henry-highland-garnet.
13   Hall, *American Religious Leaders*, p. 141. Schor says Garnet was formally ordained 1842, but that he preaching before this, p. 28.
14   'Abolitionist Newspapers': www.civilwarlibrary.org/abolitionist-newspapers.html.
15   'Garnet': www.encyclopedia.com/people/social-sciences-and-law/social-reformers/henry-highland-garnet.
16   Hall, *American Religious Leaders*, p. 141.
17   Armistead, *A Tribute for the Negro*, p. 513.
18   Schor, *Garnet*, p. 88.
19   Gregory Stephens, *On Racial Frontiers: The New Culture of Frederick Douglass, Ralph Ellison, and Bob Marley* (Cambridge University Press, 1999), pp. 75–6.
20   Schor, *Garnet*, p. 89.
21   *North Star*, 11 February 1848.
22   Henry Highland Garnet, 'Colonization and Emigration', *North Star*, 2 March 1849. Garnet did not support the aims of the American Colonization Society.
23   *North Star*, 7 September 1849.
24   Schor, *Garnet*, p. 22.
25   'Obituary', *New York Times*, 11 March 1882. Garnet's Obituary incorrectly say that he sailed to the United Kingdom on the day that the Fugitive Slave Law was passed (18 September 1850), but the Peace Congress was in August of that year.
26   General Peace Congress, *Report of the Proceedings of the third General Peace Congress, held in Frankfort 1850* (London: Charles Gilpin, 1851), pp. 2, 66. Elihu Burritt (1810–1879) was an American philanthropist and pacifist. Born in Connecticut, he was apprenticed to be a blacksmith, but his love of learning and languages resulted in his nickname, 'the learned blacksmith'. He was also known as 'the apostle of peace' for his work in organizing international peace conferences. In 1847, Burritt had travelled to Ireland to witness the Famine first-hand. He spent some time with Frederick Douglass when the latter was in England.
27   Julie L. Holcomb, *Moral Commerce: Quakers and the Transatlantic Boycott of the Slave Labor Economy* (New York: Cornell University Press, 2016), p. 181.
28   *Sheffield Independent*, 7 December 1850.

Henry Highland Garnet (1815–1882)   183

29 *Newcastle Courant*, 4 October 1850. Rev. James Pennington (1807–1870) was born into enslavement in Maryland but escaped when aged around 20 years old. In 1829, he attended the first National Negro Convention in Philadelphia. Largely self-taught, he was so learned that he became a teacher and attended classes at Yale University but, because of his colour, he could not receive a certificate. His publications include *The Origin and History of the Colored People* (1841) and his memoir, *The Fugitive Blacksmith* (1849). Pennington was a Congregationalist minister.

30 'Obituaries', *New York Times*, 11 March 1882. Some contemporary reports suggest he was a little over five foot in height.

31 Armistead, *A Tribute for the Negro*, p. 513.

32 'Alloa', *Stirling Observer*, 26 February 1852.

33 Schor, *Garnet*, pp. 117–18.

34 'Fugitive Slaves of the United States', *Monmouthshire Beacon*, 28 June 1851.

35 Francis Calder to Peter Bolton, 6 January 1851, quoted in D. Ritchie, *Isaac Nelson: Radical Abolitionist, Evangelical Presbyterian, and Irish Nationalist* (Liverpool University Press, 2018), p. 110.

36 'The Rev. H. H. Garnet', *Banner of Ulster*, 14 January 1851.

37 'ANTI-SLAVERY IN IRELAND', the *Liberator*, 30 May 1851. The 'ragged' school had been established during the Famine in 1847, by several philanthropic women in the town. By the 1850s, it was being accused of proselyting Catholic children—giving them stirabout in exchange for scripture reading. *Historical Notices of Old Belfast and Its Vicinity: A Selection from the Mss. Collected by William Pinkerton, F.S.A., for His Intended History of Belfast* (Belfast: Robert Magill Young, M. Ward & Company, Limited, 1896), p. 195.

38 'Anti-Slavery Meeting', *Weekly Vindicator*, 18 January 1851.

39 See chapter on Frederick Douglass.

40 'Home Mission of the Presbyterian Society', Belfast *News-Letter*, 15 January 1851.

41 Ibid., 'Tomorrow Evening. Anti-Slavery Meeting', 20 January 1851.

42 Ibid., 'Belfast Anti-Slavery Society. Lecture by the Rev. Henry Highland Garnet', 22 January 1851.

43 Ibid.

44 Ibid.

45 Ibid.

46 Ibid.

47 'The Rev. H. H. Garnet, *Northern Whig*, 23 January 1851.

48 'This Evening', Belfast *News-Letter*, 24 January 1851.

49 Ibid., 'SLAVERY IN THE UNITED STATES', 27 January 1851.

50 William Meade (1789–1862), the third Bishop of Virginia, did not regard slavery as a sin, but believed that slaves should be given a religious education. In 1813, Meade had compiled and published a compilation of Christian proslavery tracts: *Sermons Address to Masters and Servants, and Published in the Year 1743, by the Rev. Thomas Bacon, Minister of the Protestant Episcopal Church in Maryland, Now Republished with other Tracts and Dialogues on the Same Subject, and Recommended to all Masters and Mistresses to Be Used in Their Families* (Winchester, VA: John Heiskell, 1813).

51 'Slavery in THE UNITED STATES', Belfast *News-Letter*, 27 January 1851.

52 Ibid. A separate report in the same paper stated that he had lectured in Townsend Street Presbyterian Church.

53 'A Case for Humane Consideration', *Newry Telegraph*, 13 February 1851. The author of the letter was S. Stewart.

54 The *News-Letter* gave this higher figure, saying it was 15,000; *Ulster General Advertiser, Herald of Business and General Information*, 1 February 1851.

55 Belfast *News-Letter*, 3 February 1851.

184   *Henry Highland Garnet (1815–1882)*

56 'THE TENANT LEAGUE, AN ANTI-SLAVERY SOCIETY. BLACK AND WHITE SLAVERY', *Nation*, 15 February 1851.
57 Probably the Rev. Dr John Coulter, Presbyterian minister of the Gilnahirk Church, which was located about seven miles from Newtownards. He was also Moderator of the General Assembly of the Presbyterian Church in Ireland.
58 'THE TENANT LEAGUE, AN ANTI-SLAVERY SOCIETY. BLACK AND WHITE SLAVERY', *Nation*, 15 February 1851.
59 'American Slavery', Belfast *News-Letter*, 24 October 1851.
60 His Ballymena lecture took place on 30 January. *Coleraine Chronicle*, 1 February 1851.
61 William W. Brown, *The Anti-Slavery Harp: A Collection of Songs for Anti-Slavery Meetings* (Boston, MA: Bela Marsh, 1848).
62 His Ballymena lecture took place on 30 January. *Coleraine Chronicle*, 1 February 1851.
63 'Rev. H. H. Garnet', Belfast *News-Letter*, 31 January 1851.
64 'REV. JOHN L. RENTOUL AT THE ANTI-SLAVERY MEETING', the *Liberator*, 30 May 1851. The meeting was held in the Donegall Place Primitive Wesleyan Methodist Church, Belfast, on 5 February 1851.
65 'The Rev. Garnet in Ballymoney', Belfast *News-Letter*, 19 February 1851. Garnet's lectures raised £53–10s for Trinity Church.
66 Ibid., 'Slavery in the United States', 7 February 1851.
67 'The Rev. H.H. Garnet on American Slavery', *Banner of Ulster*, 7 February 1851.
68 Rentoul's speech was carried in the *Liberator*, 30 May 1851.
69 'The Rev. H. H. Garnet on American Slavery', *Banner of Ulster*, 7 February 1851.
70 'Mr Garnet', the *Liberator*, 30 May 1851.
71 'Slavery in the United States', Belfast *News-Letter*, 7 February 1851.
72 'AMERICAN SLAVERY', *Freeman's Journal*, 6 February 1851, 7 February 1851. The story about the meeting was carried by the anti-slavery *Kerry Evening Post*, 12 February 1851.
73 Although born in a Free State and operating a number of successful boarding houses in the New York area, in 1851, William P. Powell, Sr., decided to relocate his family to England to escape the harsh fugitive slave laws. His son, who shared the same name, studied medicine while overseas, and served as a doctor during the American Civil War. The older Powell had established The Colored Sailor's Home in New York in 1840, which was a target of racist attacks during the Draft Riots of 1863. See: https://portsidenewyork.org/afam-maritime.
74 Samuel Ringgold Ward, *Autobiography of a Fugitive Negro: His Anti-Slavery Labours in the United States, Canada, & England* (London: John Snow, 1855), p. 331.
75 'American slavery. Meeting at the Rotundo', *Freeman's Journal*, 8 February 1851.
76 Ibid., 'Anti-Slavery Meeting', 12 February 1851.
77 Ibid.
78 Ibid.
79 An exception to this might have been the Rev. Isaac Nelson who, in 1873, attended a Home Rule meeting in Dublin. He served as a member of the Irish Parliamentary Party for County Mayo in the British House of Commons from 1880 to 1885.
80 For example, long extracts were reproduced in Belfast *News-Letter*, 12 February 1851; *Ulster General Advertiser, Herald of Business and General Information*, 1 March 1851.
81 Armistead, *A Tribute for the Negro*.
82 'LABORS OF H. H. GARNET', *Frederick Douglass' Paper*, 11 March 1852.
83 'Foreign Correspondence. From our *Dublin* Correspondent', *National Anti-Slavery Standard*, 13 September 1849.
84 The 'lady' was Anna Richardson of Newcastle, who had also befriended Douglass.

Henry Highland Garnet (1815–1882) 185

85 'Foreign Correspondence. From our Dublin Correspondent. LIVERPOOL, Letter from Webb to S. H. Gay, 20 February 1851', *National Anti-Slavery Standard*, 20 March 1851.

86 Parker Pillsbury to Samuel May, 5 October 1854, reprinted in Clare Taylor, *British and American Abolitionists* (Edinburgh University Press, 1974), p. 412.

87 'BRITISH AND FOREIGN ANTI-SLAVERY SOCIETY', *Frederick Douglass' Paper*, 21 August 1851.

88 'London Peace Congress', in *Advocate of Peace* (1847–1884), vol. 9, no. 9/11 (Sept., Oct. and Nov. 1851), p. 125. The London Congress was held in Exeter Hall from 22 to 24 July 1851.

89 Diana Winkelman, 'The rhetoric of Henry Highland Garnet' (Masters' Dissertation), p. 20. Available at: https://baylor-ir.tdl.org/handle/2104/5095.

90 'Anti-slavery meeting', *Belfast Mercury*, 16 August 1851.

91 'Anti-Slavery meeting at Bangor', *Northern Whig*, 16 August 1851.

92 'Anti-slavery meeting in Bangor', *Belfast Mercury*, 16 August 1851.

93 Rev. W. D. Killen, *History of congregations of the Presbyterian Church in Ireland and biographical notices of eminent Presbyterian ministers and laymen, with the signification of names of places* (Belfast: James Cleeland, 1886), p. 56.

94 'Anti-slavery meeting', *Belfast Mercury*, 16 August 1851. The paper said the poem was authored by 'Mrs Bailey'. More usually rendered as 'The Blind Slave Boy', it appeared in William Wells Brown's collection, *The Anti-Slavery Harp* (Boston, MA: Bela Marsh, 1848).

95 'The Fugitive Slave Law', *Banner of Ulster*, 15 August 1851.

96 'Anti-slavery meeting', *Belfast Mercury*, 16 August 1851.

97 'American Slavery', Belfast *News-Letter*, 3 September 1851.

98 Ibid., 'Lisburn', 12 September 1851.

99 'The Rev. H.H. Garnet in Dromore', *Banner of Ulster*, 19 September 1851.

100 Ibid.

101 'The Rev. H. Hyland [sic] Garnet in Cargygreevy', Belfast *News-Letter*, 1 October 1851.

102 Ibid., 'Rev. Henry Garnet', 27 October 1851.

103 'A lecture', *Ulster General Advertiser, Herald of Business and General Information*, 18 October 1851.

104 Ibid.

105 The second Irish reprint appeared in 1846.

106 'Soirée', Belfast *News-Letter*, 27 October 1851.

107 Ibid., 'American slavery', 24 October 1851.

108 No title, *Northern Whig*, 25 October 1851.

109 'American Slavery', Ulster General Advertiser, Herald of Business and General Information, 27 November 1851; 'Rev. Mr Garnet in Edinburgh', *Falkirk Herald*, 6 December 1851; 'Alloa', *Stirling Observer*, 26 February 1852.

110 Schor, *Garnet*, p. 126.

111 'Designation of a Missionary', *Northern Whig*, 23 October 1852; *The Advocate: or, Irish Industrial Journal*, 27 October 1852.

112 Shortly after leaving England, their ship was badly damaged by storms, forcing them to take shelter in Madeira, 'The Rev. H. H. Garnet', *Scottish Guardian*, 18 January 1853.

113 'Illustration of Uncle Tom's Cabin', *Aris's Birmingham Gazette*, 1 November 1852.

114 'A slave case', *Dumfries and Galloway Standard*, 27 October 1852; 'Slavery in the US', *Worcester Journal*, 4 November 1852.

115 'Rev. H. H. Garnet', *Banner of Ulster*, 25 January 1853, included a letter from Garnet from Madeira.

116 'Lecture on the Origin, History and Hopes of the Negro Race [S Ward]', *Cheltenham Journal and Gloucestershire Fashionable Weekly Gazette*, 26 November 1853.

186 *Henry Highland Garnet (1815–1882)*

117 *Saunder's News-Letter*, 21 January 1853; *Longford Journal*, 29 January 1853; *Wexford Independent*, 26 January 1853; the *Dundee, Perth, and Cupar Advertiser*, 1 February 1853, all carried reports stating that Garnet had given several lectures in Jamaica on the Fugitive Slave Law.
118 'The Rev. H. W. [sic] Garnet in Jamaica', *Northern Whig*, 28 April 1853.
119 Quoted in *Frederick Douglass' Paper*, 31 July 1851; Schor, 'Garnet', p. 128.
120 Schor, *Garnet*, p. 130.
121 *Frederick Douglass' Paper*, 21 March 1856.
122 'A Slave Girl redeemed from Slavery', *Shrewsbury Chronicle*, 19 March 1858.
123 Ibid., 'A work of real charity', 14 August 1857.
124 Ibid., 'A Slave Girl redeemed from Slavery', 19 March 1858.
125 *Derbyshire Advertiser and Journal*, 1 April 1858: *Kentish Mercury*, 3 April 1858; *Durham Chronicle*, 2 April 1858; *Lancaster Gazette*, 3 April 1858; 'A Girl redeemed from slavery', *The Advocate: Or, Irish Industrial Journal*, 3 April 1858; *Belfast Mercury*, 30 March 1858.
126 Schor, *Garnet*, p. 163.
127 Winkelman, in 'Rhetoric', praised Garnet for believing that 'emigration to Africa would complete his vision of building a black nationality', p. 6.
128 Constitution of a Civilizing Society: www.blackpast.org/african-american-history/constitution-african-civilization-society-1796/.
129 William Seraile, 'The Brief Diplomatic Career of Henry Highland Garnet', in *Phylon*, vol. 46, no. 1 (1st Qtr. 1985), 71–81.
130 African Civilization Society: www.encyclopedia.com/history/encyclopedias-almanacs-transcripts-and-maps/african-civilization-society-afcs.
131 For the complexity and evolution of Douglass's views on Haiti see, Millery Polyné, 'Douglass at the Intersection of U.S. and Caribbean Pan-Americanism', in *Caribbean Studies*, vol. 34, no. 2 (Jul.–Dec., 2006), pp. 3–45.
132 'African Aid Society', *Hereford Times*, 23 March 1861.
133 *Wells Journal*, 4 May 1861.
134 'Appeal of Manchester Auxiliary to the London Committee', *Manchester Courier and Lancashire General Advertiser*, 20 July 1861.
135 Schor, *Garnet*, p. 178.
136 'Henry Garnet', *Newcastle Daily Chronicle*, 26 November 1861.
137 'Passport', *North & South Shields Gazette and Northumberland and Durham Advertiser*, 10 October 1861.
138 Schor, *Garnet*, p. 179.
139 'War in America', *Northern Whig*, 11 October 1861.
140 James McCune Smith, *Sketch of the Life and Labors of Rev. Henry Highland Garnet* (Philadelphia, PA: Philip M. Wilson, 1865), p. 52.
141 'Obituary', *New York Times*, 11 March 1882.
142 *Proceedings of the National Convention of Colored Men, Held in the City of Syracuse, N.Y., October 4, 5, 6, and 7, 1864; with the Bill of Wrongs and Rights, and the Address to the American People* (New York: Syracuse, 1864), p. 20.
143 Ibid.
144 Ibid.
145 Christine Kinealy, *Frederick Douglass and Ireland. In His Own Words* (London: Routledge, 2018).
146 Syracuse Convention, 1864, p. 20.
147 Schor, *Garnet*, pp. 202–3.
148 Ibid., p. 210.
149 For Julia's obituary, see: 'Died', *The Christian Recorder*, 22 January 1870.

Henry Highland Garnet (1815–1882) 187

150 *Slavery in Cuba. A Report of the Proceedings of the Meeting Held at Cooper Institute, New York City*, 13 December 1872 (New York: Cuban Anti-Slavery Committee, 1872), pp. 15–18. Garnet was Secretary of this Society.
151 Garnet, 'An Address to the Slaves of the United States of America, Buffalo', National Convention of Colored Citizens, Park Presbyterian Church, Buffalo, August 1843.
152 Quoted in the *New York Times*, 11 March 1882.
153 Ibid.
154 The eulogy was reprinted in Alexander Crummell, *Africa and America: Addresses and Discourses* (Springfield, MA: Willey and Co., 1891), pp. 272–305.
155 José Martí, *La Opinion Nacional* (Caracas), 31 March 1882.
156 'Ex-Slave Henry Garnet Addressed U.S. House': www.christianity.com/church/church-history/timeline/1801-1900/ex-slave-henry-garnet-addressed-us-house-11630536.html.
157 Henry Highland Garnet, *'Let the Monster* Perish', 12 February 1865. At: www.blackpast.org/african-american-history/1865-henry-highland-garnet-let-monster-perish/.
158 Ibid.
159 William Gustavus Allen (1820–1888) was born free in Virginia to a mixed-race mother and a white father. He was a scholar who taught Rhetoric and Greek in the newly established New York Central College. In 1853, he married a white woman, Mary King, in the face of much opposition and threatened violence. They immediately sought exile in England, never to return to the United States.
160 In other contemporary accounts, he was described as over six foot in height.
161 'ORATORS AND ORATORY. AN ADDRESS BY PROF. WM. G. ALLEN', *Frederick Douglass' Paper*, 22 October 1852. The address was delivered before the Dialexian Society of New York, Central College, 22 June 1852.
162 Earl Ofari, *'Let your motto be resistance'. The Life and Thought of Henry Highland Garnet* (Boston, MA: Beacon Press, 1972), p. 98.
163 Schor, *Garnet*, pp. 166–7.
164 Ibid., p. 120.
165 Ibid., p. 229.
166 Hall, *American Religious Leaders*, p. 143.

7 Edmund Kelly (1817–1884)
'A family redeemed from bondage'

Born into enslavement but having a public career that included meeting with two American Presidents, Edmund Kelly is not only relatively forgotten in transatlantic abolitionist history, but he remains one of the more puzzling figures in regard to his personal story. This is possibly because during his lifetime, his name was spelt in a variety of ways—variously appearing as Edmund/Edmond and Kelly/Kelley.[1] Some of the confusion was caused by Kelly himself. For example, in his 1851 publication, he used the name Edmond Kelley, but elsewhere he used Edmund Kelly. In the same book, Kelly gave his birth date as 10 June 1817—a precision that was unusual amongst enslaved people; elsewhere, he talked about being born in 1818.[2] In other regards, he was less forthcoming. While many enslaved people could not provide precise details about their early years, Kelly seemed especially vague, with few personal insights being offered in his writings or lectures. Who was Edmund Kelly and what was his contribution to transatlantic abolition?

Early life

Kelly was born around the same time as Frederick Douglass and, in several ways, Kelly's life mirrored that of the more famous abolitionist.[3] Like Douglass, he had a white father and an enslaved mother, Kittie White. Kittie's owner was also named White. Kelly's father was an Irish immigrant from Dublin, Edmund Kelly, who had tried, unsuccessfully, to purchase the freedom of his family.[4] When lecturing in Ireland, Kelly mentioned that his father was an Irishman, but he did not suggest that he felt any special affinity with the country or its people.[5] As a teenager, Kelly was determined to self-educate, informing one Irish audience that as a teenager because he possessed,

> a strong desire to learn, he induced some of the schoolboys by acts of kindness and small rewards to give him instruction, and so earnestly did apply himself that at the end of twelve months he had learned to read and write.[6]

His bribing of schoolchildren was very similar to Douglass's account of how he had learned to read.

Edmund Kelly (1817–1884) 189

In 1838, when still enslaved, Kelly underwent a religious conversion. He chose to follow his vocation and entered the church, just as many other prominent black abolitionists, including Samuel Ringgold Ward and Henry Highland Garnet, had done but, unlike them, he chose the Baptist Church.[7] Kelly was officially ordained in 1843, making him Tennessee's first black Baptist Minister.[8] His skills as a preacher led the Concord Baptist Association to attempt to purchase him, but Kelly did not want to exchange one form of enslavement for another; he wanted to be free, not just be transferred to another owner. Shortly afterwards, his owner, Nancy White, who was in financial difficulties and feared that Kelly might be sold to pay her debts, gave him a pass, thus enabling him to move around the country to preach without fear of being captured or sold.[9] In 1847, Kelly used this new-found freedom to travel to Boston and, in doing so, emancipated himself. He made it clear that he did not intend to return to the South.[10] In 1848, he moved to New Bedford, a Quaker and abolitionist enclave, to become pastor of the Second Baptist Church.

Although he escaped alone, Kelly had a family. In 1839, he had married Paralee Walker. They had four children together, but they lived in different households, Paralee's owner being James Walker. Paralee and the children —Dolly Ophelia, Robert Edmond, William Dempsey and Alfred remained enslaved.[11] Kelly, therefore, devoted his first years of freedom to the complex and expensive process of purchasing their freedom, largely by fundraising through his Baptist network. Walker, who was probably Paralee's father, was reluctant to sell the family, claiming to have great affection for them.[12] He responded to Kelly's request:

> if they were offered for sale here at the present prices of such servants, they would command in each $2,800. No price, however, could be offered by anyone that would induce me to permit them to be the slaves or servants of any but my own family. To part with them, with certain knowledge that they were to be free, and their condition bettered, is a matter I might take into consideration. But it is useless to do so until you inform me you can command $2,800, to be applied to that object.[13]

Walker went on to explain that his interest in the family was not simply a monetary one:

> Dolly, the mother of your wife, was my nurse, took the tenderest care of me when I was an orphan child. The attachment which this has produced on my part, and on the part of my wife and children to her and her children and their children, and their treatment, is altogether different from what is ordinarily termed slavery. Although they occupy the position of servants to me and my family, they in reality, in the tie of affection and regard for their comfort and happiness which exists, are not slaves at all. They, if they are colored, stand next in my affections to my own wife and children and children's children. The affection I believe to be mutual.[14]

190 *Edmund Kelly (1817–1884)*

Regardless of these bonds of affection, Walker insisted that Kelly pay him the full $2,800; moreover, that payment should be in cash.[15] Through a combination of donations and loans, Kelly did raise the money. Upon being released, Kelly's family travelled to New York City, arriving on 29 May 1851, a journey which Kelly also had to fund. The following day, they joined him in New Bedford, where Kelly was earning an income through preaching.[16] Paralee and Kelly were re-married there, as marriages between enslaved people were not recognized in Tennessee. Although his family were now legally free, Kelly remained a fugitive slave. Moreover, his situation had become more precarious since he first escaped because of the passage of the 1850 Fugitive Slave Law.

In 1851, partly to raise money to pay his debts, Kelly self-published '*A Family Redeemed from Bondage; Being Rev. Edmond Kelly, (the Author,) His Wife, and Four Children*'.[17] Kelly's publication differed from most narratives written by formerly enslaved people in a number of ways. The fact it was self-published suggested considerable agency and enterprise, but also that Kelly did not have the backing of any influential abolitionist group or individual. Unusually, no image of the author was provided, despite contemporary accounts attesting to Kelly's 'highly intellectual and gentlemanly appearance'.[18] The book was short, only 19 pages, and contained relatively few personal details. Rather than providing a narrative account of his life, it comprised primarily of a series of letters presenting key junctures in his life, especially his attempts to raise money to purchase his family's freedom.[19] They were mostly self-explanatory, with little additional clarification offered. Kelly's transactions with Walker featured prominently. Regarding Kelly's self-emancipation, Walker had written:

> I never blamed you for exercising the natural right of securing your freedom if you could. This was your natural right, and in exercising it you committed no offence against your God, whose approbation alone is to be looked to. But in doing this, have you made yourself happier and in better circumstances than you would have been here?[20]

This paternalistic view was at variance with many other more popular narratives that sought to depict slavery as unfailingly cruel and unchristian. The narrative concluded with a copy of the official affidavit legally declaring the family's freedom. Overall, the contents of Kelly's book were dry, legalistic and transactional, with little of the passion, anger or even sensationalism that was present in several other narratives. Moreover, it suggested that some slave owners were protective and reasonable, rather than evil. Only a few months later, the publication of a new book took the abolitionist world by storm. *Uncle Tom's Cabin, or, Life among the Lowly*, published in 1852, rekindled support for the abolitionist movement by showing the horrors of enslavement. The two publications—one written by a fugitive slave, the other by a white woman—offered very different insights into slavery, with Kelly providing the more moderate approach.

In mid-1852, Kelly sailed from Boston to Liverpool, a journey taken by many black abolitionists before and after him. Officially a fugitive slave, he travelled to

Edmund Kelly (1817–1884) 191

England to raise funds to repay for the purchase of his family and to purchase his own. The publication of *Uncle Tom's Cabin* and the expected visit by its author, Harriet Beecher Stowe, had revived interest in abolition.[21] However, the timing of Kelly's arrival was not totally auspicious as, while the Fugitive Slave Law and Stowe's novel had outraged abolitionists on both sides of the Atlantic, it had also led to a wave of black immigrants, some of whom were impoverished—a fact that had concerned William Wells Brown.[22] Not being affiliated to any abolitionist group, Kelly arrived in Britain with no official sponsor or patron on either side of the Atlantic, but he used his Baptist network as an introduction to British and Irish society. Consequently, the articulate Rev. Kelly, with his compelling story, was well received when lecturing to generous audiences in Britain and Ireland. His personal appearance was also regarded favourably, one paper reporting, 'He is a fine-looking man, carrying a very intelligent countenance, and altogether prepossessing in his manner and appearance'.[23] One of his hosts in England even flippantly wondered whether his female owner, 'was as handsome a woman as he (Mr. Kelly) was a man (but without the beard)'.[24]

In his narrative, Kelly had provided virtually no insights into his personal history. The usual approach by visiting abolitionists, however, especially those who had been formerly enslaved, was to share their personal history with the audience. Without this context, it would be hard to expect donations, and audiences had come to expect that they would be told about the horrors of slavery. Kelly did not disappoint them. His life story—and the emotional appeal on behalf of his family that accompanied it—formed the core of Kelly's lectures while overseas.[25] On several occasions, Kelly lectured to women abolitionists, his story of separation from his wife and family particularly resonating with them. A female audience in Bradford expressed their disdain 'against the iniquities, the heart-rending separation, and the rile immoralities' explained by Kelly.[26] Kelly also spoke of his childhood, telling one audience that:

> When he was about six years of age he and his sisters were put to bed, and in the morning when they awoke, his mother was gone. His sister and brother had disappeared in the same way. He did not expect to hear of them again … he did not expect to meet them on this side the judgment seat.[27]

After recounting his life story, an appeal was then made for donations. Kelly's hosts were sympathetic to this necessity, the Mayor of Leicester, when introducing him, alluded to, 'the great anomaly of a man having to stand before an audience to ask for money to buy himself'.[28] Kelly also elaborated on this theme explaining that a further motive for wishing to be free was so that he could continue with his work as a minister to his people:

> I should render such efforts unnecessary once placing myself beyond the reach of the fugitive slave law, but believing that a solemn obligation rests upon me to devote myself to the promotion of the spiritual and eternal interests of the coloured population in America, I earnestly and affectionately

192   *Edmund Kelly (1817–1884)*

appeal to the kindness and liberality of those who are the friends of the down trodden, to enable me to return under such circumstances as shall secure me against the above iniquitous enactment.[29]

How much Kelly raised at various meetings is not known, but the amount seems to have been substantial. In January 1853, for example, following a meeting in Leicester, an amount of £18 was raised, which he described as the largest sum donated.[30] Reports in local newspapers predicted that the amount would rise to £30.[31] By February 1853, Kelly had paid the debts associated with the purchase of his family's freedom. He now explained to audiences that the reason for staying in Britain was to purchase his own freedom—the cost of which he estimated to be £106 13*s.* 4*d.*[32]

Kelly did not limit his fundraising activities to just lecturing. Shortly after arriving in England, he issued a circular to accompany his tour that contained four closely printed quarto pages in small type, embellished with woodcut portraits of his wife, their four children and Ward. The first woodcut raised £237 in England. A second circular, issued approximately six months later, stated that the required amount had been reached to pay Kelly's debts, so he was now collecting money 'to purchase himself', and so return to the United States as, 'A solemn obligation rests upon him to devote himself to the promotion of the spiritual and eternal interests of the coloured population in America'. The circular also explained that Kelly was anxious to return to New Bedford, where he had lived before the passage of the Fugitive Slave Law, and where his family resided.[33]

Kelly's unorthodox way of presenting himself and of raising money in England was disapproved of by leading Irish abolitionists. The *Anti-Slavery Advocate*, a monthly paper issued out of London, but the brainchild of Dublin-based Richard Webb, published details of Kelly's travels, but expressed caution when doing so. In April 1853, it questioned some of his motives, especially regarding religious matters, pointing out:

> The Rev. Mr. Kelly [sic] is connected with a religious body which fellowships with slaveholders, and we can learn of nothing he has done to free himself or his sect from their control. He is recommended to the public by the Rev. Dr. Sharp of Boston, notorious for his advocacy of the Fugitive Slave Law.[34]

More pointedly, the article alluded to the fact that as Kelly was his own collector, and as his circulars were not dated, 'there is apparently nothing in his arrangements to prevent him from raising £1000 instead of £166 13*s.* 4*d*, (the sum named as needful for his purchase) to take him home to America'. Warning against abolitionist 'huxters', it added:

> When persons representing themselves as fugitive slaves travel as petitioners, we would suggest the propriety of close enquiry into their antecedents. They should be required to produce introductory certificates from well-known friends of the antislavery cause, and all collections made on their

behalf should be forwarded to some person in Great Britain or Ireland who is willing to act as trustee, and whose name will be a guarantee that no more than the sum required shall be solicited, and that it shall be fairly appropriated to the object specified. These precautions would protect the public against fraud, and the coloured race and the anti-slavery cause against the odium to which both are subjected when benevolent persons are swindled in their name.[35]

Kelly may have not been aware that the controversy about his fundraising methods had reached the other side of the Atlantic, with a letter from an 'English friend' appearing in the *Liberator* asking, 'Who is Rev. Edmund Kelly of New Bedford, Mass?' It suggested that Kelly was a 'humbug'. The query was answered by J. Girdwood, also of New Bedford, who described himself as Kelly's agent and said that he would be happy to receive the money that had been donated to help Kelly's mission. He described Kelly as 'a true man, a faithful and affectionate husband, a kind father, a genuine Christian and a good minister of the Gospel of Christ'. Interestingly, it referred to him as the father to five children.[36] As the controversies about Kelly were unfolding on both sides of the Atlantic, abolitionists in England were diverted by the arrival of a new champion —Harriet Beecher Stowe—a white woman who had never been a slave, but who had written a bestseller on the topic. Her arrival in Liverpool on 10 April 1853 was greeted by cheering crowds and guns being fired.[37] Kelly, at this stage, was in Dublin, where he had gone to reach new audiences and fresh donors.

Ireland

Kelly arrived in Dublin in spring 1853. In keeping with his religious beliefs, Kelly's first public appearance in the city, on Sunday morning, 3 April, saw him preach in the Baptist Chapel on Lower Abbey Street in Dublin. One local newspaper describing him as 'THE REV. EDMUND KELLY, A Coloured Man and formerly a slave', announced that, on Wednesday evening, 6 April, he would lecture on slavery at that location. It added, 'It is hoped that all who sympathize with the down-trodden slave will favour the meeting with their attendance and influence'.[38] Kelly gave a second lecture on slavery at the same venue on 7 April. It was covered by both the local and the provincial press.[39] Kelly's appearance and mien were highly praised, he being described as presenting, 'a highly intellectual and gentlemanly appearance'. Moreover, his lecture was 'of a most interesting description, and, from the simple but very impressive and persuasive manner in which it was delivered, it appeared to produce great *effect* upon the numerous and highly respectable audience present', they listening 'with great attention'.[40] At the outset of his lecture, Kelly presented his own Irish credentials by explaining that his father was an Irishman, but because his mother was a slave, according to American law, all of her children were the property of the slaveholder. Similarly, when he became a Baptist preacher, all the money that he earned reverted to his owner.[41] Kelly then

194   *Edmund Kelly (1817–1884)*

provided more details of his life story, explaining how his owner's imminent bankruptcy had led him to escape to the northern states where he hoped to make some arrangements to purchase his manumission. As he had done to audiences in England, Kelly outlined how, through his labours and loans, he had raised the money to purchase his family's freedom. While all this was in taking place, the Fugitive Slave Law had passed and he had been forced to flee. In order to return to the United States and to his family without fear of recapture, he needed to purchase his own freedom. During his talk, Kelly also spoke about American slavery in general. He described the institution as being, 'in open violation of the letter and spirit of the declaration of independence'. Moreover, by denying slaves the right to an education, 'Not only were they kept in barbarous ignorance, but their animal appetites and passions were cultivated and excited, so that they almost immediately became even more degraded than the beasts of the field'.[42]

Unusually, Kelly's final lecture was in a secular venue. On 12 April, he spoke at an Anti-Slavery meeting in the Mechanics Institute, also on Lower Abbey Street.[43] The event, which was free, was advertised widely in the Dublin press and was hosted by the Hibernian Anti-Slavery Society.[44] The lecture was also reported in the regional press in England, which noted the fact that Kelly's father had been an Irish man.[45] The audience was described as 'respectable', and they greeted Kelly with loud applause both at the commencement and conclusion of this talk. The event was chaired by James Haughton, a stalwart of the Anti-Slavery Society and an erstwhile host to many other visiting abolitionists. Richard Allen also spoke and referred to the fact that Kelly was the son of an Irish man, 'and yet he was a slave'.[46] The contents of Kelly's lecture were described as 'most interesting, and in some respects painful'.[47] During his talk, he referred to *Uncle Tom's Cabin* saying, 'that the worst characters sketched ... were far from being unfair'. Kelly concluded with a financial appeal saying that it was his intention 'to return as soon as possible to his native country, and that for the purpose of enabling him to do so, [he] was raising by contributions a sum of money to purchase his own freedom to bear his expenses home'.[48] He further explained that

> he desired to return there for many reasons. He was a native of that country, and besides, there were 3,000,000 slaves in the slave states, and he could not rest until the system was abolished; indeed, it was, he considered, his bounden duty to return.[49]

Although he did not lecture outside of Dublin, a number of Kelly's lectures were published in the provincial press, thus extending awareness about his visit.[50] Unlike many of his fellow lecturers, who provided concrete examples of cruelty, displayed items used to torture slaves and excelled in the use of literary flourishes and other rhetorical devices in order to engage and animate their audiences, Kelly's delivery and content appeared mundane and measured. One Dublin newspaper observed that, 'The discourse, which was strictly confined to the subject as announced, and which might have been delivered to any mixed audience'.[51] The clapping, cheering and gasps of horror that accompanied other abolitionist lectures were absent from Kelly's performances. During his short time in Ireland, Kelly had lectured mostly in religious venues; in contrast, Douglass's passionate denunciations of many churches in America had been considered too intemperate for such venues. After only a few weeks in the country, Kelly left Dublin and returned to Britain. Over the summer, he returned to the United States, but his departure was not reported in the British or Irish press. Kelly's brief Irish tour had completed his mission to raise the funds to liberate himself.[52] His departure from the United Kingdom roughly coincided with the arrival of another black abolitionist, who had been enslaved, and who was also a minister—the Reverend Samuel Ringgold Ward.

Later life

On his return home, Kelly continued to work in the Second Baptist Church in New Bedford. During this time, he also became a prominent member of the National Baptist Church, attending many of their conventions and often leading the prayers.[53] Kelly was elected vice-president of the American Missionary Baptist Convention in 1854. In 1855, he was based in Philadelphia, where he served as minister of the Oak Street Baptist Church, a black church founded in 1826. He remained there until 1859, successfully increasing the congregation by 120. As a proponent of education for black people, Kelly proved to be innovative. He promoted attendance at Sunday Schools and wrote and published materials in furtherance of this end.[54] This included pioneering the use of cards that had questions on one side and the corresponding answers on the other.[55] Throughout the 1850s, Kelly combined his work as a minister with political work relating to abolition, writing letters to the press arguing against colonization and attending the annual coloured conventions. Kelly spoke at the 1855 National Coloured Convention in Philadelphia as a representative for Pennsylvania. He proposed a motion that the Business Committee:

> amend that document by striking out every proscriptive feature, and inserting others more liberal, and to simplify it as much as possible, so as to make it as a whole acceptable to this Convention, and to the people generally.

His suggestion was defeated.[56]

In March 1861, Kelly and two of his children witnessed the inauguration of President Abraham Lincoln. Like many black abolitionists, he was disappointed that Lincoln was not more proactive in ending slavery, although he was less critical of the war than several of his contemporaries. Following the Emancipation Proclamation, Kelly published a long letter entitled, 'The Colored Man's Interest in the Present War'. He concluded it by suggesting that if people had observed the precepts of God more, the war would not have occurred.[57] Tellingly, Kelly sent the same letter to President Lincoln in August 1863, it becoming immortalized by being included in the President's archive.[58]

196   *Edmund Kelly (1817–1884)*

The Emancipation Proclamation had made it possible for black men to serve in the military. In February 1863, Kelly led a public prayer over the 1,000-member, 54th Massachusetts Regiment, United States Colored Troops. There was a personal interest. One of Kelly's sons, William Dempsey Kelly, was serving in that Regiment, he being amongst the 32 men from New Bedford to volunteer.[59] Kelly, now back residing in New Bedford, also worked in his home town to overcome white prejudice to black men serving in the military, a reminder that Emancipation did not mean equality.[60] Kelly was one of a delegation of religious ministers who met with President Lincoln to ask permission to go within military lines and minister to their brother soldiers.[61] It was no small achievement that Kelly was one of a number of formerly enslaved men who advised the President of the United States on matters of national importance.

The ending of the War resulted in a change of focus for Kelly and other abolitionists as they fought for equality for black people. In August 1865, Kelly was again part of a 14-man delegation representing the American Baptist Missionary Convention, who met with the President in the White House—but now President Andrew Johnson. Although the President was a fellow Tennessean, the meeting did not go well. According to Kelly:

> As the result of all that I have seen and heard, I believe President Johnson's want of faith in the immutability and ultimate triumph of right over wrong prevents him from giving the colored people a fair chance in the race, the first division of which, as he stated, we have entered. We do most heartily commend the President to the affectionate remembrance and prayers and well wishes of all Christians, and to the American people; first that he become a Christian, and secondly that he may be convinced that not anything is expedient that is not right; that to do right is our duty, leaving the consequence with God.[62]

In December 1865, Kelly wrote to the Senate highlighting the injustice of not granting African Americans full citizenship and suffrage. His letter was reprinted in the *Christian Recorder*.[63]

In the following 20 years, Kelly devoted much of his time to promoting his view of evangelical Christianity.[64] He remained active in preaching and continued to be influential within the governing body of the Baptist Church.[65] In 1867, he took time off from his ministry to tour in the south, notably Tennessee and Georgia, to establish free schools in rural areas, which he hoped would be financed by northern benevolence. To this end, Kelly, not for the first time, appealed for money to be sent to him.[66] He also worked 'zealously ... to educate and Christianize his race', by setting up 'coloured schools' in some of the poorest parts of the south, including his state of origin, Tennessee.[67] He argued that education and temperance were the keys to successful reconstruction. During this time, together with white abolitionist Charles Sumner, Kelly authored, 'Edmund Kelly, upon the condition, wants, and agencies best adapted to build up the South: and more especially the destitute regions among the colored people there, with an appeal'. In it, he argued for more Sabbath Schools as a way of educating black children.[68]

Like Douglass, Kelly lived to an old age, dying in October 1884, aged 76. Unlike Douglass, he died in relative obscurity. He was buried in Oak Grove Cemetery, New Bedford; his name being spelt as Edmund Kelly on his grave.

Conclusion

Regardless of his multiple achievements, Kelly remains an obscure presence in the story of abolition, although during his lifetime he was a well-known public figure who broke many barriers, including becoming Tennessee's first ordained black Baptist Minister.[69] As one author commented:

> By the time of his death on October 4, 1894, Kelly had purchased his family out of slavery, founded at least six churches, written scores of newspaper articles and pamphlets, traveled to Britain to speak against slavery, had received permission from one U.S. president to pass through Union lines to minister to his race, shaken the hand of another president, and labored to unify the various black Baptist groups into what later became the National Baptist Convention.[70]

In many accounts of Kelly, his time spent overseas is not mentioned. Kelly's time in Britain was relatively brief, and he only spent a few weeks in Ireland where he gave three lectures in Dublin. Perhaps more than any other visiting abolitionist, Kelly seemed unchanged and unmoved by his time there. This is particularly surprising given his paternal lineage. Unusually also, while in the United Kingdom, he attracted no notable abolitionist patrons or sponsors, nor did he align himself with Garrisonians or the British and Foreign Anti-Slavery Society. Instead, his Baptist community provided him with a limited network. Although during his tour he spoke against slavery, and did so effectively, Kelly's main reason for visiting the United Kingdom was to raise money rather than to promote transatlantic abolition. Regardless of its brevity and limited scope, he was successful in this mission. Kelly's tour and his determined, and unashamed, fundraising efforts allowed him to purchase his freedom.[71] This approach and focus mark him as very different from Douglass, Wells Brown and others, who never asked for money on their own behalf. Kelly, in contrast, advocated on behalf of himself, and he used religion as his channel for engaging with his audiences. For Kelly, Christianity, rather than agitation, was the way to end slavery and inequality. While many abolitionists challenged enslavement with polemics, politics, the press and even photographs, Kelly used predominantly prayer.

Notes

1 In his narrative he spelled it as Edmond Kelley.
2 Edmond Kelley, *A Family Redeemed from Bondage; Being Rev. Edmond Kelley, (the Author,) His Wife, and Four Children* (New Bedford, MA: The Author, 1851), p. 5. When lecturing in Leicester in England, he gave his birth year as 1818, 'AMERICAN SLAVERY: MEETING IN LEICESTER', *Leicester Chronicle*, 29 January 1853.

198 Edmund Kelly (1817–1884)

3 Some accounts give 1818, his memoir says 1817. Kelly's owner, Nancy White, had inherited the family from her mother, Ann White.
4 William J. Simmons and Henry McNeal Turner, 'Rev. Edmund Kelly. Christian Letter-Writer, Lecturer and Author', in *Men of Mark: Eminent, Progressive and Rising* (Cleveland, OH: G. M. Rewell & Company, 1887), chapter XXXII, p. 291.
5 Speech by Kelly in Baptist Chapel in Dublin, 7 April 1852, *Freeman's Journal*, 8 April 1853.
6 'LECTURE on AMERICAN SLAVERY', *Evening Freeman*, 8 April 1853.
7 Kelly's license to preach was reproduced in *A Family Redeemed*, p. 5; *Bristol Times and Mirror*, 26 February 1853.
8 Lewis L. Laska, 'Edmond Kelley, Tennessee's First African-American Ordained Baptist Minister', in *Tennessee Baptist History*, (Fall 2004), 7–28. Available at: https://archive.org/stream/tbhs25/tbhs25_djvu.txt.
9 Edmund Kelly: http://coloredconventions.org/exhibits/show/mobilitymigration1855/delegates/edmund-kelly.
10 Kelly, *A Family Redeemed*, pp. 88–90.
11 Ibid., p. 15.
12 Peter C. Ripley (ed.), *The Black Abolitionist Papers, 1830–1865*, vol. 1 (Chapel Hill: University of North Carolina Press, 1987), p. 334.
13 James Walker, Columbia, 24 February 1850, reprinted in Kelly, *A Family Redeemed*, p. 9.
14 Ibid.
15 Laska, 'Edmond Kelly', p. 11.
16 Kelly, *A Family Redeemed*, p. 18.
17 Ibid.
18 *Freeman's Journal*, 8 April 1853.
19 Kelly, *A Family Redeemed*, p. 18.
20 Ibid., p. 10.
21 Stowe arrived in Liverpool on 10 April 1853, 'Mrs Harriet Beecher Stowe in Liverpool', *Liverpool Mercury*, 12 April 1853.
22 Wells Brown wrote about these encounters with poor black immigrants in William Wells Brown, *Three Years in Europe: Or, Places I Have Seen and People I Have Met* (London: Charles Gilpin, 5 Bishopsgate Street, Without; Edinburgh: Oliver and Boyd, 1852).
23 'AMERICAN SLAVERY: MEETING IN LEICESTER', *Leicester Chronicle*, 29 January 1853.
24 Ibid.
25 *Bristol Times and Mirror*, 26 February 1853.
26 For example, in Bradford Kelly lectured to the local women's Anti-Slavery Society, 'Anti-Slavery Movement', *Halifax Courier*, 8 January 1853.
27 'AMERICAN SLAVERY: MEETING IN LEICESTER', *Leicester Chronicle*, 29 January 1853.
28 Ibid.
29 *Bristol Times and Mirror*, 26 February 1853.
30 'AMERICAN SLAVERY: MEETING IN LEICESTER', *Leicester Chronicle*, 29 January 1853.
31 *Illustrated London News*, 5 February 1853; 'Fugitive Slave in Leicester', *Morning Advertiser*, 2 February 1853. The higher amount was also stated in the *Morning Advertiser*, 2 February 1853.
32 *Bristol Times and Mirror*, 26 February 1853.
33 'COLLECTIONS IN ENGLAND FOR THE BENEFIT OF AMERICAN SLAVE-HOLDERS', *Anti-Slavery Advocate*, 1 April 1853.
34 Ibid.
35 Ibid.

Edmund Kelly (1817–1884) 199

36 'J. A. Girdwood. Question Answered', the *Liberator*, 29 April 1853. The author was probably Rev. John Girdwood, minister in First Baptist Church in New Bedford.

37 *Liverpool Mercury*, 12 April 1853.

38 'THE REV. EDMUND KELLY', *Saunders's News-Letter*, 2 April 1853.

39 'AMERICAN SLAVERY', *Kilkenny Journal, and Leinster Commercial and Literary Advertiser*, 13 April 1853; *Tipperary Free Press*, 16 April 1853; *Dublin Mercantile Advertiser*, 8 April 1853.

40 'LECTURE ON AMERICAN SLAVERY', *Freeman's Journal*, 8 April 1853.

41 Kelly told an Irish audience that he had been paid two pounds a week, which was given to the person who claimed him as her property, 'Dublin', *Limerick Chronicle*, 20 April 1853.

42 'LECTURE ON AMERICAN SLAVERY', *Freeman's Journal*, 8 April 1853.

43 Admission was free.

44 'American Slavery', *Freeman's Journal*, 9 April 1853; *Saunders's News-Letter*, 12 April 1853.

45 No title, *Wilts and Gloucestershire Standard*, 23 April 1853.

46 'AMERICAN SLAVERY-MEETING IN THE MECHANICS' INSTITUTE', *Freeman's Journal*, 13 April 1853.

47 'SLAVERY IN THE UNITED STATES—MEETING IN MECHANICS' INSTITUTE', *Weekly Freeman's Journal*, 16 April 1853.

48 'AMERICAN SLAVERY MEETING IN THE MECHANICS' INSTITUTE in DUBLIN', *Limerick Reporter*, 15 April 1853.

49 'AMERICAN SLAVERY: MEETING IN LEICESTER', *Leicester Chronicle*, 29 January 1853.

50 'AMERICAN SLAVERY MEETING IN THE MECHANICS' INSTITUTE in DUBLIN', *Limerick Reporter*, 15 April 1853; Ibid., 20 April 1853; *Kilkenny Journal, and Leinster Commercial and Literary Advertiser*, 13 April 1853; *Tipperary Free Press*, 16 April 1853

51 *Freeman's Journal*, 8 April 1853.

52 Ripley, *Abolitionist Papers*, p. 334.

53 'The American Colored Convention at Boston', *New-York Tribune*, 21 August 1857; 'Annual Meeting of the Colored Baptist American Missionary Society', *The Baltimore Sun*, 23 August 1864.

54 'Monumental Baptist Church': www.thembc.org/history.

55 La Tanya Kelly Douet, 'The Success of my father. From slavery to the present day'. Available at: https://thesuccessofmyfathers.wordpress.com/author/latanyadouet/.

56 Ibid., pp. 25–6.

57 Edmund Kelly to President Lincoln, 21 August 1863, 'The Coloured Man's interest in the Present'. Available at: https://picryl.com/media/edmund-kelly-to-abraham-lincoln-friday-august-21-1863-sends-speech-on-the-colored-2?zoom=true.

58 Abraham Lincoln Papers at the Library of Congress, LOC: www.loc.gov/teachers/classroommaterials/connections/abraham-lincoln-papers/history6.html.

59 Simmons, *Men of Mark*, p. 294.

60 Earl F. Mulderink, *New Bedford's Civil War* (New York: Fordham University Press, 2012), p. 103.

61 La Tanya Kelly Douet, 'The Success of My Father. From Slavery to the Present Day'. Available at: https://thesuccessofmyfathers.wordpress.com/author/latanyadouet.

62 'Baptists and the American Civil War: August 25, 1865'. Available at: http://civilwarbaptists.com/thisdayinhistory/1865-august-25/.

63 '*To the Honorable Senate and House of Representatives of the United States of America, in Congress assembled*', the *Christian Recorder*, 9 December 1865.

64 La Tanya Kelly Douet, 'The Success of my father. From slavery to the present day'. https://thesuccessofmyfathers.wordpress.com/author/latanyadouet/.

200 Edmund Kelly (1817–1884)

65 'Sunday Services', *Hartford Courant*, 29 August 1874; 'Meeting of the Baptist Conference', *Philadelphia Inquirer*, 31 October 1876.
66 Letter from E. Kelly, 28 January 1868, reprinted in Thomas Conway, *An Appeal to Loyal Religious People in Behalf of Kentucky* (Printed in New Orleans Times Office, 1865), p. 34.
67 'Colored School', *The Herald and Mail* (Tennessee), 20 May 1870.
68 World Cat lists this publication, but could not identify any libraries that have a copy: [New Bedford, MA?]: [publisher not identified], [186–?]
69 Laska, 'Tennessee's First African-American'.
70 Ibid., p. 8.
71 http://coloredconventions.org/exhibits/show/mobilitymigration1855/delegates/edmund-kelly.

8 Samuel Ringgold Ward (1817–c.1866)

'A Christian abolitionist'?

Samuel Ringgold Ward, though largely forgotten today, was one of the most talented and intriguing black abolitionists to cross the Atlantic in the mid-nineteenth century.[1] Both contemporaries and historians have judged him to be one of the most brilliant of that generation of activists.[2] Ward referred to himself as a Christian abolitionist,[3] explaining that as 'a man, a Christian, especially as a black man, my labours must be anti-slavery labours, because mine must be an anti-slavery life'.[4] Unusually, he combined radical abolitionism with social and religious conservatism. Moreover, his time in Ireland and later in Jamaica revealed a narrowness and elitism that suggested Ward's humanity was selective.

While Ward's time in Jamaica has been explored by a number of historians, his time in Ireland has been ignored.[5] However, his observations on the Irish peasantry, especially the Catholic peasantry, are suggestive of some deep-rooted prejudices that help to explain his subsequent actions in Jamaica. They further suggest that this gifted black abolitionist was not simply complex, but lived a life that was full of contradictions and that ended ignobly. Other incidents in his life reveal a dishonesty that was out of line with his religious calling.

Early life

Unlike many black abolitionists and fugitive slaves who travelled to the United Kingdom, Ward's knowledge of slavery was largely second-hand. He was born in Maryland in October 1817 to two enslaved parents. His family escaped to New Jersey in 1820, later relocating to New York City. There, and in contrast to other formerly enslaved abolitionists, he received an education in New York's African Free School. Consequently, Ward grew up as a free black man and it was not until he was in his mid-20s, at which stage he was working as a teacher, was married and (since 1839) had been licensed to preach as a Congregationalist minister, that he learnt of his origins and his consequent fugitive status.[6] This fact was sometimes overlooked by his fellow abolitionists. At a convention in 1854, a white abolitionist stated:

> No man is qualified to speak of it and show what a hateful thing it is unless its chains have been around his limbs and its lash upon his back.

202 Samuel Ringgold Ward (1817–c.1866)

Such men as Frederick Douglass and Samuel R. Ward, who have themselves felt the oppressor's rod, can give a true picture of Slavery, can describe it as it deserves to be described.[7]

While Douglass frequently referred to his back being scarred by the lash, Ward did not, and could only speak of slavery in the abstract.

Growing up with two parents, and in relative freedom, meant that Ward knew more about his ancestry than most enslaved people. He claimed that his father was descended from African royalty. On his mother's side, he maintained that he had Irish ancestry, his maternal grandmother being

a woman of light complexion; her grandmother, a mulattress; her greatgrandmother, the daughter of an Irishman, named Martin, one of the largest slaveholders in Maryland—a man whose slaves were so numerous, that he did not know the number of them.[8]

Regardless of his mixed heritage—albeit some generations removed—he was often praised for being a 'pure' negro.[9]

Ward's path to becoming an abolitionist was gradual. He attended his first antislavery lecture in New Haven in Connecticut in 1834. Shortly afterwards, he was present when a mob in New York City attacked an anti-slavery meeting.[10] Even though they were the group being attacked, it was the black abolitionists who were subsequently arrested and imprisoned, including Ward himself. It proved to be a watershed, he later stated: 'That imprisonment initiated me into the antislavery fraternity'.[11] In July 1837, Ward gave his first public lecture before the Literary Society. Among those present was Lewis Tappan, one of the founders and financers of the American Anti-Slavery Society.[12] Two years later, in November 1839, Ward found himself as a paid travelling agent for the Society.[13] He was only 22 years old. Prior to this, Ward had taught in schools in New Jersey and New York, but he seemed happy to leave this career behind and embark on a new one. Ward's anti-slavery message was clear, 'That the best interests of the North and the South, the now and of posterity, demand the immediate and entire and unconditional Abolition of American slavery'.[14]

In the same year that Ward became an abolitionist agent, he was licensed to preach by the New York Congregational Association. From this point, Ward combined his Christian evangelical mission with his devotion to abolition. Unlike Garrisonians who believed that the churches were complicit in slavery, Ward held that it was necessary to persuade slaveowners to liberate all enslaved peoples by appealing to their Christianity. Ward's approach to abolition and to moral reform in general, was shaped by his early vocation as a minister and religious reformer. According to Ronald Burke, a few factors had produced this outlook:

He was reared by devoutly religious parents, he received his education at the religiously orientated New York African Free School, he found himself

Samuel Ringgold Ward (1817–c.1866) 203

regularly in the presence of the leading black church activists of the day, and, as a young man he participated in church connected reform activities.[15]

Ward's religious beliefs inevitably meant that he was closer to New York abolitionists and the Tappan brothers, the Garrisonians being noted for their anti-Sabbatarian views and their repeated vocal condemnation of much organized religion, in particular, the American churches.[16] Following the split in the American Anti-Slavery Society, Ward worked with the more moderate American and Foreign Anti-Slavery Society rather than the Garrisonians, although he admitted that he was careful to avoid being embroiled in the 'quarrels' and 'dissensions' within the movement.[17]

Ward's religious duties included a ministry with an all-white congregation in Wayne County in New York. He was full of praise for the members of the Church who had defied convention by choosing him, praising them for 'The manly courage they showed, in calling and sustaining and honouring as their pastor a black man, in that day, in spite of the too general Negro-hate everywhere rife'.[18] In the 1840s, therefore, Ward combined a successful career as a preacher with being an abolitionist. There was a considerable overlap. He frequently signed his abolitionist letters with the phrase, 'yours in Gospel bonds'.[19] Additionally, Ward was frequently called on to open abolitionist meetings with an invocation.[20] Within the newly formed Liberty Party, he served on the 'Committee for Prayer'.[21]

After 1839, Ward also worked as a travelling agent, initially for the American, and afterwards, for the New York Anti-Slavery Society.[22] It was a calling not without its perils and its sacrifices. Ward explained that, leaving his young wife and infant son, lecturing hundreds of miles away from his home, and often facing hostile crowds, 'cost me a great deal of effort and self-denial'.[23] Speaking in Cortlandville in New York in 1849, in a speech on character, he started by revealing something about his own, telling the audience that within the preceding week he had lectured in ten different places on as many different topics, admitting 'it is such a task upon a very small modicum of power'.[24]

Ward quickly became recognized as one of the movements' most talented champions, he belonging to a second generation of black abolitionists who were confident, visible and vocal. His intellect, imposing presence (he was over six-foot-tall) and oratorical skills drew him much praise. As early as 1842, he was even being referred to as 'the black Daniel Webster'.[25] Moreover, as fellow black abolitionist, William Wells Brown, pointed out, 'No detractor of the negro's abilities ever attributed his talents to his having Anglo-Saxon Blood in his veins'.[26] In this sense, Ward's background was important as he provided a powerful rebuttal to the suggestion that the ability of Frederick Douglass and others was due to their having a mixed race heritage. During a heated debate in New York City in 1850, for example, a pro-slavery provocateur, Captain Isaiah Rynders, had challenged Douglass by shouting 'O, You are not a n——! You are half-blooded; a real n——can't reason'. It was left to Ward to provide a rational, lucid, refutation.[27] In 1852, Ward publicly defended Douglass's right

204 *Samuel Ringgold Ward (1817–c.1866)*

to speak at an American Anti-Slavery Society convention—an objection being made that Douglass was 'not a negro, but half white'.[28] This incident revealed the complexity of, and internal tensions within, American anti-slavery.

Throughout the 1840s, Ward was involved in national politics, primarily the Liberty Party and, after 1848, the Free-Soil Party, which he had helped to found. At the Liberty Party's National Convention in June 1848, Gerrit Smith, a white abolitionist who was a friend of Ward's, was nominated to stand for President of the United States. Ward was selected for Vice President, making him the first black person to be proposed for national office.[29] It was shortly after this that Ward and Douglass openly disagreed at a political convention in Buffalo in August 1848.[30] Ward clearly admired the more famous abolitionist, even though they represented the two different wings of the anti-slavery movement:

> Mr. Douglass, as an orator, is winning for himself and his people not only fame, but what is far better, the power of great and varied usefulness. Among his most honest admirers are persons in the highest walks of life: distinguished alike for their high positions, and their entire fitness for them.
>
> At the risk of seeming immodest, I may say, that my own short career engaged for me the personal friendship of persons who have no superiors; and whose friendship was the more highly prized, as it was the result of my own efforts—the acknowledgment of an equality previously denied to the Negro, on their part—and a favourable sign for the future of my people. The same is true of every prominent coloured man in that country.[31]

In addition to Ward, other prominent black abolitionists present included Henry Highland Garnet (Ward's second cousin), Charles Remond and Henry Bibb. However, it was Ward who impressed Douglass the most; he later recalled:

> Mr. Ward especially attracted attention at that convention. As an orator and thinker, he was vastly superior, I thought, to any of us, and being perfectly black and of unmixed African descent, the splendors of his intellect went directly to the glory of race.[32]

Regardless of the high regard the two men held each other in, they clashed intellectually on a number of issues, including the Constitution, with Ward denying that it was a pro-slavery document, believing that it was the people, not the document, that needed to change. In contrast, Douglass—like Garrison —believed the opposite. Ward challenged Douglass to debate publicly on the topic. The event took place on 18 May 1849 in the Broadway Tabernacle in New York City. Each man spoke five times for thirty minutes in a terse, intellectual and mutually respectful debate.[33] On the day, neither man conceded, but two years later, Douglass changed sides, and in doing so, rejected the Garrisonian viewpoint. The debate was significant for showcasing the ability and agency of these two black abolitionists, and for consolidating their contributions to abolitionist debate. Similar to Douglass, Ward's arguments were reasoned, cogent and logic, with both men drawing widely from literature, history and the Bible. Both men also favoured the same British poets—William Cowper and Robert Burns.[34]

Ward and Douglass both spoke at the Sixteenth Anniversary of the American Anti-Slavery Society in May 1850, at the Broadway Tabernacle in New York. Ward's speech was described as 'a brilliant stream of wit and humor, and argument'.[35] Even Parker Pillsbury, who sided with Garrison, acknowledged the power of Ward's oratory.[36] He was the final speaker at the end of a one-day debate, the *National Anti-Slavery Standard* averring:

> At the close, a speech of some length, a good deal of power, and much original wit and humor, was made by Samuel R. Ward, a Methodist clergyman, and another relic of the old Liberty party. It was decidedly the happiest and most effectual effort on that side of the question.[37]

Despite disagreeing on fundamental questions,[38] in 1850, Douglass and Ward helped to found the American League of Colored Laborers in New York, recognizing that black workers were often excluded from trade unions. It was the first black American labour union. At its inaugural meeting in the Zion Church on the corner of Leonard and Church streets, Ward was appointed its president, Henry Bibb of Michigan its secretary and Douglass its vice-president.[39] In the same year, Ward joined Douglass in criticizing Lajos Kossuth, a Hungarian nationalist who refused to condemn slavery when he visited the United States.[40] The two men's paths crossed on many other occasions, Ward lecturing in Rochester, Douglass's hometown, in the summer of 1851.[41] Increasingly, the mutual admiration of the two men and Douglass's own intellectual journey was leading him to reject Garrisonian principles and move closer to those espoused by Ward.

Like other abolitionists, Ward understood the importance of the media and the written word. Between 1849 and 1851, he edited the *Impartial Citizen*, Syracuse's first black newspaper, which he had helped to found. In 1851, he and Douglass discussed amalgamating the *Impartial Citizen* with *Frederick Douglass' Paper*. In the end, Ward decided not to do so, but agreed to act as the New England correspondent for the latter, Douglass informing his readers, 'His racy letters will do much to impart interest to our new paper'.[42] Following his self-imposed exile in British Canada, Ward continued to write both for the *Anti-Slavery Standard* and *Frederick Douglass'* newspaper.[43] The *Impartial Citizen*, however, ceased publication.[44]

The more draconian approach to fugitive slaves, embodied in the 1850 legislation, was regarded as unconstitutional by Ward. His opposition was evident when he assisted another fugitive slave, William 'Jerry' McHenry, to escape in October 1851 from Syracuse to British Canada, thereby putting himself in danger of arrest and imprisonment.[45] To protect McHenry, a crowd had gathered and 'their time was beguiled by a stirring speech from the Rev. Samuel R. Ward, the colored preacher and abolitionist'.[46] Nonetheless, this very public act of defiance led Ward to flee to Ontario in Canada in November 1851—'in

206 *Samuel Ringgold Ward (1817–c.1866)*

some haste'.[47] His family followed a month later. Ward's gratitude for this sanctuary was evident: 'I went; and a month or two after, my family followed: since which time we have each and severally been, *con amore*, the most loyal and grateful of British subjects'.[48] Following his relocation to Canada, there were suggestions that Ward had left owing money to the subscribers of his newspaper.[49] This was a sad foretaste of subsequent financial impropriety.

Ward was welcomed in Canada, where he was employed as a travelling agent of the newly formed Canadian Anti-Slavery Society, who paid his travel expenses and a full-time salary.[50] He also was made editor of the *Alienated American*. However, he resigned following its inaugural edition.[51] This action was perhaps an indication of the contradictions that Ward seemed to battle within his later years. On behalf of the Canadian Anti-Slavery Society, Ward journeyed to Britain in April 1853 to raise money for fugitive slaves in Canada. When he left Britain in 1855, he did not return to Canada, choosing to relocate to Jamaica where he worked as a minister and farmer until his death in 1866. For the final 15 years of his life, therefore, Ward lived on British soil.

The United Kingdom

Ward sailed for England on 20 April 1853 as the official agent of the Canadian Anti-Slavery Society. In advance of going, he would have been familiar with the activities of the British and Irish anti-slavery societies, as his cousin, the Rev. Henry Garnet, had been travelling there from 1850 to 1852 and had sent reports back to Ward for publication in the *Impartial Citizen*.[52] Ward's own mission was twofold: to increase awareness about the consequences of the Fugitive Slave Law and to raise funds for those who sought sanctuary in Canada. For the latter objective, a collection was made at the end of each of his public meetings.[53] This activity was not without irony as, in the previous year, Ward had opposed the establishment of a Refugee Home Society in Canada to raise funds to purchase farmland for recently arrived fugitives.[54] He had objected to it on the grounds that it promoted begging—but he was now travelling to Britain to do just that.

Like Remond and Douglass, Ward was reminded of his inferior status on the voyage over to Liverpool, he not being allowed to take his meals with other passengers. When challenged, Cunard, the transatlantic steamship company, defended the policy on the grounds that 'we cannot allow our ships to be the arena of constant quarrels on the subject'.[55] Similarly to other abolitionists, Ward was an advocate of temperance and, like Douglass and Wells Brown some years earlier, he stayed at Brown's Temperance Hotel in Liverpool.[56] On occasion though, Ward suggested that he was not a total abstainer.[57] Ward's arrival was noted in the *Anti-Slavery Reporter*, which informed its readers that 'he proposes to solicit contributions in aid of the funds of the Society which he represents', and assured them that he 'brings letters of recommendation from the officers and the committee of the society'.[58]

Being on British soil proved to be a liberating experience for many black abolitionists—both in reality and psychologically. Ward, however, felt differently, writing, 'I did not feel as some blacks say they felt, upon landing, that

Samuel Ringgold Ward (1817–c.1866) 207

I was, for the first time in my life, a man'. He further explained 'No, I always felt that; however wronged, maltreated, outraged—still, a man'.[59] Ward's self-assurance may have had its origins in the fact that he had no memory of what it was like to be a slave, and as he had chosen Canada to be his home, he no longer lived as a fugitive in a country where slavery was legal. Just as those black abolitionists who had preceded him, Ward was received in a way that would not have been possible on the other side of the Atlantic. Within weeks of arriving in London, he was invited by the Prussian Ambassador to a party in his Regent's Park residence, something unthinkable in the United States.[60] Fellow abolitionist William G. Allen, who was of mixed-race origin and had been driven from America because of his own interracial marriage, happened to be in London at the same time. He was astonished by the lack of prejudice against people of colour. He informed his friend, Garrison:

> Reverend Samuel R. Ward of Canada, than whom it is hardly possible to be blacker, and who is an honor to the race in intellectual ability, has been in London for several weeks and can amply testify to the fact that his skin, though 'deepest dyed', has been no barrier to the best society in the kingdom.[61]

Ward himself believed that the timing of his arrival in England could not have been more judicious because the anti-slavery novel, *Uncle Tom's Cabin*,[62] had been published in 1852 and was 'in everybody's hand and heart'.[63] Moreover, the author was herself visiting the country. The publication had re-energized the abolition movement and had resulted in an anti-slavery address from the women of England to 'the Christian women of America'.[64]

Possibly more than any other black abolitionist, Ward was able to garner the attention and support of many influential patrons shortly after arriving in England. These relationships provide an insight into the process and importance of white patronage and Ward's skilful negotiation of it. Early on, he found a sympathetic patron in the Duchess of Sutherland, to whom he dedicated his 1855 autobiography.[65] Other notable patrons included Lord Shaftsbury, the Duke of Argyll, the Earl of Harrowby, the Earl Waldegrave and Lord Brougham. Some of these introductions were made possible through the support of a fellow Congregationalist minister, Rev. James Sherman, minister at the Surrey Chapel in Blackfriars in London. Ward explained that, 'the Rev. Sherman procured for me the names of Sir James K. Shuttleworth'.[66] In addition, Sherman provided Ward with a home and helped him in his work of raising money for the Canadian Anti-Slavery Society. Ward was not Sherman's only protégé. Sherman had written an Introduction to Harriet Beecher Stowe's bestselling *Uncle Tom's Cabin* and he was helping to organize Stowe's promotional tour.[67] Ward's presence in England and his illustrious company was noted in 1853 by an Irish provincial newspaper, which informed its readers that: 'Professor and Mrs. Stowe, the Rev. C. Beecher and the Rev. Samuel Ward are now residing with the Rev. J. Sherman'.[68]

Beecher Stowe was not the only distinguished visitor from the United States in London. She was accompanied by her own protégé, Elizabeth Taylor Greenfield,

208   Samuel Ringgold Ward (1817–c.1866)

born into enslavement, but now a singer enjoying transatlantic success.[69] Ward wrote in his autobiography, 'When I arrived in England, I found Miss Greenfield, known in America by the soubriquet of "Black Swan," a black singer'.[70] Both Ward and Greenfield attended various events to honour Beecher Stowe.[71] Together, they transgressed many social and cultural boundaries and presented a compelling argument against the continuation of slavery.

Ward may have been the most feted, but he was not the only Canadian abolitionist to lecture in Britain in the mid-1850s. Professor Michael Willis, Doctor of Divinity in Toronto College, was also on a lecture tour. Scottish-born Willis was the first and only president of the Anti-Slavery Society of Canada.[72] It was Willis who had first employed Ward as an agent in Canada and sent him to Britain on behalf of the Society.[73] He had provided Ward with letters of recommendation.[74] Willis gave a talk in Glasgow at the end of 1855 about former slaves to whom he had lectured in Canada. He praised them for being 'attentive and devout'.[75] There is no record of Willis and Ward meeting on British soil.

In 1853, 1854 and early 1855 Ward lectured throughout England. In keeping with his vocation, he performed Sunday service in the local Baptist churches on a number of occasions.[76] Ward travelled to Scotland in 1853 and 1855. Although he was not enthralled with either Scottish food or weather, Ward was impressed with the Scottish people's devotion to anti-slavery, writing:

> There is far more of active, organized, anti-slavery vitality, among the three millions of Scottish population, than among the seventeen millions of English people.[77] As I travelled about Scotland, both in 1853 and 1855, I found the anti-slavery feeling prevalent, deep, earnest, and intelligent. It is incorporated in the feelings, habits, and characteristics of the people. They are abolitionists from intelligent conviction, human sympathy, and religious principle.[78]

Following only ten months of touring in England and Scotland, Ward had raised £1,200 for the Canadian Anti-Slavery Society.[79] However, what is less well known is that only £400 was sent to Canada, the remainder of the money being used to pay Ward's salary, traveling expenses and the cost of meetings.[80] At this point, Ward seemed to arbitrarily end his connection with his colleagues in Canada and he raised no further money on their behalf. Indirectly though, his visit had encouraged other people to send money to Canada: in 1855, the Ladies' Anti-Slavery Society in Canada reported they had received a total of £11,000 to help fugitive slaves, and they thanked Ward, 'our late agent', for the part that he had played.[81]

Ward's movements were followed in the British press. He was frequently referred to as 'a coloured gentleman from America'.[82] Elsewhere, he was described as 'a man of colour', who had been compelled to leave America when the Fugitive Slave Law was passed, and to make his home in Toronto.[83] His lineage was occasionally alluded to, he often being 'of pure African descent'.[84] Ward's lectures were well received, he delivering them in what was described as 'very eloquent

Samuel Ringgold Ward (1817–c.1866) 209

and impassioned language', which was listened to 'with deep attention by a numerous and respectable audiences'.[85] Although he had no plans to travel to Ireland, a number of his early lectures were covered by the Irish press.[86]

Ward's arrival and lecture schedule in England were noted with approval in the *Frederick Douglass' Paper*, it informing its readers, 'His speeches are characteristic of the man, abounding in excellent sense, with more than occasional flashes of merriment' adding, 'He will become more sober as he grows older'.[87] Ward's activities overseas were intermittently discussed in the columns of the *Liberator*. At a meeting of the Massachusetts Anti-Slavery Society in 1854, members from the Canadian Association informed those present that: 'Mr. Ward was soon expected home from England, with some four or five thousand dollars collected there, which would meet the wants and extend the efforts of the Society'.[88] They were to be sadly disappointed.

Ward's outlook meant that he was closer to the British and Foreign Anti-Slavery Society than to the supporters of Garrison and in both 1853 and 1854 he spoke at their annual meetings. At the end of November 1854, he attended their annual conference in London.[89] It was chaired by Lord Shaftsbury.[90] Parker Pillsbury, a white abolitionist and a Congregationalist minister, was also present. Pillsbury, a Garrisonian, informed the audience that: 'The only means by which slavery could be abolished in the States was by the exertions of the American Anti-Slavery Society. Such was the Constitution of America, that politically nothing could be done'. In keeping with his movement's support of women's equality, during his speech, Pillsbury praised the activities of the women.[91] Elihu Burritt, the 'Learned Blacksmith' from Connecticut, was also present, and he advocated abstinence, 'as far as possible, from the consumption of slave labour produces, the four principal articles of which were sugar, coffee, cotton and tobacco'.[92] Using only free labour produce had been popularized as a consequence of Garnet's visit to Britain and Ireland three years earlier.[93] The presence of these Americans at these conferences and other anti-slavery meetings, despite differences in approach, kept the abolition movement energized on both sides of the Atlantic. Ward spoke about the condition of fugitive slaves in Canada and the need for Congressional representation and 'the elevation of the free coloured population'.[94] He informed the audience that there were now 40,000 fugitive slaves in Upper Canada, who had fled there seeking liberty, with a single ferry between Detroit and Windsor in the previous year carrying 1,100 fugitive slaves crossing over from the States to Canada. He contended that 'under equally favourable circumstances, the black free population were as industrious and as capable of mental elevation as the whites'. Ward concluded by moving a resolution embodying the points referred to in his speech.[95] At this point, and what the audience may not have realized, Ward was now acting as a free agent, with no affiliation to any organization in Canada.

Ireland

Despite Ward devoting a chapter of his autobiography to Ireland, his time in the country is now largely forgotten.[96] However, he travelled to Ireland twice—in

210   *Samuel Ringgold Ward (1817–c.1866)*

September 1854 and in mid-1855, spending a total of 20 days in the country. During his first visit, Ward's purpose was to rest. He did not lecture in Ireland until 1855, by which time he had been in Britain for almost two years. When this visit is mentioned, it is assumed that, like other abolitionist visitors, he was well disposed to the Irish poor, but this was not the case. According to one sympathetic biographer, Ward believed that:

> ... while the Irish were not technically enslaved their association with the established ruling powers came close to the master-slave relationship of American blacks. The Irish peasants were ensnared in conditions where their basic economic needs were far below the marginal. Oppression, said Ward, came in many forms.[97]

Ward's attitude towards the Irish poor was both more complex and more unsympathetic, he viewing them through an evangelical, anti-Catholic lens.

Ward's first visit to Ireland took him to some of the most scenic tourist spots in the country. He sailed from Holyhead to Kingstown,[98] spent a few days in the Dublin area and then travelled to Cork by train. He stayed one night there, and then journeyed to Killarney, a popular tourist destination. Ward admitted that, 'There, like others, I did, as nearly as possible, nothing: in fact, I went there for that very purpose'.[99] As a tourist, he felt that the Irish landscape and lakes were not as impressive as those in Canada and New York State, stating that he was not as 'perfectly captivated, charmed, delighted, overwhelmed' as his guides expected him to be.[100] The purpose of Ward's second visit to Ireland was to undertake a brief anti-slavery tour. This time, he sailed from Scotland to Belfast. From there, he travelled to Sligo, a journey that proved to be arduous and exhausting.[101] On the coach part of his journey, he met Mrs. Caldwell of Clogher and she introduced him to Mrs. Maxwell, the Secretary of Clogher Anti-Slavery Society. Thus, by this circuitous coincidence, Ward was invited to speak in Clogher with Professor Allen,[102] but other commitments meant that he could not attend.[103] On Sunday morning, Ward preached at the chapel of the Rev. Noble Shepherd in Sligo. Shephard was a member of the Congregationist Union of Ireland and the Irish Evangelical Society.[104] The next day, 4 June, Ward spoke in the church again, but this time on slavery. The place was full, with Ward observing that, 'no small proportion of them being Episcopalians'.[105]

Like Douglass, Ward visited Limerick, travelling from Sligo via Mullingar, a reminder of how enervating the anti-slavery travelling circuit could be.[106] There, he was hosted by the Rev. William Tarbotton, also a Protestant evangelical minister.[107] One provincial newspaper advertised his visit thus:

> The Rev. S. W. Ward, a coloured man from Canada, is to lecture this evening at the Independent Chapel, Limerick, on American slavery; he is, we understand, one of the most powerful and eloquent speakers the public ever heard.[108]

The independent chapel on Bedford Street was where Douglass had lectured in 1845. The meeting was full and chaired by William Cochrane, Esq., a fellow

Samuel Ringgold Ward (1817–c.1866)   211

evangelical.[109] The following evening, on 7 June, Ward lectured in the Independent Chapel on George's Street in Cork. His host was Rev. A. M. Henderson.[110] Henderson had recently left the Wesleyan Connexion and joined the Congregation ministry in Cork.[111] The advance publicity notice described Ward as being from Toronto and 'the eloquent advocate of the fugitive from American Slavery'. It added that Ward 'creates a great sensation wherever he is heard'.[112] The meeting was chaired by Sir John Gordon, the Mayor of Cork. A number of professors from the university attended 'and these learned gentlemen kindly participated in the proceedings of the meeting, which was the most enthusiastic one I ever held, even in Ireland'.[113] In Cork, Ward stayed with the Jennings family, who had hosted Douglass almost ten years earlier.[114]

Like Douglass, Ward was an admirer of Father Mathew, the Cork-based 'apostle of temperance', whom he had met in the United States. Unlike Douglass, however, he did not have time to meet him in person, merely sending the Catholic priest his card and good wishes.[115] Regardless of his admiration for Father Mathew, Ward's greatest admiration was for Protestant proselytizers in Ireland, especially Rev. Joseph Denham Smith, an English evangelical. Smith was one of a number of evangelicals who had viewed the Great Famine and its aftermath as an opportunity to 'free slaves of Romish intolerance'.[116] Ward openly admired Smith's labours at conversion:

> In no country is this more manifest than in Ireland, where the class of ministers to which Mr. Smith and his co-labourers belong are obliged to compete with State Churchism in so many forms. This remark is not made offensively. I am giving utterance to my own religious opinions, without disguise; and repeat, that their correctness, in practical working, never struck me so forcibly as during my last visit to Ireland: nor can I bring myself to believe that any honest, honourable Christian, of whatever denomination, will find fault with my refusing so far to play the neutral, as to write as if I had no opinions or were too unmanly to express them.[117]

The Cork meeting was Ward's final one in Ireland. In contrast to Remond, Douglass and other visitors, Ward had chosen religious locations only, in keeping with his vocation and outlook, and he had avoided the east coast, the more usual circuit of visiting abolitionists. During his time in the country, Ward received little coverage in the Irish press. Nevertheless, in his autobiography, Ward spoke extensively of his time in Ireland, devoting 24 pages to his stay.

After he had left the country, Ward wrote further reflections on his time in Ireland. His comments were based on a much more limited experience and a much narrower cultural lens than other visiting abolitionists. Inevitably, his prism was a religious one, but it was also a combative one, he viewing Ireland in terms of the struggle for the heart, minds and souls of the Catholic population. The ministers who had hosted him—all evangelical Protestants—were each engaged on their own crusade, which was 'one of real issue with Papal Catholicism'.[118] Ireland's progress, Ward believed, depended on 'the utter overthrow of the Papal power in Ireland'.[119] He explained:

212 *Samuel Ringgold Ward (1817–c.1866)*

In no part of Europe, Protestant or Papal, is that system, either temporally or spiritually, what it was a hundred years ago. It can never regain its lost prestige, but it must certainly lose its hold, upon the minds of its own votaries. It has no elements adaptable to the middle of the nineteenth century. Its doom is sealed in Ireland, as elsewhere. It is menaced by the emigration of Irishmen, by the spread of education, by the elevation of tenants, by landlords, by Agricultural Societies, and by the onward, rolling tide of progress, which, having once set in upon Ireland, will never ebb, but sweep before it all systems and customs which accord not with itself. Yet it is right and dutiful to do what has to be done in the very best way: and one who loves Ireland as I do, cannot but grieve that among Protestants things should exist which weaken their power to do good; while one rejoices to know that other and better ideas prevail to some extent, and that, in spite of the defects hinted at, good is being done—the proclamation of the gospel is being blessed, and its truths will finally become triumphant—in that island gem.[120]

Ward also commented on the social condition of Ireland, acknowledging its potential, but criticizing its people. Like Douglass, Ward was beset by beggars, but he proved to be less compassionate.[121] Furthermore, he drew unfavourable comparisons between Ireland and both Scotland and Wales:

The neatly trimmed hedge, the smoothly turned furrow, the air of industry and thrift, with their abundant reward smiling on every hand, were left behind, on the other side. The neglected broken hedge, the slovenly-looking field, the air of neglect, and their legitimate consequences, frowned on every hand upon us and around us, with the rarest exceptions, from Belfast to Sligo, from Sligo to Mullingar, from Dublin to Cork. Like frowns upon the face of beauty, these Irish farms gave abundant evidence that they were capable of presenting a very different aspect.[122]

Ward acknowledged that by speaking so frankly he had perhaps offended some people, but he posited:

Roman Catholics freely express their opinions: why should not one of the humblest of Protestants? I am conscious of doing so kindly and should be sorry to speak otherwise. After all, I expect less fault-finding with what is said on this and a preceding page, from Romanists, than from squeamish, timid Protestants. Be that as it may, 'I have believed, therefore have I spoken'.[123]

In a rare political comment, he added:

I may be told, on the one hand, of Saxon rule as the prolific parent of this terrible state of things; on the other hand, I am told of Papal religion as the producing cause of it. I will not discuss either of these but admit the force of both. Who can deny the fact of Saxon rule? Who can deny the fact of

Samuel Ringgold Ward (1817–c.1866) 213

Papal religion? Who denies that the Irish peasantry have for generations been subject to both? Neither is perfect. All that is true. I will not stop to compare dates as to the priority of these; nor inquire what have been the tendencies of either, or both, in other countries.[124]

After Ireland, Ward travelled to Wales where he stayed for only a few days. It was, however, long enough for him to form a favourable opinion of the country and its people, leading him to state, '[I] must say that little with very great pleasure; for no country, no people, ever pleased me so much—excepting black people, of course'.[125] He concluded that, 'Wales is the most moral and most religious country, and her peasantry the best peasantry, that I know'.[126] In praising Wales, however, he drew unfavourable comparisons with Ireland—pointing to the higher crime rates in the latter, the proliferation of beggars, the excessive drinking, the lack of morality and stating bluntly in regard to Irish poverty:

> The Welsh are poor as well as the Irish; and their landlords sufficiently neglect them, as to their dwellings: but the cleanliness of the peasantry is most striking. The contrast betwixt Holyhead and Kingstown, within four hours' sail of each other, is most remarkable. One can scarcely believe that he has not been to two opposite sides of the globe, instead of across a narrow channel. The reader will now see why I blame the Irish for their defects, in contrast with the Welsh.[127]

Inevitably, Ward praised the devotion of the Welsh to the Calvinist Methodism denomination, and the sincerity of their ministers, adding 'Compare these sturdy, honest preachers, with the priests of Romanism!'[128]

In regard to the topic of the Irish in America, Ward was more aligned to the views of other abolitionists in despairing of their attitudes. Unlike other visitors, he expressed his opinions in openly offensive terms:

> Of all Europeans, the Irish immigrant becomes, as a rule, the readiest dupe of the pro-slavery men ... It turns out, that the man who on his native bog is unwashed and unshaved, a fellow lodger with his pig in a cabin too filthy for most people's stables or styes, is, when arriving in America, the Negro's birthplace, the free country for which the Negro fought and bled, one of the first to ridicule and abuse the free Negro—the Negro, who has yet to learn how to sink into such depths of degradation as the Irishman has just escaped from! The bitterest, most heartless, most malignant, enemy of the Negro, is the Irish immigrant.[129]

In a long letter to *Frederick Douglass' Paper*, printed in April 1855, on the eve of Ward's second visit to Ireland, he compared 'the Negro with the Anglo-Saxon race', Ward's dislike of the lower classes, especially the Irish lower classes, was evident:

> I can give people on this side the Atlantic, no better explanation of Negro hate than the following. In England, the lowest classes stare impudently at

214 *Samuel Ringgold Ward (1817–c.1866)*

a black person, and frequently make some stupid, vulgar remark concerning him. The same is true in Ireland, but, strange to say, not in Scotland or Wales. Of course, I speak of my personal experience only. But a well-bred Englishman or Irishman is quite incapable of anything of the sort. In Canada, and other portions of British America, the prejudice is confined, to the lowest, dirtiest, most contemptible except those beneath the reach of contempt of all Her Gracious Majesty's humblest subjects, and the immediate descendants of such like Judge Haliburton, for instance. In the United States, you find prejudice less in refined New England, greater among the stolid Dutch and their descendants. There, too, you find the refined and educated English and Irish, as a rule maintaining their impartiality, while the low pauper, scum, offscourings from here and Ireland, become the bitterest persecutors of the Negro. Putting all these parts together, I infer from them that our disparagement had its origin where it now has its chief seat, in the low degraded minds of the early semi-savage settlers of America; and they having once fixed the fashion, those following them to their new homes, were made of stuff just about malleable enough to be molded into the same shape.[130]

Towards the end of Ward's stay in Britain, his life story, *Autobiography of a Fugitive Negro: His Anti-Slavery Labours in the United States, Canada and England*, was published in London.[131] Interestingly and unusually, in the title, Ward does not refer to himself as a 'slave', but as a 'negro' who was fighting against slavery. Nele Sawallisch argued that the use of fugitive in the title is misleading as Ward grew up as a free black man who received a formal education. Consequently, this text cannot be considered 'a traditional slave narrative, but ... it is, in fact, autobiography, travel report and *anti-slavery* narrative'.[132] Because of the timing of its publication—towards the conclusion of Ward's time overseas—it included extensive details of his travels, with relatively little written about his early life.[133] Moreover, unlike other narratives published in the United States, this publication was aimed primarily at a British audience. Ward wrote his own Preface to his autobiography—something that Douglass did not feel comfortable in doing until the second Irish reprinting of his book. Moreover, the Dedication to the Duchess of Sutherland, in the form of a letter, was a pointed reminder that during his time away, Ward moved within social circles that included the English upper classes.[134]

Despite having spent a relatively short period in Ireland, Ward included a chapter on his time there. Elsewhere, the publication showed the author's familiarity with Irish history; when talking about 'Negro-Hate' shown by a judge in Canada, he illustrated it with this quote:

I see a recent traveller says, 'there is not a respectable coloured family in Toronto'. That is like 'Sam Slick' (Judge Haliburton) saying, 'a Negro gentleman is out of the question'. I would say to that bold false writer, and to that Negro-disparaging judge, what Robert Emmett [sic] said to Judge Norbury—'There are men united with me ... who are superior to your own conceptions of yourself, my Lord'.[135]

On other occasions, Ward, like Douglass before him, praised earlier Irish patriots, including John Philpot Curran, a Protestant lawyer who (unlike Ward) had defended the rights of Irish Catholics.[136] His admiration for Irish patriots (most of whom were Protestant) was in stark contrast to his antipathy to the poor Irish peasantry.

Later life

Following his tour of Britain and Ireland, Ward did not return to Canada but relocated to Jamaica. His narrative gives some indication of his motive—he considered the life of the travelling agent to be full of 'a great many disagreeables'.[137] Moreover, he was able to do so because an English Quaker friend, John Candler of Chelmsford, who had travelled extensively in the West Indies, offered him 50 acres of land there for a nominal fee.[138] Ward explained that his motive for emigrating was to relieve his family 'from a position of dependence'. He added that his longer-term plan would be, 'The duty of spending a portion of every year in Jamaica, until my son shall be old enough to attend to that property, is thus made clear to me'.[139] He did not fulfil this plan, however, as his relocation proved to be full-time. Consequently, from 1851, Ward had chosen to live on British soil—in Canada, the United Kingdom and Jamaica—and, more importantly, to reinvent himself as a loyal subject of the British Empire.

The approach of Ward and several other abolitionists, who blatantly appealed for money while in the United Kingdom, angered some of their fellow activists. Parker Pillsbury, writing from Belfast to Samuel May in October 1854, lambasted a number of them, saying:

> The thing that troubles me most here is to find so many is to find all sorts of creatures travelling in the name of the American Anti-Slavery Society, and picking the people's pockets for vigilance committees, Canada Missions, chaplain funds, colored schools in the West, and colored churches in Canada. Pennington, Garnet, Ward, Hemming, Gloucester & that fry are an outrage on all decency & a scandal to the name of anti-slavery.[140]

Pillsbury believed that Ward was damaging, rather than helping, the cause of abolition.[141] Ward's behaviour was also admonished by Richard Webb, still unapologetically Garrisonian, in his Dublin paper, *The Anti-Slavery Advocate*. At the beginning of 1856 he wrote:

> Black, portly, fluent, *reverend* and clever,—a lion unmistakably African—he found his way into white circles where a white man, with much greater claims to the respect and gratitude of mankind, could hardly have gained access.

Because of this privileged access, in his first ten months overseas, Ward was able to collect £1,200 for the Canadian Anti-Slavery Society, his employers. But, according to Webb:

216 *Samuel Ringgold Ward (1817–c.1866)*

As he remained in the country at least as much longer, on the same comfortable terms with the benevolent, the wealthy, and the powerful, the report is probably correct that he did very well on his own particular behalf, before he left our shores to take possession of small estate in Jamaica, which, he tells us, was made over to him by a philanthropic Quaker, John Candler, Esq., on such easy terms as almost to constitute it a gift.[142]

It was a damning indictment of somebody who claimed to be a Christian and to be leading 'an anti-slavery life'.[143]

Following Ward's successful and lucrative tour of the United Kingdom, he departed for Kingston in late 1855. Ward apparently left without paying debts to a London tradesman and to the Canadian Anti-Slavery Society.[144] In regard to the former, Ward had been loaned £140 by Richard Baynham, with a promise that the debt would be paid when Ward returned to Toronto. He never, however, returned to Canada. His motivations for acting in this way remain unclear. Both the Canadian and the London Anti-Slavery Societies were aware of Ward's actions but maintained a discreet silence in public.[145] Nonetheless, Ward's dishonesty suggests a more troubling side to his character. Moreover, it was not the first time that there had been suggestions of financial impropriety and of his exploiting his status for personal gain. These accusations paint a picture of a flawed man, however brilliant he was.

Ward's time in Jamaica was marked by the same restiveness that he had demonstrated throughout his life. Many accounts suggest he preached for a few years, before turning his attention to farming. Ward had arrived on the island as a Congregationalist minister, but at some stage he 'immersed' and converted to become an Independent Baptist.[146] However, there is no mention of him in the religious directories for the island for either 1857 or 1865, but in 1861 he was listed as a Baptist Minister in Kingston.[147] In this year, he moved to St David's and there, with his daughter, he set up a small school that operated out of his home.[148] Ward's time in Jamaica was not without controversy—he took a case of libel against a man whom he accused of 'Making an attack on my moral character in a publication'. The man, a member of Ward's congregation, had accused the minister of immoral behaviour with other members of the congregation. Ward lost the action.[149]

Ward's arrival in Jamaica coincided with a period of increasing tensions between the black, the mixed race and the white populations of the island. These tensions culminated in a rebellion in Morant Bay in October 1865. In advance of this, Ward had been 'recruited by planters to counteract the influence of [George William] Ganordon', one of the leaders of the insurgents. Ward's presence at one of the meetings resulted in him being booed.[150] Following the brutal repression of the rebellion, Ward sided with the authorities, again revealing the conservative side to his nature.[151] He even published a pamphlet, 'Reflections upon the Gordon Rebellion' explaining his stance on 'this diabolical affair'.[152] In 1866, he gave evidence before a Royal Commission, his focus being on the apparent 'insolence' of the local peasantry. The lack of empathy

Samuel Ringgold Ward (1817–c.1866)   217

that he displayed towards the poor natives of Jamaica had parallels with his unsympathetic views of the Irish peasantry. When giving evidence before the Commission, he even made the unfavourable comparison:

> I remember ten years ago when there was a row between any persons on the road, I could go up and stop it at once, a thing I dare not do in Ireland, but now I could not do that.[153]

When questioned about his time in the United Kingdom, his answer was perplexing and seemingly out of character:

> [qu] 28,223. (Mr. Payne) I think you are the celebrated gentleman who escaped from American slavery, are you not, and visited England?
> No, I am not the celebrated gentleman. I am not the man who escaped from slavery: I was one of many others.
> 28, 224. But you are the gentleman who was received by the Duke and Duchess of Sutherland.
> Yes.[154]

Ward's minimalist answers were a strange reversal of his earlier attempts to cultivate, celebrate and publicize his associations with the wealthy and influential English upper classes. His curt answers suggest that Samuel Ward was reinventing himself, yet again, as an English loyalist who had not used his slavery background as a passport to celebrity.

By publicly stating his support of the authorities' actions in Jamaica, Ward was out of step with his former anti-slavery colleagues in the United States and in Britain, one abolitionist newspaper opining that:

> THE readers of the STANDARD are already aware of the recent terrible outrages by the government authorities in Jamaica on the colored population of the island under pretence of suppressing an insurrection or rebellion. The last arrivals from Great Britain have brought full accounts of that most remarkable occurrence. From the statements made and not contradicted, the only wonder is that downright revolution has not desolated the island long ago.[155]

Liberals in Britain condemned the violent response by the establishment. In England, John Stuart Mill, MP, convened a meeting in London 'to express condemnation of the massacre in Jamaica'.[156] The action of the British authorities was also roundly and publicly criticized by both Ellen Craft and Sarah Parker Remond.[157] Ward's response in Jamaica has perplexed historians. Tom Watson, writing in 2008, argued that his actions can only be understood 'within the framework of the British empire and Victorian respectability'.[158] Jeffrey Kerr-Ritchie has suggested that Ward's reaction shows how fully he had embraced being an 'imperial subject' who defended and upheld the British Empire.[159] Elsewhere, Kerr-Ritchie argues that Ward's opposition to the rising 'was the logical consequence of the

218 *Samuel Ringgold Ward (1817–c.1866)*

thoughts and actions of a long-term black loyalist for whom a powerful Empire guaranteed freedom and promised future reform'.[160]

In contrast with Jamaica, Ward's relationship with Ireland has largely been ignored. He differed from other black abolitionists by being impatient with the poverty of the people—in 1846, Douglass had expressed a more sympathetic view, although, at that stage, he attributed much of the poverty to intemperance. For Ward, Irish poverty arose from a moral defect, which he implicitly attributed to the religion of the peasants and their priests. Tellingly, when visiting the country for the second time to lecture, he was mostly hosted by English evangelical ministers who were in Ireland to proselytize. This was in stark contrast to Equiano, Remond, Douglass, Wells Brown and others, who had moved easily across religious, political and anti-slavery divides. Additionally, Ward's views on Ireland were shaped by his positioning himself since 1851 as being, 'among the most loyal of Her Majesty's subjects'.[161] Ireland did not fit comfortably into his vision of British benevolence and liberty.

Ward died shortly after the rebellion in Jamaica. His death passed by largely unnoticed, the year being given variously as 1866 and 1867.[162] He also appeared to die in poverty and obscurity, and his burial place remains unknown.[163] Ward's passing was not observed in the abolitionist community on whom he had largely turned his back. In contrast, Douglass, with whom he was often compared, died a wealthy man, whose death was widely noted, including in Ireland.

Conclusion

Ward and Douglass were frequently considered the intellectual giants of abolitionism, and models for their fellow black men. In 1851, it was even incorrectly suggested that they were both running for office together as President and Vice-President.[164] One newspaper report in 1855, calling for suffrage, opined, 'If the Blacks of today were all, or mainly all, such men as Samuel R. Ward or Frederick Douglass, nobody would consider "Negro" an invidious or reproachful designation'.[165] Even years after Ward had left the United States, he and Douglass were spoken of as the two men who had, 'magnificently vindicated the ability of the black man'.[166] Inevitably, perhaps, the two superstars of the movement had public disagreements; in 1850 when the *North Star* joined in with criticizing Ward for giving a sermon in a segregated church, Ward accused the paper of being motivated by 'jealousy, envy, and mean ambition'.[167]

Regardless of differences, Douglass often admitted his intellectual debt to Ward in moving him away from Garrisonianism, his first introduction to abolition:

> The main points were, that the views entertained and promulgated by the American Society, were those to which he was first introduced, after his exodus from slavery, and as a natural consequence, because of the confidence he reposed in the men, he embraced them. But when he went West,

Samuel Ringgold Ward (1817–c.1866)   219

and came in contact with such men as Beriah Green. Wm. Goodell, Gerrit Smith, and the powerful Samuel R. Ward, and met them in debate, both public and private, he was introduced to a different set of ideas was forced to submit his mind to a new training to defend his positions; and the end was, that from inquiry to inquiry, he, finally, in open conviction, came to believe in the anti-slavery character of the United States Constitution, and thereupon he left the old platform of belief to stand where he stands tonight.[168]

Although Ward is largely forgotten today, his contribution to anti-slavery and to showing the intellectual prowess of his people was immense. Sadly, his personal life revealed ambiguities regarding financial dealings, while his short time in Ireland and his final years in Jamaica were a betrayal of the principles of social justice. Unusually, amongst black abolitionists, while in Ireland, he demonstrated little sympathy or empathy with its people, his praise being reserved for Protestant evangelicals. Regardless of his flaws, to his contemporaries, Ward was of immense importance. Douglass, in particular, maintained his admiration for his fellow abolitionist. When writing in 1884, on the passing of the black Congressman, Robert Elliot,[169] Douglass added:

> I have known but one other black man to be compared with Elliott, and that was Samuel R. Ward, who, like Elliott, died in the midst of his years. The thought of both men makes me sad. We are not over rich with such men, and we may well mourn when one such has fallen.[170]

In Douglass's third and final autobiography, he elaborated further on Ward's contribution saying:

> In depth of thought, fluency of speech, readiness of wit, logical exactness, and general intelligence, Samuel R. Ward has left no successor among the colored men amongst us, and it was a sad day for our cause when he was laid low in the soil of a foreign country.[171]

In the early parts of their careers, these two men were often spoken of as equals. There were many parallels in their approaches: they both argued for an immediate ending to slavery, but both men saw beyond this goal, realizing that the fight for equality and ending racism and prejudice would take a lot longer. The latter parts of their careers, however, were widely divergent. While Douglass chose to fight slavery from within his native land, Ward chose to relocate within the British Empire, where he viewed himself as a British citizen and became a defender of the imperial project, repeatedly stating his loyalty to the British Empire.[172] Ward's devotion to evangelical Christianity, similar to his support for imperialism, was also part of his civilizing mission.

Ward's time in America, Canada, Britain, Ireland and Jamaica provide an example of the transnational nature of abolition. Yet his life and his lifestyle

220 *Samuel Ringgold Ward (1817–c.1866)*

choices suggested a restlessness and a recklessness, which meant that he could never commit wholly to a cause. Frequently also, his actions appeared to be prompted by self-interest rather than a desire for justice. Ward's later years, particularly his time in Ireland and Jamaica, indicated a more conservative and less palatable side to his character that were inconsistent with his early radicalism and his professed Christianity. Ward's life was a powerful reminder of the complexity and diversity of the abolition movement, and of the abolitionists who shaped it.

Notes

1 A map of Abolitionists who visited the British Isles does not mention Ward but includes Frederick Douglass; William Wells Brown; William and Ellen Craft; William Lloyd Garrison; Josiah Henson; Charles Remond; Sarah Remond; Moses Roper; George Thompson; Harriet Tubman; Ida B. Wells; Henry C. Wright. See: http://frederickdouglassinbritain.com/ Few, with the exception of Douglass and Garnet, rivalled Ward's impact in terms of leadership and intellectual contribution to anti-slavery.
2 Joel Schor refers to Ward as 'a brilliant antislavery intellectual', *Henry Highland Garnet* (CT: Greenwood Press, 1977), p. 5.
3 Samuel Ringgold Ward, *Autobiography of a Fugitive Negro: His Anti-Slavery Labours in the United States, Canada, & England* (London: John Snow, 1855), p. 47. This phrase is also used in the title of a biography of Ward, Ronald K. Burke, *Samuel Ringgold Ward: Christian Abolitionist* (London: Routledge, 1995). Burke states that Ward followed the doctrine of Christology—the belief that Jesus Christ was the perfect man. The African America Registry described Ward as a 'spiritual abolitionist': https://aaregistry.org/story/rev-samuel-r-ward-spiritual-abolitionist/.
4 Ibid., p. 33.
5 In an otherwise fine chapter on Ward's autobiography, Nele Sawallisch repeatedly refers to Ward's tour of Great Britain, ignoring his time in Ireland, *Fugitive Borders: Black Canadian Cross-Border Literature at Mid-Nineteenth Century* (New York: Columbia University Press, 2019), p. 105.
6 Ward to Gerrit Smith, 18 April 1842, in C. Peter Ripley (ed.), *The Black Abolitionist Papers*, The British Isles, 1830–1865, vol. 1 (Chapel Hill: University of North Carolina Press, 2015), p. 384; Ward, *Autobiography*, p. 4.
7 'FIRST OF AUGUST AT FLUSHING', *National Anti-Slavery Standard*, 5 August 1854.
8 Ward, *Autobiography*, p. 8.
9 William Wells Brown, *The Black Man: His Antecedents, His Genius, and His Achievements* (New York: Thomas Hamilton; Boston, MA: R.F. Wallcut, 1863), p. 285.
10 Ward, *Autobiography*, p. 35.
11 Ibid., p. 37.
12 Ibid., p. 49.
13 Ibid., p. 51.
14 Letter from Samuel Ringgold Ward [Oswego, New York], to Amos Augustus Phelps, 1846 Apr[il] 15, Anti-Slavery Collection, Boston Public Library. Available at: www.digitalcommonwealth.org/search/commonwealth:2v23xh536.
15 Burke, *Christian Abolitionist*, p. 3.
16 Ibid., pp. 116–17.
17 Ward, *Autobiography*, p. 31.
18 Ibid. p. 32.

Samuel Ringgold Ward (1817–c.1866) 221

19 Letter from Samuel Ringgold Ward, Oswego, [New York], to Amos Augustus Phelps, 1846 Apr[il] 18, BPL. Available at: www.digitalcommonwealth.org/search/commonwealth:2v23xh76h.
20 Ward opened the 1849 meeting of the American and Foreign Anti-Slavery Society in this way, see, Herbert Aptheker, 'The Negro in the Abolitionist Movement', in *Science & Society*, vol. 5, no. 2 (Spring 1941), 148–72, p. 167.
21 Hanes Walton Jr, Sherman Puckett, Donald R. Deskins Jr, *The African American Electorate* (Los Angeles, CA: Sage, 2012), p. 181.
22 Ward, *Autobiography*, p. 31.
23 Ibid., p. 52.
24 The speech 'On Character', delivered in the Cortlandville Academy Lyceum on 22 January 1849, reprinted in Burke, *Christian Abolitionist*, p. 123.
25 Wells Brown, *Black Man*, p. 284.
26 Ibid., p. 285.
27 *New York Tribune*, 8 May 1850.
28 Wells Brown, *Black Man*, p. 285.
29 Syracuse abolitionist Samuel Ringgold Ward was the first black man nominated for national office, *Central New York News*: www.syracuse.com/news/index.ssf/2012/02/samuel_ringgold_ward_oswego.html.
30 Throughout the 1840s, there were multiple conventions held throughout the Free States and it is possible that the men had met earlier. Schor states that both Douglass (already a star in the movement) and Ward were present at the 1843 convention in Buffalo, *Garnet*, p. 58, but no mention is made of Ward in the Proceedings: *Minutes of the National Convention of Coloured Citizens Held at Buffalo, 15, 16, 17, 18 and 19 August 1843 for Purpose of Considering Their Moral and Political Condition as American Citizens* (New York: Piercy and Reed, 1843).
31 Ward, *Narrative*, p. 96.
32 Frederick Douglass, *Life and Times of Frederick Douglass, Written by Himself* (Boston, MA: De Wolfe and Fiske, 1892), p. 345.
33 *North Star*, 25 May 1849.
34 Ward, *Autobiography*, p. 158.
35 'Letter from the Editor', *North Star*, 16 May 1850.
36 Parker Pillsbury (1809–1898) was a Congregationalist minister and abolitionist, known for his waspish personality. In 1854, he travelled to Britain on behalf of the American Anti-Slavery Society.
37 'The Massachusetts Annual Meeting', *National Anti-Slavery Standard*, 31 January 1850.
38 In addition to the Constitution, they also disagree on the use of physical force and the value of being involved in political organizations.
39 American League of Coloured Labourers: www.blackpast.org/african-american-history/american-league-colored-laborers-1850/.
40 *National Anti-Slavery Standard*, 31 January 1850.
41 'Samuel R. Ward', *Frederick Douglass' Paper*, 21 August 1851.
42 Ibid., 'Samuel R. Ward', 26 June 1851.
43 Ibid., 'The Needs of the Fugitives', 20 January 1853.
44 For more information of this newspaper, see the Library of Congress: www.loc.gov/item/sn84022610/.
45 Ward, *Autobiography*, pp. 33–4.
46 'The Slave Crime at Syracuse', *New York Daily Times*, 4 October 1851.
47 Ward, *Autobiography*, p. 33.
48 Ibid., p. 127.
49 Burke, *Christian Abolitionist*, p. 39.
50 'No Union with Slaveholders', the *Liberator*, 4 August 1854.

51 This is according to Burke, *Christian Abolitionist*, p. 43. No other evidence of this brief association could be located, but an abolitionist newspaper of this name was founded in Cleveland, Ohio, in 1853 by William Day and his wife, Lucy Stanton Day, and Ward contributed to it.
52 Garnet, Newcastle-Upon-Tyne, to Ward, 4 September 1850, reprinted in Ripley, *Black Abolitionist Papers*, p. 225.
53 'ANTI-SLAVERY Lecture', *Bradford Observer*, 22 February 1855.
54 John R. McKivigan (ed.), *The Frederick Douglass Papers: Series Three: Correspondence, vol. 2: 1853–1865* (New Haven, CT: Yale University Press, 2018), pp. 3–4.
55 Ward, *Autobiography*, p. 229.
56 Ibid., p. 237.
57 Ibid., p. 359.
58 'Samuel R. Ward of Canada', *Anti-Slavery Reporter* (London), 1 June 1853.
59 Ward, *Autobiography*, p. 236.
60 William Allen, London, to Garrison, 20 June 1853: https://atlanticslaverydebate.stanford.edu/sites/default/files/shared/ASD/Module1/WmGAllentoGarrison1853.pdf.
61 Ibid.
62 Harriet Beecher Stowe, *Uncle Tom's Cabin; or, Life Among the Lowly*, was published in 1852 by John Jewett and Co. in Boston. It sold in millions and was influential within the abolitionist debate. Though ground-breaking at the time, it is now regarded as sentimental and full of stereotypes.
63 Ward, *Autobiography*, p. 248.
64 The petition was organized by the Duchess of Sutherland. The wife of a former American President issued a public response: Julia Gardiner Tyler, *The Women of England versus the Women of America. Mrs. Ex-President Tyler's Letter to the Duchess of Sutherland on American Slavery* (London: W. Davy and Son, 1853).
65 Ward, *Autobiography*, pp. iii–iv.
66 Ibid., p. 250.
67 Harriet Beecher Stowe, *Uncle Tom's Cabin; or life among the lowly ... with introductory remarks by J. Sherman* (London: H.G. Bohn, 1852).
68 *Waterford News and Star*, 27 May 1853.
69 After England, Greenfield performed in Ireland, 'Rotunda Black Swan Concerts', *Freeman's Journal*, 22 August 1853. Elizabeth Taylor Greenfield (c.1820–1876) was known as 'The Black Swan', a play on Jenny Lind's pet-name, The Swedish Nightingale. Greenwald had been born in slavery, but as a child her family had been emancipated by their female owner. In England, Harriet Beecher Stowe acted as her patron. In England, Greenfield sang in front of Queen Victoria. During the American Civil War, she performed alongside Douglass.
70 Ward, *Autobiography*, p. 304.
71 'Presentation of a testimonial to Mrs Stowe', *Illustrated London News*, 25 June 1853. Harriet was travelling with her brother. After England, they visited Switzerland.
72 *Dictionary of Canadian Biography*: www.biographi.ca/en/bio/willis_michael_10E.html.
73 *Dictionary of Canadian Biography*: www.biographi.ca/en/bio/ward_samuel_ringgold_9E.html.
74 Ward, *Autobiography*, p. 237.
75 *Nation*, 3 November 1855; 'Coloured refugees in Canada', *Kerry Evening Post*, 3 November 1855.
76 'Rev. Ward', *Bradford Observer*, 22 February 1855. The Bradford meeting was chaired by Rev. Dr Godwin of the Sion Baptist Church, which is probably where Ward preached at during his visit there.
77 Ward, *Autobiography*, p. 337.
78 Ibid., p. 338.

Samuel Ringgold Ward (1817–c.1866)   223

79 Ibid., p. 253; 'Canadian Anti-Slavery Society', in the Canadian Encyclopedia: www.thecanadianencyclopedia.ca/en/article/anti-slavery-society-of-canada.
80 'Fugitive Slaves in Canada', *Anti-Slavery Reporter* (London), 1 May 1854, p. 103.
81 Ibid., 'Canadian Anti-Slavery Society', 2 July 1855.
82 *London Daily News*, 1 December 1854.
83 'Lecture on Slavery', *Hampshire Advertiser*, 18 November 1854.
84 'Escaped slaves to Freedom', *Birmingham Journal*, 15 October 1853.
85 'Lecture on Slavery', *Hampshire Advertiser*, 18 November 1854.
86 'Fugitive Slaves in Canada', *Longford Journal*, 2 July 1853.
87 'SAMUEL RINGOLD WARD has safely landed in England', *Frederick Douglass' Paper*, 3 June 1853.
88 'No Union with Slaveholders', the *Liberator*, 4 August 1854.
89 Anti-Slavery Conference, *Papers Read and Statements Made on the Principal Subjects Submitted to the Anti-Slavery Conference: Held at the London Tavern on the 29th and 30th of November 1854* (London: Anti-Slavery Conference, 1854).
90 Ward, *Autobiography*, p. 289.
91 *London Daily News*, 1 December 1854.
92 Ibid.
93 See chapter on Henry Highland Garnet.
94 *Anti-Slavery Reporter* (British and Foreign Anti-Slavery Society), vol. 3, 1855, pp. 10–11. Ward represented himself as being there on behalf of Jamaica. Richard Madden from Ireland was also present.
95 *London Daily News*, 1 December 1854.
96 The African American Registry states, 'In April 1853, Ward went to England on a fund-raising mission. During his two-year stay, he gave many speeches and published his life story', https://aaregistry.org/story/rev-samuel-r-ward-spiritual-abolitionist.
97 Burke, *Christian Abolitionist*, p. 56.
98 The name given to Dun Laoghaire, a port just outside Dublin. Ward spells it as 'Kingston'.
99 Ward, *Autobiography*, pp. 360–1.
100 Ibid., 262. Joseph Denham Smith, 1817–1889. In 1848, Smith published a small pamphlet *A Voice from the West; or, the Condition and Claims of Connaught, Ireland* (London: John Snow, 1848), which was addressed to the Dublin and London Committees of the Irish Evangelical Society.
101 Ward, *Autobiography*, p. 365.
102 William G. Allen, known in his day as 'the coloured professor'. He had left the United States in 1853 due to opposition to his mixed-race marriage.
103 Ward, *Autobiography*, p. 365.
104 *The Scottish Congregational Magazine*, 1844, p. 180.
105 Ward, *Autobiography*, pp. 365–6.
106 Ibid., p. 367.
107 *The Evangelical Magazine and Missionary Chronicle*, 1848, p. 593.
108 'The Church. American Slavery', *Nenagh Guardian*, 6 June 1855.
109 Ward, *Autobiography*, p. 368. William Cochrane was a member of the Evangelical Alliance which had been found in 1846 in the UK, they believing that they were the true followers of Jesus Christ (London: J.S. Phillips, 1857); *Evangelical Christendom*, vols. 11–12, p. 160. Cochrane was a financial contributor to missions that sought to convert Catholics, *The Wesleyan Missionary Notices, Relating Principally to the Foreign Missions* (London: Wesleyan Methodist Missionary Society, 1872), p. 5.
110 In his *Autobiography*, Ward incorrectly gives the initials of his host as M. A. Henderson. Anketell Matthew Henderson (1820–1876) was born in the north of Ireland. He served with the Wesleyans for 11 years before moving to the

224   *Samuel Ringgold Ward (1817–c.1866)*

Congregationalists. Following his time in Cork, he moved to a ministry in London and in 1865 he and his family moved to Australia to take charge of the Congregational Theological College, *Christian World*, 9 June 1865.

111 *Evangelical Magazine and Missionary Chronicle*, vol. 30, 1852, p. 733.

112 'American Slavery', *Cork Examiner*, 6 June 1855.

113 Ward, *Autobiography*, p. 369.

114 Ibid.

115 Ibid., p. 362.

116 Quoted in William Williams, *Tourism, Landscape, and the Irish Character: British Travel Writers in Pre-Famine Ireland* (Madison: University of Wisconsin Press, 2012), p. 174.

117 Ward, *Autobiography*, p. 364.

118 Ibid., p. 371.

119 Ibid., p. 372.

120 Ibid., pp. 372–3.

121 Ibid., p. 381.

122 Ibid., pp. 374–5.

123 Ibid., p. 378.

124 Ibid., p. 380.

125 Ibid., p. 385.

126 Ibid., p. 391.

127 Ibid., pp. 392–3.

128 Ibid., p. 395.

129 Ibid., pp. 382–3.

130 'The Modern Negro, No. 3', *Frederick Douglass' Paper*, 20 April 1855.

131 John Snow of Paternoster Row in London was the publisher. Snow specialized in publishing evangelical and Christian texts.

132 Sawallisch, *Fugitive Borders*, p. 104.

133 The 1855 version of Ward's *Autobiography* was published by John Snow in 1855. It cost 6*s* 6*d*, was cloth bound and included a portrait. Ward devoted one chapter to Ireland—only four focus on his personal story, the remaining chapters on his travels.

134 Ward, *Autobiography*, pp. iii–iv.

135 Ibid., pp. 156–7.

136 Ibid., p. 279.

137 Ibid., p. 348.

138 Ibid., pp. 405–6.

139 Ibid., p. 406.

140 Letter from Parker Pillsbury, Belfast, to Samuel May, 5 October 1854, BPL. Available online at: www.digitalcommonwealth.org/search/commonwealth:dv144j632.

141 *Anti-Slavery Advocate*, 1 November 1854.

142 Ibid., 1 February 1856.

143 Ward, *Autobiography*, p. 33.

144 Dictionary of Canadian Biography: www.biographi.ca/en/bio/ward_samuel_ring gold_9E.html.

145 Burke, *Christian Abolitionist*, pp. 56–7.

146 *Report of the Jamaica Royal Commission 1866*, parts 1 & 2 (London: H. M. Stationery Office, 1866), p. 558.

147 The *Jamaica Almanac* for 1857 and 1865, list all religious denominations and ministers of the island. They make no reference to Ward: www.jamaicanfamilysearch.com/Members/alm1857_06.htm www.jamaicanfamilysearch.com/Members/a1865_06.htm. However, he does appear in t he 1861 listing as a Baptist Minister in Kingston: www.jamaicanfamilysearch.com/Members/al61c07.htm.

148 Evidence of Rev. S. R. Ward, *Report of the Jamaica Royal Commission*, pp. 554–5.

Samuel Ringgold Ward (1817–c.1866) 225

149 Ibid., qu. 28223–30, pp. 557–8.
150 Swithin Wilmot, 'The Politics of Samuel Clarke: Black Creole Politician in Free Jamaica, 1851–1865', in *Caribbean Quarterly*, vol. 44, no. 1–2, 129–44, p. 142.
151 Dictionary of Canadian Biography: www.biographi.ca/en/bio/ward_samuel_ring gold_9E.html.
152 Samuel Ringgold Ward, *Reflections upon the Gordon Rebellion* (Publisher and place of publication not identified), p. 1.
153 *Royal Commission*, qu. 28, 150, p. 555.
154 Ibid., p. 557.
155 'The Jamaica Imbroglio', *National Anti-Slavery Standard*, 16 December 1865. The paper ran several similar articles, eg, 3 March 1866.
156 Ibid., 13 January 1866.
157 See chapter on Sarah Parker Remond.
158 Tom Watson, *Caribbean Culture and British Fiction in the Atlantic World 1780–1860* (Cambridge University Press, 2008), p. 106.
159 Jeffrey Kerr-Ritchie, 'Samuel Ward and the Making of an Imperial Subject', in *Slavery and Abolition*, vol. 33, no. 2 (2012), 205–19.
160 Jeffrey Kerr-Ritchie, 'Samuel Ward and the Gordon Rebellion', in *The Journal of Caribbean History*, vol. 50, no. 1 (January 2016), pp. 36–51, 36.
161 Ward, *Autobiography*, p. 322.
162 An online biography of Ward gives it as 1867: https://mdahgp.genealogyvillage. com/biography_of_samuel_ringgold_ward.html most sources give it as 1866.
163 Kerr-Ritchie, 'Imperial Subject', states that the location of Ward's grave is unknown, p. 211. No reference to Ward's death could be found from an extensive search in American, British and Irish newspapers by this author for both 1866 and 1867.
164 This story appeared in *Frederick Douglass' Paper*, it adding 'They ought to be good friends, for they may sit together', 21 August 1851.
165 Ibid., 'Unpalatable Counsel', 28 September 1855.
166 'Speech of Rev. W. H. Furness. Third decade of Anti-slavery Society', *National Anti-Slavery Standard*, 19 December 1863.
167 'The letter of M. R. Delany', *North Star*, 27 June 1850.
168 'FREDERICK DOUGLASS IN PHILADELPHIA', *Frederick Douglass' Paper*, 6 April 1855.
169 Although born in Liverpool, Robert Brown Elliott (1842–1884) established a law practice in the United States. He went on to become a black member of the United States House of Representatives for South Carolina, serving from 1871 to 1874.
170 'Hon. Robert B. Elliot' (chapter lxii), in Rev. William J. Simmons, D. D. *Men of Mark: Eminent, Progressive and Rising* (Cleveland: Geo. M. Rewell and Co., 1887), p. 473.
171 Douglass, *Life and Times*, p. 345.
172 Kerr-Ritchie, 'Imperial Subject'.

9 Benjamin Benson (1818–?)

'Drunkenness ... worse than slavery'

Benjamin Benson is an enigma.[1] An enslaved person with a unique story, he clearly preferred his role as a promoter of temperance and evangelism to that of being a champion of abolition. Moreover, he remains virtually invisible in abolitionist histories. If he is mentioned, it is only regarding his presence at a large meeting in London in August 1851 to celebrate West Indian Emancipation Day. No further information is provided, only his surname is given and the fact that he joined William Wells Brown and his daughters as one of the (non-speaking) platform party.[2] For historians and contemporary abolitionists, it seems that Benson disappeared after this.[3] Yet, Benson's story was in print. His thrilling *Narrative* had been published in England in 1847, although not penned by the eponymous hero. And throughout the 1850s, Benson lectured on slavery and temperance in small, usually Protestant and temperance, venues in England. He remained unaligned to the main abolitionist groups and to his fellow lecturers. He reappeared in Ireland in the end of the 1850s, not in the guise of an abolitionist, but as an evangelical preacher and temperance agent. In this role, he came into contact with many Irish abolitionists, and his origins as a slave were often cited. But who was Benjamin Benson? Why was he so temperate and evasive on the topic of slavery? How authentic was his *Narrative*? Why did he fail so spectacularly in business?

Benson's life story and escape from enslavement were dramatic, even by the standard of his contemporaries, given that he was enslaved twice and escaped twice. A narrative of his life was published, but it had been written by somebody else—an English doctor named Andrew Welch. In the 1830s, Welch had lived in Florida, where he had become an opponent of slavery and of the treatment of Native Americans. Following his return to England in 1840, he had come across a young black man handing out religious tracts on the streets of Worcester. The man, Benjamin Benson, was described as 'a lone Negro, a stranger, in poor health and with no skill or trade'. Welch invited 'the forlorn figure' to his London home.[4] It was not the first time that Welch had shown sympathy to a vulnerable male. While in Florida, he had become interested in the fate of a Native American Seminole child, Oceola Nikkanochee. Welch had provided for the boy's education and, to avoid ostracization, had brought the boy back to England to live with him and his family. After three years, the boy ran away at sea, probably to Australia.[5] Welch published a narrative of Oceola's life in 1841.

In 1847, Welch wrote and self-published Benson's life story. It was melodramatic, but Welch claimed that he had checked the story out where possible and, in his opinion, 'IT IS A TALE OF TRUTH'.[6] The title of the narrative encapsulated the arc of the story; *A Narrative of the Life of Benjamin Benson, Who Was Born a Slave in the Island of Bermuda, Emancipated by the English Government, August 1, 1838, and Subsequently Sold as a Slave in the United States of America.* Benson's life story was made even more extraordinary in that not only was he enslaved twice, but he had been enslaved under both British and American jurisdiction.

Early life

According to Welch's narrative, Benson had been born into enslavement in Bermuda in the West Indies, which was part of the British Empire. Unusually, he knew his precise date of birth, 16 December 1818.[7] His father had been abducted from Gambia in Africa, his mother had been born into slavery on Long Island but sold when aged 12. Together, they had 22 children, but the family were then broken up and the members repeatedly sold.[8] Benson's experiences as an enslaved child were harrowing: he had been scarred over his left eye and branded on his right shoulder to ensure that he could be identified if he ever escaped. When aged 12, he had been sold to a plantation in Mobile.[9] During the next few years, he worked in the cotton and rice fields. He was frequently whipped.[10] Benson was subsequently sold to slaveholders in Washington and when they went bankrupt, he was sent to St Kitts Island. His return to the West Indies enabled him to see his mother again. An added joy was that Britain was on the verge of ending slavery in its empire. This took place on 1 August 1833, although a period of transition was considered necessary and therefore a system of apprenticeship was put in place. Benson used his freedom to work aboard ships which frequently took him back to the United States. During one voyage, he was accused of mutiny and imprisoned in New Orleans. Having been freed from enslavement in the British Empire, he now became a slave in America.[11] Helped by an English man, Benson escaped on a steamship to New Providence.[12] He then worked as a sailor and, during this time, made many voyages to Britain. In 1844, during one of these journeys, he disembarked in England where he started a new life.[13] Initially, he was assisted by some English Quakers. He then found employment as a miner and a waiter but left both due to poor health.[14]

It was sometime afterwards, that Welch encountered Benson in the streets of Worcester, about 100 miles north of London. Benson, who had inherited his evangelical beliefs from his mother and was extremely pious, was distributing religious tracts.[15] One of Benson's brothers, Anthony, was in New York studying to be a minister in the Zion Church. For some reason, Benson gave Welch a letter from his brother Anthony, sent from New York in March 1846, which Welch described as being 'well written'. Anthony informed Benjamin that he was following this vocation so that he could, 'save souls from eternal ruin'. He further added, 'I am a temperate man, and go for teetotalism, and

228 *Benjamin Benson (1818–?)*

hope you may be temperate in all things. I lecture upon that subject'.[16] There is no evidence that Anthony completed his studies or ever became a minister because, like Benjamin was to do on a number of occasions, he disappeared from public view. Regarding Benjamin, religion and temperance remained central to his mission, and throughout his three decades in the United Kingdom, he leaned consistently more towards fellow evangelicals rather than fellow abolitionists.

Little is known about the subsequent relationship between Welch and Benson, the former only saying that:

> The writer met him on the streets of Worcester, procuring a scanty existence by the sale of religious tracts, and invited him to call at his residence, when he obtained this eventful history. Benson accompanied the writer in his visit to several other towns, but at length left him with the intention of proceeding to Liverpool to procure a passage back to his native island of Bermuda.[17]

When the narrative was published in 1847, Benson had disappeared, leading Welch to conclude by saying:

> Should this little work chance to meet the eyes of Benjamin, the writer begs to assure him he will gladly share with him any profit that may arise from the sale.[18]

It is not known whether the two men met again, or if Benson had returned to Bermuda before reappearing in England in 1851. It is known that Welch died in January 1852, aged 54.[19]

An interesting feature of the 1847 *Narrative* is the three testimonials, provided by George Gilfillan, a Scottish writer who was also a Presbyterian minister, Thomas Drew, an evangelical Anglican minister in Belfast and Isaac Nelson, a Presbyterian minister in Belfast. Both Drew and Nelson had written glowing testimonials for the second Irish edition of Frederick Douglass's *Narrative*, published in 1846.[20] They knew Douglass personally, but they had not met Benson. Regardless, they wrote:

> Belfast, August 20, 1847.
>
> I have read Dr Welch's narrative of the negro Benjamin Benson's eventful life: it has the fullest internal evidence of a truthful relation. To circulate such a narrative is the more useful, because it is no very singular story, but may go forward as the duplicate of many an injured, outraged, and fearfully wronged negro's destiny. Three millions of the family of Benson yet live to appeal to humanity for mitigation of their sufferings, and to the God of love for that compassion which men desire for themselves, but deny to slaves.
>
> Thomas Drew D.D.

And:

Belfast, 23 August, 1847

By the publication of the narrative of the life of Benjamin Benson, Dr Welch has deserved the thanks of those who wait and labour for the overthrow of slavery.

The graphic picture of one slave's life and sufferings, does more to make the reader acquainted with the atrocity of the system, than the most profound and elaborate disquisitions on the evils of slavery. We are brought near to the features of the monster by such simple and touching recitals. Individual Christians will pause and contemplate, and churches will feel the responsibility of encouraging such enormities.

What man in his most untutored state will do for freedom, may be learned from such biography, and the impossibility of crushing the love of liberty demonstrated. The sad reflection, however, must arise, how many such drinks at this moment the bitter cup, whose tales have never been told, except in sighs, heard only by the God of Sabaoth! The truth of the narrative will not be doubted by those who are familiar with the condition of the slave.

Isaac Nelson, Presbyterian Minister.[21]

Clearly, the story of Benson, whose whereabouts at this time were unknown, had reached and impressed abolitionists in Ireland.

Benson appeared again in London in 1851, when anti-slavery sentiment was peaking due to the recent passing of the Fugitive Slave Law.[22] He was part of the platform party at a large gathering on 1 August in London to celebrate West Indian Emancipation. The meeting was chaired by William Wells Brown and a number of prominent American and British abolitionists attended, including Maria Weston Chapman and Caroline Weston of Boston, and George Thompson.[23] Wells Brown's two daughters, who had recently arrived from America, were also present.[24] Towards the end, 'An Appeal to the people of Great Britain and of the World' was made. Benson, who was described as 'a man of colour' supported the resolution.[25] This appears to be his only verbal contribution to the meeting. Following this, a resolution was adopted praising Garrison.[26] The meeting had been convened by a newly formed 'American Fugitive Slaves in the British Metropolis', of which Benson appeared to be a founder.[27]

Benson continued to lecture on slavery in Britain, but he did not attract the same attention as his colleagues who were touring at the same time, including Wells Brown, Henry Highland Garnet, James Pennington and Alexander Crummell. He did, however, create a distinctive niche. A few days after the London meeting, Benson's presence at a Temperance Festival in Dunstable was noted. He was described as 'a fugitive slave from North America'.[28] Later that month, Benson chaired an anti-slavery meeting at a temperance hall in Camden to hear from John Brown, a fugitive slave from Georgia.[29] The two men appeared in a number of other venues, with Benson's role being confined to chairing, rather than sharing, his own life story, his comments being described as 'hasty'. At

230 *Benjamin Benson (1818–?)*

these meetings, collections were made to help Brown return to Canada, where he would be safe from recapture.[30] More mysteriously, a 'B. Benson lectured on American slavery in Whitney in November of the same year. He was described as being from Long Island.[31] In December 'B. Benson, a man of Colour from America' lectured in the temperance hall, Leighton Buzzard in Bedfordshire'.[32] Overall, the venues were small, and the newspaper coverage was scant and brief, with none of the positive adjectives being used to describe Benson's performances. Benson may have had a thrilling life story but neither the audiences nor the newspapers seemed to be aware of it. Throughout the next few years, Benson continued to lecture on slavery. He sometimes spoke alongside the Rev. Edward Mathews, a Baptist minister who was an agent of the American Baptist Free Mission Society.[33] In May 1854, Mrs Elizabeth Doyle recorded in her diary that 'Benjamin Benson a black man' had visited Crimplesham School rooms to talk about the 'horrors of slavery'.[34]

Ireland

Around this time, Benson met Jonathan Revel, who had introduced the Band of Hope, a temperance movement aimed at young persons, into Ireland in 1856.[35] It was at Revel's invitation that Benson travelled to Ireland in the summer of 1858. In August of that year, Benson attended a meeting of the Band of Hope and Temperance Association in the Joymount Presbyterian Church in Carrickfergus. Referred to as 'the Rev. Mr. Benson, a coloured man', his address to the children was received warmly:

> The audience were especially well pleased with the splendid style in which Mr. Benson related several amusing anecdotes concerning his own experience and knowledge of the evils of intemperance, and gave ample evidence of their pleasure by their hearty applause.[36]

These comments suggested that Benson had had his own struggles with alcoholism.

A few days later, Benson lectured in the Second Presbyterian Church in Carrickfergus, but this time on American Slavery. The church was full and he was well received. Although the lecture was entitled, 'The Horrors of American Slavery', Benson's description of the system was at variance with the graphic descriptions of cruelty given by other former slaves. He informed the audience that:

> the slave's complaint was not, as is generally supposed, hard labour, or bad food, or clothing. On the contrary, he said, the slaves were both well fed and clothed, and as to labour, he said there were men in England and Ireland who worked harder than any slaves do. The complaints they do make were that they got nothing for their labour, and that they were deprived of liberty.[37]

In response to a question, he stated that *Uncle Tom's Cabin* 'was a very fair representation of the system'.[38] Those listening to Benson's lecture, however, might have got the impression that the horrors of slavery had been exaggerated.

In October, Benson lectured to the Total Abstinence Society in Armagh. When he was introduced, the chairman, Mr Weir, compared, 'the horrors of slavery and the great evils resulting from intemperance'. Benson was received with 'hearty cheering'. He then gave 'a slight sketch of his life; his knowledge of the system of slavery ... contrasting the degradation it produced with that which was seen in connection with drunkenness'.[39] In regard to temperance, Benson's 'speech was interspersed with numerous interesting anecdotes, and was attentively listened to throughout'.[40] Given Benson's interest and skills, it was not surprising that towards the end of the year he was appointed the first agent of the newly formed Irish Temperance League, his main mission being to form county associations throughout the country.[41] He was subsequently described as 'the coloured evangelist, preacher and temperance agent'.[42] Although Benson appeared to have had no contact with them previously, the committee included two leading Dublin abolitionists, James Haughton and Richard Allen.[43] Unlike Father Mathew's movement, which had been preeminent in the 1840s, this new association had Protestant roots and outreach. Moreover, its formation coincided with a Protestant religious revival, centred in Ulster, which benefitted Benson and other evangelical preachers.[44] Consequently, Benson's appointment combined his passions of religion and temperance. He may not have been a clergyman, but Benson out-preached his ordained colleagues in terms of his devotion to religion and temperance.

Benson's first year as a temperance agent was very successful; in the first three months he visited 30 towns and villages in the north of Ireland.[45] By the end of his first twelve months, he had formed 18 auxiliary societies, giving 40 lectures and holding 224 public meetings.[46] In June 1860, Benson was invited to speak at a temperance festival in Jersey. He had agreed to give only four lectures, explaining that he was too busy to give any more. The organizers were confident that his presence would 'draw large crowds'.[47] In August, Benson gave a number of lectures in Dublin.[48] Around this time, he made a decision to leave Belfast and move to the capital city permanently. The reasons are not fully clear but it appears that regardless of Benson's intense schedule of lectures in Ulster and the positive reception he received, the income to the Society was less than expected. Towards the end of 1860, therefore, Benson relocated to Dublin.[49] At the beginning of January 1861, Benson along with Revel, held a large temperance meeting in the Metropolitan Hall in Dublin. Benson was warmly greeted. His only reference to his origins was in his opening statement that, 'no one would have expected in past times that an Ethiopian would stand on a platform to address enlightened Irishmen and Englishmen upon a subject like temperance. But so it was'.[50]

Despite having employment as an itinerant agent, Benson continued to give occasional lectures on slavery, but usually in small venues. He claimed that he wanted to end slavery and drunkenness.[51] The following newspaper report from Clones provided a rare amount of detail on the content of the lecture and the man presenting it:

A lecture on the present condition of slaves in America, and the evil effect of slavery on the free people of colour, was delivered in the Wesleyan

232   *Benjamin Benson (1818–?)*

Church, Farnham-street, on Wednesday evening. Mr Benson, a gentle man of colour, and one of the accredited agents of the Irish Temperance League, who delivered similar lectures and others on temperance in the neighbourhood of Clones several days last week. The admission was free, and the attendance was large and respectable.[52]

In these and other descriptions, the evangelical Benson was apparent; the meeting starting and ending with prayers, while hymns were sung throughout. Although little was said of the content of the lecture, a rare insight was provided into Benson's appearance:

Mr Benson is very intelligent-look negro, apparently of almost unmixed African blood. He speaks English with considerable fluency, and his lecture was characterised by much genuine eloquence, a thorough acquaintance with his subject, and was met in retaining the unwavering attention of his hearers.

Yet again, no reference was made to his personal life story. Although admission was free, collections were made at end of each meeting to defray the expenses of the speaker.

For the next few years, Dublin remained Benson's home base, but he lectured extensively throughout the country and occasionally in Britain, where he was described as the 'agent to the Dublin Total Abstinence Society'.[53] During the summer of 1861, Benson lectured on temperance in the Irish Midlands, including in Athlone, Moate, Clara and Tullamore. The result was that 'not a few' took the pledge.[54] In late 1862, Benson spent some weeks in County Cork, lecturing in the city and county.[55] Cork had been the home of Father Mathew, the famous 'Apostle of Temperance', who had died in 1856. The movement there had been languishing for some years and it was hoped that Benson's presence would revive it.[56] In October, one of Benson's lectures was advertised as being on slavery and temperance but on the evening of lecture, it was announced that it would only be on latter theme and that Benson would give a separate lecture on slavery. The smallness of the audience was attributed to poor publicity. Again, some insights were offered into his lecturing style 'sincere and an earnest advocate ... and makes less use of declamation than of ascertained facts and statistics, from which draws reflections, the justice of which cannot be denied'. In the course of the lecture, Benson did use his knowledge of slavery as a benchmark for viewing drunkenness averring:

he had seen the slaves sold in the market and all the misery that could be inflicted upon human beings by slavery; but the effects of drunkenness were, in his opinion, worse than those of slavery. It was in the interest of the slaveowner to feed his slave with wholesome and nutritive food, to lodge him in a dry and somewhat comfortable place, and to keep his body in vigorous health; but drunkenness deprived a man of wholesome food, of comfortable lodging, and health. He never saw so much misery among slaves as he saw in Spitalfields and St. Giles's; and the greater part of the hardships suffered by the people of these places was attributable to drink.[57]

Benson also argued that the Famine of 1847 would not have happened if grain had not been used to make intoxicating liquors, as there would have been enough bread to feed everybody, 'from the Queen to her meanest subject'. Benson was praised for making so many cogent arguments in favour of sobriety.[58]

In a lecture delivered in Connaught a few months later, Benson again made a comparison between temperance and slavery, telling his audience:

We may talk about slavery in America, and pity the poor n—r who is the chattel of his white master, but the drunken slaves of this vice are far more deserving of sympathy. Both are bad, and a disgrace to human nature, but the drunkard is the most pitiable of the two. The slaves do not live in such hovels or in half the misery and degradation of the drunkard of this free and enlightened land.

Benson referred to the war raging in America, a country which he said was 'dear to his heart, and he had no doubt it was also dear to the hearts of the generality of the Irish', but 'the wicked system of slavery had brought a curse upon that fair, fertile, and prosperous country'. Unusually, he talked about his earlier life, saying that he had travelled in 'India, China, the Cape of Good Hope, Canada, the States, and the most remote parts of the world', and everywhere had encountered Irishmen. The bulk of the long lecture, however, focused on temperance and Benson peppered it with 'many amusing and interesting anecdotes'. At the end of the meeting, the audience was called on to sign the pledge.[59] Benson's impact within only a few years of moving to Ireland was evident in publicity for a meeting to be held in Bray, near Dublin, in March 1863, at which Benson was one of the speakers. A leading temperance Journal referred to him as a man 'who is so well known throughout Ireland as a temperance lecturer'.[60]

In 1864, Benson and his wife, of whom little is known, opened a coffee shop in Dublin. They did so on behalf of the Temperance League as a way of raising funds, coffee being regarded as a good alternative to alcohol.[61] The committee explained:

We are turning the coffee room at the Temperance Hall, Dublin, into a good dining depot on this plan. A number of us have taken shares of £1 each, and sufficient capital will thus be raised to fit up the place thoroughly, and make it most commodious and comfortable. Mr. B. Benson, a man of colour, who is well known as a Temperance lecturer, will be manager of it, and Mr. and Mrs. Benson are well qualified to conduct it with ability, and so as to give satisfaction. This will be a superior plan I believe, to any system of collecting funds.[62]

234 *Benjamin Benson (1818–?)*

The mention of Benson's wife in this context was deliberate, 'when advertising these positions, the league often called for a husband and wife to apply together'. By doing so, they were promoting morals that they also held dear, namely family values and social respectability.[63] Benson's more grandiose ambitions quickly became apparent. Although it commenced as a coffee shop, the premises were shortly afterwards described as a temperance coffee 'palace and restaurant'. Demonstrating Benson's marketing skills, an advertisement in a local newspaper provided an insight into the range of foodstuffs available on the premises:

> The city coffee palace, and TEMPERANCE REFRESHMENT ROOMS. DUBLIN TOTAL ABSTINENCE HALL, 2, MARLBOROUGH-STREET. LIST OF FARES. BREAKFASTS, LUNCHES, DINNERS. Coffee ... 1*d*. per Cup. Tea ... 1*d*. Cocoa ... 1d. Steak ... 4*d*. Chop ... 3*d*. ... Large ... 4*d*. Rasher Bacon ... 3*d*. Ham ... 3*d*. Herring ... 1*d*. Soup ... 1*d*. per Bowl. Vegetables ... 1*d*. Puddings, Tarts, Eggs, etc. BENJAMIN BENSON, Proprietor.[64]

Despite this additional responsibility, Benson continued to lecture. In May 1864, he spoke in a Protestant Hall in Longford, where he was described as the 'celebrated champion of temperance'. The Rev. R.J. Card who introduced Benson commenced by commenting on the restaurant in Dublin, saying that 'first-class victuals were to be obtained, at prices considerably less than they got at Hotels'. Benson then spoke about the evils of drinking but followed his lecture by introducing the new addition to his repertoire—a magic lantern. He used it to show images of the Royal Family, which greatly pleased the audience.[65]

By 1865, Benson had extended his business interests in Dublin and was now the proprietor of the Leopold Temperance Hotel at 13 Lower Abbey Street.[66] An advertisement in the *Irish Times* informed readers that he would 'continue to manage his old refreshment rooms'.[67] The following year, his advertisements notified his 'numerous friends and patrons' that he would be adding refreshment rooms to the hotel, similar to those that he had managed before, and which had been 'daily crowed to excess'.[68] It seemed at this point that Benson had parted ways with the Irish Temperance League. His mentor, Revel, was now in New York, lecturing on temperance.[69] Throughout 1865 and 1866, the Dublin newspapers carried multiple advertisements regarding the Hotel, which appeared to be thriving. In early May 1866, keeping both himself and his business in the public eye, Benson placed prominent advertisements in various Dublin newspapers informing, 'his numerous customers that the business in Marlborough street has entirely moved to 13 Lower Abbey-street where he can accommodate his kind patrons with everything that can be desired'. He further promised that, 'a reading room will be fitted up for their comfort'.[70]

It was surprising then, that concurrently with Benson's business expansion, legal Petitions were being presented against him in his capacity as 'proprietor of the temperance hotel and restaurant'.[71] Both news of the expansion and news of the legal action were carried on the same front page of the *Freeman's Journal*, as was notice of an auction:

> George Fitzgerald *v.* B. Benson
> On this day the premise on Lower Abbey-street. The defendant's interest in the lease held for a period of 44 years at an annual rent of 40 pounds. The above premises know as Leopold Dining Rooms have been recently fitted up at an outlay of £250. Terms at sale to commence at 12 o' clock. Richard Martin, High Sherriff. J.C. Bennett, Auctioneer.[72]

Things then moved rapidly and unfavourably for Benson. In September 1866, the Dublin newspapers carried the following:

> City of Dublin, W. Ward *v.* B. Benson
> TO BE SOLD BY public AUCTION, by virtue of her Majesty's writ of *fieri facias* in this case on T0-M0RROW (Wednesday), the 19 September, 1866, at the defendant's Interest in and to all that and those the House and Premises, 13 LOWER ABBEY-STREET, known as the Leopold Dining-rooms, held for a term of 50 years from the 1st June, 1865, at the yearly rent of £40. The Premises are insured in the Royal Fire and Life Insurance Company for £500, and the premium paid up to the 21st July next. A sum of £250 has been expended by the defendant in fitting up said house. Terms at sale. To commence at One o'clock. Richard Marlin, Esq., High Sheriff. JAMES C. BENNETT; Auctioneer, Upper Ormond-quay.[73]

A few days later, two lines appeared in the *Freeman's Journal* stating, 'Benjamin Benson, of 13 Lower Abbey-street, city of Dublin, proprietor of a temperance hotel and restaurant' would appear in the Insolvent Debtor's Court on 5 December.[74] The news of Benson's bankruptcy appeared in an October edition of the Boston *Pilot*.[75] Bankruptcy had increased in Ireland in the wake of the Famine necessitated the passage of the 1857 'Irish Bankrupt and Insolvent Act'.[76] Benson was tried under this new legislation in December 1866.[77] From this point, Benson disappeared from public view. In the 1867 Dublin Street Directory, Benson did not appear under merchants or hoteliers. Moreover, 13 Lower Abbey Street was no longer a temperance hotel, but, ironically, was occupied by Thomas Snow, a wine merchant.[78] What happened to Benson is not known.[79]

Conclusion

A history of the temperance movement, published in 1892, wrote, 'Mr. Benson, a man of colour, formerly in slavery, and an ardent, useful worker in the cause, had been employed as the first itinerant lecturer for the League'.[80] For almost eight years, Benson had been the poster boy of the Irish temperance movement. His fall from grace was unexpected, spectacular and total, especially for one

236 *Benjamin Benson (1818–?)*

who positioned himself as being pious and devoted to good works. What happened to him afterwards? Did the man who had apparently survived many terrible incidents in his life survive bankruptcy?

For a short period, Benson appeared in public with other more famous abolitionists. If true, Benson's life story was unique and extraordinary. He had been enslaved twice, the first time within the British Empire and the second time in America, yet, when he appeared on stage, he clearly preferred to pray and preach rather than talk about abolition or his own personal story of enslavement. His road to Ireland, and becoming a temperance agent, was also unexpected, but it demonstrated clearly that evangelism, rather than abolition, was his motivation. When called on, he did talk about his life in enslavement although, unlike other lecturers, he played down its horrors and his own suffering. Despite the publication of his narrative and his intermittent appearances on abolitionist stages, occasionally with fellow black abolitionists, Benson made no lasting impact on the movement or it seems, on his colleagues. In Ireland, however, he found his true métier and passion—temperance and God.

Benson's involvement with his fellow abolitionists was fleeting, and although he resided in Dublin for several years, he did not appear to link up with the Webb family, the go-to place for so many former slaves. His speeches and comments on slavery are also puzzling. Despite having a melodramatic story—and audiences loved to hear of daring tales of escape—it appears that he never recounted his adventures, the ones that had made Welch take pity on him and publish his thrilling biography. Furthermore, when he did speak of enslavement, it was in the abstract, and he was always anxious to show that slaves were well cared for. The cruelties that he claimed had been inflicted on him—deliberate scarring, branding and whipping—did not feature in his sanitized accounts. This absence was particularly puzzling giving the claims he had made to Welch about his own mutilation. The passion and pain that distinguished so many abolitionist lectures, were absent from his. With no corroboration other than Welch having briefly befriended and believed Benson's story (before Benson disappeared out of his life), how accurate were Benson's claims? Self-invention was not unusual amongst black abolitionists, and often necessary for survival, but Benson's public stance on his own personal enslavement and on slavery in general are peculiar.

Strangely, for a man who had such a public existence, little is known about Benson's private life. His wife is referred to fleetingly regarding managing the Dublin coffee shops. Who was Mrs Benson and what became of her following her husband's bankruptcy?[81] Although the memoir provided precise details regarding Benson's place and time of birth, multiple places were given in newspaper reports and Benson never addressed the issue directly himself. When in Belfast, for example, Benson was described as being from Delaware.[82] Did he deliberately obfuscate his origins? Was the story that he had told Welch true? What happened to the money that he earned through his lectures and his businesses? And what happened to Benson after 1866? Of all the formerly enslaved people to visit Ireland, Benjamin Benson remains the most enigmatic and perplexing.

Notes

1 There is another enslaved man with the same name, Benjamin Benson, a free black man who lived in Delaware, was kidnapped and sold as a slave to John Thompson of Greensboro. In 1817, aided by local Quakers, Benson filed a suit against Thompson to reclaim his freedom. In 1820, he was declared a free man.

2 Benson is mentioned twice in passing in Peter Ripley's *The Black Abolitionist Papers, 1830–1865* (Chapel Hill: University of North Carolina Press, 1987), pp. 285, 290, but no information is provided except for his name.

3 In Ripley's comprehensive list of Black Abolitionists in the British Isles, he states that Benson was present from 1851 to 1858, his subsequent move to Ireland being missing, p. 571.

4 Introduction by Frank Laumer and Andrew G. Welch, *A Narrative of the Early Days and Remembrances of Oceola Nikkanochee, Prince of Econchatti* (Gainesville, FL: LibraryPress@UF, 2017), p. xl.

5 Laumer, 'Introduction', Welch *Narrative of Oceola*, pp. xv–xxxix.

6 Andrew G. Welch, *A Narrative of the Life of Benjamin Benson, Who Was Born a Slave in the Island of Bermuda, Emancipated by the English Government, August 1 1838, and Subsequently Sold as a Slave in the United States of America* (London: by the Author, 1847), p. iv.

7 Ibid. p. 8.

8 Ibid., p. 1. At the time of Emancipation, there were three slaveholders with the name of Davenport in Bermuda, who received compensation for the loss of their slaves, namely, George F. Davenport (3 enslaved, £27-19-11 compensation); John Davenport (4 enslaved, £48-19-11 compensation); Sarah F. Davenport (5 enslaved, £47-2-10 compensation), Legacies of British Slave Ownership: www.ucl.ac.uk/lbs/search/.

9 Ibid., p. 9.

10 Ibid., pp. 11–13.

11 Ibid., p. 24.

12 Ibid., p. 27.

13 Ibid., p. 32.

14 Ibid., p. 34.

15 Ibid., p. 10.

16 The letter included some family information, saying that 'our dear sister', Sally, was dead of fever, while her husband John was doing well, 'as far as worldly matters are concerned. No other family members are mentioned. See, letter dated 24 March 1846, from Anthony Benson, in Welch, *Narrative*, pp. 6–7. Anthony's letter was in response to one sent by Benjamin the previous November.

17 Welch, *Narrative*, p. 35.

18 Ibid.

19 Welch, *Remembrances of Oceola*, p. xliii.

20 'Introduction', Christine Kinealy, *Frederick Douglass and Ireland. In His Own Words* (London: Routledge, 2018).

21 'Testimonials', Welch, *Narrative*.

22 Ripley incorrectly dates Benson's time in England to be from 1851 to 1858, Ripley, *Black Abolitionists*, p. 571.

23 'Anniversary of West Indian Negro Emancipation', *Morning Advertiser*, 2 August 1851; Liberator 5 September 1851.

24 'Anti-slavery Soiree', *Oxford Chronicle and Reading Gazette*, 9 August 1851.

25 'Anniversary of West Indian Emancipation', *Morning Advertiser*, 2 August 1851.

26 Ibid.

27 R. J. M. Blackett, 'Fugitive Slaves in Britain: The Odyssey of William and Ellen Craft', in *Journal of American Studies*, vol. 12, no. 1 (Apr. 1978), pp. 41–62, 45; Ripley suggests that Benson was 'probably' one of the founders, p. 290. The group

238 *Benjamin Benson (1818–?)*

was to give support to former slaves who had fled to England for sanctuary. It appears to have been short-lived.

28 'Dunstable', *Bedfordshire Mercury*, 9 August 1851.

29 'American Slavery', *Morning Advertiser*, 26 August 1851.

30 Ibid., 8 September 1851.

31 No title, *Oxford Chronicle and Reading Gazette*, 8 November 1851.

32 *Bucks Chronicle and Bucks Gazette*, 13 December 1851.

33 Thomas Mathews, *Anti-Slavery Labours in England of the Rev. Edward Mathews, Agent of the American Baptist Free Mission Society* (Bristol: Thomas Mathews, 1855); the two men lectured together in the Myrtle Street Baptist Church in Liverpool in early 1858, *Anti-Slavery Advocate*, 1 March 1858.

34 'Slavery and Abolition: The Norfolk Connections': www.bbc.co.uk/norfolk/content/articles/2007/02/27/abolition_norfolk_overview_20070227_feature.shtml.

35 Frederic Smith (ed.), *The Jubilee of the Band of Hope Movement: A Jubilee Volume* (United Kingdom Band of Hope Union, 1897), p. 59.

36 'A meeting of the Band of Hope and Temperance Association', *Banner of Ulster*, 21 August 1858.

37 Ibid., 31 August 1858.

38 Ibid., 'Slavery', 31 August 1858; 'On Tuesday Evening Last', *Belfast Weekly News*, 4 September 1858.

39 'Total Abstinence', *Armagh Guardian*, 15 October 1858.

40 Ibid.

41 'Irish Temperance League', *Banner of Ulster*, 21 December 1858. Benson was not the first formerly enslaved person to lecture in the province. In 1856, the Belfast Temperance Association employed Joseph Woodhouse to speak on temperance to school children in the town. See, Elizabeth Malcolm, *Ireland Sober, Ireland Free: Drink in Nineteenth Century Ireland* (Dublin: Gill and Macmillan, 1986), p. 163.

42 Frederick Sherlock (ed.), *Fifty Years Ago: Or, Erin's Temperance Jubilee* (Belfast: W.E. Mayne, 1879), p. 25.

43 Ibid., p. 26.

44 Orfhlaith Campbell, 'A Platform Upon Which All Could Unite? Temperance in Ulster and the Irish Temperance League, 1858–1914'. PhD thesis, The Open University (2017), p. 245.

45 Ibid.

46 Ibid., p. 115; *Portadown News*, 5 November 1859; 'Temperance Meeting', *Coleraine Chronicle*, 24 March 1860.

47 'Temperance Festival', *Jersey Independent and Daily Telegraph*, 30 June 1860.

48 *Warder and Dublin Weekly Mail*, 18 August 1860; 'Lecture', *Irish Times*, 22 August 1860.

49 Sherlock, *Fifty Years Ago*, p. 25. Sherlock said that the reason for the move was that the League did not do well in Ulster despite the initial flourish. By 1860, few subscriptions were coming in that—but this seems unlikely.

50 'TEMPERANCE DEMONSTRATION', *Dublin Daily Express*, 4 January 1861. The lecture was on 3 January 1861.

51 'A Lecture on Slavery', *Cavan Observer*, 13 October 1860.

52 Ibid.

53 'Gosforth Temperance Society', *Whitehaven News*, 6 August 1863.

54 'Speaker Visits Athlone', *Westmeath Independent*, 10 August 1861.

55 Malcolm, *Ireland Sober*, p. 178.

56 *The Irish Temperance League Journal*, vol. 1, p. 15.

57 'TEMPERANCE LECTURE', *Southern Reporter and Cork Commercial Courier*, 10 October 1862.

58 'Ibid'. The reporter references the Famine incorrectly, giving 1837 as the date.
59 'TEMPERANCE LECTURE', *Connaught Watchman*, 3 January 1863.
60 *The Irish Temperance League Journal*, vol. 1, p. 58.
61 Campbell, 'A Platform', p. 108.
62 *The Irish Temperance League Journal*, vol. 1, p. 15.
63 Campbell, 'A Platform', p. 112.
64 *Dublin Daily Express*, 23 April 1864.
65 'Longford Temperance Society', *Longford Journal*, 7 May 1864.
66 *Irish Times*, 14 October 1865.
67 Ibid., 18 July 1865.
68 Ibid., 7 February, 14 February, 21 February, 28 February 1866. Many other Dublin newspapers carried similar advertisements.
69 'JUVENILE MASS MEETING; Temperance Gathering at the Cooper Institute— Half-Yearly Meeting of the American Temperance Alliance—Over Three Thousand Children Present—Interesting Exercises', *New York Times*, 19 November 1865.
70 *Freeman's Journal*, 3 May 1866.
71 Ibid.
72 Ibid.
73 Ibid., 18 September 1866.
74 'Insolvent Debtors', *Freeman's Journal*, 29 September 1866; *Dublin Evening Post*, 29 September 1866; *Dublin Daily Express*, 29 September 1866. The *Boston Pilot* also covered information of Irish insolvent debtors.
75 *Pilot*, vol. 29, no. 43, 27 October 1866. Only after 1861, could insolvent debtors claim bankruptcy.
76 See also, Kevin Costello, *The Irish Shopkeeper and the Law of Bankruptcy 1860– 1930* (Dublin: UCD Research Depository, 2016). Available at: hdl.handle.net/10197/ 9408.
77 'Bankruptcy and insolvency', *Dublin Daily Express*, 5 December 1866.
78 Thom's Directory for 1867 lists the occupier at number 13 as being 'Thomas Snow, wine merchant', p. 1345. Nor does Benson appear under the listing for merchants and traders, p. 1621, nor under hotels, p. 1808.
79 A debtor's prison had opened in Dublin in 1784, on Green Street. Generally, debtors remained incarcerated until their debts were paid.
80 P. T. Winskill, *The temperance movement and its workers. a record of social, moral, religious, and political progress*, vol. iii (London, Glasgow, Edinburgh, and Dublin: Blackie & Son, Limited, 1892), p. 70.
81 A Catherine Benson (née Brogan of Drumgun in Donegal), wife of Benjamin Benson, was recorded under 'Deaths' in the *Boston Pilot* of 25 October 1873, but there is nothing to suggest she is the correct person.
82 D. Ritchie, *Isaac Nelson: Radical Abolitionist, Evangelical Presbyterian, and Irish Nationalist* (Liverpool University Press, 2018), p. 116.

10 Sarah Parker Remond (1826–1894)
'Remarkably feminine and graceful'

On 29 December 1858, Sarah Parker Remond sailed from Boston to Liverpool. Samuel J. May, a fellow abolitionist, was aboard the same vessel. They arrived in the English port on 12 January 1859. Sarah was following the route taken by many earlier black abolitionists. Her gender, however, marked her as different. At Liverpool, the two Americans would part ways, with May travelling on to Italy. Sarah intended to return to America after one year spent lecturing in Ireland and Britain. However, she never crossed the Atlantic again but chose to spend the remainder of her life in Europe.

Early life

Sarah Parker Remond was born in Salem, Massachusetts in 1826 to John and Nancy (neé Lenox) Remond, two freeborn blacks.[1] She was the second youngest of ten children and 16 years younger than her brother, Charles Lenox Remond. Sarah later explained that Nancy had instilled in her children the ethos of discipline and hard work:

> to enable them to meet the terrible pressure which prejudice against color would force upon them ... but it did not—could not, fit us for the scorn and contempt which met us on every hand when face to face with the world, where we met a community who hated all who were identified with an enslaved race. While our mother never excused those who unjustly persecuted those whose only crime was a dark complexion, her discipline taught us to gather strength from our own souls; and we felt the full force of the fact, that to be black was no crime, but an accident of birth.[2]

As a free black person, Sarah was able to learn to read and write. Yet, despite her family being prosperous, because of her colour, she received limited schooling, later admitting, 'My strongest desire through life has been to be educated'.[3]

Before travelling to England, Sarah was known and respected on the abolitionist circuit, being regarded as a 'zealous and able anti-slavery lecturer'.[4] She was an active member of the Salem Female Anti-Slavery Society, and, in 1856, she had been appointed an agent for the American Anti-Slavery Society.[5] She claimed

Sarah Parker Remond (1826–1894) 241

to have accepted the position reluctantly as, 'A defective education, and a pro-slavery atmosphere, are not the best incentives for such a purpose'.[6] Nonetheless, with her brother Charles, she undertook a lecture tour in New York. In May 1858, the siblings spoke at a Woman's Rights Convention in New York City. They were 'both honoured for their remarks in favour of women's suffrage'.[7] Sarah's decision to undertake this public role appears to have been encouraged by fellow woman abolitionist, Abby Kelley, suggesting a network of support amongst female abolitionists.[8] Sarah's feistiness and willingness to challenge public opinion had been evident in 1853, when she had been refused a ticket and ejected from a public theatre in Boston, on the grounds of her colour. During the process, she had been pushed down the stairs. Sarah took the matter to the press and the police. In this instance, the theatre was fined and made to pay the legal costs. Sarah's decision to publicize the issue was a tactic that she would use again, with good effect, when she was in the United Kingdom.

Travel to the United Kingdom

Sarah's stated decision to travel to the United Kingdom was 'that I might for a time enjoy freedom, and I hoped to serve the anti-slavery cause at the same time'.[9] Although associated with William Lloyd Garrison, she chose to travel as an independent abolitionist, who was not affiliated to any society. Nonetheless, William Lloyd Garrison, founder of the *Liberator*, announced her travel plans in the American abolitionist press, pointing out:

> She is much esteemed and beloved by all who know her; and she will carry with her the best wishes of them all for her safety and happiness. I can easily imagine how unutterable must be her feelings on finding herself, for the first time in her life, in a land where this dreadful spirit of caste is quite unknown; where she can travel on terms of equality with others, with no liability to insult or ostracism; where she will be estimated according to her moral worth and intellectual force. It will be to her almost like a resurrection from the dead, and to that extent a foretaste of the heavenly state.[10]

Sarah, however, demonstrating her agency and media acumen, had already self-publicized her journey. A letter written to 'Dear Friend' on 18 September 1858, appeared in the British abolitionist press in November. Sarah commenced by describing the success of her recent lectures, which had all been full. She then explained her determination to undertake the journey even though, 'I dread starting for many reasons. I do not fear the wind nor the waves, but I know that no matter how I go, the spirit of prejudice will meet me'.[11] In relation to a suggestion that she should contact the people who had welcomed her brother almost 20 years earlier, she wrote, 'It is a long time since he visited England, so I shall gather up all my courage, and endeavour to depend on myself'.[12] It was a bold statement and one that summed up the tenacity of the intrepid Miss Remond.

242   *Sarah Parker Remond (1826–1894)*

In January 1859, former slave William Powell, who was residing in Liverpool, informed the Boston abolitionists that 'our devoted collaborators' had arrived.[13] The sea crossing, however, had taken its toll and Sarah 'had suffered much from sickness on the voyage, but she was recovering her strength, remaining, in the meantime, the guest of Mr. Robson'.[14] Robson, who resided in Warrington, a town about 20 miles from Liverpool, had been introduced to Sarah by Garrison, when he had visited America the previous year.[15] During her short stay in the north of England, Sarah gave her first lecture on non-American soil in Liverpool. The chairman, the Rev. W.H. Channing, introduced her to the large and enthusiastic audience, alluding to her gender, and the unusualness of hearing a woman speak in public:

> as one who, with her family, had long taken a deep and most active part in the abolition movement—as a countrywoman who had consecrated her best gifts to the cause of heroism and humanity, and as a woman, without at all feeling that they sacrificed their womanhood, appeared on the public stage to rehearse a fictitious tragedy. There was no reason why a woman should not speak in public of a real tragedy, and on a subject upon which she so deeply felt.[16]

Sarah's lectures were covered by the local press, which reported that she had, 'a clear and musical voice … has at her command a great flow of language … is never at a loss for words admirably calculated to express her sentiments'. All of which was more impressive as she used no notes. At the end of her lecture, she was 'rapturously' applauded.[17]

Towards the end of January, Sarah spoke in Warrington, to an overflowing audience, for approximately 90 minutes, sitting down to 'enthusiastic cheering'.[18] Sarah gave two more lectures; the final one was shorter than the previous two because she was not feeling well. At her final lecture, the audience consisted only of women who presented her with a watch inscribed, 'Presented to S.P. Remond by English-women, her sisters, in Warrington. February 2nd, 1850'. Remond appeared to be overcome by this gesture, saying that a testimonial was unnecessary as, since being in England, 'I have been removed from the degradation which overhangs all persons of my complexion …. I have received a sympathy I was never offered before'.[19] While in Warrington, Sarah also received an Address signed by 3,522 people from the town, including the mayor and the local Member of Parliament. Moreover, an amount of $100 was raised on behalf of Garrison's Anti-Slavery Society.[20] This disinterested, generous gesture again marked Sarah as different from some of her male counterparts who collected sums of money clearly for their own benefit.

Ireland

When Sarah's health recovered, she travelled to Ireland, where her brother Charles had spent many happy months in the early 1840s. The decision to go there was her own, Samuel May explaining to Webb, 'she went impelled by her own soul, alone'.[21] Sarah, like so many abolitionists before her, was hosted by

Sarah Parker Remond (1826–1894) 243

Richard and Hannah Webb in Dublin. Richard was delighted with this latest visitor, writing to May:

> She is very clever—the most so of all the coloured people I ever met, except Douglass, and is a much more sensible and thoroughgoing person than he. Except Wendell Phillips, I don't think you could have a more effective agent here. She is far less crotchety than Wright or Pillsbury. She has more common sense—and her devotion to the cause and its friends is thorough. We like her very much.[22]

May, in turn, was delighted to hear Sarah praised, telling Webb, 'it gratifies me exceedingly, as it will all our friends'.[23]

Sarah's first lecture in Ireland was given in the Rotundo Rooms in Dublin on the evening of 11 March. She was there at the invitation of the Dublin Ladies' Anti-Slavery Society. Admission was free.[24] The Lord Mayor of Dublin was unable to attend but sent a letter of support. James Haughton, the chairperson, introduced Sarah by 'commenting on the due influence of the ladies in forwarding every noble and laudable purpose'. The audience was described as 'crowded and influential'.[25] When Sarah stood up she was 'hailed with long and repeated plaudits'.[26] The *Freeman's Journal* informed its readers that Sarah's appearance 'is remarkably feminine and graceful, coupled with a quiet, dignified manner, a well-toned voice and pleasing style of enunciation'.[27] Sarah commenced by talking about the cruelty and immorality of slavery, explaining to those present:

> She stood there to advocate and inculcate, with all the energy of her soul, the truly noble and upright principles avowed, taught, and defended by the 'ultra-abolitionists' of the United States, the true friends of freedom and of the human race. She would invite her audience to imitate the energy, raw zeal, the courage, and the perseverance of that noble band of philanthropists—the very salt of the American people—whose exertions and sacrifices in the cause of human liberty, and for the utter abolition of slavery in America, it was impossible to exaggerate, but which would become matter of history, yet to be read and dwelt on with pride by their descendants (cheers).

Sarah explained that on a daily basis, 'odium, obloquy and hatred' were aimed at those who spoke on behalf of enslaved people. Despite this, they were making progress, albeit slowly. When praising Garrison, she said that his name 'should ever be spoken of with respect by every lover of freedom'. Like many other Garrisonians, she was critical of the role of the Christian churches whose response to appeals for support had been met:

> At first with coolness, apathy, and indifference—then with covert sneers and injurious calumny; and at last by open and vindictive opposition. Such had been the reception 'religion' (so called) had accorded to devoted effort in the cause of human freedom (groans).

244　*Sarah Parker Remond (1826–1894)*

Sarah was also critical of the newly established Republican Party, who claimed they did not support slavery, yet did nothing to end it. She then, 'in a strain of impressive eloquence', 'pointedly dwelt on the possible mission of Great Britain in aiding to overthrow the iniquitous slavery system and showed how compatible such aid was and would be with the spirit of true liberty'. It was a clear statement of her mission overseas. She explained her motivation to advocate the cause of enslaved people was not, 'merely because she was identified with them in complexion (an accident of which she was proud), but because they were men and women'.[28] Sarah concluded by returning to a topic that she had made her own—enslaved women—appealing:

> ... to women on behalf of the female slave, the most deplorably and helplessly wretched of human sufferers. Of all who dropped and writhed under the infliction of this horrible system, the greatest sufferer was defenseless women (hear.) For the male slave, however brutally treated, there was some resources: but for the woman slave, there was neither protection nor pity.

Sarah provided several examples of the abuse of enslaved women, which included reading extracts from Harriet Beecher Stowe's 'admirable book', *Uncle Tom's Cabin*. She finished by saying:

> She could go on thus furnishing a thousand painful instances, enforcing her appeal to women on behalf of the female slave, but she felt she need not; for when were the women of this country ever backward in the cause of humanity? (cheers).

After singling out two women for praise—Elizabeth Fry and Florence Nightingale—Sarah sat down to 'enthusiastic plaudits'.[29] Her lecture was followed by speeches by several men, including Richard Webb, who passed resolutions condemning slavery. Haughton returned to what was a common theme at such meetings, namely, the role of the Irish in America, saying:

> ... he had often experienced a sinking of heart when he came to consider the conduct of Irishmen who had made America their home (hear, hear). He had asked himself, how it was that they had become in America as inconsistent and so false to the principles of freedom which they so earnestly advocated at home (hear, hear)? and why it was that men who had been accustomed to prize liberty as the first and dearest of human blessings, could, in another land, range themselves on the side of the most brutal and relentless foes of human freedom?

A thank you speech was made by a former professor of political economy at Trinity College, William Neilson Hancock, who described the lecture as 'masterly'. He also referred to Sarah's gender:

Sarah Parker Remond (1826–1894)   245

They were accustomed in this country to hear lectures on public subjects delivered by men only; but this was a great moral question. Miss Remond had identified herself with it, and had made it her own (cheers). It was also a question involving a mission of kindness and humanity, a question coming completely within woman's province.[30]

Hancock then warned that pro-slavery sentiment was growing on both sides of the Atlantic, concluding:

> This resolution expressed their grateful appreciation of Miss Remond's able elucidation of the character of American slavery, and her not less than masterly delineation of its baneful easels on the social condition of an entire people (hear). Miss Remond thought anxiously and felt deeply in connection with this subject. She had spoken as she felt, and they had all seen how she had succeeded ... it is incumbent on all who abhor a system as inhuman and unchristian as slavery, to make known its real character, and we therefore rejoice in the promulgation of such information as we have heard this evening, and cordially recommend Miss Remond to the assistance and good offices of all who desire to promote a sound anti-slavery sentiment in these kingdoms. Therefore, the friends of humanity, who longed for the extinction of America's slavery, would recommend that Miss Remond's lectures should he delivered in every town and city throughout the land.[31]

Sarah was also praised by the Rev. Dr Foley, Professor of Irish in Trinity College, who said that 'his heart had been stirred within him by the language and sentiments of the splendid address they had heard from the lips of Miss Remond'. The final words of the evening, however, belonged to Sarah:

> MISS REMOND came forward, amidst renewed plaudits, and said she wished to thank them all for the kind attention with which they had followed her through the course of a necessarily lengthened address on a painful subject (cheers). If by any means she could have conveyed the spirit as well as the matter of this meeting to America, the slaves would take courage and rejoice in renewed hope of freedom, and their advocators would work with renewed vigour, and the slaveholders would believe that the hour of retribution was at hand, that they saw '*the handwriting on the wall*,' and that their unholy power was passing away for ever (loud cheers).[32]

It was a hard-hitting denouncement of slavery and of those who allowed the system to continue. It was also a triumphant and accomplished performance, reminiscent of the appearances of Frederick Douglass two decades earlier. Sarah's long and impassioned speech was reported in full by newspapers in Ireland, Britain and America.[33] The *Freeman's Journal* described her as 'a lady of colour, a native of Salem, Massachusetts, and a particular friend of Mrs. Beecher Stowe, the popular authoress of *Uncle Tom's Cabin*'. It stated that although the audience

246 *Sarah Parker Remond (1826–1894)*

had come to hear a lecture, it had proved to be 'an able, eloquent, and comprehensive address'.[34] The *Liberator*, which covered the lecture over two editions, referred to Sarah as 'our respected friend and efficient coadjutor'.[35]

Sarah's second Dublin lecture was in the theatre of the Mechanic's Institute, three days later. The room could hold 1,000 people. Seats for non-members cost 1*s* or 6*d*.[36] Again, Sarah was introduced by Haughton. And again, the local press was fulsome in their praise:

> She commenced her discourse with all the ease and grace to be expected from an accomplished lady, and the narrative of the wrongs and injustice heaped upon the section of the human family to which she belongs was given with a force and natural truthfulness beyond the reach of art.—In all she said, there was something so persuasive, so femininely beautiful and subdued, that made her appear in the estimation of her hearers (though a free woman) one who felt the wrongs and oppression of her whole tribe, and who, in her own person, endured, through sympathy, their slavery and degradation.[37]

Demonstrating an understanding of where she was speaking and of Ireland's history, Sarah spoke of the poverty and degradation of the peasants 'with painful precision'. However, just as O'Connell and Douglass had repeatedly done, she made an important distinction between poverty, oppression and slavery, pointing out, 'all these were as nothing to the absence of the possession of freedom, and the knowledge of being the chattel property of another, to be bought and sold'. Other topics covered by Sarah included the Underground Railroad and the Fugitive Slave Act. She concluded, 'amid loud and long continued cheering'.[38]

Sarah's third Dublin lecture took place a week after her first and was again held in the Rotundo. In order to cover expenses, there was a charge of 6*d*.[39] Despite this, the audience was 'numerous and respectable'. Sarah commenced by expressing:

> ... in clear and forcible language, the evils of slavery, which she stated to be a stain on the American nation, and which one day would, unless abolished, draw down upon the slave owners and advocates of the system a fearful retribution. She denounced slavery in all its forms as contrary to every principle of justice and of morality, and to all doctrines of Christianity, which the Americans themselves professed.[40]

Yet again, she 'was listened to with marked attention throughout and was repeatedly and warmly applauded'.[41] While in Dublin, in addition to her public role in giving lectures, privately, Sarah was working to persuade Richard Whately, the Anglican Archbishop, to issue a statement condemning slavery. To this end, she was invited to his Palace to meet him, leading Samuel May to opine: 'If Archbishop Whately should be led to <u>utter a bull</u> against slavery, and all abettors of slavery, especially in the "churches," it would not be an "Irish bull," but one which would tell with mighty effect in this country'.[42] Since the

Sarah Parker Remond (1826–1894)   247

1830s, Whately had been a consistent opponent of slavery in the West Indies and latterly in America.[43] Regardless of the meeting, no further action appears to have been taken by the Archbishop.[44] Sarah's secret mission, however, provided further evidence of her importance as a transatlantic emissary of the abolition movement.

Following Dublin, Sarah travelled south, staying there for almost a month and lecturing three times in Waterford, once in Clonmel, and twice in Cork. Everywhere, she was received 'with respect and cordial hospitality'.[45] Sarah's visit to Waterford took place in early April 1859, she giving all three lectures in the Town Hall. To cover costs, there was an entrance fee: one shilling for the front seats, six pence for the back seats and three pence for the gallery. Children were half price and there was a special price for families and schools.[46] Sarah's first lecture was on 5 April, and her second, two days later. At her first appearance, she thanked her audience 'for their kind manifestations towards her', adding that 'though she was 3,000 miles from home, and from loved ones, yet she felt that a common sympathy should unite all'.[47] In a speech that lasted for 90 minutes, Sarah spoke about the evils of slavery, the corruptness of American politics and the hypocrisy of American churches. She also described the prejudice against free blacks and the particular suffering of women slaves. Sarah repeatedly drew 'enthusiastic cheers' from the audience.[48] Her lecture was favourably covered in the local press, the *Waterford Mail* reporting:

> Miss Remond, a coloured lady, who is travelling in this country, delivered a very interesting lecture on American Slavery in the Large Room, Town Hall, on Tuesday Evening. The Chair was taken by Dr. Elliott, who introduced her to the meeting with an appropriate address. Miss Remond is an excellent female lecturer, one of the best we have heard. Her manner is gentle, yet impressive; her countenance intelligent and animated, her language pure; her diction copious, and her thoughts elevated.[49]

During her second lecture, Sarah referred to the wars then taking place in the United States, with the Seminoles in Florida and with the Mexicans in Texas. She contested that these conflicts were the result of the greed of the slaveowners. She warned that unless they were stopped, 'the rights not only of the free Blacks, but also of the Whites, would be menaced'.[50] Dr Elliott, who again chaired the meeting, agreed with Sarah's comments and introduced a resolution condemning slaveowners for also encroaching on the rights of Irish emigrants to the United States. It was passed unanimously. Sarah had planned to give a third lecture in Waterford four days later, but it was announced that 'her health does not seem quite equal to it'. The meeting concluded by hoping that Sarah would get another change to lecture before she leaves the city.[51]

Sarah's final meeting in Waterford also took place in the Town Hall on 13 April. The meeting had been convened, 'in consequence of the wish that been expressed by some those who had attended Miss Remond's previous meetings that they might have the opportunity of expressing their feelings on the

248   *Sarah Parker Remond (1826–1894)*

subject of American slavery'.[52] Sarah, 'in her usual forcible and eloquent style, exposed the evils of American slavery'. She informed those present that

> she was not there as the representative of any society; she came to expose the wrongs of the people of colour; and not alone the people of colour, for the liberties of the white were now as menaced just as much as those of the coloured race by the inert aging despotism of the slave owners in the south.[53]

Again, she spoke critically of the position of the American churches, stating:

> the slaveowners had such a control of the pulpit, and dreaded so much the voice of public opinion that they removed every preacher who dared to open his mouth for the slave; and she was sorry to say that the preachers of the different sects of churches were too ready to succumb to this tyranny; and religion in America was too ready to take the side of the oppressor.[54]

The Rev. Thomas Wishere, a Baptist minister in Waterford, objected to her comments, stating that:

> she was perfectly justified in expressing and condemning the apathy and wicked silence of the northern churches; but if her just indignation led to the utterance of extreme views upon the personal character of the members of these churches, or the late religious revivals in America, she alone was accountable for them.

Joseph Fisher, who was part of a leading local Quaker family with a long tradition of anti-slavery activities, spoke in support of Sarah and her mission, asking:

> Are the people of Waterford to be silent? Are the people of Ireland to withhold their voices? Forbid it, Heaven. Erin stands with her face to the west, the nearest land to the New World, and every wave that surges from our shore, and rolls in thunder along the coast of America, shall say from us to the slave-owner—'Free your slaves' (cheers).[55]

Fisher concluded with a resolution that was unanimously adopted:

> That this meeting has listened with much interest to the eloquent appeal made by Miss Sarah Remond on behalf of the people of colour; and in returning her its sincere thanks, desires that her labours may enlist the sympathies and the energies the British public in the cause of the abolition of slavery.[56]

From Waterford, Sarah travelled to Clonmel where she lectured on the same evening in the Mechanics' Institute. The local press reported that she 'proceeded

Sarah Parker Remond (1826–1894) 249

with a heart-appealing oratory, a graceful simplicity of language, and an easy fluency to delineate the wild longings for liberty inherent in human nature'.[57] Throughout her talk, she was 'frequently and enthusiastically applauded'. A resolution was passed praising Sarah's 'spirit-stirring lecture'. A second resolution was passed wishing her 'God-Speed in her praiseworthy and humane efforts to enlist Christian sympathy'. The spirit of unanimity was spoilt by a dissenting pro-slavery voice in the audience, leading the chairperson to chastise him, averring:

> In this Emerald Isle of ours, where we were always the advocates, and when we dearly praise the name of liberty (applause) he was exceedingly sorry that there should be even one dissentient voice to the sentiments which they had all heard given expression to during the evening. He remembered the saying of the celebrated Franklin, which he had read of in his boyhood, 'where liberty dwells, there is country', and when his feelings were harrowed—when his blood curdled in his veins on hearing the recital on the horrors of slavery, he felt in his heart all the glorious attributes of freedom, and experienced consequently a still greater sympathy for the hapless victims of serfdom and oppression (loud applause). He was sorry, he repeated, to hear that expression of dissent, for feelings other than sympathy for the unfortunate race of which the lecturer treated, would be disgraceful to any man who prized liberty in his heart (loud applause).[58]

In the context of Ireland, such an incident was unusual, but it was a reminder to Sarah that the road to abolition was not always smooth.

Sarah did not remain long in Clonmel but, following her lecture, travelled 60 miles south to Cork. There, she gave two lectures. A small notice in a local newspaper stated that, 'We understand that Miss Remond, the well-known and highly gifted lecturer on American Slavery, intends visiting our city'.[59] Subsequent advertisements in the local newspapers provided a tantalizing glimpse of Sarah's visit:

> MISS S. REMOND,
> AN American Lady, who Lectured with great Success in several Towns in England (and recently in Dublin to large Audiences) will give Two Lectures in the IMPERIAL HOTEL—on FRIDAY EVENING, April 15. Eight o'clock, and on SATURDAY, April 16, at Two o'clock, on NEGRO SLAVERY in the UNITED STATES, which is rapidly becoming White Slavery.
> Admission 6*d*.[60]

A separate newspaper report explained the relevance of Sarah's presence in the city:

> Negro slavery is now attracting the attention of the civilised world. Their 'peculiar institution' is still sustained in the slave holding States by all the aids and sanctions of tradition, religious teaching, and legislative enactment.

250 *Sarah Parker Remond (1826–1894)*

Various agencies, however, are fast producing a powerful reaction against slavery. Its abolition in many countries, the popularity of Mrs. Beecher Stowe's writings, and the influence of eloquent lecturers, are combining to weaken and undermine this terrible evil. We understand that Mrs. S. Remond, an American lady, has acquired a distinguished reputation as a lecturer on this subject; and she is to lecture here at the Imperial Hotel, this evening, and on tomorrow, we anticipate that her efforts in the cause of humanity will be rewarded by the attendance of a numerous auditory.[61]

Sarah lectured twice in the Imperial Hotel, which had opened in 1816. In 1845, it had been the site of a lecture by Frederick Douglass.[62] Because her lectures had been arranged at short notice, unusually, the size of the audience was 'limited'. The second lecture was chaired by Francis Beamish, a Member of Parliament and President of the Cork Anti-Slavery Society. Sarah told the audience that every hour the division between the northern and southern states was becoming wider: that even if slaves were well fed and well looked after, slavery was wrong, with its core principle being, 'thinking, reasoning beings, daily sold by an auctioneer; women and children struck off to the highest bidder'. She asked those present to 'give to the cause your sympathy and moral suasion'.[63] This lecture marked the end of Sarah's tour of the south of Ireland. In the final four days, she had given four lectures in three different locations. It had been a punishing schedule, but Sarah had won many new friends, and energized old ones in the cause of abolition. Sarah's hardline attack on organized religions had proved to be contentious. Yet, like Douglass before her, she had repeatedly returned to the topic, at the risk of alienating some of her audience. Not only was Sarah a gifted lecturer, she was a fearless one.

The American abolitionist press followed Sarah's progress in Ireland with clear pleasure:

Her visits have given great satisfaction both in public and in private. Her style of public speaking is easy, even, low voiced, yet clear-toned, fluent, and remarkably free from stumbling or hesitation; whilst in the social circle, from her ample information, readiness, good temper, and fidelity to the object of her mission, she is eminently suited to promote the interests of the antislavery cause. We have heard some amusing incidents of conversations in which she has been engaged.[64]

Sarah's time in Ireland coincided with the arrival of a group of six political refugees from the Italian states, who were known as the Neapolitan exiles. They arrived in Queenstown (Cobh) on 6 March, and their appearance was reported throughout the world.[65] At this stage, Italy was seeking both unification and independence. Webb sent a long letter to the *Anti-Slavery Standard* describing the 'warm sympathy' that all Irish people felt towards them. From Ireland, five of the exiles travelled to England where they were met by thousands of well-wishers, and hosted by William Gladstone.[66] The hospitable Webb played his own role in their journey

Sarah Parker Remond (1826–1894)   251

from Cork to London, he arranging to meet them on their arrival in Dublin and look after them until they could sail. Sarah was one of a group organized by Webb to greet the exiles and it proved to be a happy encounter. Webb wrote:

> I have seen fairer faces; but I have never seen one brighter, more intelligent, or better 'lit up', than was hers that whole evening. The exiles were deeply interested on being informed that she was here as the representative of a down-trodden race in a land of liberty, and their advocate before the British people. The Dacha di Cabellino begged to be presented to her, and desired that she should be informed how, as one who had himself suffered from cruel oppression, he entirely sympathized with her and her noble mission. Several of the exiles handed her their cards, and the Baron Poerio gave her some lines with his autograph. In reply to repeated expressions of grateful acknowledgment for attentions which we were only too glad to offer, we could only give the true reply that we felt honored and obliged by the opportunity.[67]

While studying in London in 1861, Sarah would meet with Giuseppe Mazzini, a leader of Italian unification.[68] They subsequently became friends and he provided Sarah with letters of introduction when she moved to Italy in 1866. As a result of these exiled acquaintances, Sarah became a fervent supporter of Italian independence and unification.[69] Sarah's support for Italy's struggle showed that her desire for reform extended beyond simply wanting equality for her own people. Like Douglass, she believed that oppression needed to be fought wherever it existed.

Return to the United Kingdom

In early summer 1859, Sarah returned to England, spending time in Bristol with the Estlin family, before travelling to London. Sarah's return to England coincided with a revival in anti-slavery activity by fellow supporters of Garrison. In June 1859, the London Emancipation Committee had been formed by the Rev. W. H. Bonner, Minister of Trinity Chapel in Southwark, who was alarmed that pro-slavery feeling appeared to be increasing in the country, especially in localities that traded with the slave states. William Craft was present at the inaugural meeting, and George Thompson was elected chairman, suggesting the society's affinity with Garrison. A resolution was unanimously adopted that:

> The committee would embrace this as its first opportunity to express to Miss Sarah P. Remond, now present, its congratulations on her arrival in this country, and on the success, which has attended her labours in England and Ireland during the last five months. The committee would also assure her of their earnest sympathy with her in her antislavery efforts and would bespeak for her the confidence and co-operation of the friends of the slave in every place she may hereafter visit during her stay in this country.[70]

252   *Sarah Parker Remond (1826–1894)*

With her usual graciousness, Sarah responded, 'It may not be inappropriate on my part, as the representative of three millions and a half of slaves in the United States, who cannot speak for themselves, to say—I thank you'.[71]

The revival in anti-slavery sentiment was matched by a renewed effort to win support for the Southern States as America moved closer to a civil war. The pro-slavery forces had sent their own emissary to Britain, Madame Lola Montez, who attracted large audiences in London. Despite her Spanish sounding name, Montez was Irish-born, her real name being Eliza Gilbert. Moreover, she was dancer and performer, renowned for her bohemian and unconventional lifestyle.[72] The lecture was reported in full in the Irish press, including several provincial papers.[73] During it, Montez had assured her listeners that:

> the anti-slavery cause in the United States was dying out, and that the once magnificent gatherings in New York during the anniversary week had dwindled down to three or four poor miserable beings with sour, crotchety faces, in some dark room ... The abolition lecturers were most of them 'unsuccessful preachers', and gained no admission into respectable or wealthy families, but put up at the houses of benevolent and simple-minded Quakers.

She went on to describe slaves as, 'fat, lazy, and contented. They pitied the condition of the white labourers of this country'. She warned the British public 'against intermeddling in the domestic affairs of their brethren across the Atlantic'.[74] Sarah was present at the meeting and, at the end, handbills were distributed advertising her upcoming lecture, when she would respond to the 'mis-statements' made by Montez.[75]

On 15 June, Sarah spoke in the Music Hall on Bedford Square in London to respond to Montez. Her skill at negotiating both sides of the anti-slavery movement was evident in that both Louis Chamerovzow, Secretary of the British and Foreign Anti-Slavery Society, and George Thompson, a Garrisonian, attended and both praised her work. Sarah was introduced by Chamerovzow, who said that he had much pleasure in performing the duty, as he had long been an admirer of her and her brother.[76] This collaboration with the rivals of Garrison suggested that Sarah was able to transcend the long-standing divisions. Sarah commenced by saying that she was:

> the representative in the first place of four millions of human beings held in slavery in a land boasting of its freedom—of 400,000 persons of colour nominally free, but treated worse than criminals. She was the representative also of that body of abolitionists in the United States, reproachfully called Garrisonians; an epithet, however, which she deemed it an honour to appropriate.

Injecting a feminist note, Sarah added that she spoke in particular on behalf of her own sex, pointing out that each enslaved woman was 'the victim of the

Sarah Parker Remond (1826–1894)   253

heartless lust of her master, and the children whom she bore were his property'.[77] It was a theme to which she would return frequently.

Sarah briefly referred to the fact that she had recently attended a lecture in defence of slavery, explaining that, 'She had listened with indignation, a few nights before, to the statement that the slaves were happy and contented'. This was untrue, but she did not allow it to distract her from her own message, especially when it came to championing the cause of enslaved women. Despite the occasion and the topic, Sarah again charmed the audience and she was listened to with great attention, much interest and 'great applause'.[78] A resolution proposed by Thompson was passed in her honour:

> That this meeting welcomes to the metropolis of England Miss Sarah P. Remond, and would assure her of their deep sympathy with her in her labours on behalf of the slave; of their detestation of the system the evils of which she has so ably exposed; and of their earnest wish that her future labours, on both sides of the Atlantic, may be crowned with success.[79]

The lectures by the two women were watched with interest on the other side of the Atlantic. The *Anti-Slavery Advocate* was unequivocal in declaring who had presented the better argument. Describing Montez as 'that lady of unenviable reputation', they claimed that her audience had been comprised of 'Americans of the true Democratic breed'. In contrast, Sarah had been listened to 'with great interest' and 'we have great reason to be grateful for Miss Remond's visit, and to anticipate that the best results will flow'.[80]

In London, Sarah stayed with the Crafts, William now supporting his family 'respectably by the sale of some useful articles of which he is the importer or inventor'. One of the visitors to meet Sarah was the much-respected long-term opponent of slavery, Lord Brougham.[81] She was also reunited with Samuel May and they lectured together on several occasions, before his return to the United States at the end of October 1859.[82] In August, both Sarah and Ellen Craft had attended an anti-slavery meeting in London to celebrate the twenty-fifth anniversary of West Indian Emancipation but neither woman had been called on to speak. The *Anti-Slavery Advocate* attributed this to innate sexism, and:

> the prejudices of some influential persons present who were unable to see that the platform is not more unbecoming the proper sphere of highly endowed women than the throne, the editorial chair, the merchant's office, the author's study, and many other positions in which the English people are accustomed to see woman occupied with credit to herself and benefit to her fellow creatures.[83]

Harriet Martineau, an admirer of Sarah, was more forthcoming, believing:

> It was done by the intervention of that kind of abolitionism which can make very fine speeches on liberty and slavery, but cannot free itself from

254 *Sarah Parker Remond (1826–1894)*

some bondage or other which stops it short, and makes it stop everybody it can reach. The objection to inviting Miss Remond to speak was that 'it might raise the much-vexed question of Woman's Rights'—an excuse too low and too irrelevant to need any exposure here.[84]

More pleasantly, part of Sarah's time in the United Kingdom coincided with Frederick Douglass's return, he having left America peremptorily to avoid arrest following John Brown's unsuccessful insurrection. Occasionally too, Sarah and Douglass lectured with English abolitionist, Wilson Armistead, the author of 'A Tribute for the Negro'.[85] Douglass was warmly received by audiences, many recalling his earlier visit. An element of sexism was evident, however, when the two American abolitionists lectured together. Following a joint lecture in Leeds, Douglass's speech was reported in full (receiving almost 3,000 words of coverage), while the only reference to Sarah's lecture was that, 'Miss Remond having also addressed the meeting, resolutions condemnatory of slavery were adopted'.[86] Similarly, a report in a local newspaper provided a full account of Douglass's speech, but only briefly noted that, 'Miss Remond having also addressed the meeting, the following resolution was carried on the motion of Alderman Richardson'.[87] It was a blatant example of the deep-rooted sexism with which even the most talented of women abolitionists were confronted.

Sarah had intended to stay away from home for only one year but, in October 1859, she enrolled as a student at the Ladies' College in Bedford Square, London, thus 'availing herself with ardor of her long-sought opportunity for reaping the advantages of a liberal education'.[88] She studied there for two years, while still giving anti-slavery lectures. Robson, who had remained in touch with Sarah after she left Warrington, informed Garrison that:

> You will be glad to hear that our dear friend, Miss S. P. Remond, is spending her Christmas vacation from College Studies in lecturing in Scotland and the north of England.[89]

In Britain, therefore, Sarah was able to become the student that she had long aspired to be.

The passport controversy

While in Britain, Sarah desired to travel to the Continent. At the end of 1859, rather than going home as had been her original plan, she applied for a visa to visit France; while visas were not required for entry to Britain, they were necessary for travel to the Continent. The right to American citizenship and to holding a passport were issues that confronted all travelling black abolitionists. The issue had been further complicated by the Supreme Court's Dred Scott Decision of 1857, which had ruled that black people, whether free or enslaved, could not be citizens.[90] Even though Sarah had an American passport, she was refused by George Mifflin Dallas, the United States Ambassador at the Court of St. James,

Sarah Parker Remond (1826–1894)   255

on the grounds that she was person of colour. Sarah, in turn, repeatedly challenged the decision, doing so in the most public of manners, in order to use the incident to throw a spotlight on American prejudice. The press in both Ireland and Britain gave the unfolding drama extensive coverage, they all expressing sympathy and outrage on behalf of Sarah.[91] Even the provincial Irish press published Sarah's correspondence in full:

> DISABILITIES OF AMERICAN PERSONS OF COLOUR. The following correspondence has been published by a London contemporary: 6, Grenville Street. Brunswick Square, W.C., December 12. Sir,—I beg to inform you that a short time since I went to the office of the American Embassy to have my passport vised for France. I should remark that my passport is an American one, granted to me in the United States, and signed by the Minister in due form. It makes the fact—that I am a citizen of the United States. I was born in Massachusetts. Upon my asking to have my passport vised at the American Embassy, the person in the office refused to affix the visa, on the ground that I am a person of colour. Being a citizen of the United States, I respectfully demand my right that my passport be vised by the Minister of my country. I am desirous of starting for the Continent, so I must request an answer at your earliest convenience.—I remain, Sir, your obedient servant, Miss Sarah P. Remond.[92]

Dallas, the minister at the centre of this dispute, had served as the Vice President of the United States between 1845 and 1849. His name might have been familiar to Irish readers because, at the beginning of 1847, he had convened a mass meeting in Washington on behalf of the victims of the Irish Famine. He also belonged to the pro-slavery wing of the Democratic Party.[93] On a day-to-day basis, the matter was handled by Benjamin Moran, the Assistant Secretary in the Legation, who doubted the authenticity of Sarah's Passport. Tellingly, in his private journal, he variously described Sarah as a 'darkie' and a 'Mulatto with woolly hair'.[94] The Irish press followed the unfolding saga and shared each stage of it in full detail with their readers, including this response from the Embassy:

> I am directed by the Minister to acknowledge the receipt of your note of the 12th inst., and to say, in reply, he must, of course, be sorry if any of his countrywomen, irrespective of colour or extraction, should think him frivolously disposed to withhold from them facilities in his power to grant for travelling on the Continent of Europe, but when the indispensable qualification for an American passport, that of the 'United States' citizenship, does not exist—when, indeed, it is manifestly an impossibility by law that it should exist—a just sense of his official obligations under instructions received from his Government as long ago as July, 1816, and since then strictly conformed to, constrains him to say that the demand of Miss Sarah L. Remond cannot be complied with.[95]

256 *Sarah Parker Remond (1826–1894)*

Sarah, undaunted, challenged the decision, again using the columns of the newspapers to do so:

> The purport of your communication is most extraordinary. You now lay down the rule that persons free-born in the United States, and who have been subjected all their lives to taxation and other burdens imposed upon American citizens, are to be deprived of their rights as such, merely because their complexions happen to be dark, and that they are to be refused the aid of the Minister of their country, whose salaries they contribute to pay.[96]

In a long editorial entitled 'FIE! ON AMERICA', the *Belfast Morning News* questioned why Sarah was granted a passport in America, yet refused a visa in London, pondering that:

> there is objection to colour at the American embassy in London, and none at the American Foreign Office at Washington, or that the ocular perception of Mr. Dallas on that subject differs from that of Mr. Cass, one would suppose that this coloured lady had surmounted any difficulty which American diplomacy could throw in her way. Such, it appears, was her own opinion, and she comes to England accordingly in the faith of Mr. Cass's passport.[97]

Interest in the visa controversy did not subside and continued to be covered by newspapers on both sides of the Atlantic, with the British and Irish press overwhelmingly siding with Sarah. The backlash against the American Embassy led Moran to despair that even Queen Victoria was opposed to their actions.[98] The issue was resolved by the British Home Office issuing Sarah with a Passport.[99] The incident and Sarah's willingness to stand up to the American authorities and to use the media to do so, demonstrated that, like Equiano, Douglass, Garnet, Wells Brown and others, Sarah was not only fearless, but sophisticated in her ability to garner publicity for her cause. It also demonstrated what Sarah and other black abolitionists had been saying for years, their fight was not simply to end slavery, but to expose and end prejudice against colour.

After she returned from France, Sarah continued with her studies. Although a student, she continued to be a presence in the transatlantic abolitionist movement. In November 1860, as America descended towards a civil war, Sarah was one of a group of powerful women abolitionists who called for a peaceful ending to slavery:

> We earnestly and cordially entreat all who love our native land in sincerity, whether Europeans or Americans, to unite with us more numerously and more generously than ever, to meet the demands of a period of crisis unparalleled in the history of our country, new, indeed, in the history of the world. For when before has it ever happened that freedom has been sought from among a dominant people for a down-trodden one, on so grand a scale as this?[100]

In August 1861, an Irish newspaper reported that 'Miss Sarah P. Remond (a lady of colour) read an interesting paper on American Slavery and its influence in Great Britain'. During the course of her lecture, she stated, as she had done on a number of earlier occasions, that war was the inevitable outcome of slavery.[101] Sadly, in April of that year, a civil war had commenced in America when secessionist forces attacked Fort Sumter in South Carolina. Sarah watched the tragedy unfold from 3,000 miles away.

Sarah's continuing impact was evident in that in March 1861, the *English Woman's Journal*, featured her in their series, 'Lives of Distinguished Women'.[102] They explained that they had chosen her because her life story, 'possesses a special interest just now that all eyes are turned towards America, and to the great struggle which had its origin in the efforts made to liberate colored people'.[103] They added:

> We will now let Miss Remond tell her own tale, only observing that she is probably personally known to many of our readers, having during her present stay in England made a tour as an antislavery lecturer through some of our principal towns, where her spontaneous appeals were listened to with respect and even with admiration.[104]

Sarah again showed herself to be a champion of the oppressed everywhere when she publicly defended the insurgents who had taken part in a rebellion in Jamaica in 1865. It prompted Sarah to write to the English press protesting against attacks on black people in London following the uprising.[105] She thus inserted herself into the debate, but took a diametrically opposing view to that of Samuel Ringgold Ward, a fellow black abolitionist.[106] The conservative Ward, who was living in Jamaica at the time, had sided publicly with the authorities and their brutal suppression of the rising.[107] For Sarah, what had happened in Jamaica was an example of systemic racism, she arguing that since the start of the Civil War prejudice against black people in England and elsewhere had increased. Consequently, the insurgents in Jamaica were being punished because of their complexion. Again, Sarah demonstrated fearlessness in her public defence of her people. The following year, Sarah was one of the 1,500 women who signed the first women-only suffrage petition, making her possibly the only black woman to do so.[108] In this regard, she mirrored what Douglass had done when he signed the Declaration of Sentiments in 1848.

Later life

In the summer of 1866, Sarah moved to Florence to study medicine, auditing classes for a year before taking an entrance exam and enrolling as a medical student.[109] She proved to be a good scholar, qualifying as a physician.[110] Sarah had only been a few weeks in Italy when she felt compelled to write to the London press in relation to prejudice on both sides of the Atlantic. Regarding post-War Reconstruction, she believed that 'Fresh hatred seems to have been

258   *Sarah Parker Remond (1826–1894)*

added to the old stock'. She believed that similar prejudice was now evident in Britain, exemplified in the writings of Thomas Carlyle, who 'has special claims to the gratitude of negro haters on both sides of the Atlantic'.[111] Her dismal view of the deepening of prejudice following the Civil War, offers an explanation as to why Sarah showed no interest in returning to the United States. Her contact with other abolitionists continued, however. During her studies, Garrison visited Europe and Sarah returned to London in June 1867 to attend a public breakfast in his honour. Her friends William and Ellen Craft were also present.[112]

Sarah remained in Italy where she was successful in her chosen profession as a doctor. Occasionally, however, she encountered both overt and covert racism. Elizabeth Buffum Chase, long-term abolitionist and women's rights activist, visited Florence in 1873 and met with Sarah. She recorded in her memoir:

> In the afternoon, we all went, by invitation, to take tea with Mrs. Putnam, Sarah Remond and Miss Sargent. We had a fine visit. Sarah Remond is a remarkable woman and by indomitable energy and perseverance is winning a fine position in Florence as a physician, and also socially; although she says Americans have used their influence to prevent her, by bringing their hateful prejudices over here. If one tenth of the American women who travel in Europe were as noble and elegant as she is, we shouldn't have to blush for our countrywomen as often as we do.[113]

In April 1877, Sarah married an Italian man, Lazzaro Pintor, an office worker from an affluent family. Sarah was 50 and Pintor was 44. At this point, the unconventional Sarah did something conventional—following marriage, she gave up her work and became a housewife.[114] Sarah and her husband, and Sarah's sisters, Caroline Remond Putnam and Maritcha Remond, all lived in Rome.[115] A rare glimpse of the covert racism that Sarah continued to face was provided by two English Quaker sisters who resided in Rome and who had witnessed Sarah on her wedding day:

> March 17, 1878. Tell Madgie that the P___s were there with their black aunt. She was a bride, having just married an Italian, and wore her bridal dress of grey silk. It must have been very trying for Mrs P____. People came up to question her. One Italian said, *'Chi e quell' Africana?'* It appears that she is very clever, and a female doctor. She was taken up a good deal in London by different people who were interested in negroes. I think she lived with the Peter Taylors. She has given lectures. I went to sit on the sofa with her, to the amusement of Franz, who cannot rise above her appearance. Dr Baedtke was much impressed to think that anyone has had the courage to marry her, and said, 'In that I should have been a coward'.[116]

In early 1887, Frederick Douglass visited Sarah in Rome, accompanied by his second wife, Helen.[117] Douglass, like Sarah, had chosen an interracial marriage, an action that was illegal in some American states. In his diary, Douglass

Sarah Parker Remond (1826–1894) 259

wrote that he was going to have lunch with the Putnams at their hotel, explaining 'the older Mrs Putnam was formerly Miss Caroline Remond, sister to the later Charles Lenox Remond'. He added:

> We met here she that I knew forty years and more ago as Miss Sarah Remond, and also Maritcha Remond … It was very delightful to meet this charming circle of Massachusetts people a way off here in the city of Rome. Like myself the Remond sisters with [the] exception of Caroline, have grown quite old, but in all of them I saw much of the fire of their eloquent Brother Charles.[118]

Douglass also wrote to his friend Amy Post about the visit, explaining that the Remond sisters, like their brother Charles, 'detest prejudice of color and say they would not live in the U. States if you would or could give them America'.[119] It was a sad indictment on the land of their birth, and an observation made over 20 years after the Proclamation to end slavery had passed. Sarah never did return to the United States, but died in Rome in 1894, where she was buried.[120]

Conclusion

A biography of Sarah, published in 2017, which focuses on her time overseas, gives little mention to the months that Sarah spent in Ireland at the commencement of what she had planned to be a twelfth month lecture tour.[121] Significantly though, Sarah chose Ireland, which had so warmly welcomed her brother almost two decades earlier, to spend her early months overseas. There, she lectured in four very different locations and there, she honed her skills as a transatlantic lecturer. In Ireland also, as her brother had done many years earlier, she came to understand what freedom and equality meant. Further continuity was provided in that it was the Webbs, James Haughton and Richard Allen, who had hosted Charles Remond, William Garrison and Frederick Douglass, who also welcomed Sarah into the Irish abolitionist community.

Sarah was among the small number of abolitionists who did not return to the United States. She had arrived in England in 1859, intending to stay for a year, instead, she spent the second half of her life in Europe. There, she received the higher education she had always longed for, first in England, then in Italy. By so doing, she was challenging multiple stereotypes. Although Sarah followed in the footsteps of her equally famous brother, she carved a pathway that was uniquely her own amongst abolitionists. Like Charles, Sarah had no first-hand knowledge of being enslaved, but she had experienced prejudice against colour from an early age. Like her brother, Douglass and others, she realized that ending slavery would mark the beginning of a renewed fight to end racism. As the visa issue showed, she was willing to take on government officials at the highest level to expose prejudice and racism, and she did so with doggedness that was effective and energizing. As a result of this stand-off, Sarah's name became well known on both sides of the Atlantic. Moreover, it ended with a victory for her, which was as much a moral victory as a practical one.

260   *Sarah Parker Remond (1826–1894)*

Sarah's contribution both to the abolition movement and to the women's question was immense. By creating a feminist abolitionist agenda, she united the 'woman's question' and abolition together in a way that her male compatriots could not. Sarah personally experienced the double disadvantage of racial and gender inequality and she proved to be an effective champion on both issues. In Ireland and Britain, Sarah felt that she had escaped from racial prejudice, but she continued to be viewed through a gendered lens. Undaunted, she not only spoke out against discrimination, but her gender made her a particularly effective speaker on the abuse of enslaved women, a topic that some of her male counterparts avoided. Moreover, she was not afraid to tackle taboo subjects such as interracial rape and the sexual exploitation of enslaved women, especially those with mixed blood.

Sarah understood that women occupying public spaces were held to a higher standard than men, in terms of dress, demeanour and language. Again, she negotiated these challenges while delivering her message powerfully on behalf of her oppressed people, especially her enslaved and sexually abused sisters. Unusually, Sarah appealed directly to women in the audiences, asking them to be active on behalf of enslaved women, thus empowering themselves in the process. Her stories about the breaking up of enslaved families, about marriages between slaves being not allowed, and about how women preferred to take their own lives rather than be separated from their children, resonated with her female listeners who viewed the family unit as sacrosanct. Yet she delivered her uncompromising discourses in a way that was deemed to be feminine and appropriate, again demonstrating her skill as somebody who could negotiate the fine lines of acceptable and unacceptable behaviour. Sarah's call to a transatlantic interracial sisterhood was significant:

> As white and black women united around common causes, they displaced dominant norms, creating a counter narrative to patriarchy and antiblackness; women assumed agency and participated in social and political struggle as they resolutely worked against discrimination and reworked conceptualizations of gendered subjectivity.[122]

By calling on other women to join her to resist oppression, Sarah became a powerful agent of change.

During Sarah's time in Ireland, she gave some of her most mesmerizing speeches against enslavement. Her presence re-energized the Irish abolitionist movement and strengthened its transatlantic ties. For abolitionists on both sides of the Atlantic, the timing of her visit was important with a civil war within America appearing inevitable. As an articulate and talented black woman, Sarah provided a constant reminder of the cruelty and injustice of the system of slavery. As one recent biographer has written, her:

> female agency offered a new, distinct model of blackness, one of empowered and elaborated identity. In Europe, Remond reinvented herself as a representative of female versatility, activism and black acculturation.[123]

Sarah Parker Remond (1826–1894) 261

Sarah's long European journey had commenced in Ireland where, like a number of other black abolitionists, she found her own voice and experienced the transformative power of being treated as an equal. Regardless of the constraints imposed by her gender, Sarah showed herself to be more gifted than many of the male abolitionists in whose footsteps she followed. Moreover, in her chosen role as the transatlantic champion of enslaved women everywhere, her contribution to abolition and to social justice proved to be unique and truly groundbreaking.

Notes

1 A 1935 article on Sarah gives her year of birth as 1815 and says she was well educated at Salem public schools: Dorothy B. Porter, 'Sarah Parker Remond, Abolitionist and Physician', *The Journal of Negro History*, vol. 20, no. 3 (Jul. 1935), 287–93, p. 287.
2 'Lives of Distinguished Women', *English Woman's Journal*, vol. vii, no. 37 (Mar. 1, 1861).
3 Ibid.
4 'Letter from Miss Remond', *Anti-Slavery Advocate*, 1 November 1858.
5 Sarah claimed it was 1857, but it was probably the previous year, C. Peter Ripley (ed.), *The Black Abolitionist Papers, The British Isles*, vol. 1 (Chapel Hill: University of North Carolina Press, 2015), p. 441.
6 'Lives of Distinguished Women'.
7 Rosalyn Terborg-Penn, *African American Women in the Struggle for the Vote, 1850–1920* (Bloomington: Indiana University Press, 1998), p. 19.
8 Sirpa Salenius, 'Transatlantic Interracial Sisterhoods: Sarah Remond, Ellen Craft, and Harriet Jacobs in England', *Frontiers: A Journal of Women Studies*, vol. 38, no. 1 (2017), 166–96, p. 169.
9 Quoted in Sirpa Salenius, *An Abolitionist Abroad. Sarah Parker Remond in Cosmopolitan Europe* (Amherst: University of Massachusetts Press, 2016), p. 75.
10 'LETTER FROM MR. GARRISON. To the Editor of the Anti-Slavery Advocate', 28 December 1858, *Anti-Slavery Advocate*, 1 February 1859.
11 'Letter from Sarah Remond', 18 September 1858, reprinted in *Anti-Slavery Advocate*, vol. 2, no. xxiii (Nov. 1858), pp. 179–80.
12 Ibid.
13 William P. Powell to Maria Chapman, 21 January 1859, Claire Taylor, *British and American Abolitionists: An Episode in Transatlantic Understanding* (Edinburgh University Press, 1974), pp. 436–7.
14 'A letter from our friends William Robson, dated from Warrington, dated 16 January 1859', the *Liberator*, 4 February 1859.
15 'Letter from Sarah Remond', 18 September 1858, reprinted in *Anti-Slavery Advocate*, vol. 2, no. xxiii (Nov. 1858), pp. 179–80.
16 'MISS SARAH P. REMOND in Liverpool', the *Liberator*, 18 February 1859.
17 *Anti-Slavery Bugle*, 26 February 1859.
18 *Warrington Times*, 29 January 1859 reprinted in Ripley, *Abolitionist* Papers, pp. 435–40.
19 Ibid., *Warrington Times*, 5 February 1859, reprinted in Ripley pp. 445–6.
20 *Anti-Slavery Advocate*, vol. 2, no. xxxviii (Apr. 1859), p. 221.
21 Samuel May Jr. to Richard Webb, 22 May 1859, Available at: www.digitalcommon wealth.org/book_viewer/commonwealth:dv144x36f#1/1.
22 Webb to May, 3 May 1859, Taylor, *British and American Abolitionists*, p. 440.

262   *Sarah Parker Remond (1826–1894)*

23 May to Webb, 22 May 1859, Available at: www.digitalcommonwealth.org/book_
    viewer/commonwealth:dv144x36f#1/1.
24 *Freeman's Journal*, 10 March 1859, 11 March 1859.
25 'THE U.S. CONSTITUTION AND FUGITIVE SLAVE LAW', the *Liberator*,
    8 April 1859.
26 From the *Freeman's Journal* reprinted in the *Liberator*, 8 April 1859.
27 Ibid.
28 Ibid., 'MISS REMOND IN DUBLIN', 22 April 1859.
29 Ibid.
30 'Miss Remond's First Lecture in Dublin', *Anti-Slavery Advocate*, 1 April 1859.
31 'MISS *REMOND* IN DUBLIN', the *Liberator*, based on the reports in the Dublin
    Freeman's Journal and Anti-Slavery Advocate from London, 22 April 1859.
32 Ibid.
33 Ibid.
34 'Miss Remond's Anti-Slavery Lecture', *Freeman's Journal*, 15 March 1859.
35 'THE U.S. CONSTITUTION AND THE FUGITIVE SLAVE LAW', the *Liberator*,
    8 April 1859.
36 'DUBLIN MECHANICS' INSTITUTE' (advertisement), *Freeman's Journal*,
    12 March 1859. The Institute offered classes to the people of Dublin at the time of
    Sarah's lecture and, included in the same advert, 'The Classes in connexion with
    the Institute are now in full operation, under the direction of the following distin-
    guished Masters:—English, Mr. Ryan; Drawing, Mr. Dowling; French, under Mon-
    sieur DePontot; German, D. Schuitheis; Music, Mr. Rogers; Mr. Chamberlain; An
    Irish Class has recently opened under Dr. O'Brennan'.
37 'THE U.S. CONSTITUTION AND THE FUGITIVE SLAVE LAW', *Freeman's
    Journal* reprinted in the *Liberator*, 8 April 1859.
38 Ibid.
39 'LECTURE ON AMERICAN SLAVERY' (advertisement), *Freeman's Journal*,
    18 March 1859.
40 Ibid.
41 Ibid.
42 May to Webb, 22 May 1859, Available at: www.digitalcommonwealth.org/book_
    viewer/commonwealth:dv144x36f#1/1.
43 'Archbishop Richard Whately', *Compendium of Irish Biography*. Available at:
    www.libraryireland.com/biography/ArchbishopRichardWhately.php.
44 There is no mention of the meeting in his biography, Elizabeth Jane Whately, *Life
    and Correspondence of Richard Whately, D.D.: Late Archbishop of Dublin*, vol. 2
    (Dublin: Longmans, Green, and Company, 1866).
45 'MISS SARAH P. REMOND IN IRELAND', *Anti-Slavery Advocate*, 2 May 1859.
46 'American Slavery' (advertisement), *Waterford News*, 1 April 1859.
47 'Lecture on American Slavery', *Waterford Mail*, 9 April 1859.
48 Ibid.
49 Ibid., 'Lecture on American Slavery', 7 April 1859.
50 Ibid; 'Irish Temperance League', Belfast *News-Letter*, 12 April 1859.
51 'Lecture on Slavery', *Waterford Mail*, 12 April 1859.
52 Ibid., 'American Slavery' 19 April 1859.
53 Ibid.
54 Ibid. Because of her criticism of the American churches, Sarah was accused of
    being an 'infidel'; 'MISS SARAH P. REMOND IN IRELAND', *Anti-Slavery Advo-
    cate*, 2 May 1859.
55 History of Kinsalebeg Fishers of Pilltown: Available at: http://kinsalebeg.com/chap
    ters/fishers/fishers.html; American Slavery', *Waterford Mail*, 19 April 1859.
56 Ibid.

Sarah Parker Remond (1826–1894) 263

57 American Slavery, *Tipperary Free Press and Clonmel General Advertiser*, 15 April 1859.
58 Ibid.
59 *Cork Advertising Gazette*, 6 April 1859.
60 'Miss S Remond', advertisement, *Morning Advertiser*, 28 April 1859, *Southern Reporter and Cork Commercial Courier*, 14 April 1859; 'Miss S Remond', *Cork Constitution*, 14 April 1859.
61 'Negro Slavery—America—Public Lectures', *Southern Reporter and Cork Commercial Courier*, 15 April 1859.
62 See chapter on Frederick Douglass. The hotel has a plaque commemorating the visit by Douglass.
63 'Slavery in the United States', *Southern Reporter and Cork Commercial Courier*, 18 April 1859.
64 'MISS SARAH P. REMOND IN IRELAND', *Anti-Slavery Advocate*, 2 May 1859.
65 'The Neapolitan Exiles', the *Liberator*, 13 May 1859; 'The Neapolitan Exiles', *The Argus* (Melbourne, Australia), 10 June 1859.
66 Due to ill-health, Baron Toerio remained in Cork, 'The Neapolitan Exiles', the *Spectator*, 26 March 1859.
67 'THE NEAPOLITAN EXILES', From the *Anti-slavery Standard*, reprinted in the *Liberator*, 13 May 1859.
68 In 1859, a letter from Joseph Mazzini, then residing in London, had appeared in the *New York Tribune*, saying he was striving to end white bondage just as people in the U.S. were fighting to end negro bondage, 'Mazzini on Slavery', *Morning Advertiser*, 28 April 1859.
69 Salensius, *Abolitionist Abroad*, pp. 9–11.
70 The Anti-Slavery Advocate, vol. 2, no. 31, 1 July 1859.
71 'London Emancipation Committee', the *Liberator*, 1 July 1859.
72 Bruce Seymour, *Lola Montez: a life* (New Haven, CT: Yale University Press, 1996). Montez was alleged to have been the mistress of the former mistress of Ludwig I of Bavaria. She died aged 39, probably of syphilis. In the late 1850s, Montez's agent was journalist and writer, Charles Chauncey Burr (1817–1883) who had changed from being opposed to slavery, to being proslavery.
73 'Lola Montez on American Slavery', *Waterford Mail*, 15 June 1859; *Leeds Times*, 15 June 1859; *Liverpool Mercury*, 17 June 1859; *The Advocate: or, Irish Industrial Journal*, 18 June 1859; *Derbyshire Advertiser and Journal*, 1 July 1859.
74 'C. LOLA MONTEZ ON AMERICAN SLAVERY', *Anti-Slavery Advocate*, 1 July 1859. no. 31, vol. 2, 1 July 1859.
75 'Lola Montez on American Slavery', *Waterford Mail*, 15 June 1859; *Leeds Times*, 15 June 1859; *Liverpool Mercury*, 17 June 1859; *The Advocate: or, Irish Industrial Journal*, 18 June 1859; *Derbyshire Advertiser and Journal*, 1 July 1859.
76 'MISS SARAH P. REMOND IN LONDON', *Anti-Slavery Advocate*, vol. 2, no. 31, 1 July 1859.
77 Ibid.
78 'MISS *REMOND* ON AMERICAN SLAVERY', from the *London Morning Star* of 16 June, the *Liberator*, 8 July 1859.
79 Ibid.
80 Editorial, *Anti-Slavery Advocate*, 1 July 1859.
81 Ibid., 'MISS SARAH P. REMOND', 1 September 1859.
82 Letter from Sarah Parker Remond, Warrington, [England], to Maria Weston Chapman, 6 October 1859, BPL. Available at: www.digitalcommonwealth.org/search/commonwealth:cv43pt345.
83 *Anti-Slavery Advocate*, vol., no. 33, 1 September 1859.

264 *Sarah Parker Remond (1826–1894)*

84 'Our European Correspondence. LETTERS FROM HARRIET MARTINEAU', *National Anti-Slavery Standard*, 3 September 1859.
85 'AMERICAN SLAVERY', *Barnsley Chronicle*, 7 January 1860.
86 'MR FREDERICK DOUGLASS THE HARPER'S FERRY INSURRECTION', *Southern Reporter*, 5 January 1860.
87 'MR FREDERICK DOUGLASS ON THE HARPER'S FERRY INSURRECTION', *Leeds Times*, 24 December 1859.
88 Sarah Parker Remond, 'Lives of Distinguished Women', in *English Woman's Journal*, vol. vii, no. 37, (1 March 1861).
89 Letter from William Robson, Warrington [England], to William Lloyd Garrison, 25 January 1860, BPL. Available at: www.digitalcommonwealth.org/search/commonwealth:2v23x262g.
     When Garrison visited England in 1877, Robson arranged a banquet in his honour.
90 *Dred Scott v. Sandford*, 60 U.S. (19 How.) 393 (1857).
91 *Dublin Evening Packet and Correspondent*, 10 January 1860.
92 'DISABILITIES OF AMERICAN PERSONS OF COLOUR', *Tipperary Vindicator*, 18 December 1860. Also, Ibid., 'AN AMERICAN LADY OF COLOUR IN A STRANGE POSITION', 18 December 1860. The story was covered in many other Irish newspapers including, *Belfast Mercury*, 9 January 1860; *Dublin Evening Packet and Correspondent*, 10 January 1860; *Belfast Morning News*, 11 January 1860; Ibid., 12 January 1860; *Londonderry Sentinel*, 13 January 1860; *Ballymena Observer*, 14 January 1860; *Warder and Dublin Weekly Mail*, 14 January 1860; *Clare Journal, and Ennis Advertiser*, 16 January 1860.
93 Christine Kinealy, *Charity and the Great Hunger. The Kindness of Strangers* (London: Bloomsbury, 2013), passim.
94 Benjamin Moran, *The Journal of Benjamin Moran, 1857–1865*, vol. 2 (University of Chicago Press, 1949), pp. 608–15.
95 'DISABILITIES OF AMERICAN PERSONS OF COLOUR', *Banner of Ulster*, 12 January 1860.
96 Ibid.
97 'FIE! ON AMERICA', from the *Standard*, reprinted in *Belfast Morning News*, 12 January 1860.
98 Moran, *Journal*, entry for 25 February 1860.
99 Salenius, *Abolitionist Abroad*, p. 111.
100 'THE TWENTY-SEVENTH NATIONAL ANTI-SLAVERY ANNIVERSARY', *Anti-Slavery Advocate*, 1 November 1860.
101 'Social Economy', Miss Sarah Remond (a lady of colour) read an interesting paper on American Slavery and Its influence in Great Britain', *Freeman's Journal*, 20 August 1861.
102 *English Woman's Journal*.
103 Ibid.
104 Sarah's story had first appeared in Matthew Davenport Hill, *Our Exemplars Poor and Rich: Or Biographical Sketches of Men and Women Who Have by an Extraordinary Use of Their Opportunities Benefited Their Fellow-creatures* (London: Cassell, Petter and Galpin, 1861), pp. 276–86. This writing of her life story is sometimes referred to as her 'narrative'.
105 *London Daily News*, 7 November 1865.
106 See chapter on Samuel Ringgold Ward.
107 See chapter on Moses Roper.
108 www.bbc.co.uk/history/british/abolition/abolition_women_article_01.shtml.
     Sarah does not provide a street address but simply says she resides in London. For a list of the signatures see: Available at: www.parliament.uk/documents/parliamentary-archives/1866SuffragePetitionNamesWebJune16.pdf.

Sarah Parker Remond (1826–1894) 265

109 Salenius, *Abolitionist Abroad*, pp. 169–72.
110 Some accounts say she trained to be a nurse, others, a physician.
111 Letter from Sarah Parker Remond, Florence, 19 September 1859, *London Daily News*, 22 September 1866.
112 Wendell Phillips Garrison and Francis Jackson, *William Lloyd Garrison, 1805–1879: The Story of His Life Told by His Children* (New York: Century Co., 1885–1889), pp. 196–8.
113 Lillie Buffum Chace Wynian and Arthur Crawford Wyman, *Elizabeth Buffum Chace, 1806–1899: Her Life and Its Environment*, vol. 2 (Boston, MA: W. B. Clarke Co. 1914), pp. 48–9.
114 Salenius, *Abolitionist Abroad*, pp. 185–6.
115 See: Available at: https://books.google.com/books?id=rVLOhGt1BX0C&dq=Sarah+P+Remond+google+book&q=remond#v=onepage&q=remond&f=true.
     Little more is known of Sarah's subsequent life or death.
116 Mathilda Lucas, *Two Englishwomen in Rome, 1871–1900* (Rome: Methuen, 1938). The sisters were Anne (1841–1928) and Matilda Lucas (1849–1943) who were the daughters of Samuel Lucas, a brewer from Hitchin in Hertfordshire.
117 In *Life and Times* (1881), Douglass wrote extensively about the architecture and history of Rome, but not about the people he had visited, Chapter ix.
118 Frederick Douglass's Diary (Tour of Europe and Africa), 25 January 1887, Library of Congress. Available at: www.loc.gov/resource/mfd.01001/?sp=23.
119 Douglass to Amy Post, 10 June 1887, quoted in Salenius, 'Transatlantic Interracial Sisterhoods', p. 186.
120 Connie A. Miller, *Frederick Douglass American Hero: And International Icon of the Nineteenth* (Bloomington, IN: Xlibris, 2008), p. 341.
121 Salenius, *An Abolitionist Abroad*.
122 Salenius, 'Transatlantic Interracial Sisterhoods', p. 167.
123 Salenius, *An Abolitionist Abroad*, p. 73.

Bibliography

Archives

Boston Public Library.
Cork City and County Archives.
Library of Congress, Washington.
National Archives, England.
National Archives of Ireland, Dublin.
National Library of Ireland.
New York Public Library.
Pearse Street Library, Dublin.
Royal Irish Academy, Dublin.

Newspapers

Abolitionist Paper (U.S.).
The Advocate: or, Irish Industrial Journal.
Anti-Slavery Advocate (England/Ireland).
Anti-Slavery Bugle (U.S.).
Anti-Slavery Reporter (England).
The Argus (Australia).
Aris's Birmingham Gazette (England).
Athlone Sentinel.
The Atlantic (U.S.).
Ballymena Observer.
Banner of Ulster.
Barnsley Chronicle (England).
Bath Chronicle and Weekly Gazette (England).
Bedfordshire Mercury (England).
Belfast Commercial Chronicle.
Belfast Mercury.
Belfast Morning News.
Belfast News-Letter.
Belfast Protestant Journal.
Belfast Vindicator.
Berkshire Chronicle (England).
Boston Globe (U.S.).

Bibliography 267

Boston Pilot (U.S.).
Bradford Observer (England).
Bristol Times and Mirror (England).
British and Foreign Anti-Slavery Reporter (England).
Bucks Herald (England).
Burnley Gazette (England).
Bury Free Press (England).
Bury and Norwich Post (England).
Caledonian Mercury (Scotland).
Cambridge General Advertiser (England).
Cambridge Independent Press (England).
Carlisle Journal (England).
Cavan Observer.
Cheltenham Journal and Gloucestershire Fashionable Weekly Gazette (England).
Christian Recorder (U.S.).
Christian World (England).
Clare Journal and Ennis Advertiser.
Clinton Republican (U.S.).
Coleraine Chronicle.
The Colored American (U.S.).
Connaught Watchman.
Cork Advertising Gazette.
Cork Constitution.
Cork Examiner.
Daily Bee (U.S.).
Derbyshire Advertiser and Journal (England).
Downpatrick Recorder.
Dublin Daily Express.
Dublin Evening Mail.
Dublin Evening Packet and Correspondent.
Dublin Evening Post.
Dublin Monitor.
Dublin Morning Register.
Dumfries and Galloway Standard (Scotland).
Dundee Courier (Scotland).
Dundee, Perth, and Cupar Advertiser (Scotland).
Durham Chronicle (England).
Edinburgh Evening News (Scotland).
Elgin Courier (Scotland).
Emancipator (U.S.).
Essex Standard (England).
Evangelical Magazine and Missionary Chronicle (England).
Evening Freeman.
Falkirk Herald (Scotland).
Fife Herald (Scotland).
Fife Journal (Scotland).
Finn's Leinster Journal.
Frederick Douglass' Monthly (U.S.).
Frederick Douglass' Paper (U.S.).

268   *Bibliography*

The Freed-man (U.S.).
Freeman's Journal.
Galignani's Messenger (France).
Galway Mercury, and Connaught Weekly Advertiser.
Galway Vindicator, and Connaught Advertiser.
Glasgow Herald (Scotland).
Gloucester Journal (England).
Hampshire Advertiser (England).
Hampshire Chronicle (England).
Hartford Courant (U.S.).
Herald and Mail (U.S.).
Herald of Freedom (U.S.).
Hereford Journal (England).
Hereford Times (England).
Hertford Mercury and Reformer (England).
Illustrated London News (England).
Ipswich Journal (England).
Irish Temperance League Journal.
Irish Temperance Shield.
Irish Times.
Jersey Independent and Daily Telegraph (UK).
Kendal Mercury (England).
Kentish Mercury (England).
Kerry Evening Post.
Kerry Examiner.
Kilkenny Journal, and Leinster Commercial and Literary Advertiser.
La Opinion Nacional (Venezuela).
Lancaster Gazette (England).
Leeds Intelligencer (England).
Leeds Times (England).
Leicester Chronicle (England).
Leinster Express.
Liberator (U.S.).
Limerick Chronicle.
Limerick Reporter.
Liverpool Daily Post (England).
Liverpool Mercury (England).
London Daily News (England).
London Morning Star (England).
London Standard (England).
Londonderry Sentinel.
Londonderry Standard.
Longford Journal.
Manchester Times (England).
Manchester Mercury (England).
Monmouthshire Beacon (Scotland).
Morning Advertiser (England).
Nation.
National Anti-Slavery Standard (U.S.).

Bibliography 269

Nenagh Guardian.
New York Daily Times (U.S.).
New York Times (U.S.).
New York Tribune (U.S.).
Newcastle Courant (England).
Newcastle Daily Chronicle (England).
Newcastle Guardian and Tyne Mercury (England).
Newry Times.
Newcastle Journal (England).
Norfolk Chronicle (England).
Norfolk News (England).
North and South Shields Gazette (England).
North Star (U.S.).
Northampton Mercury (England).
Northern Warder and General Advertiser for the Counties of Fife, Perth and Forfar
  (Scotland).
Northern Whig.
Oxford Journal (England).
Oxford Chronicle and Reading Gazette (England).
Paisley Herald and Renfrewshire Advertiser (Scotland).
Pennsylvania National Anti-Slavery Standard (U.S.).
The Pilot.
Portadown News.
Salisbury and Winchester Journal (England).
Saunders's News-Letter.
Scottish Congregational Magazine (Scotland).
Scottish Guardian (Scotland).
The Scotsman (Scotland).
Sheffield Independent (England).
Sheffield Register (England).
Sherborne Mercury (England).
Shrewsbury Chronicle (England).
Spirit of Liberty (U.S.).
Southern Reporter and Cork Commercial Courier.
The Spectator (England).
Stamford Mercury (England).
Statesman and Dublin Christian Record.
Stirling Observer (Scotland).
Suffolk Chronicle; or Weekly General Advertiser & County Express (England).
Telegraph or Connaught Ranger.
Time (U.S.).
Tipperary Free Press and Clonmel General Advertiser.
Tipperary Vindicator.
Tralee Mercury.
Tuam Herald.
Tyrone Constitution.
Ulster General Advertiser.
Ulster Times.
Vindicator.

270 *Bibliography*

Warder and Dublin Weekly Mail.
Warrington Times (England).
Waterford Chronicle.
Waterford Mail.
Waterford News and Star.
Weekly Vindicator.
Wells Journal (England).
Westmeath Independent.
Wexford Independent.
Wilts and Gloucestershire Standard (England).
Wiltshire Independent (England).
Worcestershire Chronicle (England).

Primary Sources

Annual Meeting of the Colored Baptist American Missionary Society (Baltimore, MD, 23 August 1864).

Armistead, W., *A Tribute for the Negro: Being a Vindication of the Moral, Intellectual, and Religious Capabilities of the Colored Portion of Mankind; with Particular Reference to the African Race* (Manchester and London: W. Irwin, 1848).

Beecher Stowe, H., *Uncle Tom's Cabin; or, Life among the Lowly* (Boston, MA: John P. Jewitt, 1852).

Conway, T., *An Appeal to Loyal Religious People in Behalf of Kentucky* (Louisiana: Printed in New Orleans Times Office, 1865).

Cooke, H., *The Repealer Repulsed. A Correct Narrative of the Rise and Progress of the Repeal Invasion of Ulster* (Belfast: William McComb, 1841).

Craft, W., *Running a Thousand Miles for Freedom; or, the Escape of William and Ellen Craft from Slavery* (London: William Tweedie, 1860).

Crummell, A., *Africa and America: Addresses and Discourses* (Springfield, MA: Willey and Co., 1891).

Cugoano, O., *Thoughts and Sentiments on the Evil and Wicked Traffic of the Slavery and Commerce of the Human Species* (London, July 1787).

Davenport, H. M., *Our Exemplars Poor and Rich: Or Biographical Sketches of Men and Women Who Have by an Extraordinary Use of Their Opportunities Benefited Their Fellow-Creatures* (London: Cassell, Petter and Galpin, 1861).

Douglass, F., *Narrative of the Life of Frederick Douglass, an American Slave, Written by Himself* (Boston, MA: Anti-Slavery Office, 1845).

———, *Farewell Speech of Mr. Frederick Douglass upon His Return to America, Delivered at the Valedictory Soiree Given to Him at the London Tavern on March 30, 1847* (London: R. Yorke, Clarke and Co., 1847).

———, *Frederick Douglass's Diary* (Tour of Europe and Africa), 25 January 1887, Library of Congress (available online).

———, *Life and Times of Frederick Douglass, Written by Himself* (Boston, MA: De Wolfe & Fiske, 1892).

———, *'Lecture on Haiti', Delivered on 2 January 1893 at World's Fair, Chicago* (Chicago, IL: Violet Agents, 1893).

Emmet, T. A., *Memoir of Thomas Addis and Robert Emmet: With Their Ancestors and Their Immediate Family*, vol. 2 (New York: The Emmet Press, 1915).

English Woman's Journal (London: Victoria Press, 1858–64).

Bibliography 271

Foner, P. S., and G. E. Walker (eds.), *Proceedings of the Black State Conventions, 1840–1865* (2 vols, Philadelphia, PA: Temple University Press, 1979).

Freed-Men's Aid Society in the United States, *The Freed-Man. A Monthly Magazine Devoted to the Interests of the Freed Colored People* (London: S. W. Partridge, 1866).

Garnet, H. H., 'The Past and the Present Condition, and the Destiny, of the Coloured Race' (1848).

———, *Let the Monster Perish* (Philadelphia, PA: Joseph M. Wilson, 1865).

Grandy, M., *Narrative of the Life of Moses Grandy; Late a Slave in the United States of America* (London: C. Gilpin, 5, Bishopsgate-Street, 1843).

Grimes, W., *Life of William Grimes, the Runaway Slave. Written by Himself* (New York: W. Grimes, 1825).

Hallowell, D. A. (ed.), *James and Lucretia Mott: Life and Letters* (Boston, MA: Houghton, Mifflin and Company, 1890).

Hansard (London: T.C. Hansard).

Haughton, S., *Memoir of James Haughton: With Extracts from His Private and Published Letters* (Dublin: E. Ponsonby, 1877).

Hibernian Anti-Slavery Society, *Address of the Hibernian Anti-Slavery Society to the People of Ireland* (Dublin: Webb and Chapman, 1837).

'Investigations by Commissioners of Enquiry into the Case of James Williams, and Other Apprenticed Labourers', *Papers Presented to Parliament ... for the Abolition of Slavery throughout the British Colonies*, part v, Jamaica, 1838, vol. xlix (1837–1838).

Jacobs, H., and L. M. F. Child, *Incidents in the Live of a Slave girl, Written by Herself* (Boston, MA: Published for the Author, 1861).

Jamaica Almanac (Kingston: Stevenson and Aikman, 1672–1880).

Kelley, E., *A Family Redeemed from Bondage; Being Rev. Edmond Kelley, (The Author,) His Wife, and Four Children* (New Bedford, MA: The Author, 1851).

Lane, L., *The Narrative of Lunsford Lane, Formerly of Raleigh, N.C. Embracing an Account of His Early Life, the Redemption by Purchase of Himself and Family from Slavery, and His Banishment from the Place of His Birth for the Crime of Wearing a Colored Skin* (Boston, MA: J.G. Torrey, 1842).

Lowe, J. (of Manchester), 'The Ship-Wreck of a Slave-Ship', in *Poems* (Manchester: R. and W. Dean, 1803).

Madden, R. R., *The United Irishmen: Their Lives and Times*, etc., vol. 4 (Dublin: James Duffy, 1860).

Manchester Guardian, *Address to President Lincoln by the Working-Men of Manchester, England, 31 December 1862*, 1 January 1863.

Mathews, T., *Anti-Slavery Labours in England of the Rev. Edward Mathews, Agent of the American Baptist Free Mission Society* (Bristol: Thomas Mathews, 1855).

McCune Smith, J., *Sketch of the Life and Labors of Rev. Henry Highland Garnet* (Philadelphia, PA: Philip M. Wilson, 1865).

Meade, W., *Sermons Address to Masters and Servants, and Published in the Year 1743, by the Rev. Thomas Bacon, Minister of the Protestant Episcopal Church in Maryland, Now Republished with Other Tracts and Dialogues on the Same Subject, and Recommended to All Masters and Mistresses to Be Used in Their Families* (Winchester, VA: John Heiskell, 1813).

Minutes of the National Convention of Coloured Citizens Held at Buffalo, 15, 16, 17, 18 and 19 August 1843 for Purpose of Considering Their Moral and Political Condition as American Citizens (New York: Piercy and Reed, 1843).

Mott, J., *Three Months in Great Britain* (Philadelphia, PA: J. Miller McKim, 1841).

272 Bibliography

Papers Read and Statements Made on the Principal Subjects Submitted to the Anti-Slavery Conference: Held at the London Tavern on the 29th and 30th of November 1854 (London: Anti-Slavery Conference, 1854).

Pillsbury, P., *Acts of the Anti-Slavery Apostles* (Boston, MA: Cupples, Upham, & Company, 1884).

Prince, M., *The History of Mary Prince, a West Indian Slave. Related by Herself* (London: published by F. Westley and A. H. Davis, Stationers' Hall Court; And by Waught & Innes, Edinburgh: and supplied at trade price to Anti-Slavery Associations by Joseph Phillips, 18, Aldermanbury, 1831).

Proceedings of a Public Meeting for the Formation of the Northern Central British India Society Held in the Corn Exchange, Manchester, on Wednesday Evening, 26 August 1840 (Manchester: Printed at Society's Office, 1840).

Proceedings of the World Anti-Slavery Convention (London: British and Foreign Anti-Slavery Society, 1840).

Proceedings of the National Convention of Colored Men, Held in the City of Syracuse, N.Y., October 4, 5, 6, and 7, 1864; with the Bill of Wrongs and Rights, and the Address to the American People (New York: Syracuse, 1864).

Reporatory of Patent Inventions, July to December 1854, vol. xxiv (London: Macintosh, 1855).

Report of the Jamaica Royal Commission 1866, parts 1 & 2 (London: H. M. Stationery Office, 1866).

Rogers, N. P., *Miscellaneous Writings of Nathaniel Rogers* (New Hampshire: W. H. Fisk, 1849).

Roper, M., *A Narrative of the Adventures and Escapes of Moses Roper from American Slavery, with a Preface by the Rev. T. Price, D.D.* (London: Darton: Harvey, and Darton, 55 Gracechurch-Street. Birmingham: B. Hudson, 18, Bull-Street, and of the Author, 31, Cherry-Street, 1837).

———, *Hanes bywyd a ffoedigaeth Moses Roper, o gaethiwed Americanaidd* (Aberystwyth: Argraphwyd dros y cyhoeddwr gan; Aberystwyth: J. Cox., 1842).

———, *A Narrative of the Adventures and Escape of Moses Roper, from American Slavery* (Berwick-upon-Tweed: Published for the Author, and Printed at the Warder Office, 1848).

———, *An Intellectual Entertainment! Moral, Instructive and Amusing, Spiced with Humor* (Rutland, VT: Tuttle & Co., 1882).

Sanborn, G., 'The Plagiarist's Craft: Fugitivity and Theatricality in *Running a Thousand Miles for Freedom*', in *PMLA*, vol. 128, no. 4 (October, 2013), 907–922.

Seymour, B., *Lola Montez: A Life* (New Haven, CT: Yale University Press, 1996).

Simmons, W. J., *Men of Mark: Eminent, Progressive and Rising* (Cleveland: Geo. M. Rewell and Co., 1887).

Smith, J. D., *A Voice from the West; or, the Condition and Claims of Connaught, Ireland* (London: John Snow, 1848).

The County and City of Cork almanac, Calculated & Adapted by C. Thompson (Cork: Jackson, 1843).

The Wesleyan Missionary Notices, Relating Principally to the Foreign Missions (London: Wesleyan Methodist Missionary Society, 1872).

Thom's Directory for Ireland (Dublin: Alexander Thom, 1844–1900).

Tone, T. W., *An Argument on Behalf of the Catholics of Ireland* (Belfast: Society of United Irishman of Belfast, 1791).

Tyler, J. G., *The Women of England versus the Women of America. Mrs. Ex-President Tyler's Letter to the Duchess of Sutherland on American Slavery* (London: W. Davy and Son, 1853).

Bibliography 273

Walker, D., *Walker's Appeal, in Four* Articles; Together with a Preamble, to the Coloured Citizens of the World, but in Particular, *and Very* Expressly, *to Those of the United States of America*, Written *in Boston*, State *of Massachusetts, September 28, 1829* (Boston, MA: Revised and Published by David Walker, 1830).

Ward, S. R., *Autobiography of a Fugitive Negro: His Anti-Slavery Labours in the United States, Canada, & England* (London: John Snow, 1855).

————, *Reflections upon the Gordon Rebellion* (Publisher and place of publication not identified).

Webb, A., and M.-L. Kegge (ed.) *The Autobiography of a Quaker Nationalist* (Cork: Cork University Press, 1999).

Welch, A. G., *A Narrative of the Life of Benjamin Benson, Who Was Born a Slave in the Island of Bermuda, Emancipated by the English Government, August 1 1838, and Subsequently Sold as a Slave in the United States of America* (London: By the Author, 1847).

Wells Brown, J., *Biography of an American Bondman, by His Daughter* (Boston, MA: R. F. Wallcut 1856).

Wells Brown, W., *Narrative of William W. Brown, a Fugitive Slave. Written by Himself* (Boston, MA: Anti-Slavery Office, 1847).

————, *Anti Slavery Harp: A Collection of Songs for Anti-Slavery Meetings* (Boston, MA: Bella Marsh, 1848).

————, *Narrative of William W. Brown, a Fugitive Slave. Written by Himself* (London: Charles Gilpin, 1849).

————, *Three Years in Europe: Or, Places I Have Seen and People I Have Met* (London: Charles Gilpin, 5 Bishopsgate Street, Without; Edinburgh: Oliver and Boyd, 1852).

————, *Clotel* (London: Partridge and Oakey, 1853).

————, *The American Fugitive in Europe. Sketches of Places and People Abroad, with a Memoir of the Author* (Boston, MA: John P. Jewett and Company, 1855).

————, *The Black Man, His Antecedents, His Genius, and His Achievements* (New York: Thomas Hamilton; Boston: R. F. Wallcut, 1863).

Whately, E. J., *Life and Correspondence of Richard Whately, D.D.: Late Archbishop of Dublin*, vol. 2 (Dublin: Longmans, Green, and Company, 1866).

Williams, J., *A Narrative of Events, Since the First of August, 1834, by James Williams, an Apprenticed Labourer in Jamaica* (London: Rider, 1837).

Young, R. M. et al. *Historical Notices of Old Belfast and Its Vicinity: A Selection from the Mss. Collected by William Pinkerton, F.S.A., for His Intended History of Belfast* (Belfast: Robert Magill Young, M. Ward & Company, Limited, 1896).

Secondary sources

Aptheker, H., *The Negro in the Abolitionist Movement* (New York: International Publishers, 1941).

Baraw, C., 'William Wells Brown, Three Years in Europe, and Fugitive Tourism', in *African American Review*, vol. 44, no. 3 (Fall, 2011), 453–470.

Barnes, G., 'Revolutionary Jamaica: Interpreting the Politics of the Baptist War'. Available at: https://ageofrevolutions.com/2017/01/23/revolutionary-jamaica-interpreting-the-politics-of-the-baptist-war/

Blackburn, R., 'Haiti, Slavery, and the Age of the Democratic Revolution', in *The William and Mary Quarterly*, Third Series, vol. 63, no. 4 (October, 2006), 643–674.

Blackett, R. J. M., 'Fugitive Slaves in Britain: The Odyssey of William and Ellen Craft', in *Journal of American Studies*, vol. 12, no. 1 (April, 1978), 41–62.

274   *Bibliography*

————, *Divided Hearts: Britain and the American Civil War* (Baton Rouge: Louisiana State University Press, 2000).

————, *Building an Antislavery Wall: Black Americans in the Atlantic Abolitionist movement, 1830–1860* (Baton Rouge: Louisiana State University Press, 2002).

Bradley, I., 'Wilberforce the Saint', in J. Hayward (ed.), *Out of Slavery: Abolition and After* (London: Frank Cass, 1985).

Brewer, W. M., 'Henry Highland Garnet', in *The Journal of African American History*, vol. 13, no. 1 (January, 1928), 36–52.

Bric, M., 'Daniel O Connell and the Debate on Anti-Slavery, Daniel O'Connell and the Debate on Anti-Slavery, 1820–50', in *History and the Public sphere, Essays in Honour of John A. Murphy*, edited by T. Dunne and L. M. Geary (Cork: Cork University Press, 2005).

Bugg, J., 'The Other Interesting Narrative: Olaudah Equiano's Public Book Tour', in *Journal of Modern Language Association*, vol. 121, no. 5 (October, 2006), 1424–1442.

Burke, R. K., *Samuel Ringgold Ward: Christian Abolitionist* (London: Routledge, 1995).

Campbell, O., 'A Platform upon Which All Could Unite? Temperance in Ulster and the Irish Temperance League, 1858–1914'. PhD thesis, The Open University (2017).

Carretta, V., 'Olaudah Equiano or Gustavus Vassa? New Light on an Eighteenth-Century Question of Identity', in *Slavery and Abolition*, vol. 20, no. 3 (1999), 96–105.

————, *Equiano, the African: Biography of a Self-Made Man* (Athens, GA: University of Georgia Press, 2005).

Chaffin, T., *Giant's Causeway: Frederick Douglass's Irish Odyssey and the Making of an American Visionary* (Charlottesville: University of Virginia Press, 2014).

Cleal, E. E., *The Story of Congregationalism in Surrey* (London: James Clarke & Co., 13 & 14 Fleet Street, 1908).

Costello, K., *The Irish Shopkeeper and the Law of Bankruptcy 1860–1930* (Dublin: UCD Research Depository, 2016).

Cotter, W. R., 'The Somerset Case and the Abolition of Slavery in England', in *History*, vol. 79, no. 255 (February, 1994), 31–56.

Cutter, M. J., 'Revising Torture: Moses Roper and the Visual Rhetoric of the Slave's Body in the Transatlantic Abolition Movement', in *ESQ: A Journal of the American Renaissance*, vol. 60, no. 3 (2014) (No. 236 O.S.), 371–411.

Darity, W. A., 'Eric Williams and Slavery: A West Indian Viewpoint', in *Callaloo*, vol. 20, no. 4 (Fall, 1997), 801–816.

Douglass, F., W. Wells Brown, and H. E. Wilson, *Three Great African-American Novels* (New York: Dover Publications, 2008).

Drescher, S., 'People and Parliament: The Rhetoric of the British Slave Trade', in *Journal of Interdisciplinary History, MIT Press*, vol. 20, no. 4 (Spring, 1990), 561–580.

Dryden, J., 'Pas de Six Ans!', in *Seven Slaves & Slavery: Trinidad and Tobago 1777–1838*, edited by A. de Verteuil (Port of Spain, 1992).

Emmet, T. A., *Memoir of Thomas Addis and Robert Emmet: With Their Ancestors and Their Immediate Family*, vol. 2 (New York: The Emmet Press, 1915).

Fagan, 'Reclaiming Revolution: William Wells Brown's Irreducible Haitian Heroes', in *Comparative American Studies. An International Journal*, vol. 5, no. 4 (2007), 367–383.

Falk, L. A., 'Black Abolitionist Doctors and Healers, 1810–1885', in *Bulletin of the History of Medicine*, vol. 54, no. 2 (Summer, 1980), 258–272.

Farrell, S., 'Going to Extremes: Anti-Catholicism and Anti-Slavery in Early Victorian Belfast', in *European Romantic Review*, vol. 28, no. 4 (2017), 461–472.

Bibliography 275

Featherstone, D., '"We Will Have Equality and Liberty in Ireland": The Contested Geographies of Irish Democratic Political Cultures in the 1790s', in *Historical Geography*, vol. 41 (2013), 121–136.

Ferreira, P. J., 'Frederick Douglass in Ireland: The Dublin Edition of His *Narrative*', in *New Hibernia Review*, vol. 5, no. 1 (Earrach/Spring, 2001), 53–67.

Garrison, W. L., *The Letters of William Lloyd Garrison. A House Dividing against Itself*, vol. 2 (Cambridge, MA: Harvard University Press, 1971).

———, *The Letters of William Lloyd Garrison: No Union with the Slaveholders, 1841–1849* (Cambridge, MA: Harvard University Press, 1973).

Garrison, W. P., and F. Jackson, *William Lloyd Garrison, 1805–1879: The Story of His Life Told by His Children* (New York: Century Co., 1885–1889).

Gates, H. L., Jr., and E. B. Higginbotham (eds.), *African American Lives* (Oxford: Oxford University Press, 2004).

Goddu, T. A., 'Anti-Slavery's Panoramic Perspective', in *Multi-Ethnic Literature of the U.S.*, vol. 39, no. 2 (Summer, 2014), 12–41.

———, 'Visual Culture and Race', in *The Society for the Study of the Multi-Ethnic Literature of the United States*, vol. 39, no. 2 (Summer, 2014), 12–41.

Gosse, V. E., '"As a Nation, the English Are Our Friends": The Emergence of African American Politics in the British Atlantic World, 1772–1861", in *The American Historical Review*, vol. 113, no. 4 (October, 2008), 1003–1028.

Gough, K., *Haptic Allegories: Kinship and Performance in the Black and Green Atlantic* (London: Routledge, 2013).

Greenspan, E., *William Wells Brown: A Reader* (Athens, GA: University of Georgia Press, 2008).

———, *William Wells Brown: An African American Life* (New York: Norton and Co., 2014).

Gregory, J., *Victorians against the Gallows: Capital Punishment and the Abolitionist Movement in Nineteenth Century Britain* (London: I. B. Taurus, 2011).

Hall, T. L., *American Religious Leaders* (New York: Infobase Publishing, 2014).

Hamilton, C. S., 'Hercules Subdued: The Visual Rhetoric of the Kneeling Slave', in *Slavery and Abolition. A Journal of Slave and Post-Slavery Studies*, vol. 34, no. 4 (2013), 631–652.

Harris, L. M., *In the Shadow of Slavery: African Americans in New York City, 1626–1863* (Chicago, IL: University of Chicago Press, 2003).

Harrison, R. S., 'Irish Quaker Perspectives on the Anti-Slavery Movement', in *The Journal of the Friends Historical Society*, vol. 56, no. 2 (1991), 106–125.

Harry, T., *Summary of Moses Roper's Narrative* (2011) in *Documenting the American South*. Available at: https://docsouth.unc.edu/neh/roper/summary.html

Hogan, L., 'Frederick Douglass's Journey from Slavery to Limerick', in *The Old Limerick Journal*, no. 49 (Winter, 2015), 21–26. Available at: www.limerickcity.ie/media/olj%2049%202015%20p021%20to%20p026.pdf

———, '*"Treat the Coloured People as Your Equals"*: Charles Lenox Remond in Limerick and the Failure of the Anti-Slavery Irish Address', in *Old Limerick Journal*, no. 52 (Winter, 2017), 8–11.

Holcomb, J. L., *Moral Commerce: Quakers and the Transatlantic Boycott of the Slave Labor Economy* (New York: Cornell University Press, 2016).

Holman, H. B., *A Survey of the Negro Convention Movement, 1830–1861* (New York: Arno Press, 1969).

Horton, J. O., '"What Business Has the World with the Color of My Wife?" A Letter from Frederick Douglass', in *Magazine of History*, vol. 19, no. 1 (January, 2005), 52–55.

276 Bibliography

Hulsebosch, D. J., 'Nothing but Liberty: "Somerset's Case" and the British Empire', in *Law and History Review*, vol. 24, no. 3 (Fall, 2006), 647–657.

Jenkins, L. M., 'Beyond the Pale: Frederick Douglass in Cork', in *Irish Review*, no. 24 (Autumn, 1999), 80–95.

Kerr-Richie, J., 'Samuel Ward and the Making of an Imperial Subject', in *Slavery and Abolition*, vol. 33, no. 2 (2012), 205–219.

———, 'Black Abolitionists, Irish Supporters, and the Brotherhood of Man', in *Slavery & Abolition. A Journal of Slave and Post-Slave Studies*, vol. 37, no. 3 (2016), 599–621.

———, 'Samuel Ward and the Gordon Rebellion', in *The Journal of Caribbean History*, vol. 50, no. 1 (January, 2016), 205–219.

Killen, W. D., *History of Congregations of the Presbyterian Church in Ireland and Biographical Notices of Eminent Presbyterian Ministers and Laymen, with the Signification of Names of Places* (Belfast: James Cleeland, 1886).

Kinealy, C., *Daniel O'Connell and the Anti-Slavery Movement. The Saddest People the Sun Sees* (London: Routledge, 2011).

———, *Charity and the Great Hunger. The Kindness of Strangers* (London: Bloomsbury, 2013).

———, *Frederick Douglass. In His Own Words*, 2 vols (London: Routledge, 2019).

Landy, C. T. A., 'Society of United Irishmen Revolutionary and New-York Manumission Society Lawyer: Thomas Addis Emmet and the Irish Contributions to the Antislavery Movement in New York', in *New York History*, vol. 95, no. 2 (Cornell University Press, Spring, 2014), 193–222.

Laska, L. L., 'Edmond Kelley, Tennessee's First African-American Ordained Baptist Minister', in *Tennessee Baptist History*, vol. 6 (Fall, 2004), 7–28.

Laumer, F., and A. G. Welch, *A Narrative of the Early Days and Remembrances of Oceola Nikkanochee, Prince of Econchatti* (Tallahassee, FL: LibraryPress@UF, 2017).

Leeman, R. W., *African-American Orators: A Bio-Critical Sourcebook* (Westport, CT: Greenwood Press, 1996).

Levine, R. S. (ed.), *Martin R. Delany: A Documentary Reader* (Chapel Hill: University of North Carolina Press, 2003).

Lovejoy, P. E., 'Autobiography and Memory: Gustavus Vassa, Alias Olaudah Equiano, the African', in *Slavery and Abolition*, vol. 27, no. 3 (2006), 317–347.

Lucas, M., *Two Englishwomen in Rome, 1871–1900* (Rome: Methuen, 1938).

Maclear, J. F., 'The Evangelical Alliance and the Antislavery Crusade', in *Huntington Library Quarterly*, vol. 42, no. 2 (Spring, 1979), 141–164.

Maynard, D. H., 'The World's Anti-Slavery Convention of 1840', in *The Mississippi Valley Historical Review*, vol. 47, no. 3 (December, 1960), 452–471.

McDaniel, W. C., 'Repealing Unions: American Abolitionists, Irish Repeal, and the Origins of Garrisonian Disunionism', in *Journal of the Early Republic*, vol. 28, no. 2 (Summer, 2008), 243–269.

McKivigen, J. R., *Frederick Douglass Papers* (New Haven, NC: Yale University Press, 2009).

Meem, J., *Print, Publicity, and Popular Radicalism in the 1790s. The Laurel of Liberty* (Cambridge: Cambridge University Press, 2017).

Midgely, C., *Women against Slavery: The British Campaigns, 1780–1870* (London: Routledge, 1995).

Miller, C. A., *Frederick Douglass. American Hero: And International Icon of the Nineteenth Century* (Bloomington, IN: Xlibris, 2008).

Moran, B., *The Journal of Benjamin Moran, 1857–1865*, vol. 2 (Chicago, IL: University of Chicago Press, 1949).

Bibliography   277

Mott, L., *Slavery and 'The Woman Question'. Lucretia Mott's Diary of Her Visit to Great Britain to Attend the World's Anti-Slavery Convention of 1840*, edited by F. B. Tolles Mott (Swarthmore, PA: Friends' Historical Association & Friends' Historical Society, 1952).

Obama, B., 'Remarks by President Obama, Vice President Biden, and Prime Minister Enda Kenny of Ireland at a St. Patrick's Day Reception', *Press Release*, White House, 17 March 2011.

Ofari, E., *'Let Your Motto Be Resistance'. The Life and Thought of Henry Highland Garnet* (Boston, MA: Beacon Press, 1972).

O'Ferrall, F., 'Daniel O'Connell and Henry Cooke: The Conflict of Civil and Religious Liberty in Modern Ireland', in *The Irish Review*, no. 1 (1986), 20–26.

Peckover, A., *Life of Joseph Sturge* (London: Swan Sonnenschein, 1890).

Pettinger, A., *Frederick Douglass and Scotland,1846: Living an Antislavery Life* (Edinburgh: Edinburgh University Press, 2018).

Phillips, W., *Lectures and Speeches* (New York and London: Street and Smith, 1902).

Phillips, W., and F. J. Garrison, *William Lloyd Garrison, 1805–1879: The Story of His Life Told by His Children* (New York: Century Co., 1885).

Polyné, M., 'Douglass at the Intersection of U.S. and Caribbean Pan-Americanism', in *Caribbean Studies*, vol. 34, no. 2 (July–December, 2006), 3–45.

Porter, D. B., 'Sarah Parker Remond, Abolitionist and Physician', in *The Journal of Negro History*, vol. 20, no. 3 (July, 1935), 287–293.

Pryor, E. S., *Colored Travelers: Mobility and the Fight for Citizenship before the Civil War* (Chapel Hill, NC: University of North Carolina Press, 2016).

Pugh, E. L., 'Women and Slavery: Julia Gardiner Tyler and the Duchess of Sutherland', in *The Virginia Magazine of History and Biography*, vol. 88, no. 2 (April, 1980), 186–202.

Ripley, P. C. (ed.), *The Black Abolitionist Papers, 1830–1865* (Chapel Hill: University of North Carolina Press, 1987).

Ritchie, D., *Isaac Nelson: Radical Abolitionist, Evangelical Presbyterian, and Irish Nationalist* (Liverpool: Liverpool University Press, 2018).

Robertson, S. M., *Parker Pillsbury: Radical Abolitionist, Male Feminist* (New York: Cornell University Press, 2000).

Rodgers, N., *Equiano and Anti-Slavery in Eighteenth-Century Belfast* (Belfast: Ulster Historical Foundation, 2000).

———, 'Ireland and the Black Atlantic in the Eighteenth Century', in *Irish Historical Studies*, vol. 32, no. 126 (November, 2000), 174–192.

Salenius, S., *An Abolitionist Abroad. Sarah Parker Remond in Cosmopolitan Europe* (Amherst, MA: University of Massachusetts Press, 2016).

———, 'Transatlantic Interracial Sisterhoods: Sarah Remond, Ellen Craft, and Harriet Jacobs in England', in *Frontiers: A Journal of Women Studies*, vol. 38, no. 1 (2017), 166–196.

Sawallisch, N., *Fugitive Borders: Black Canadian Cross-Border Literature at Mid-Nineteenth Century* (New York: Columbia University Press, 2019).

Schor, J., *Henry Highland Garnet. A Voice of Black Radicalism in the Nineteenth Century* (Westport, CT: Greenwood Press, 1977).

———, 'The Rivalry between Frederick Douglass and Henry Highland Garnet', in *Journal of Negro History*, vol. 64, no. 1 (Winter, 1979), 30–38.

Scott, M., and N. Megoran, 'The Newcastle Upon Tyne Peace Society (1817–50)', in *Northern History*, vol. 54, no. 2 (2017), 211–227.

Seraile, W., 'The Brief Diplomatic Career of Henry Highland Garnet', in *Phylon*, vol. 46, no. 1 (1st Qtr., 1985), 71–81.

278   *Bibliography*

Shillington, K., 'British Made. Abolition and the Africa Trade', in *History Today*, vol. 57, no. 3 (January, 2007), 21–22.

Stephens, G., *On Racial Frontiers: The New Culture of Frederick Douglass, Ralph Ellison, and Bob Marley* (Cambridge: Cambridge University Press, 1999).

Stouffer, A. P., *Light of Nature and the Law of God: Antislavery in Ontario, 1833–1877* (Montreal: McGill-Queen's Press, 1992).

Sweeney, F., '"The Republic of Letters": Frederick Douglass, Ireland, and the Irish *Narratives*', in *Éire-Ireland*, vol. 36, no. 1 & 2 (*Earrach/Samhradh* Spring/Summer, 2001), 47–65.

Taylor, C., *British and American Abolitionists: An Episode in Transatlantic Understanding* (Edinburgh: Edinburgh University Press, 1974).

Terborg-Penn, R., *African American Women in the Struggle for the Vote, 1850–1920* (Bloomington, IN: Indiana University Press, 1998).

Thompson, E. P., *The Making of the English Working Class* (New York: Vintage Books, 1963).

Tolles, F. B. M., *Slavery and 'The Woman Question'. Lucretia Mott's Diary of Her Visit to Great Britain to Attend the World's Anti-Slavery Convention of 1840* (Philadelphia, PA: Friends' Historical Association & Friends Historical Society, 1952).

Wallace, L., 'Charles Lenox Remond: The Lost Prince of Abolitionism', in *Negro History Bulletin*, vol. 40, no. 3 (May–June, 1977), 696–701.

Walton, H., Jr., S. Puckett, and D. R. Deskins, Jr., *The African American Electorate* (Los Angeles, CA: Sage, 2012).

Watson, *Caribbean Culture and British Fiction in the Atlantic World, 1780–1860* (Cambridge: Cambridge University Press, 2008).

Wayland, F. F., 'Slavebreeding in America: The Stevenson-O'Connell Imbroglio of 1838', in *The Virginia Magazine of History and Biography*, vol. 50, no. 1 (January, 1942), 47–54.

Wheaton, P. G., and C. M. Condit, 'Charles Lenox Remond (1810–1873), Abolitionist, Reform Activist', in *African-American Orators: A Bio-Critical Sourcebook*, edited by R. W. Leeman (Westport, CT: Greenwood Press, 1996).

Whyte, I., *'Send Back the Money!': The Free Church of Scotland and American Slavery* (Cambridge: James Clarke & Co, 2012).

Williams, E., *Capitalism and Slavery* (Chapel Hill: University of North Carolina Press, 1944).

Williams, W., *Tourism, Landscape, and the Irish Character: British Travel Writers in Pre-Famine Ireland* (Madison, WI: University of Wisconsin Press, 2012).

Wilmot, S., 'The Politics of Samuel Clarke: Black Creole Politician in Free Jamaica, 1851–1865, in *Caribbean Quarterly*, vol. 44, no. 1–2 (2017), 129–144.

Winkelman, G., 'The Rhetoric of Henry Highland Garnet' (Masters' Dissertation). Available at: https://baylor-ir.tdl.org/handle/2104/5095

Winskill, P. T., *The Temperance Movement and Its Workers. A Record of Social, Moral, Religious, and Political Progress*, vol. iii (London, Glasgow, Edinburgh, and Dublin: Blackie & Son, Limited, 1892).

Woodson, C. G., *Negro Orators and Their Orations* (New York: Simon and Schuster, 2016).

Wyman, L. B. C., and A. C. Wyman, *Elizabeth Buffum Chace, 1806–1899: Her Life and Its Environment* (Boston, MA: W. B. Clarke Co., 1914).

Index

Abeokuta 177
Act of Union 6
Address to the American Congress (1841) 85–6
Address to the Women of England (1863) 29
Africa 2, 31, 41, 67, 87, 162, 177, 201, 208
African Civilization Society 174–5, 176
Age of revolutions 8
agency of black people 5, 6–7, 8, 10, 17, 19–20, 21–22, 31–2, 43, 49, 51, 62, 106–7, 118, 136, 147–8, 149, 204, 150, 163, 196, 240, 241, 256
Allen, Richard 9, 11, 15, 29, 79, 85, 87, 109, 120, 126, 170, 194, 231, 259
Allen, William 26, 29, 163, 180, 207
Amazing Grace 53
American Anti-Slavery Society 11, 13, 15, 27, 30, 60, 62, 76, 77, 97, 98, 108, 109, 115, 119, 120, 123, 125, 137, 140, 141, 142, 163, 172, 202, 203, 204, 205, 209, 215, 240, 242
American Civil War 1, 3, 5, 6, 28–30, 98, 126, 177, 178, 252, 256, 257, 258, 260
American Colonization Society 176, 179
American Constitution 22, 125, 204, 209, 219
American and Foreign Anti-Slavery Society 11, 78, 115, 140, 163, 203
American Fugitive Slaves in the British Metropolis 229
American League of Colored Laborers 205
American Revolution 46, 48
An Address to the People of Ireland (1837) 9
Anderson, Francis 148
Annexation of Texas 114
antagonisms 22–3, 24

anti-Catholicism 7–8, 23, 43, 46, 88, 126, 181, 210, 211–13
Anti-Slavery Conventions (1840) 5, 10, 11, 76–8; (1843) 14
Anti-Slavery League 120, 122
Appeal to Colored People (1829) 6–7
Apprenticeship system 8–11, 14, 89, 227
Aptheker, Herbert 31
Arabin, Mayor John 110
Armagh 231
Armistead, Wilson 254
Atlantic crossing 24–5
attacks on abolitionists 26–7
Auld, Hugh 113
Auld, Sophia 106
Auld, Thomas 106, 113

Bailey, Frederick Augustus Washington 106
Bailey, Harriet (Frederick's mother) 106
Bailey, Harriet 119
Ball, Presley 21
Ballymacarrett 90
Ballymena 168
Ballymoney 168, 169
Baltimore 107
Band of Hope 230
Bangor 77, 120, 173
Bangor Female Anti-Slavery Society 77
Baptist Church 8, 61, 66, 69, 146, 189, 191, 193, 195, 196, 197, 208, 216, 230, 248
Baptist War 8
Baraw, Charles 153
bazaars 23, 87, 92, 93, 94, 124
Beale, Joshua 85
Beamish MP, Francis 250
Belfast 5, 9, 24–5, 46, 47–8, 49, 88, 89, 98, 114–17, 120, 121, 165–8, 169

280   *Index*

Belfast Anti-Slavery Society 5, 115, 165–7, 173
Belfast Ladies' Anti-Slavery Society 117, 124, 166, 175
Benson, Benjamin 2, 18, 19, 118, 148, 226–39; childhood 127; described 232; evangelicism 231–2; Ireland 230–6; marriage 233; *Narrative* 226–7, 228–9; temperance 229–33, 234–5
Bermuda 2, 5, 10, 227, 228
Bewley, Joseph 82
Bibb, Henry 204, 206
Bible 20, 42, 54, 69, 90, 117, 172, 175, 205
Birney, James 13–14
Black Atlantic 54, 85
Black History Month 162
Black Negro Conventions 6, 163
'blackface' performers 21, 114
Blind Slave Boy 168, 173
Bonner, Rev. W.H 251
Boston 15–17, 87, 92, 93, 94, 107, 119, 188, 229
boycotts 47, 48, 166, 168; *see also* Free Produce Movement
Bradburn, George 95
Bray 233
Brewer, W.M. 162
Bristol 26, 251
British and Foreign Anti-Slavery Society 9, 11, 15, 25, 26, 61, 67, 78–9, 82, 88, 109, 115, 117, 119, 120, 142, 144, 148, 172, 197, 209, 252
'British' India 3, 13, 77, 78, 88, 110
British Museum 145
Broadway Tabernacle 204, 205
Brougham, Lord Henry 253
Brown, Clarissa 147, 148
Brown, Henry Box 18, 21, 147
Brown, John 125, 176, 229
Brown, Josephine 145, 147, 148, 149, 152
Brown, William Wells 2, 18, 21, 26, 27, 135–61, 168, 229; death 152; described 140–1; in Ireland 138–43; marriages 136, 145–6, 151–2, 191; *Narrative* 19, 135, 136, 138, 141, 142, 143, 144–5, 153; purchase of freedom 146, 149; return to Ireland 151
Buffalo 136
Buffum, James 23, 68, 108, 110, 113, 117, 119
Burritt, Elihu 143, 164, 173, 209
Burs, Anthony 21
Buxton, Fowell 9

Calder, Commander Francis 28–9, 115, 116, 166, 167
'Call to Rebellion' 163
Cambria 108, 137
Canaan Institute 163
Canada 67, 69, 85, 136, 148, 205–6, 209
Canadian Anti-Slavery Society 206, 208, 216
Canadian Ladies' Anti-Slavery Society 208
Carlyle, Thomas 149, 258
Carretta, Vincent 41
Carrickfergus 48, 230
Catholic Emancipation 7, 28, 49, 109, 124
Catholics, prejudice against 49, 88
Chamerovzow, Louis 25, 29, 252
Chapman, Maria Weston 12, 21, 26, 87, 92, 98, 229
Chase, Elizabeth Buffum 258
children 10, 21, 26, 28, 53, 65, 83, 96, 112, 126, 147, 151, 154, 163, 166, 169, 170, 173, 179, 188, 189, 190, 192, 193, 195, 196, 227, 230, 240, 247, 250, 253, 260
Christianity 42–3
churches: criticized 23, 26, 65, 68, 90, 110, 113, 115, 141, 167, 169, 243, 247, 248
Clarke, Rev. Owen 121
Clarkson, Thomas 11, 42, 77, 78
Clonmel 47, 92, 247, 248, 249–50
Clogher Anti-Slavery Association 69, 125, 210
Cochrane, William 210
Collins, John A. 95
Conciliation Hall 111–12
Congregationalists 52, 82, 170, 201, 207, 209, 216
Connaught 233
Cooke, Rev Henry 91
Cork 8, 29, 62, 85–6, 112–13, 211, 232, 247, 249–50
Cork Anti-Slavery Society 85, 86, 125, 250
Cork Ladies' Anti-Slavery Society 92, 112, 125
Coulter, Rev. John 168, 175
County Clare 83
Cox, Rev. Francis 61
Cox, Rev. Samuel 121
Craft, Ellen 18, 24, 25, 26, 137, 147, 148, 217, 253, 258
Craft, William 18, 24, 25, 26, 137, 147, 148, 251, 253, 258
Crawford MP, William Sharman 117, 120, 173
crop failures 29, 30

Index   281

Crown and Anchor Tavern 120
Crummell, Rev. Alexander 162, 179, 229
Crystal Palace 147
Cuba 179
Cugoano, Ottobah 42, 44
Cullen, Susannah 50, 51
Cunard 137, 206
Curran, John Philpot 170, 179–80, 215

Dallas, George Mifflin 254–5
Declaration of Independence 166, 194
Declaration of Sentiments 257
Delany, Martin 22, 24
Democratic Party 30, 96, 97, 126, 255
Derry 69
Digges, Thomas 48
disagreements 163–4, 171–2, 180, 204,
    205, 218
Donahoe, Patrick 95
Douglass, Frederick 2, 3, 4, 5, 14, 15, 17,
    18, 21, 22, 23–4, 25, 26–7, 29, 30, 32,
    60, 94, 97, 98, 100, 106–34, 135, 139,
    152, 163, 176, 177, 178, 188, 201, 204,
    210, 218, 228, 243, 245, 250, 251, 254,
    258–9; in Ireland 108–20; marriages 50,
    107, 126; *Narrative* 19–20, 108, 109,
    116, 118, 128, 166; purchase of freedom
    123; remembered 54; return to Ireland
    126–7; Send Back the Money 68, 117
Dowden, Mayor Richard 29, 114
Downpatrick 70
Draft Riots 30, 177–9
Dred Scott Decision 18, 177, 254
Drew, Rev. Thomas 88, 118, 175, 228
Dromore 174
Dublin 4, 6, 7, 8, 9, 12, 13, 47, 79, 87–8,
    119, 136, 138, 143, 149, 151, 169, 188,
    193, 231, 243
Dublin Negro's Friend Society 7
Dublin Ladies' Anti-Slavery Society
    125, 243
Dublin Total Abstinence Society 232
Duval, Alexander 148

Edgar, Rev. John 89
education 24, 54, 61, 106, 135, 136, 141,
    162, 188, 201, 240
Elliot, Congressman Robert 219
Emancipation Proclamation (1863) 3, 29,
    151, 195, 196, 259
emigration 30, 86, 91, 139
Emmet, Robert 52, 214
Emmet, Thomas Addis 28, 52–3

Equiano, Olaudah 2, 4, 6, 14, 15, 18, 21,
    41–54, 114, 117; baptism 42, 43; in
    Ireland 45–9; marriage 50–1; *Narrative*
    19–21, 41–3, 44–5, 47, 50–1, 54;
    remembered 53–4
Estlin, John 26, 146, 148, 151, 251
Evangelical Alliance 121, 122
evangelicism 2, 4, 7–8, 23, 60, 70, 121,
    177, 180, 196, 202, 210–11, 218, 219,
    226, 227, 228, 231, 232
Evans, Samuel 82
Exeter Hall 26, 77, 78, 108, 172

Fagan, Benjamin 150
Faneuil Hall 15–16, 94, 108
Fifty-fourth Massachusetts Infantry 99,
    151, 196
finances 23, 27, 51, 67, 70, 145, 148–9,
    191–2, 242
Fisher, Benjamin Clarke 81–2, 113
Fisher, Joseph 248
Fisher, Rebecca 113
Fisher, Susanna 113
Fisherwick Place Presbyterian Church 91
Florence 257, 258
Foley, Rev. Dr Daniel 245
Fort Sumter 257
France 254
Frankfurt 164
Frederick Douglass' Paper 171, 205, 213
Free Church 68, 115–17, 119, 120, 121,
    122, 169
Free Produce Movement 164, 165, 166,
    170, 176
Free Soil Party 204
French Revolution 45–6, 141
Fry, Elizabeth 92, 244
Fugitive Slave Law (1793) 108
Fugitive Slave Law (1850) 18, 26, 28,
    98, 108, 137, 145, 146, 148, 149, 152,
    164, 165, 166, 168, 169, 170, 172, 173,
    176, 190, 191, 192, 194, 206, 208,
    229, 246
fugitive status 27

Gambia 227
Garnet, Henry Highland 2, 17, 18, 19, 22,
    97, 162–87, 189; criticized 171–2; death
    179; described 165, 180, 204, 206, 229;
    Draft Riots 177–9; evangelicism 177,
    180, 181; Ireland 165–172; and Jamaica
    175–7; marriage 163, 169, 173, 175, 176,
    179; return to Ireland 173–5

282   *Index*

Garrison, William Lloyd 8, 12–13, 15–16, 19, 26, 30, 60, 76, 77, 78, 81, 87, 94, 96, 97, 107, 108, 110, 117, 119, 120–21, 128, 136, 137, 140, 144, 148, 169, 205, 207, 229, 241, 242, 254, 258
Gay, Sydney Howard 149, 172
German Anti-Slavery Society 164
Ghana 42
Gibson, Rev. William 174
Gladstone, William 250
Glasgow Anti-Slavery Society 119
Gordon, Mayor Sir John 211
Gordon Rebellion 216
Grandy, Moses 1, 142
Great Exhibition (1851) 147
Great Famine 124–5, 128, 139, 175, 181, 211, 233, 235, 255
Green Atlantic 54
Greenfield, Elizabeth Taylor 207–8
Greenspan, Ezra 135
Grimes, William 19
Griffiths, Julia 125, 154
Guerin sisters 43

Haiti 24, 30, 32, 49, 51, 87, 91, 127, 150, 151, 177, 180
Haitian Emigration Bureau 177
Hamilton, Alexander 108
Hancock, William Neilson 244
Hanna, Rev. Samuel 90
Hardy, Thomas 50–1
Harpers Ferry 176
Haughton, James 9, 11, 12, 13, 29, 79, 80, 93, 109, 120, 126, 138, 140, 142, 154, 170, 231, 243, 244, 246
Henderson, Rev. A.M. 211
Hibernian Anti-Slavery Society 9, 11, 15, 79, 80, 82, 85, 88, 109, 110, 118, 135, 165, 170, 172, 194
Hibernian Negro's Friend Society 7, 8
Home Rule 127
Hughes, Bishop John 95, 96
Hugo, Victor 143
human rights 8, 9, 16, 17, 24, 32, 45–6, 50, 53, 54, 88, 106, 107, 128, 173, 251

Imperial Hotel, Cork 249, 250
instruments of torture 20, 62, 65, 66, 114, 137–8, 145, 194
intellectuals 19, 22, 23, 24, 83, 84, 162, 175, 190, 193, 203, 204, 205, 207, 218, 219, 241

Ireland: abolition in 3–4; Catholics in 46; as a colony 3, 4, 7, 27–8, 107; poverty in 4, 29, 128, 138–9, 143, 175, 210
Irish Address 12, 15–17, 79, 80–1, 86, 93–7, 108; opposition to 16–17, 95–6
Irish Americans 12, 13–14, 15–17, 27, 28, 30, 52, 79, 91, 92, 93, 95–7, 126, 166, 213, 214, 244; Draft Riots 177–9
Irish Evangelical Society 210
Irish people: as slaves 3–4, 27–8, 46, 83, 114, 168, 210, 246
Irish Temperance League 231, 232, 233, 234
Irish Volunteers 46
Italy 24, 99, 240, 250, 251, 257, 258, 259

Jacobs, Harriet 18, 19, 25, 28; *Narrative* 19
Jamaica 8, 10, 24, 82, 85, 88, 89, 149, 175–177, 179, 181, 201, 215, 216, 217, 218, 219, 220, 257
Jamaican Emigration Scheme 82, 85, 88–9
jealousies 22–3, 98, 113, 164, 178, 218
Jennings, Ann 123
Jennings family 112, 211
Jennings, Isabel 112
Jim Crow 3, 30, 126, 141
Johnson, President Andrew 196

Kelley, Abby 241
Kelly, Edmund 2, 18, 21, 188–200; death 197; described 191, 193; evangelicism 196, 197; financial dealings 190–2; Ireland 194–5; marriage 189–92; *Narrative* 190; purchase of freedom 189–92
Kerr-Ritchie, Jeffrey 217–18
Kerry 80
Killarney 210
Kingston 216
Kossuth, Lajos 205

Ladies' College, Bedford Square 254
Lancashire cotton workers 29
Landy, Craig 52
Lane, Lunsford 19, 20
Leeds 254
Let the Monster Perish 179
Liberia 179
Liberty Party 172, 203, 204, 205
Limerick 21, 28, 62, 81, 84–5, 113–14
Limerick Anti-Slavery Society 82, 113
Lincoln, Mary Todd 178
Lincoln, President Abraham 3, 29, 30, 126, 151, 178, 195, 196

Index 283

L'Instant de Pradine, Monsieur 87, 91
Lisburn 47, 174
Liverpool 7, 25, 47, 61, 67, 77, 92, 108,
  120, 137, 138, 143, 144, 145, 147,
  151, 164, 172, 177, 190, 193, 206,
  228, 240, 242
London 21, 24, 119, 123, 143–4, 177,
  227, 251, 252
London Anti-Slavery Society 216
London Corresponding Society 50–3
London Emancipation Society 251
loneliness 26–7, 87, 117, 119, 122, 143,
  146, 148, 203
Longford 234
L'ouverture, Toussaint 108
Lovejoy, Paul 41
Lowe, John 53
lynchings 3, 30, 151

M'Afee, Rev. Daniel 91
McCracken, Henry Joy 52, 117
McCracken, Mary Ann 52, 117
McHenry, William 'Jerry' 205
McNevin, William James 52
Madden, Dr Richard 11, 14, 16, 17, 87,
  92, 93
magic lantern slides 149, 152, 234
male suffrage 50, 99
Manchester 29, 53, 78, 93, 149–50
Mandingo tribe 162
Mansion House 110
Marlborough 234
Martin, William 86–7
Martineau, Harriet 30, 66, 154, 253–4
Maryborough 70
Massachusetts Anti-Slavery Society 209
Mathew, Father Theobald 15–16, 92, 93,
  95, 112, 211, 231, 232
Mathews, Rev. Edward 230
Maxwell, Isabella Waring 69, 210
May, Samuel J. 240, 242, 246, 253
Mazzini, Giuseppe 251
Meade, Bishop William 167
medicine 24, 151, 257–8
memorials 51–2, 53–4
Methodism 43, 90, 110, 115, 169, 175, 205
middle passage 42
Mill, John Stuart 217
mob attacks 26, 77, 108, 111, 124, 162–3,
  178, 202
Montez, Madame Lola 252, 253
Moore, Thomas 92, 139
Moran, Benjamin 255

Morant Bay 216
Mott, James 110
Mott, Lucretia 12, 26, 77–8, 110
Mount Hope Cemetery 127
Mulholland, Mayor Andrew 116
Mullingar 210
Murray, Anna 107, 113, 119, 125, 127
music 20, 27, 70, 83–4, 135, 146, 148, 152

Nantucket 107
narratives 1–2, 10, 19–21, 54, 67, 136,
  142, 150, 171, 179, 181, 190, 214,
  226, 228
National Convention of Colored Men
  178, 195
National Negro Conventions 6, 163
Neapolitan Exiles 250–1
Neilson, Samuel 48, 49, 52
Nelson, Rev. Isaac 118, 121, 166, 169, 175,
  228–9
New Bedford 107, 188, 190, 192, 193, 195,
  196, 197
New England Anti-Slavery Society 76, 150
New Haven 201
New Ross 81
New York 30, 107, 176, 177, 178, 190,
  201, 203, 227
New York African Free School 162, 201
New York Anti-Slavery Society 69,
  136, 203
Newcastle 122, 144, 146, 149, 164, 165,
  171, 176
Nigeria 43
Nightingale, Florence 244
Nixon, Reuben 25
North Star 123, 124, 142, 144, 164,
  171, 218
Northern Star 48, 52
Noyes College 163

Obama, President Barack 128
O'Connell, Daniel 3, 7–8, 9, 10–11, 12,
  15–17, 77–8, 79, 83, 88, 91, 93, 94–5,
  96, 109, 110–11, 112, 123, 124, 126,
  127, 128, 140, 141, 154, 170–1, 178,
  246; praised 78–9, 83, 88, 109, 110,
  111, 112
O'Connell, John 3, 11, 111
Ofari, Earl 180–1
Opium Wars 110
Oregon Question 114
Orpen, Charles 7
Ortiz, Paul 162

284 *Index*

pacifism 110, 136
Paine, Thomas 49
Painter, Nell Irvin 31, 152
panoramas 21, 138, 146–147, 149, 152
Paris 137, 143
Parker, Theodore 20
passports 4, 18, 126, 145, 177, 217, 254–7
patronage 25–6, 43, 44–5, 47, 61, 62, 207, 214
Patteson, Rev. William 173
Peabody, Nathaniel 12, 27
Peace Congresses 137, 142, 143, 164, 165, 172–3
Pennington, Rev. James 25, 143, 172, 177, 215
Pennsylvania Peace Society 164
Penrose, Cooper 85
petitions 7, 9, 11, 14, 15–16, 125, 257
Philadelphia 6, 141, 150, 195
Phillipe, Dr Jean Baptiste 10
Phillips, Wendell 30, 94, 99, 118, 144, 243
photography 152
Pillsbury, Parker 12, 26, 27, 107, 172, 205, 209, 215, 243
Pintor, Lazzaro 258
Pitts, Helen 50, 126, 258–9
Pittsburg 97
poetry 62–4, 168, 205
poets quoted 20, 48, 69, 139, 168
Portarlington 70
Post, Amy 259
Powell, William P. 170, 171, 242
prayer 1, 17, 175, 196, 197, 203, 236
prejudice 24–5, 50, 76–7, 79, 90, 93–4, 97, 150, 167, 241, 257–8, 259; absence of 12, 24, 25, 78, 87, 92, 142, 207, 241, 242
Presbyterian Church 69–70, 88, 91, 115, 120, 163, 165–9, 173–5, 176, 228, 230
Price, Rev. Thomas 62, 67
Prince, Mary 1, 19
Proclamation of Neutrality (1861) 29
Protestant Ascendancy 3, 46
Protestant churches 2, 70
Prussian Ambassador 207
Putnam, Caroline Remond 258, 259

Quakers 7, 80, 81, 82, 85, 88, 96, 110, 112, 113, 140, 144, 170, 188, 252, 258; restrictions on 27, 28
Queen Victoria 9, 25–6, 29, 139–40, 256
Queenstown 250
Quincy, Edmund 94–5

racism 3, 18, 30, 44, 65–6, 90, 93–4, 123–4, 149, 150, 151, 167, 176, 219, 255, 258, 259
Ray, Charles 78
Refugee Home Society of Canada 206
Remond, Charles Lenox 2, 3, 5, 11, 12, 14, 15–16, 19, 22, 24–5, 27, 28, 108, 112, 124, 137, 204, 240, 241, 259; death 99; described 79, 80, 82, 83, 84, 89; in Ireland 79–93; Irish Address 79, 80–1, 85, 86, 87, 92, 93–7
Remond, Maritcha 258, 259
Remond, Nancy 24
Remond, Sarah Parker 2, 5, 8, 9, 18, 21, 24, 29, 72, 98–9, 125, 149, 217, 240–65; criticized 248, 249; described 243, 246, 247, 250, 258; feminist agenda 260; gender 244–5, 260–1; Ireland 242–51; Jamaica 257; marriage 258; use of press 21, 241, 255–7; visa controversy 254–7, 259; visit by the Douglasses 258–9
Rentoul, Rev. John 168–9
Repeal Association 15, 16, 19, 28, 95, 111
Republican Party 244
Revel, Jonathan 230, 231
Richardson, Anna 122, 144, 146, 164, 176
Richardson, Ellen 149
Richardson, Henry 144, 149, 164
Rights of Man 49
Rising (1798) 4, 6, 28
rivalries 163–4, 180, 218
Robson, William 242, 254
Roche, Andrew 29
Rochester 23, 123, 124, 125, 127, 205
Rogers, Nathaniel Peabody 77, 108
Rome 259
Roper, Moses 2, 18, 20, 23, 24, 60–75; criticized 65–66, 67; death 71; described 61, 65, 69, 70–1; evangelicism of 60, 61; in Ireland 69–71; marriages 67, 69; *Narrative* 60, 61–2, 67
Rosemary Street Meeting House 90, 115, 168
Rotundo Rooms 9, 140, 151, 169, 243, 246
Royal Exchange 79, 80, 87, 110
Ruggles, David 24
Rynders, Captain Isaiah 203

Salam Female Anti-Slavery Society 240
Sampson, William 52
Sawallisch, Nele 214
Schor, Joel 22, 29, 178, 181
Scoble, John 13–14, 61

Index 285

Scotland 49, 50, 51, 68, 117, 119, 121, 125, 147, 165
sectarianism 88, 118
self-education 1, 18, 24
Seminoles 126, 147
Send Back the Money 11, 68, 115–16, 117, 119, 120, 121, 122
Seneca Falls Convention 12, 124
Seven Years' War 43
Sewell, Stacy Kinlock 99
sexism 254
Shaftsbury, Lord 207, 209
Sharp, Granville 4, 42, 44, 45, 48, 50
Shepherd, Rev. Noble 210
Sheridan, Richard Brinsley 107, 154
Sherman, Rev. James 207
Shillington, Kevin 31
Shuttleworth, Sir James 207
Sierra Leone 44
singing 20–21, 70, 142, 168
slave-trade 4; anniversary 41; ending of 2–3, 4, 6, 54
slavery: ending in British Empire 8–9, 10–11, 54
Sligo 210, 212
Sligo, Marquis of 17
Smith, Gerrit 125, 204, 219
Smith, James Boxer 147
Smith, Dr James McCune 24, 162, 178
Smith, Robert 122
social justice 8, 9, 23–4, 53, 54, 76, 99, 107, 110, 127–8, 166, 173, 219, 244, 251, 261
Society for the Abolition of the Slave Trade (1787) 44, 46, 50
Society for the Mitigation and Gradual Abolition of Slavery throughout the British Dominions (1823) 6, 31
Society of Friends *see* Quakers
soirées 91, 113, 169, 175
Somerset case 4, 179
Sons of Africa 44
St Kitts Island 227
Standfield, James 29, 88–9, 90, 92, 115, 121, 166, 167, 168, 173
Stanton, Elizabeth Cady 12, 13, 26, 124
Stanton, Henry 13–14
Stevenson, Ambassador Andrew 11, 88, 90, 109, 141
Stowe, Harriet Beecher 20, 26, 29, 191, 193, 207, 208, 244, 245
Stowe, Rev. Calvin 26
Stuart, Captain Charles 8

Sturge, Joseph 9, 25, 127
Sumner, Charles 196
Sutherland, Duchess of 25–6, 207, 214, 217
Synod of Ulster 50

Tappan, Lewis 202, 203
Taylor, William 4–5
temperance 12, 87, 110, 112, 136, 138, 163, 227, 228, 229, 231–2
Tennant, James 121
Texas 85, 114, 247
Thirteenth Amendment 179
Tompkins, Sarah Smith 179
Thompson, George 21, 68, 144, 147, 148, 150, 251, 253
Total Abstinence Society 231
Tone, Theobald Wolfe 46
Toronto College 208
Townley, Rev. Charles Gostling 82
Tramore 81
travel visas 18, 21, 254–7, 259
Trinidad 10
Trinity College, Dublin 244, 245
Tubman, Harriet 24
Tuckey, Mary 62–4

Uncle Tom's Cabin 20, 26, 69, 149, 190, 191, 194, 207, 230, 244, 245
Underground Railroad 246
United Irishmen 6, 28, 46, 47, 48, 49, 51, 52, 54, 114
United Presbyterian Church of Scotland 175
United States 20, 52, 81, 82, 90, 92, 147, 151
University College, London 61
Urwick, Rev. William 170

Vassa, Gustavus *see* Olaudah Equiano
Vassa, Joanna 51–2, 53
Vassa, Maria 51–2

Wales 181, 213
Walker, David 6–7
Walker, James 189–90
Walker, Paralee 189–90
Ward, Rev. Samuel Ringgold 2, 8, 17, 18, 21, 22, 24, 26, 60, 150, 162, 175, 181, 189, 195, 201–25; anti-Catholicism 211–14, 218, 219; controversy 216; death 218; dishonesty of 215–6; evangelicism 202–3, 210, 211, 218;

286   *Index*

Ireland 209–15; Jamaica 215–17, 257; *Narrative* 17, 214; praised 26, 219
Waring, Maria 112
Warrington 242, 254
Washington 127
Waterford 5, 9, 47, 81, 92, 112, 126, 247–9
Watson, Tom 217
Webb, Alfred 126–7
Webb family 7, 9, 12, 81, 82, 112, 114, 140, 170
Webb, Hannah 12, 80, 110, 112, 138, 147, 243
Webb, Maria 124, 125
Webb, Richard 9, 11, 12, 13, 19, 24, 27, 29, 80, 81, 83, 84, 85, 108–9, 110, 113, 115, 119, 120, 126, 135, 138, 139–40, 141, 143, 148, 171–2, 242, 243, 244, 250–1
Webster, Daniel 203
Wedgwood, Josiah 31
Weims, Stella 175, 176
Welch, Andrew 226, 227, 228, 236
Wells, Ida B. 30
Welsh language 62, 67
West Indian Emancipation Day 21, 147–8, 226
West Indies 4–5, 6, 10, 11, 13, 14, 43, 45, 48, 85, 88–9, 147, 148, 149, 150, 164, 169, 175, 215, 227, 229, 247, 253
Weston, Caroline 229

Wexford 81, 112
Whatley, Archbishop Richard 246–7
Whitehaven 165
Whitman, Walt 96
Whittier, John Greenleaf 118
Wilberforce, William 2, 6, 7, 23, 42, 45, 50, 154, 180
Williams, Eric 31–2
Williams, James 10
Williams, Julia 163, 176, 179
Willis, Professor Michael 208
Wishere, Rev. Thomas 248
women: abolitionists 25, 26, 29, 47, 50, 67, 77–8, 127, 147, 163, 191, 207, 242, 256; enslaved 5, 243, 247, 252–3, 260; Irish 9, 62–4, 69, 77, 82, 85, 86, 90, 92–3, 112, 113, 117, 124, 169, 170, 175
women's rights 12, 13, 81, 97, 110, 124, 127, 136, 163, 241, 254, 257, 258, 260
Women's Rights Convention 241
woodcuts 192
Woodson, Carter 99
Wright, Henry Clarke 68, 110, 115, 122, 123, 243

Youghal 112–13

Zong Massacre 44

Printed in the United States
by Baker & Taylor Publisher Services